Kuki Shūzō

Kuki Shūzō

A Philosopher's Poetry and Poetics

Translated and Edited by
MICHAEL F. MARRA

University of Hawai'i Press
HONOLULU

© 2004 University of Hawai'i Press
All rights reserved
Printed in the United States of America
04 05 06 07 08 09   6 5 4 3 2 1

Library of Congress Cataloging-in-Publication Data
Kuki, Shūzō, 1888–1941.
Kuki Shūzō : a philosopher's poetry and poetics /
translated and edited by Michael F. Marra.
p. cm.
Includes bibliographical references and index.
ISBN 0-8248-2755-4 (hardcover : alk. paper)
1. Kuki, Shūzō, 1888–1941—Translations into English.
I. Title: Philosopher's poetry and poetics. II. Marra, Michele. III. Title.
PL810.U45M27 2004
181'.82—dc22
2003020639

Designed by inari information services
Printed by The Maple-Vail Book Manufacturing Group

A Padrino

Contents

Acknowledgments   xi

Introduction   1
Worlds in Tension: An Essay on Kuki Shūzō's
   Poetry and Poetics   6

POETRY
Free Verse *(Shi)*

Paris Mindscapes   45

   Wind   45
   Recollections   46
   Seafood Restaurant   46
   The Gatekeeper's Son   47
   An Autumn Day   49

Fragments (From Paris)   51

   The Negative Dimension   51
   Contingency   51
   The Dialectical Method   52
   Pure Duration   53
   The Human Dance   54

Sleep Talking in Paris   54

   Self-Questioning   54
   The Tango   55
   Yellow Face   55
   Serenade   57

Monte Carlo   58
Ginkgo Leaf   58
Loneliness   59
Pig   60

Windows of Paris   60

Guest   60
A Walk   61
The Russian Song   61
Heine's Tomb   63
My Heart   64
Vomiting   65

Short Poems *(Tanka)*

Paris Mindscapes   66

Sonnets from Paris   79

Andantino   79
Nocturne   83
Variations   85
Scherzo   89
Serenade   93

Winter in Kyoto   97

Last Poems   99

Rhyming Poems: Poems Appended to *Rhyme in Japanese Poetry*

Thoughts Originating from Herbs   100
To Ms. D   101
A Solitary Life   101
Onogoro and Intercourse   102
Konohana no Sakuyabime   102
Poetry   103
Journey   103
One Night   104
Squirrel   104
Bookbinder   105
Bat   105
The Sleepy Inland Sea   106
Heart   106
Meeting Bridge   107

Monte Carlo   107
The Carnival of Nice   108
A Wish   109
Wind   109
Farewell to Paris   110
Grieving Mr. Iwashita Sōichi   110
Credo Quia Absurdum   111
A Stroll   112
Renunciation   112
Cointreau   113
Luxor   113
Fontainebleau   114
The Geometry of Gray   114
Arabesque   115
Tango   115
Mediterranean Sunset   116
Repentance   116
Evening in the Alps   117
Dialectic   118
The Ruins of Karnak   118
Flower Picking   119
Three Comma-Shaped Figures in a Circle   120
Destiny   120

Essays on Poetry

The Genealogy of Feelings: A Guide to Poetry   125
The Metaphysics of Literature   174

Selected Essays

My Family Name   217
Negishi   228
Remembering Mr. Okakura Kakuzō   235
Remembering Mr. Iwashita Sōichi   241
A Recollection of Henri Bergson   248
Tokyo and Kyoto   253
Contingency and Destiny   257
Contingency and Surprise   264
A Joke Born from Contingency   271
Sound and Smell: The Sound of Contingency
    and the Smell of Possibility   273

A Record of Short Songs   275
My Thoughts on Loanwords   277
Tradition and Progressivism   284

Notes   287
Bibliography   349
Index   355

Acknowledgments

I want to express my gratitude to Professor Iwaki Ken'ichi for inviting me to teach a course on Japanese aesthetics in the Department of Aesthetics and Art History of Kyoto University in fall 2000. The stay in Kyoto allowed me to retrace Kuki Shūzō's steps through the ancient capital while discussing his philosophy with Professors Fujita Masakatsu and Yoshioka Kenjirō of the University of Kyoto, Professor Ōhashi Ryōsuke of the University of Osaka, Professor Hamashita Masahiro of Kobe College, and Professor Muroi Hisashi of Yokohama National University whose tenure as a visiting professor at Kyoto University took place at the same time as mine. I am also indebted to Usui Michiko for a substantial amount of administrative work done on my behalf at Kyōdai.

Several years ago the University of Kyoto brought me into contact with Professor Iwakura Tomotada and his wife Shōko with whose friendship I have been blessed for over two decades. They have generously shared with me their knowledge of Kuki and provided useful information on Kuki's days in Kyoto.

I also want to thank Professor William R. LaFleur, for inviting me to the University of Pennsylvania to talk about Kuki's poetry, and Professor Eiji Sekine of Purdue University for allowing me to present a paper on Kuki at the 2002 meeting of the Association for Japanese Literary Studies.

The UCLA Center for Japanese Studies and the UCLA Council on Research have generously supported the present work. To all of them goes my gratitude and to me alone the blame for any shortcoming.

Introduction

Kuki Shūzō (1888-1941), one of Japan's most original thinkers of the twentieth century, has been the object of divided critical evaluations since the time he published a work that was destined to make him a truly popular philosopher, rather than simply an academic one: *Iki no Kōzō* (The structure of *iki*; 1930).[1] As Kuki himself noticed in a short essay titled "Dentō to Shinshu" (Tradition and progressivism; 1936),[2] as soon as *The Structure of Iki* appeared, first in the pages of the journal *Shisō* (Thought) and then as a monograph eight months later,[3] he was immediately attacked by Marxist critics as a "fervent traditionalist." Kuki accepted the charges, but only after qualifying his position toward tradition. He would hardly have spent eight years in Europe and dedicated most of his life to the study of Western philosophy—he argued—if he wanted simply to promote the maintenance of "the old customs of tradition" in his land. The simple mentioning of the issue was, in his opinion, "obvious, banal, and almost ludicrous." But if by "traditionalism" one meant the realization of the role played by tradition in the formation of one's "Being," then the charge of traditionalism was not only justified but actually welcome. Kuki's commitment to an understanding of language—a topic that is central to the articulation of *Sein* (Being)—was reduced by Marxist critics to an avowal of nationalism, particularly in light of the changed political circumstances that were silencing all opposition in the name of military expansionism.

This charge has haunted Kuki's reputation to this day, threatening to obfuscate the originality of a truly cosmopolitan philosopher whose "guilt" has been established chiefly by association. In Japan no one dared to talk about Kuki after the war because of his association with the "Kyoto school," which was accused of providing the government with the intellectual justification for nationalistic and expansionistic policies. This argument is based on the premise that Kuki worked in the department of philosophy at Kyoto Imperial University together with Nishida Kitarō (1870–1945), Tanabe Hajime (1885–1962), and other members of the Kyoto school whose thought was deeply affected by Nishida's system. Not until the 1980s did Kuki become the focus of scholarly attention in Japan and the West, at the same time as a reevaluation of the alleged war responsibilities of members of the Kyoto school.[4] It is ironic, however, to notice that while Kuki's association with the Kyoto school hurt him to a considerable degree, he is seldom included in discussions of the school—and appropriately so, since he was intellectually rooted in the philosophy department of Tokyo Imperial University and seldom took a public stand on the issue of imperialism.[5]

Furthermore, Kuki's association with the German philosopher Martin Heidegger (1889–1976), with whom he studied in the fall of 1927 and the spring of 1928, has led several critics to see a commonality of aims between the two philosophers, who are thus presented as "typical ideologues of nineteenth-century imperialism." This is the position taken by Karatani Kōjin, who has had a particular influence on historians and literary critics writing on Kuki in the West. Karatani sees Kuki's and Heidegger's speculations on Being as developments of nineteenth-century discourses on "spirit," which led both thinkers to arrive, "respectively, at the 'Great East Asian Coprosperity Sphere' and the 'Third Reich.'"[6] Karatani's "hermeneutics of national being" is a rehearsal of the Marxist critiques that Kuki himself talked about in "Tradition and Progressivism." Karatani follows an argument made by the Marxist critic Tosaka Jun (1900–1945) in *Nihon Ideorogīron* (Essay on Japanese ideology; 1935), in which Tosaka highlighted the parallels between the aesthetic practices of German romanticism and the aesthetic ideology of Japan's ultranationalism.

Tosaka's and Karatani's arguments are fully at work in Leslie Pincus's *Authenticating Culture in Imperial Japan*, the most extensive work on Kuki in English, published in 1996. In this monograph Kuki is

accused of following a methodology—the hermeneutical method—
that, allegedly, "has lent itself to conservative, even reactionary, per-
spectives on history."[7] The reference is to Heidegger,[8] of course, who
provided Kuki with a "cultural hermeneutic," "a national ontology,"[9]
and a "logic of organicism" that made Kuki intellectually responsible
for the government's expansionistic policies in China.[10] Pincus reads
Kuki's philosophy in light of Marxist interpretations of Heidegger,
especially interpretations by one of Heidegger's most severe French
critics, Philippe Lacoue-Labarthe, who created the term "national aes-
theticism" to define Heidegger's views of cultural organicism and from
whom Pincus derived the subtitle of her book, *Kuki Shūzō and the Rise
of National Aesthetics.*[11] Karatani's and Pincus's interpretations of
Kuki have become quite authoritative among scholars of literature in
the West, who tend to rely on their assessments when referring to
Kuki's thought.[12] This does not mean that no effort has been made to
point out how difficult it is to substantiate these claims when one looks
at Kuki's actual body of work.[13] It simply indicates that the voices call-
ing for more attention to the writings of Kuki Shūzō tend to be ignored.

Realizing that inattentively conceived links between the philoso-
phies of Heidegger and Kuki have significantly distorted the latter,
some critics have attempted to detach Kuki's thought from Heidegger's
philosophy of Being, pointing out Kuki's predominant use of French
thought, in which he specialized and lectured extensively at the Univer-
sity of Kyoto.[14] Research in this direction has contributed powerful
analyses of the differences between Kuki's and Heidegger's hermeneu-
tical phenomenology.[15] The answer to the question of relationships lies
ultimately with Kuki himself who, in the essay "Tōkyō to Kyōto" (To-
kyo and Kyoto),[16] compares his links with Henri Bergson (1859–1941)
and Martin Heidegger to his relationship with the two cities most dear
to him, the city where he was born and raised (Tokyo) and the city
where he spent the second half of his life (Kyoto). If, as Goethe pointed
out, talent is built in quietness while character develops in the midst of
activity, then Kuki could argue that his personal experience was a fer-
tile ground for the development of both. Raised in the modernity of Ja-
pan's capital, the city of Bergsonian and Parisian vitalism, he was
developing his philosophy in the stillness of the ancient capital Kyoto,
which afforded him the quietness of Heidegger's Black Forest. The

names of the two philosophers can hardly be separated in Kuki's thought. His cosmopolitanism was the result of fortunate circumstances that brought him into the world as a member of one of Japan's most distinguished and influential families, both culturally and politically, and allowed him an unusually lengthy stay in Europe where he could engage in conversation with the major philosophical figures active in France and Germany.[17] As I argue in the following chapter, this cosmopolitanism did not come without a price. But this was a price that most Japanese intellectuals born in the Meiji period had to pay in order to make sense of an intellectual tradition into which they were born and which was profoundly challenged by new configurations of knowledge flooding Japan from the West. Beginning with the Meiji Restoration (1868), Japanese thinkers engaged in tremendous efforts to come to grips with new Western vocabularies and sets of ideas in art, literature, philosophy, aesthetics, and more. This was a history of anxious assimilation, angry rejection, and, eventually, detached speculation that came about as a result of unimaginable efforts made by Japan's intellectual pioneers of modernization.[18] No wonder, therefore, that we find "tensions" in Kuki's system reflected in the competing positions taken by his critics. These positions are interesting to me not so much for the grain of truth they may contain but for exemplifying with their performative acts the complexities of Kuki's thought.

In this book I will not be adding my voice to the debate on the political responsibilities of Kuki's philosophy. My aim is much more modest and very much related to my own interests in literary matters. I agree with the characterization that the editors of *Sourcebook for Modern Japanese Philosophy* give of Kuki in the preface to their book. They state: "Indeed, Kuki Shūzō must be considered not only a philosopher of art but also an artist in his own right, especially in the realm of poetry. As such a philosopher-poet, Kuki emerges as one of the most appealing and sensitive modern Japanese philosophers."[19] In the present book I offer Kuki's poetic production in translation: his collections of free verse, *Parī Shinkei* (Paris mindscapes; 1925–1926), *Hahen* (Fragments; 1927), *Parī no Negoto* (Sleep talking in Paris; 1926), and *Parī no Mado* (Windows of Paris; 1925), as well as his 31-syllable poems *(tanka)* written in Paris during the second half of the 1920s. I have also translated additional poems that Kuki appended to a long essay on rhyme in poetry, "Nihonshi no Ōin" (Rhyme in Japanese poetry; 1931). The poems are followed by translations of two essays on poetry that Kuki wrote in Kyoto in the late 1930s and early 1940s: "Jōcho no Keizu: Uta o Tebiki to Shite" (The genealogy of feelings: A guide to poetry; 1938) and "Bungaku no Keijijōgaku" (The metaphysics of literature; 1940). I have chosen to provide readers with textual samples of Kuki's poetry and poetics because it seems to me that the slippage between practice and theory—the production and the discussion of poetry—is another example of Kuki's divided loyalties on which critics have focused. In the introductory essay I discuss what I perceive to be an unresolved tension between, on the one hand, the philosophy espoused in Kuki's poetry dealing with issues related to Bergsonian thought (contingency, freedom, and pure duration) and, on the other, much more conservative theories that he followed in discussing poetry, especially his notion of temporality—theories not unrelated to German thought.

I have appended a translation of selected essays by Kuki that, hopefully, will give readers additional materials for a better understanding of his poetry. I have chosen to include a few essays related to Kuki's life ("Negishi," "Remembering Mr. Okakura Kakuzō," "Remembering Mr. Iwashita Sōichi," "A Recollection of Henri Bergson," "Tokyo and Kyoto," "A Record of Short Songs," and "Tradition and Progressivism"), to his discussions of language ("My Family Name" and "My Thoughts on Loanwords"), and to the notion of contingency ("Contingency and Destiny," "Contingency and Surprise," "A Joke Born from Contingency," and "Sound and Smell: The Sound of Contingency and the Smell of Possibility"), a notion which informs Kuki's philosophy deeply and which he developed in one of his most distinctive poems.

Worlds in Tension

An Essay on Kuki Shūzō's Poetry and Poetics

In his monograph on Kuki Shūzō, the intellectual historian Tanaka Kyūbun takes the notion of "tension" to be a major feature of Kuki's thought. Tanaka's psychological analysis begins with the portrayal of a boy divided between the two households of divorced parents, the highly influential baron Kuki Ryūichi (1852–1931) and the former Gion geisha Hoshizaki Hatsu, to whom Shūzō was born the fourth son. Tanaka also describes the divided loyalties that Shūzō feels for two paternal figures: the stern father who held a major position in the Meiji government and was later appointed Japanese ambassador to Washington, on the one hand, and the charismatic Okakura Kakuzō (or Tenshin; 1861–1913), on the other, a major intellectual figure of the Meiji period who often visited Shūzō's mother in Negishi.[1]

Readers might be skeptical of the basis on which a study relates a philosopher's childhood memories to the development of his thought. But Tanaka's focus on tension *(kinchō)* is perfectly justified by Kuki Shūzō's own focus on it in one of his most popular works, *Iki no Kōzō* (The structure of *iki;* 1930). In this work Kuki defines the aesthetic category of *iki*—which, in his opinion, summarizes the Being of the Japanese people—as a tension between a man and a woman that must be maintained in order for their relationship not to stagnate or die out into an unauthentic experience. According to Kuki, *iki* is embodied by the Japanese geisha whose continuously changing interactions with customers teach her that the ideal relationship is one of possibility rather than fulfillment, a relationship that is free from the shackles of love, a transcendental possibility *(chōetsuteki kanōsei)* rather than a necessity of reality *(genjitsuteki hitsuzensei)*. Kuki introduces the notion of allure *(bitai)*, one of the three main ingredients of *iki,* as follows:

> This dualistic possibility is the fundamental determinant for the being of allure, and allure disappears on its own accord when the opposite sexes unite totally and lose that source of tension. This is because the hypothetical goal of allure is conquest, destined to disappear when this goal is fulfilled. As Nagai Kafū says in his short story "Kanraku" (Pleasure), "there is nothing more pathetic than a woman one has had after the successful attempt to have her." He must surely have had in mind the "boredom, despair, and aversion" arising from the disappearance of allure that once played such an active role in both sexes. For this reason, the main concern of allure—and the essence of pleasure—is maintaining a dualistic relationship, that is to say, preserving the possibility as a possibility.[2]

Kuki is not arguing that the union of the couple should not be consummated. He is simply stating that in order to avoid the pain resulting from an unsuccessful union, or in order to avoid making such a union unsuccessful, the couple must master the arts of pride *(ikiji)* and renunciation *(akirame)* in order to avoid the illusion that a relationship could or should last forever. Seen from the perspective of *The Structure of Iki,* in which Kuki attempts to articulate a description of the local Being, the ideal love relationship is the one that actors share on the kabuki stage, in which man and woman (actually a male actor impersonating a woman) pledge their love by standing shoulder to shoulder while turning their heads toward each other without ever reaching one another. The idea stands in perfect antithesis to the kiss scenes immortalized in Hollywood movies—and in opposition, too, to the Neo-Kantian philosophy of values postulated by Heinrich Rickert (1863–1936), who saw in marriage a universal value sustaining eternally the love of the couple. For Rickert, who was appealing to an ethics that would help reconstruct bourgeois values in Germany after the catastrophic World War I, each sex supplemented the other: while the wife brought coziness to the marriage, the man brought to it the dimension of public life.

Kuki, who bases his explanation of local Being on the difference between local Being and Western versions of Being, appeals to the idea of tension between two entities whose individuality and specificity should not be offered as victims to the god of harmony. Whether his personal experience as the son of divorced parents (and later as a divorced husband himself) had anything to do with Kuki's peculiar idealization of heterosexual relationships, as Tanaka implies, is for others to decide.[3] Instead of questioning the source of Kuki's use of tension, I would like to point out how scholars such as Yasuda Takeshi and Tada Michitarō have discussed several variations on the theme of tension between individuated entities that run through Kuki's thought. They stress Kuki's ambivalent position in *Iki no Kōzō* between stoicism and epicurism, for example, grounding their argument in a statement that Kuki himself made when he confessed his personal tendency toward a philosophy of pleasure rather than a philosophy of will.[4] Moreover, they indicate the presence in *Iki no Kōzō* of a tension between Japan and the West, between the dialects and customs of Japan's eastern (Kantō) and western (Kansai) areas, and between the city (Edo) and the countryside *(inaka)*.[5]

Another commentator on Kuki, the philosopher Sakabe Megumi, considers Kuki's increasingly conservative stance after his return to Japan from Europe to be the result of a relaxation of that very tension which culminated in the writing of *Iki no Kōzō*—a tension that was particularly visible at a time when Kuki was physically removed from his homeland during his lengthy stay in Europe from 1921 to 1928. Apparently such a tension had diminished with the transformation of a physical Other into an increasingly fading memory.[6]

I am in complete agreement with all these scholars on the relevance of tension in the interpretation of Kuki's thought. After all, Kuki was well versed in the work of Martin Heidegger who, in *The Introduction to Metaphysics,* argued that Being shows itself in the tension of opposites:

> Thus Being, logos, as the gathered harmony, is not easily available for everyone at the same price, but is concealed, as opposed to that harmony which is always a mere equalizing, the elimination of tension, leveling: *armoniē afanēs fanerēs kreítton,* "the harmony that does not show itself (immediately and without further ado) is more powerful than the harmony that is (always) evident" (fragment 54).[7]

Here I would like to analyze another kind of tension that becomes particularly apparent when we read Kuki's poetry in connection with his essays on the arts: French and German philosophies—an unresolved pull to which Kuki was directly exposed during his studies in Heidelberg (October 1921–September 1923), Paris (at the Sorbonne, October 1925–March 1927), Freiburg (April–October 1927), and Marburg (November 1927–May 1928). In France Kuki met with Henri Bergson and Émile Bréhier (1876–1952), then professor of philosophy at the Sorbonne, who apparently introduced him to a young Jean-Paul Sartre (1905–1980).[8] In Paris Kuki read the books of Émile Boutroux extensively, especially Boutroux's work on the challenges that contingency continuously poses to the realm of necessity. Sartre later developed this topic into a philosophy of action, freedom, and responsibility.[9] Kuki discussed the work of Boutroux's student, Bergson, on the relationship between temporality (of which contingency is a major element) and freedom *(liberté)*.[10]

In Germany Kuki attended Rickert's lectures, "From Kant to Nietzsche: A Historical Introduction to the Problem of the Present" at the University of Heidelberg in October 1921. Unsatisfied with Rickert's philosophy of values,[11] Kuki turned to the phenomenological school of Freiburg where he met Edmund Husserl (1859–1938), Oskar Becker (1889–1964), and Martin Heidegger. In November 1927 Kuki attended Heidegger's lectures at the University of Marburg on the "Phenomenological Investigations of Kant's *Critique of Pure Reason*" and his seminar on "Schelling's *Treatise on the Essence of Human Freedom*." In spring 1928 Kuki saw Heidegger lecturing on "Leibniz's Logic" while also attending his seminar on "Phenomenological Studies: Interpretation of Aristotle's *Physics*." Whether or not we agree with French valuations of the German hermeneutical school in general and Heidegger's philosophy in particular, we cannot neglect the strong critiques from the land of enlightenment that label Heidegger's thought a "conservative revolution,"[12] an "aestheticization of politics,"[13] a "neoconservative" thought.[14] These judgments indicate the difficulty of reconciling a philosophy of chance and freedom—Kuki's French inheritance—with a philosophy of Being, universality, and particularity, which came to Kuki from Germany. The tension between apparently irreconcilable intellectual trends emerges quite clearly when we compare Kuki's work on contingency, especially his poetic work written in Paris in 1925,[15] with the theory of temporality on which he relied to distinguish art from knowledge and morality and to distinguish poetry from the other arts.[16]

Contingency

Kuki's reading of Émile Boutroux's *De la Contingence des Lois de la Nature* (1908) and Émile Borel's *Le Hasard* (1920) prompted him to ponder philosophically over the idea that human beings are born by chance and thrown into a situation over which they have no control. Moreover, every day one keeps being faced with chance encounters and all sorts of chance occurrences. Kuki presented his major thoughts on contingency in *Gūzensei no Mondai* (The problem of contingency; 1935), in which he provided a theoretical answer to a very basic question, a question he had repeatedly posed to himself during his stay in Paris: why was I born Japanese rather than, say, American or Chinese? He called this event "categorical contingency" *(teigenteki gūzen)*, a contingency that makes the individuality of race and nationality over come the generality of being born a human being (Kuki's "categorical necessity"). Contingency challenges the self-sameness *(dōitsusei)* of the general category of the human being by introducing splits and conflicts into it, thus giving a specific particularity to an otherwise unmarked, anonymous generality. Categorical contingency is related to individuals *(kobutsu)* and opposes general concepts or rules.

Seen from the viewpoint of cause and effect, however, categorical contingency—the fact of being born Japanese—is nothing but a necessity *(hitsuzensei)*, the result of the relationship between cause and effect. He was born Japanese because both parents were Japanese—a fact that Kuki called "hypothetical necessity." In turn, this necessity is predicated on a new kind of contingency—an encounter *(sōgū)* or chance meeting *(kaikō)* between the parents that led to their decision to get together and make a family. This is what Kuki called "hypothetical contingency" *(kasetsuteki gūzen)*. Again, once the chance meeting is analyzed in the light of cause and effect, the cause ceases to be contingent. A "chance meeting" cannot be called totally contingent since, although the two Japanese parents met by chance, they actually worked in the same factory—what Kuki referred to as "disjunctive necessity" *(risetsuteki hitsuzen)*. The whole process comes to a halt in "disjunctive contingency" *(risetsuteki gūzen)*, the possibility of death that breaks the totality of all possibilities, a final contingency containing the destiny of all human beings in their specific particularities, an opening to nothingness *(mu)* that brings reality to life by denying life. In other words, human existence is a reality created by a series of contingencies: an individual is characterized by its difference from another for no necessary reason (categorical contingency); it meets by chance with another for no necessary reason (hypothetical contingency); and it eventually fades into nothingness for no necessary reason (disjunctive contingency).

Kuki discusses the topic of contingency in one of his poems, a poem that challenges attempts to explain human life in terms of the inflexible rules of necessity. Kuki included this poem, appropriately titled "Contingency" (Gūzensei), in a collection known as *Fragments (From Paris) (Hahen, Parī yori):*[17]

Contingency

Could you find a proof to the design
Of parallel straight lines?
That was your aim:
Did you withdraw your fundamental claim?
Did the central issue become
That to the angles of a triangle's sum
Two right angles are equal?
Or was it less than a 180-degree sequel?
In Alexandria the old book was found,
Principles of Geometry two thousand years ago bound,
No matter whether the worms ate it or not,
Euclid is a great man, never forgot,
Who with lines and points the shape of the universe drew!
You and I, I and you,
The secret of a chance encounter I saw,
Of love the anti-law.
This is the geometry of life's retribution,
Won't you bring it for me to some solution?
At the straight line of cause and effect A we look!
The straight line of cause and effect B we took!

The principle that two parallel lines do not intersect,
To the intersection of parallel lines don't you object?
With this, contingency is fulfilled,
With chaos Venus is filled,
Two people a string of pearls detect
Brought by the waves of cause and effect.

In this poem Kuki seems to concentrate on the second type of contingency, hypothetical contingency, the chance encounter between a man and a woman that breaks the law of cause and effect, introducing the element of fortuitousness which challenges the rationality of Euclid's geometry and disrupts the notion that parallel lines theoretically do not come together. They do come together in practice, however, when two people who are unknown to each other and who—although they travel toward the same destination (death) and do it on separate, parallel paths—meet by chance and their paths come to intersect. The event is unforeseeable and geometry has a hard time conceptualizing it. Poetry seems to be a more appropriate tool for bringing life to contingency by giving it form, as Kuki explained in the lectures he gave at the University of Kyoto in 1933 (published as *Bungaku no Gairon,* or Outline of literature). In the section on contingency and poetry, Kuki appeals to Paul Valéry's (1871-1945) definition of poetry as a "pure system of the chances of language" in order to theorize the importance that rhetorical techniques such as "pivot words" *(kakekotoba),* alliteration, "pillow words" *(makura kotoba),* and end rhymes *(kyakuin)* have played and, in Kuki's opinion, should continue to play in the composition of poetry.

In "Nihon Shi no Ōin" (Rhyme in Japanese poetry)—an essay published in 1931 that appeared in an extensively revised version in his later *Bungeiron* (Essays on the literary arts; 1941)—Kuki translated his philosophy of contingency into a full-grown poetics.[18] In this essay he stresses the importance of sound *(oto)* in poetic language, defining rhythm as the "number of sound" *(onsū)* and defining rhyme as the "color of sound" *(neiro).* Kuki proposed a revival in Japan of "rhythmic poetry" endowed with both rhythm and rhyme. A lack of attention to the sound of poetry by modern poets—who, since the Meiji period, had been following the new free style *(shintaishi)*—was an obstacle in raising Japanese poetry to world standards.[19] Puns and word play *(da-*

jare) were essential elements of poetic language developing from the repetition of sounds. For Kuki the success of poetry was found in its ability to express contingency (meaninglessness, nonsense, the unconscious, dreams) in a world of necessity known as the world of meaning. Rhyme was "the awakening of *logos* as *melos* (song)," a *melos* that provided an opening to a more authentic perception of reality. "Language as content of meaning" pointed at necessity and the self-sameness of a subject, whereas "language as sound" referred to contingency and the continuous disruption of a solid, unified subject. Kuki argued that rhyme was the chance encounter of two sounds—"the twin smiles" of Paul Valéry, who had called rhymes "philosophical beauty." The fact that rhyme, besides bringing to life a chance encounter of sounds, was also the medium for the repetition of the same sound indicated to Kuki that rhymes contain at the same time necessity and contingency (same sound, different words), sameness and difference. Thus rhyming poetry was "freedom following reason" based on "objective rules," while free poetry was an "arbitrariness following drive." The chance encounter of rhyming sounds was a good symbol for the recurring cycles of necessity and contingency.

How could contingency be better voiced than by exploiting the chance meeting of sounds that interpret the necessity of meaning in terms of the reality of contingency? My translation of the poem "Contingency" only vaguely reproduces Kuki's efforts to articulate the notion of chance—most properly voiced by a series of rhymes describing the unstructured and unstructurable flow of life. The original text is built around several sets of head rhymes, internal rhymes, end rhymes, and parallels. A reading of the romanized version of the poem reveals Kuki's determination to reproduce the topic of the poem in its very language, as the reader can see from the following highlighted words:

> *Heikō chokusen no* **kōri**,*/nozomidōri/shōmei ga dekita?/Iya, kihon yōkyū o tekkai shita?...Arekisandoria de mitsuketa* **furuhon**/*nisennen mae no kikagaku* **genron**,*/mushi ga kutte iyō to kutte imai* **to**/ *Yuukuriddo wa erai hito...*

The reversed parallel of "you and I/I and you" *(omae to ore/ore to omae)* provides a phonetic representation of the parallel lines of man and woman running on parallel tracks that do not intersect initially but will do so eventually. Moreover Kuki weaves the law of causation into the linguistic pattern of the poem, as we can see in the parallelism (which is not a simple repetition) of the verses *"kō naru inga no chokusen o miyo/otsu naru inga no chokusen o miyo."*

Far from being limited to the sphere of rhetoric, contingency for Kuki had profound consequences with respect to ethics and morality. Because of contingency, human existence is something in which one is thrown by chance, whose only law is that it could have been totally different. One cannot consider other people's existence to be alien to oneself, since others bear the destiny that could have been one's own. By understanding that one's own existence could be exchanged—that one might have lived someone else's existence—one realizes the wondrous nature of the meeting with others. According to Kuki, one should respect one's own destiny, as well as others', as something to be grateful for *(arigatai)* in the literal sense of the word, "difficult to be." This should be an encouragement to develop a sympathy for the existence of others. At the same time, understanding the nature of contingency should enable the conduct of a free and flexible life that is continuously open to what may occur and to those whom one has the chance of meeting.

Kuki's intellectual journey is constantly informed by the limitations of his personal "throwness" (Heidegger's *Geworfenheit*). His meditations on contingency and necessity, however theoretical and abstruse they might sound to a contemporary reader, are deeply rooted in his personal history. A privileged man by birth—he was born the fourth son of the wealthy and powerful baron Kuki Ryūichi—Kuki spent eight years in Europe, from October 1921 to January 1929, at a time when fear of the unknown Other often translated into prejudice and racism. Kuki's aristocratic education and economic stability undoubtedly won him access to the major philosophical voices in France and Germany. Yet even words of praise for the intellectual curiosity of a distinguished Japanese gentleman become an eloquent statement of how difficult it must have been to be Japanese in Europe during the 1920s. When, in 1921, Kuki arrived in Heidelberg to ask the most renowned Neo-Kantian philosopher of the time, Heinrich Rickert (1863–1936), for a private tutorial, a famous student of Rickert who lived in Rickert's house, Hermann Glockner, describes the arrival of the thirty-four-year-old Japanese man as follows:

One day Rickert surprised me with the news that he had just decided to give private lessons to a Japanese, a fabulously wealthy samurai who had asked him to read Kant's *Critique of Pure Reason* with him. This unusually distinguished gentleman looked totally different from the rest of his countrymen. He was tall and slender, with a relatively narrow face, a nose almost like that of Europeans, and unusually delicate hands. His name was Kuki, which meant something like "Nine Devils" (as he himself told us).[20]

To the question "Why was I born Japanese?" Kuki gave this answer: "Because of the rolling of the dice"—a purely contingent act breaking the chain of necessity. He accepted Aristotle's terminology: a human being lives for himself *(kathautó)* since his essence is to be an organism, a living thing. At the same time, however, he happens to be born by accident *(katà sumbebekós)* in a specific historical situation with specific racial characteristics. Kuki addresses the issue of racial difference in a poem titled "Yellow Face" (Ōshūjin) in which he presents the opinions of four scholars: a European, an Asian positivist thinker, an Asian metaphysician, and a European critical philosopher. They challenge each other in search of an explanation for the existence of different skin pigmentation. The poem, which comes from a collection titled *Sleep Talking in Paris (Parī no Negoto),* was originally published in the journal *Myōjō* (Morning star) in October 1926:[21]

Yellow Face

The European:
Your face is so yellow!
Inhabitants of the southern countries of Spain
And Italy,
Unable to stand strong sunlight,
Have a brown face but
Not yellow.
It might be rude to say but
The Chinese and the Japanese have contracted
Something like a chronic jaundice...
This is what we Europeans
Actually think.

The Positivist:

This seems a little harsh.
The place where we find skin pigments and
The layer where the yellow color of jaundice
Is present are different.
It seems that our ancestors
Somehow overate
Pumpkins and tangerines.
Maybe they also drank too much
Of the Yellow River and Yellow Sea.

The Metaphysician:

The distinction between races is inborn.
In a former life we committed mischief,
The gods got terribly upset,
Then the demons came upon us,
Caught us while we were running away,
Forced on our heads the filth of urine and feces.
Our yellow face
Stands as eternal memorial
To the merciless curse
Of just gods.

The Kritik Philosopher:

I am not going to mimic the arguments
Of the birdcatcher in the Magic Flute, but
There are yellow persons
As there are yellow birds.
The issue of becoming is a different complexity,
Reality is given as reality.
In short, we should establish appropriate categories
For the concept of a yellow race
And look at it from the standpoint of value.
Well, how can a yellow face become white?
Let's turn this problem from pure reason
To the realm of the practical.

Well aware that a poet never answers his questions, Kuki did not intervene with personal remarks on a topic that was at the center of personal experience and suffering. His writings on human life and temporality, however, are clear indications of Kuki's stand on this subject. For Kuki the issue of race was directly related to "human existence" *(jitsuzon)*, which is contingent *(gūzen;* Japanese translation of the Latin words *"quod potest non esse"),* since human existence *(existentia)* is particular *(kotaiteki)* and temporal *(jikanteki).* As contingency, human existence is the result of particularity and temporality—the opposite of necessity *(hitsuzen,* which translates the Latin expression *"quod non potest non esse").* The determination of pigmentation is basically a matter related to particularity and time, since it is an individual phenomenon taking place within a temporal instant. Kuki's powerful critique of racism indicates the potential that a philosophy of contingency has to accommodate differences whose distinction is constantly threatened by the ghost of homogeneity. It is not at all clear whether Kuki followed through with his own philosophy, as the years following his return to Japan in 1929 seem to indicate that he distanced himself from the promising ideas he had developed during his European stay.

Kuki's philosophy of contingency contains all the major ingredients of a postmodern philosophy of difference, including a move to deconstruct the pillars of metaphysical thought: necessity, causality, the primacy of identity, sameness, and completion. The dialectical method becomes the target of Kuki's critique in a poem titled "The Dialectical Method" (Benshōronteki Hōhō) in which Kuki disparagingly compares the Hegelian logic of thesis, antithesis, and synthesis to the three rhythmic measures of a waltz:[22]

The Dialectical Method

Spirit!
Hell, paradise
Sobbing out a counterpoint.
Glaring at each other are clouds of rain,
Not even a canon
Is born!

Living in a field at dawn
Hornets and red starlilies
Entwine to make honey,
Who can explain this?
God and witch
Plight their promise and give birth to humanity.

These are the rules of life,

Thesis, antithesis, synthesis,
The tone of logos,
The singer a priest,
How good, a triple time
Dancing the waltz.

In this poem Kuki challenges the complacent geometricity of a dia-
lectical method that arrogantly pretends to reduce the rules of life to a
preestablished order which he sarcastically compares to the triple pat-
tern of a waltz. Here Kuki followed Henri Bergson who in *La Pensée et
le Mouvant* argued as follows: "Hence a thesis and an antithesis which
it would be vain for us to try logically to reconcile, for the simple reason
that never, with concepts or points of view, will you make a thing."[23]
Being shaped by the ungeometric paradigm of contingency (the destiny
of suddenness and unexpectedness), human nature is much too com-
plex to be reduced to a law, a method, whether Hegelian dialectics or
Kantian categories. Kuki expresses this hesitation to entrust the vitality
of human life to philosophical laws in one of his short poems *(tanka)*
from the collection *Sonnets from Paris (Parī Shōkyoku):*

Hanchū ni	How many years have I spent
Toraegatakaru	Lamenting to myself
Onogami o	This body of mine—
Ware to nagekite	As difficult to grasp
Hetsuru ikutose	As a category?[24]

Nothingness

In his poetry, Kuki returned to the fundamental question of metaphys-
ics: why are there beings at all instead of nothing?—a question that was
later discussed by Martin Heidegger in *Introduction to Metaphysics*
and Jean-Paul Sartre in *Being and Nothingness.*[25] Kuki's mentor on this
subject was undoubtedly Nishida Kitarō, who was responsible for
Kuki's appointment as lecturer in the history of philosophy at Kyoto
Imperial University in April 1929. Western logic had either excluded
the notion of nothingness from its system or had reduced it to absence
and irrationality. Nishida Kitarō's philosophy of nothingness *(mu)*,
which Nishida posited as the East Asian counterpart of the Greek phi-

losophy of Being, provided Kuki with a basic framework for his recuperation of what Western philosophy tended to perceive as negative, contradictory, nihilistic. At the same time, Kuki relied on Western thought, especially Kantian, in talking about Being and its opposite.

In *An Outline of Literature* Kuki followed Western ontology in his definition of Being, which he saw as a bifurcation of "possible being" *(ens possibile,* or *essentia)* and "real being" *(ens reale, ens actuale,* or *existentia).* The former was related to Plato's notion of idea *(eidos)* and to form, corresponding to the Japanese expression *"ga aru"* (to be as an absolute); the latter corresponded to the Japanese expression *"de aru"* (to be relatively speaking). With regard to the classification of the opposite of Being—nothing *(mu)*—Kuki structured it into three types along Kantian lines: *nihil privativum* (privative nothing, or minus), *nihil positivum* (positive nothing, *quod potest esse,* or possibility), and *nihil negativum* (negative nothing, *quod non potest esse,* or impossibility).[26] Kuki derived the notion of *nihil privativum* from Kant's idea of negative dimension or minus (-) *(negative Grösse),* which Kant set up as real opposition (plus and minus, thesis and heterothesis) in order to explain what the logical negation of the law of noncontradiction (plus and zero, thesis and antithesis) could not explain.[27] To elucidate this point we can say that, according to the law of contradiction, one cannot possess a property and, at the same time, not possess it. In reality, however, it is quite possible that someone who possesses property also possesses a debt. A real opposition between two equally positive substances succeeds in explaining what a logical negation does not. According to Kuki, literature voices *nihil privativum* by dealing with topics such as error, crime, or evil. He points out that Baudelaire's *Les Fleurs du Mal* gives life not only to the beauty of good but also to the beauty of evil. In other words, the *nihil privativum* is a reality that comes into being in literature as real beauty.

In contrast to privative nothing, Kuki took *nihil positivum* to mean a reality that is present in the *essentia* of things rather than in their *existentia.* We find positive nothing in the world of images and ideas rather than in what we perceive to be the real world. *Nihil positivum* is the result of the skepticism following from Descartes's entreaty to question everything and be suspicious of everything. Why should the real world be more real than the world of dreams? Is there not a reality to the world of dreams, the world of the artist, and the hallucinatory world of the insane? From the perspective of the present world, such an illusory world does not exist. And yet we cannot deny that such a world of images which takes a form of its own, independently from the limits of reality, does indeed exist. All major East Asian philosophical traditions provide variations on the theme of undecidability with regard to the nature of reality.[28] In this regard Kuki refers to a poem from the *Kokinshū* in which the anonymous poet cannot decide whether the world is actually dream or reality since, although this world is *(arite)*, it is as if it were not *(nakereba)*:

Yo no naka wa	Might this world be real,
Yume ka utsutsu ka	Or might it be but a dream?
Utsutsu to mo	Whether it be a dream
Yume to mo shirazu	Or reality I know not,
Arite nakereba	For we are here and not here.[29]

The dreamer, the poet, and the mad person—and the three might well be combined into one—hold the key to the representation of this positive nothing, since they all create their own fictions within a world of nonreality, or nothing, which stand out as positive signs.[30] The surrealist is a visionary whose dreams are the concrete presence of a world that is beyond reality.[31]

Unlike positive nothing, *nihil negativum* is not possible in the world of *essentia*. As Kant says, it is "an empty object without concept" *(Nichts als leerer Gegenstand ohne Begriff)*. In other words, the principle of noncontradiction has no potential for impossibility—an example of *nihil negativum* would be a round square. The fact that such a nothing has no concept does not mean it does not have an object; we can still think it despite its being impossible in reality. Its possibility lies in the fact that negative nothing is nonreal. Although, logically speaking, it is a nothing, it might well find its way into poetry. Thus Kuki quotes from Aristotle's *Poetics:* "Let us first take the charges against the art of poetry itself. If an impossibility has been portrayed, an error has been made. But it is justifiable if the poet thus achieves the object of poetry—and makes that part or some other part of the poem more striking."[32] Poetry presents not simply what does not exist in reality *(nihil positivum);* it also includes what is impossible *(nihil negativum).* Kuki refers to Chikamatsu Monzaemon's (1653–1724) idea that "art is found in the skin membrane between reality and lie."[33] "Nothing" cannot be understood in absolute terms; it always possesses an existence that literature brings into being.[34] Literature begins by expressing the realm of possibility *(nihil positivum)* and then proceeds to conquer expressively even the realm of impossibility *(nihil negativum).* In other words, literature occupies the entire sphere of being *(ens):* rooted in existence, it subjugates nonexistence. It originates from Being *(yū)* and fills Nonbeing *(mu,* or nothing).[35] Although rooted in existence, literature develops in the realm of nonexistence *(quod non est).*

The positivity of the negative and the restoration of dignity and autonomy to what had been sacrificed on the altar of rationalism are the major themes of the poem opening Kuki's Parisian *Fragments,* which he titled "The Negative Dimension" *("Fugōryō,"* the Japanese translation of Kant's *"negative Grösse").* In this poem, a real opposition between two equally positive substances succeeds in explaining what a logical negation does not. Thus Kuki stresses the positive value of privative nothing, the blessing that can be found in a shadow—the glory of the female, negative, moonlike image of yin which stood in Chinese philosophy as the equally powerful pair of the solar, male, positive yang. As Kuki's poem says, plus and minus are both affirmations second to none.[36]

The Negative Dimension

In a shadow there is the blessing of a shadow,
It is not just that the shadow is not exposed to sunlight.
Ice has the taste of ice,
It is not the same as cooled hot water.
You can pull out your white hair,
Black hair won't grow.
A eunuch
Cannot become a lady-in-waiting.
Plus and minus—both extremes
Are affirmations second to none.
The law of contradiction regrettably
Is an odd pair, a one-eyed man, a man with one arm.
Glory to yin!

Glory to yang!
Good,
Smell the fragrance!
Evil,
Let the flower bloom!

As Kuki himself revealed in his *Outline of Literature,* this poem was also inspired by another source he used to explain the concept of *nihil privativum:* Goethe's theory of colors *(Farbenlehre),* which Goethe set up in opposition to Newton's. Whereas for Newton color was the product of light only, for Goethe colors resulted from the combined activity of light and darkness. Rather than positing darkness as the negation of light, Goethe considered darkness an equally positive and independent partner in the constitution of colors.[37] Goethe's theory of colors stands on the premise that colors are "bodily" *(körperlich)* and "shady" *(schattig).* In his writings on the natural sciences Goethe emphasized the true role played in reality by both the positive (yellow, operation, light, clear, strength, hot, proximity, push) and the negative (blue, deprivation, shade, dark, feebleness, cold, distance, pull).[38]

In developing the idea of the positivity of the negative we cannot disregard Kuki's indebtedness to Henri Bergson's theory of colors. The following quotation from Bergson comes from the *Essai sur les Données Immédiates de la Conscience,* a publication to which Kuki refers on several occasions:

We have grown accustomed, through the combined influence of our past experience and of physical theories, to regard black as the absence, or at least as the minimum, of luminous sensation, and the successive shades of grey as decreasing intensities of white light. But, in point of fact, black has just as much reality for our consciousness as white, and the decreasing intensities of white light illuminating a given surface would appear to an unprejudiced consciousness as so many different shades, not unlike the various colors of the spectrum....The variations in brightness of a given color—the affective sensations of which we have spoken above being left aside—would thus be nothing but qualitative changes, were it not our custom to transfer the cause to the effect and to replace our immediate impressions by what we learn from experience and science....

Every color, we might say, can be regarded under two aspects, from the point of view of black and from the point of view of white. And black is then to intensity what white is to saturation.[39]

Quality and Quantity

Variations in brightness—Bergson reminds us—are qualitative rather than quantitative changes. This differentiation is essential to understanding Kuki's philosophy of heterogeneity, which is profoundly rooted in Bergson's thought. For Bergson, the difference between qualitative and quantitative is equivalent to the difference between authenticity and inauthenticity. According to Bergson, the world of human sensations and consciousness can only be caught in the inner experience of real time, which he called "pure duration" *(durée pure)*—a time that is qualitative *(temps-qualité),* heterogeneous, dynamic, and creative. The time of pure duration provides an explanation for the heterogeneity of life. It is the time of contingency and the space of difference. In the real time of duration, the states of consciousness permeate one another. Pure duration is "the form which the succession of our conscious states assumes when our ego lets itself *live,* when it refrains from separating its present state from its former states."[40] Pure duration is the flowing of inner life *(fluidité même de notre vie intérieure),* the notes of a tune "melting, so to speak, into one another,"[41] "the effect of a musical phrase which is constantly on the point of ending and constantly altered in its totality by the addition of some new note."[42] Real time is characterized by "mutual penetration" *(pénétration mutuelle),* "multiplicity without possibility of being divided" *(multiplicité sans divisibilité),* "succession without separation" *(succession sans séparation).* Pure duration cannot be contained in one set of boundaries since it is "pure heterogeneity" *(pure hétérogénéité);* it anticipates a before and an after that are bridged by memory. Without memory, before and after cannot come into being. In other words, it would be impossible to distinguish duration from memory, since duration continues to exist in things when it ceases to exist in its essence.

People live in "quantitative time" *(temps-quantité),* however, the homogeneous time of the watch that can be measured easily, the time of sameness, a spatialized time, a time made into space. It is an emptying of the content of time into "a space of four dimensions in which past, present, and future are juxtaposed or superimposed for all eternity."[43] Quantitative time is a mathematical replacement of duration with a series of simultaneities that can be counted, instantaneities that do not endure. This time is made of the same kind of measures since it has to be measurable and, as a result, it can be separated; it is "homogeneous time" *(temps homogène)*. Rather than being real time, quantitative time is the product of time and space; it is "the fourth dimension of space" *(quatrième dimension de l'espace)*. By indicating "a numerical multiplicity" *(multiplicité numérique)*, homogeneous time is the time of the clock. This nonflowing time is a calculation of "a simultaneity within the instant" *(simultanéité dans l'instant)*. When we look at the hand of the clock calculating the seconds, we see that every instant is separated. Imaginary time is not "a flowing time" *(temps qui s'écoule)*; it is a "flown time" *(temps écoulé)*. Real time is duration; imaginary time is simultaneity.

In other words, quantitative time is "the ghost of space," the space of science in which real change is eliminated and human beings are made into machines rather than being analyzed as free individuals. Real time has no time to count itself, although we do it all the time, living outside ourselves, hardly perceiving anything but our own ghost, a colorless shadow, thus living for the external world rather than for ourselves—thus speaking rather than thinking. To the time of the clock we can, then, apply Bergson's definition of space: "Space is what enables us to distinguish a number of identical and simultaneous sensations from one another; it is thus a principle of differentiation other than that of qualitative differentiation, and consequently it is a reality with no quality."[44]

We find in Kuki's collection of poetic *Fragments* a song dedicated to Bergson's idea of *"durée pure,"* titled "Pure Duration" (Junsui Jizoku), in which Kuki attacks the measurable inauthentic time of quantity as "the shabby illegitimate child" of space, the cause of daily worries that makes people regret their decisions. To be imprisoned in quantitative time means to regret one's own destiny and to grieve over missed opportunities, a continuous lament in the name of compromise and at the cost of enjoying the value of one's own decisions irrespective of their final outcome.[45]

Pure Duration

Falling in love with space
Time, what a shabby illegitimate child!
To give birth was a mistake in the first place,
To repent for it, a good-for-nothing goblin,
The cause of your worries night in and night out.
Hello tortoise, dear tortoise!
To lose to a rabbit in a race, isn't that a victory?
A gull floating on the water says,
I will not be outrun by a duck!
You are thirty-something,
Still studying 31-syllable poems?
You say it is a 5/7/5/7/7 syllable poem?
That two stanzas 17/14 is the norm?
That three stanzas 12/12/7 is the poem's original form?
Aren't you rewriting the poem since the caesura splitting verses is bad?
Don't mistake "line" for "nine"![46]
A stanza is not made of numbers.
Since homogeneity is the foundation of compromise,
Respect the tune of pure heterogeneity!
Recollection of the past as well
Depends on time:
To curl your fingers[47] around moldy possibilities
Is the habit of the loser.[48]
Shout in your heart!
A meteor
A flash of lightning
A melody
A color.

As Bergson had argued in the *Essai,* "time, conceived under the form of an unbounded and homogeneous medium, is nothing but the ghost of space haunting the reflective consciousness."[49] Bergson had defined pure duration as "a succession of qualitative changes, which melt into and permeate one another, without precise outlines, without any tendency to externalize themselves in relation to one another, without any affiliation with number: a pure heterogeneity."[50] "Space," by contrast, "is the material with which the mind builds up number, the medium in which the mind places it."[51]

The reference in the poem to the rabbit addressing the tortoise (*"moshi moshi kame yo kame san yo"*) is not simply the echo of an Aesopian fable praising the determination of a steadily advancing tortoise who wins the race with a rabbit because of the latter's overconfidence and sluggishness—a fable that became a popular song during the Meiji period.[52] Kuki had also in mind the paradox of the Eleatic philosopher Zeno (ca. 495–430 B.C.), according to which Achilles will never reach the tortoise in a race if the tortoise is given a proper advantage—since by the time Achilles reaches the point where the tortoise started the race, the tortoise will have already moved ahead beyond that point. Zeno had challenged appearance, reducing movement to absurdity. Bergson explained the paradox as the result of a confusion between motion and space. Although motion takes place in space, the successive positions of the moving body do not occupy space; they are rather a process by which the body passes from one position to another, a process that is related to duration. Movement is more like a melody eluding space than a homogeneous and divisible object. Bergson explained Zeno's paradox as follows:

> It is to this confusion between motion and the space traversed that the paradoxes of the Eleatics are due; for the interval which separates two points is infinitely divisible, and if motion consisted of parts like those of the interval itself, the interval would never be crossed. But the truth is that each of Achilles' steps is a simple indivisible act, and that, after a given number of these acts, Achilles will have passed the tortoise. The mistake of the Eleatics arises from their identification of this series of acts, each of which is *of a definite kind* and *indivisible,* with the homogeneous space which underlies them....Why does Achilles outstrip the tortoise? Because each of Achilles' steps and each of the tortoise's steps are indivisible acts in so far as they are movements, and are different magnitudes in so far as they are space: so that addition will soon give a greater length for the space traversed by Achilles than is obtained by adding together the space traversed by the tortoise and the handicap with which it started. This is what Zeno leaves out of account when he reconstructs the movement of Achilles according to the same law as the movement of the tortoise, forgetting that space alone can be divided and put together again in any way we like, and thus confusing space with motion.[53]

The problem of Zeno's paradox lies in the illusion that a series of indivisible acts can be identified with homogeneous space. Bergson argued that Achilles, after all, was not a tortoise chasing after another tortoise. Achilles' movement was irreducibly individuated by its character as an action. We cannot reduce action to a spatialized present for all of time. For a tortoise, therefore, to lose to a rabbit in a race can only be a victory, if the event is seen from the perspective of the tortoise's authenticity, for the sake of the nature of the tortoise itself, and not for the sake of the nature of speed. Likewise, Kuki argued, poetry rejects any compromise with measurability—the strict form of a *tanka* made of 31 syllables in five verses distributed according to the pattern of 5/7/5/7/ 7 syllables—unless the "tune of pure heterogeneity" is able to spring forth from such a pattern. The elements of contingency must be accounted for if we want to grasp life and poetry in their ultimate nature of fortuitousness, suddenness, unexpectedness, duration, change, and heterogeneity—a meteor, a flash of lightning, a melody, a color.[54]

Kuki shared with Bergson an unmistakable suspicion of a modernity privileging numbers, quantities, productions, over the quality of life that was increasingly threatened by the development of industrial capitalism. It is no accident that Kuki saw in quantitative time the commodified time of the clock, a temporality measured by production and money.[55] While living in Paris, Kuki witnessed the backlash of anti-American sentiment in Paris during the 1920s when the city was flooded, not only by American writers such as John Dos Passos, Ernest Hemingway, Gertrude Stein, and Francis Scott Fitzgerald, musicians such as Aaron Copland and Josephine Baker, and many jazz players trying their fortune in Paris, but also by American banks and corporations investing heavily in the French economy. In the following short poem Kuki catches the Parisians' indignation over the invasion of their land by American capital and values:

Amerika no	People indignant
Hito ni kawareshi	At hearing the rumor
Gekijō no	That the theater
Uwasa o kikite	Was bought
Ikidohoru hito	By an American.[56]

The quantification of time is the target of Kuki's vitriolic critique in an essay discussing the Western proverb "Time is money"—a short piece originally written in French and published in a collection titled *Choses Japonaises* (Things Japanese). While daydreaming at the view of sweet mimosas during a winter sojourn in Nice, Kuki's reverie was interrupted by the words of a wealthy lady who, looking at "a bracelet encrusted with emeralds on her wrist," kept repeating to her neighbor, "Very expensive! Very expensive!" The following is Kuki's comment:

> Even with all goodwill, it is difficult to imagine this kind of mentality which always acts and speaks according to the law of the dollar's weight, this necessity of the mind to bring everything down to the level of money. For our taste, the ugliest proverb imaginable would be: Time is money. Nevertheless, it is this proverb which is adopted and worshipped in all parts of the world. Born in the new world, it victoriously invades the old.[57]

Kuki's reaction to the numerical reality of quantitative time was not simply a hypocritical rhetorical outburst by a privileged member of Japan's high society for whom "the law of the dollar's weight" was his very last concern. We find in Kuki's words the echo of a stern Meiji upbringing, a pride in the values of a temporality that is not measured by money, the same pride that led to the starvation of an unknown Japanese painter by the name of Toda who was in Paris at the same time Kuki was there, although Kuki never had the chance to meet him. Toda was one of many destitute Japanese artists who had fled to Paris in the 1920s in order to join the avant-garde movements of the time. We know of him thanks to the account of Robert McAlmon (1896–1956), a prolific American novelist who found himself in Paris in those years and who, in his modestly titled memoir, *Being Geniuses Together*, tells the sad story of a Japanese painter by the name of Toda who arrived in Paris around 1927 and let himself starve to death rather than ask his friends for help. Toda's traditional "fishes and flower-women pictures" reminded McAlmon of the work of Hokusai, Utamaro, and Hiroshige. Unable to speak any language beyond his native dialect, Toda did not mingle with other well-known Japanese artists such as Fujita Tsuguji (1886–1968), although they might have been sitting in the same bistro. Toda had "a wild, primitive quality…that made one think of legends of the Samurai knights in

the days before upstarts from the Western world invaded Japan." A
heavy drinker, Toda was soon appreciated for his talent, good looks, and
humor. After a while, however, he disappeared from the bars and cafés
of the French capital. McAlmon describes the tragic event of Toda's
death with a sense of surprise but respect for his fatal pride:

> Then he was discovered dead of starvation. Possibly his friends had not
> known that he was without money. Because of the old Japanese tradition
> of honor, he had told no one of his troubles. Certainly there were people
> who would have helped him had they known, myself among them, but his
> pride kept him silent. There seems to me no reason for sentimentality about
> suicide, and generally the suicides of people I have known do no more to
> me than make me wonder a little more about life. But Toda's death, and
> the suicide of the little French girl, Rita, did depress me. Both were needless.
> Rita killed herself when she was wild with drink, and Toda died because he
> was too proud to ask for momentary financial help or food.[58]

Kuki was not faced with the concerns of starving artists. He dined at
the exclusive Prunier, one of Paris's foremost seafood restaurants on
Victor Hugo Avenue;[59] he was a frequent guest at the Opéra;[60] he trav-
eled to the Italian shores of Lake Como[61] in order to rest from his fre-
quent dances chez Maxim;[62] he gambled at the casino of Monte Carlo.[63]
He was also a regular customer of the Sphinx, the first high-class brothel
on the Left Bank in the somber neighborhood of the Montparnasse cem-
etery. It was a palace of unrivaled opulence characterized by its stucco
sphinx added to the façade and by its Art Déco interiors with an Egyp-
tian theme. Established by Marthe Lemestre, known as "Martoune,"
this three-star house of rendesvouz began with a staff of fifteen *filles de
joie,* girls of reputedly superior gifts. Eventually it employed as many as
sixty charming hostesses entertaining hundreds of clients every night,
"not only as bed partners but often simply as salon companions, grace-
ful tablemates with whom one discussed art and the issues of the day
over a bottle of Taittinger."[64]

The world of Kuki's short poems *(tanka)* is filled with Parisian demi-
mondaines or women of pleasure *(asobi onna).*[65] We find Yvonne,[66] De-
nise,[67] Rina,[68] Marianne,[69] Louise,[70] Henriette,[71] Jeannine,[72] Renée,[73]
and Yvette.[74] As for Suzanne, who might well be the same Suzanne in

"The Russian Song,"[75] we find her standing together with Yvonne on a street corner of Paris trying to keep warm by eating chestnuts—all indications that leave no doubt about their nightly profession:

Yakiguri ga	An evening
Parī no tsuji ni	When roasted chestnuts perfume
Kaoru yoi	The street corners of Paris—
Tachite kuri hamu	Yvonne, Suzanne
Ivonnu, Suzannu	Stand and eat chestnuts.[76]

Later, living in Kyoto, Kuki will be chasing his memories of Paris while spending the evenings in Gion, the district populated by clubs, parlors, coffee shops, and teahouses where geisha performed their arts.[77] In Kyoto he wrote a series of poems titled *Winter in Kyoto (Kyō no Fuyu)* in which he sings the great poetic voice of the medieval recluse Saigyō (1118-1190),[78] as well as the voice of Kyoto's most revered river, the Kamogawa.[79] Kuki also hinted at historical events unfolding in front of his eyes, some casual, such as the loss of a student in philosophy who opted for the theological life of the monastery,[80] others poignant, such as the deaths of friends and relatives in battle during World War II.[81] Kuki spent the last twelve years of his life from 1929, when he was appointed lecturer in the department of philosophy of Kyoto Imperial University, until his death in 1941, in Kyoto, a city that had served Japan as capital from 794 until 1868. Filled with historical traces that stood as a rebuke to reckless modernization, Kyoto presented Kuki with the perfect setting for the articulation of an alternative qualitative temporality in opposition to the quantitative time of the modern, capitalistic world. The personal experience of tasting the vestiges of the past in the present was a direct appeal to explore the notion of temporality. Such a notion formed the core of the philosophies of the Western thinkers who had the most impact on Kuki's thought: Henri Bergson, Martin Heidegger, Augustine (354-430), and Edmund Husserl (1859-1938).[82]

Temporality

In "Bungaku no Keijijōgaku" (The metaphysics of literature) Kuki introduces three types of temporality based on past, future, and present.

In the first type, time originates in the past, flowing from the past toward the future; it is the temporality of history. Past and future are bridged by memory since "time as continuation is nothing but memory," a memory whose task is to connect a before and an after. Calling this view of time "biological," Kuki linked it to the genres of novels and *monogatari* (tales) in which the author "tells" *(noberu)* a story or, playing on a homophonous word, "stretches" *(noberu)* the story in time while unrolling the scroll in space, thus presenting "a past present" *(kakoteki genzai)*. According to Kuki, the same temporality characterizes scholarship *(gakumon)* since scholarship adapts new theories to old observations and is grounded in a knowledge that has been previously acquired.[83]

The privileging of the past was directly related to the philosophy of Bergson, who had raised the past to ontological status by considering it being-in-itself.[84] The present cannot be considered Being since it no longer exists; it has already ceased to be. People tend to confuse Being with being-present. Although the present acts, it does not exist. Rather than Being, the being of the present is active or useful. The past, by contrast, has ceased to act or to be useful. Useless and inactive, the present exists in the true sense of the word: it is identical with being-in-itself. Bergson disclosed the paradox that common sense tends to neglect when it considers temporality: of the present we should say that at every instant "it was"; of the past we should say that "it is," that it is for all times, eternally. With Bergson we perceive the past in the place where it is in itself, not in our present or in ourselves. We leap into being-in-itself—into the being-in- itself of the past. The past is contemporaneous with the present that it has been. Past and present coexist: "One is the present, which does not cease to pass, and the other is the past, which does not cease to be but through which all presents pass."[85] Bergson's notion of duration is grounded in the authority of the past, since "duration is the continuous progress of the past which gnaws into the future and which swells as it advances."[86]

The second type of temporality emphasizes the future and makes the future its starting point. Here memory is replaced by anticipation since "time is born in the future and flows in reverse back to the present and the past." According to this view, the difference between time and everything else is found in the fact that only time has a future. Kuki calls this view "ethical," since within this temporality we struggle after a moral purpose located in the future by having our consciousness anticipate a goal in the realm of the future. He associates this temporality with drama—a genre that develops from the future since it is premised on a crisis preceding the tragic conclusion of a tragedy or on a joyful resolution coming before the final act of a comedy. The Aristotelian theory of pathos, according to which drama has a purifying and pacifying effect, reinforced Kuki's belief that the temporal structure of drama is similar to the temporal structure of morality, since drama brings about an ethical effect. Kuki defined the temporality of drama as a "futural present" *(miraiteki genzai).*[87]

Kuki's source for this future-oriented temporality was Heidegger, for whom human beings exist in the etymological sense of the word (ek-sist): they "stand out" into future possibilities, into a past heritage, and into a present world. Heidegger stresses the futural aspect of our *Da-sein.* Human life begins with the future since authentic existence involves facing up to mortality and accepting the finitude of one's possibilities. By freeing human beings from everydayness, death is actually liberating. The key to Heidegger's temporality is "anticipatory resoluteness," which indicates one's responsibility to take a stance and make an authentic choice of a way to be. Paradoxically, for Heidegger, the future is the source of the past since our past gets its meaning from our projection of a future. In inauthenticity, past (as forgetting) and future (as awaiting) are subordinated to the present (as making-present); in authenticity, the present (as a moment of vision) gains a deeper meaning from the past (as retrieval) and, especially, from the future (as anticipation).[88]

Kuki's third model of temporality privileges the present. This view is based on the consideration that neither past nor future actually exists: while the past is already gone, the future has not yet come; only the present exists. In the past and the future, only the memory of the former and the anticipation of the latter exist. Kuki called this temporality "psychological" because "it is based on the original impression within the present of the phenomenon of time."[89] This is the general temporality of art. In the lecture course *Bungaku no Gairon,* Kuki indicated his indebtedness to Augustine and Husserl in formulating this theory of time centered on the present. In the *Confessions,* Augustine argues that since neither the future nor the past is present, we cannot talk about the three times of past, present, and future. We should rather talk about "the present of the past" *(praesens de praeteritis),* "the present of the present" *(praesens de praesentibus),* and "the present of the future" *(praesens de futuris).* These three times are found only in the human soul *(anima):* the present of the past is "memory" *(memoria);* the present of the present is "intuition" *(contuitus);* the present of the future is "anticipation" *(expectatio).* Through "attention/care" *(adtendit),* anticipation *(expectat)* changes into memory *(meminit).* Although the future is not yet, the expectation of the future is already in the soul. Although the past is already gone, the soul is endowed with the memory of the past. Although the present lacks continuity since it is already gone at any singular moment, attention endures *(perdurat).* As a result, what is going to be becomes what is not any longer. Augustine did not acknowledge the being of future and past; he only acknowledged the being of the present. In other words, future and past live only in the present and in its modalities: the future lies in the form of expectation; the past lies in the form of memory. Expectation and memory are the modalities of the present; for Augustine the essence of time is unmistakenly the present.

Kuki pointed out similarities between Augustine and Husserl on the relevance of the present in the analysis of time. Husserl describes the original spheres of time as (1) presentation *(Präsentation)* or present *(Gegenwärtigung);* (2) retention *(Retention);* (3) anticipation *(Protention).* The center of Husserl's temporal scheme is the "now" *(Jetzt).* An "impression" *(Impression)* originates in the now. The now is an abiding form *(verharrende Form)* that is opposed to a substance *(Materie).* In addition to the now there is also the form of the "just now" *(Soeben).* In other words, an impression is followed by other new impressions. Impressions transform into retention, and retention changes into a retention of retention *(Retention von Retention).* Here we find the continuity *(Kontinuum)* of retention. In the opposite direction we have the continuity of anticipation. While the continuity of retention is "before" *(Vorher),* the continuity of anticipation is "after" *(Nachher).* The now of experience *(Erlebnisjetz)* possesses the horizon of before *(Horizont des Vorhin),* that is, the now that has become past. It also possesses the horizon of after *(Horizont des Nachher),* that is, it becomes a new now. The consciousness of the now is necessarily linked to the consciousness of what has gone just now *(das soeben Vergangen),* which is another now. At the end of an experience we have the consciousness of the end. This new consciousness is a newly fulfilled now. Presentation, retention, and anticipation come with a content since, for Husserl, "an empty form without content is a nonsense"—an idea that indicates the volition of time.[90]

Kuki found in the work of Augustine and Husserl inspiration for the development of a fourth type of temporality—a temporality that he made the structural pillar of his essays on poetics: time as a circle, a "recurrent time" *(kaikiteki jikan),* an "infinite present" *(mugen no genzai),* the "eternal now" *(eien no ima):*

> We can add a fourth theory of time. The past is not simply something that has already gone. The future is not simply something that has not yet come. The past comes again in the future; the future has already come in the past. If we follow the past far enough, we return to the future; if we follow the future far enough, we return to the past. Time forms a circle; it is recurrent. If we locate time in the present, we can say that this present possesses as present an infinite past and an infinite future and, moreover, that it is identical with a limitless present. The present is the eternal present with an infinite depth; in short, time is nothing but the infinite present, the eternal now.[91]

Kuki called this fourth kind of temporality "a metaphysical theory." In *Bungaku no Gairon,* Kuki stresses the metaphysical coloring of Augustine's and Husserl's theories of time in which the now is considered a beginning *(Anfang)*—a source *(Quellpunkt)* from which past and future flow and spread. Husserl calls the now "the primary source" *(die Urquelle),* "the primary impression" *(Urimpression),* "the spontaneous generation" *(Urzeugung),* "the original creation" *(Urschöpfung).* Kuki argues that the now, as the primary source and the original creation, can be considered "an eternal present," which can be described as a circle. The now keeps repeating itself endlessly—an infinite series of spirals. The now, then, possesses unlimited depth. In the lectures on literature Kuki also refers to the notion of *samsāra* (Jpn. *rinne)* found in Indian philosophy and in Greek thought (Pythagoras, Plato, the Stoa), as well as to Nietzsche's "eternal return" *(ewige Wiederkehr).*

Kuki uses the following quotation from Confucius's *Analects* as an example of metaphysical time: "Once when the Master was standing by a stream, he said, Could one but go on and on like this, never ceasing day or night."[92]

To privilege the past is for Kuki like going down a river on a ship. To privilege the future is like towing a boat upstream against the current. To privilege the present is like staring at the river while standing on the shore. The privileging of the present presupposes the idea of stepping outside of time in order to stare time in the face. While the spectator looks at the river from the shore, the water enters into the sea, evaporates, rises to the sky, and eventually returns to earth as rain, nurturing the mountain and flowing again into the river down the valley. The eternal cycle of the river's water is for Kuki a perfect symbol of the concept of metaphysical time.[93]

Kuki did not agree with Heidegger, who approached time as "human time," "finite time," the time between birth and death, the time whose being makes itself visible, "is out there" *(Da-sein)*. In "Der Begriff der Zeit" (The concept of time), a lecture delivered to the Marburg Theological Society in July 1924, Heidegger had challenged the notion of eternal time whose explanation required an act of faith, a belief in an eternal God. Quoting from Einstein's theory of relativity, Heidegger argued that absolute space and absolute time do not exist in themselves since space exists only "by way of the bodies and energies contained in it" and time "persists merely as a consequence of the events taking place in it." Accordingly, Heidegger defined time as "that within which events take place." In the lecture Heidegger not only took issue with the theologians but also challenged the physicists' practice of measuring time. Borrowing from Bergson's idea of quantitative time (although he himself reached different conclusions), Heidegger argued that the clock reduces time to a temporal sequence that is not subject to change; it degrades time to an identical duration that constantly repeats itself. Time, then, becomes an arbitrarily fixed now-point—a uniform, homogeneous time. Such a view ignores the fact that *"Da-sein* as human life *is primarily being possible,* the Being of the possibility of its certain yet indeterminate past." Unlike the physicist's (or the historian's) approach to time, Heidegger's questioning seizes the indeterminacy of the certainty of the past rather than wishing to determine indeterminate time.

The clock loses the futuricity of time or, as Heidegger put it, "only if I say that time authentically has no time to calculate time is this an appropriate assertion." The clock is the concern of "everydayness." Rather than reducing time to a continuous present—in which the past is interpreted as a no-longer present and the future as indeterminate not-yet present—Heidegger reminded his audience that "the possibility of access to history is grounded in the possibility according to which any specific present understands how to be futural. This is the first principle of all hermeneutics."[94]

Kuki was not ready to accept Heidegger's notion of "horizontal time," time seen as an integral unity of its ecstasies. Kuki never fully integrated into his philosophy Heidegger's deconstruction of the metaphysics of presence. The safety net of metaphysics was one that Kuki never agreed to give up. As he confesses in the poem "An Autumn Day" (Aki no Ichinichi):

> After all, I am lonesome,
> The loneliness of one who follows darkness, the grief of one
>   who pursues an invisible shadow,
> A philosophy without metaphysics is sad—
> I wish for a metaphysics that problematizes human
>   existence and death.[95]

Kuki associates metaphysical time, the time of Kuki's temporality, with poetry, by which he means lyrical poetry. For Kuki, poetry is the intuition *(chokkan)* and the emotion *(kandō)* of the present instant. By singing the "eternal present," the rhythm of poetry is an indication of the "eternal return of the present." Rhymes, repetitions, and other rhetorical devices were means for the reader to stop at the place of the same present and concentrate on the unending instant of the eternal present. Kuki calls the temporal structure of poetry "the present present" *(genzaiteki genzai),* the same structure found in all arts.[96] In *Bungaku no Gairon,* Kuki argues that the temporal stipulation of art is the present in the sense of Augustine's *praesens de praesentibus* (present of present), that is, a present which has a duration made of intuition *(contuitus)* and attention *(attentio).* It is not the present of the natural sciences, Augustine's *praesens* (present), a point lacking extension. To explain the present of art, Kuki offers the example of a painting of a horse by the French painter Théodore Géricault (1791–1824) that is kept at the Louvre museum. Géricault was criticized because in his painting the legs of the horse are fully extended in front of and behind the horse's body. A snapshot of a horse would demonstrate the impossibility of such a posture and the painter's alleged error. Kuki sided with the French sculptor Auguste Rodin (1840–1917), who had defended Géricault's artistic representation of the horse. According to Rodin, the painter portrayed a continuity of instants using his intuition. The snapshot presents a single instant that in actuality does not exist. Géricault had portrayed Augustine's *praesens de praesentibus*, whereas the snapshot was only able to catch the *praesens,* a point with neither extension, continuity, nor duration.[97]

In the first lecture that he gave at Pontigny, on the outskirts of Paris, on his way back to Japan, "La Notion du Temps et la Reprise sur le Temps en Orient" (The notion of time and repetition in oriental time; 11 August 1928), Kuki articulated a notion of time that he hoped would bring the depth of metaphysics back to time. Instead of Heidegger's "horizontal time" he introduced the view of a "self-escaping vertical time," a mystical time seen as an eternal present. This was a critique of modern time as a time "alienated toward the future," in which the present is always meaningless, time being always directed toward a future purpose—a straight, infinite, abstract line. Kuki presented what he believed to be the structure of Eastern time, a returning/recurring time, the cyclical time of transmigration *(rinne),* in which what he called the "great cosmic year" *(daiuchū nen)* repeats itself infinitely. The same instant that takes place in the present is found in the infinite "great cosmic year" of past and present; as a result, every instant is "the eternal present" *(eien no genzai).* The awakening to the truth that each instant actually is "the eternal present" Kuki called "the vertical casting off the self" *(suichokuteki datsuga),* that is, the experience of mystical time.

Kuki structured his theory of time as a response to the growing nihilism in Europe following World War I, which Kuki had personally witnessed, particularly during his stay in Germany. Following the example of his European colleagues who were struggling to give a fullness of meaning back to the notion of time, Kuki moved toward an articulation of time in which every single instant is granted a plenitude of meaning.

In this respect, Kuki's sources were not simply Asian notions of cyclical time; he also imported back into his notion of "oriental time" the interpretation of Buddhist time that Nietzsche had developed in the theory of the "eternal return." Like Nietzsche, Kuki turned his attention to finding a way liberated from quantitative, inauthentic time. Unlike Nietzsche, however, Kuki relied on the full strength of metaphysics in his reworking of temporality. He referred to two native and traditional, though mutually contradictory, ways of liberation: one was Buddhist liberation, that is, a denial of the will leading to the realization of nirvana (extinction, the suppression of the world), resulting from belief that "annihilation is beatitude"; the other was the liberation of the way of the warrior *(bushidō),* that is, an affirmation of the will conducive to the development of the skill of not fearing time. This latter liberation was the negation of negation: the abolition of nirvana. The perpetual repetition of the will, which for Buddhist thinkers is the supreme evil, becomes the supreme good for the warriors. In *bushidō* the good-will in itself has an absolute value, even if it is an unsatisfied will, an unrealizable ideal, "that time lost perpetually repeating itself." It is to find *Unendlichkeit* in Hegel's notion of *Endlosigkeit,* to find infinity in the indefinite, to find eternity in succession without end. Kuki defines cyclical time using the example of love that loves something by a process of repetition, a love within the repetition of the same in which the subject is a subject of sameness *(dōitsusei).* As Kuki concludes at the end of the lecture:

> The time which could be called oriental is the time of transmigration, that is to say, that time which repeats itself, periodic and identical time. There are two methods, two means of liberating oneself from this time: (1) *transcendent, intellectualist liberation* and (2) *immanent, voluntarist liberation.* Transcendent, intellectualist liberation is the *nirvāna* of the religion of Indian inspiration. Immanent, voluntarist liberation is *bushidō,* the way of the *bushi,* the moral ideal of Japan. The first consists in denying time by means of the intellect in order to live, or rather to die, in nontemporal "deliverance," in "eternal repose." The second consists in an unconcern with time, in order to live, truly live, in the indefinite repetition of the arduous search for the true, the good, and the beautiful. One is the consequence of that hedonism which seeks to escape from misfortune; the other is the expression of moral idealism, always valiantly determined to

put itself in the service of the God within us, struggling without respite and, thus, transforming misfortune into happiness.[98]

In the second Pontigny lecture, "L'Expression de l'Infini dans l'Art Japonais" (The expression of the infinite in Japanese art; 17 August 1928), Kuki connected "vertical time" to art by arguing that vertical time is the time of art, especially the time experienced in poetry. Kuki reminded his audience that in addition to being further informed by *bushidō* ("the cult of the absolute spirit, contempt for what is material"), Japanese art had developed under the influence of Indian mysticism and Chinese pantheism (the pervasive Tao informing all matters and all beings). Art, then, is a perfect example of liberation from time, since the mysticism of Indian Buddhism and the pantheism of Chinese Taoism are allegedly expressions of the liberation from time and space. Kuki defined Japanese art as "the idealist expression of the infinite in the finite." In its attempt to seize the absolute, art must destroy the natural forms in order to create aesthetic and absolute forms, often incomplete and empty, "forms without form," achieved by art's power to suggest rather than to state. Kuki emphasizes in the lecture: "It is not necessary to express and disclose everything; it is only necessary to indicate with several essential lines and leave the rest to the active play of the imagination." Silence is more eloquent than eloquence itself.

Poetry *(tanka* and *haiku)* liberates the infinite from time. The infinite realizes itself "in an asymmetric and fluid form" (the 5-7-5-7-7 pattern is not symmetric). In such an asymmetric form, "the idea of liberation from measurable time is realized." In the circular time of Japanese poetry, time past is brought back to the present so that ordinary time is broken. The "infinite present" of poetry gives concreteness to Kuki's notion of the "great cosmic year": poetry brings vertical time (ecstatic time / the outside of time / past / the eternal present) into the present, inauthentic, spatial, horizontal time. As an example of poetry's ability, Kuki quotes a verse by Japan's most revered *haiku* poet, Matsuo Bashō (1644-1694):

Tachibana ya	Oh, mandarin orange!
Itsu no no naka no	In the field of what time,
Hototogisu	The cuckoo bird.[99]

The fragrance of mandarin oranges and the cry of the cuckoo bird (a traditional association in classical Japanese poetry) remind the poet of a time past and an unknown place in which he went through the same experience as the present one. Kuki interprets the poem in light of the notions of memory and the recreation of time as Marcel Proust had expressed them in *Remembrance of Things Past:* "A sound already heard or an odor caught in bygone years are sensed anew, simultaneously in the present and in the past, real without being of the present moment, ideal but not abstract, and immediately the permanent essence of things, usually concealed, is set free and our true self, which had long seemed dead but was not dead in other ways, awakes, takes on fresh life as it receives the celestial nourishment brought to it."[100]

Like poetry, Japanese music is a liberation from measurable time. For Kuki, all multiplicity is founded in music's simplicity—music is another expression of pantheistic mysticism. Music is simplicity after the disappearance of the multiplicity of sounds. In a related essay, "Oto to Nioi" (Sound and smell), Kuki argues that the sound of a blossoming lotus flower brings back a time long past, thus making possible the experience of recapturing that past.[101] By participating in the work of art, the appreciator experiences a giant leap into a bottomless metaphysical pool, the pool of the eternal present. Eternal beauty for Kuki exists only in the human heart. True art, therefore, is an inner art: "the expression of the mystical voice of eternity coming from the bottom of the soul."[102]

Closing the Circle

Kuki uses the notion of the "the eternal present" in discussing poetry and the arts, but his poetry foregrounds the very different idea of "duration." Kuki's circle of eternal time does not present the characteristics of Bergson's expanding circle—a circle that by expanding shows openness but by remaining at any instant a circle affirms that it is still closed. Kuki's circle is closed at all times—marking the boundaries of a circumscribed space in which time is frozen in an ahistorical eternity, the eternity of the "reigns of the gods" *(kami no yo)* of mythical memory. Kuki's fourth type of temporality presents all the characteristics of imperial time, the Japanese emperor a reminder of his sacred ancestors, all living in the eternal present. Before drawing a hasty conclusion, however, we should not forget that Kuki was deeply imbued with the education of the Meiji period, a time when the emperor stood as the symbol that had crushed the feudalism of the shogunal regime, rather than the symbol justifying the atrocities of the contemporary military regime. If I may borrow the language that Bergson developed in *Les Deux Sources de la Morale et de la Religion* (The two sources of morality and religion; 1932),[103] a book with which Kuki was familiar, Kuki's spatialized temporality is ambiguously located between the closed society of moral obligation and the open society of moral aspiration. His philosophy of contingency is a centrifugal movement involving open sociability and dynamic spirituality. Its potential was somehow silenced by his philosophy of necessity (recurring time and eternal present), which is a centripetal movement of closure. In the philosophy of necessity, the in-group of family, nation, and race excludes the differences of the out-group. Space, once again, is privileged over time.

Kuki passed away on 6 May 1941 at 11:50 P.M. His mentor and colleague Nishida Kitarō translated a poem from Goethe's *Lieder* titled "Ein Gleiches" (The same) and prepared a calligraphic sample that was carved on one side of Kuki's tomb at the Hōnen-in temple in Kyoto, along the "path of philosophy" (Tetsugaku no Michi) that Nishida and Kuki had walked countless times. The poem is Nishida's homage to his own philosophy of "nothingness," a philosophy that, while opening Kuki's thought to the possibility of overcoming necessity and singing the tune of heterogeneity, also helped to freeze once again the world of contingency in the eternal repetition of the same:

Miharukasu yamayama no chō
Kozue ni wa kaze mo ugokazu tori mo nakazu
Mateshibashi yagate nare mo yasurawan[104]

The top of the mountains looking far in the distance,
No wind makes the treetops sway, no bird sings.
Wait a moment! In the end, you too will be resting.

POETRY

Free Verse
[Shi]

Paris Mindscapes
[Parī Shinkei]

Wind

O autumn wind
Blowing through the sycamores' treetops,
Let me blow
As freely as you do!

Let me speak of unsightly things as well
With no embellishment,
Let me tell of shameful actions as well
With no hiding,

As they are,
Just as they are,
With no fear of man,
Unfrightened by the world,

Let me speak
The confession of my heart!
Let me sing
The grief of my heart!

O autumn wind
Blowing through the sycamores' treetops,
Let me blow
As freely as you do![1]

Recollections

Shadowy is the path
Of man's world;
Lonesome is the shade of a tree
At dusk.
That fragrance
I cannot forget;
That shape
Looks like a phantom to me.

My heart injured
At recollecting;
My life distressed
At yearning.

Shadowy is the path
Of man's world;
Lonesome is the present body
When night falls.[2]

Seafood Restaurant

[Man]
Oh, the sea, the sea
Born in an island country in the Far East
I pine for the blue sea,
The shore scattered with seashells,
White sand bathing in the morning sun,
The smell of seaweed, the sound of waves,
I wonder, you who grew up in Paris,
Do you understand my feelings?
Tonight let us go to Prunier[3]
On Victor Hugo Avenue.

Pillars designed with the pattern of scallops,
Lamps shaped as sea crabs,

Watery foam on the walls,
Fish on the counters,
The ceiling a light turquoise,
The rug the crimson color of seaweed,
A faint floating light,
A scent more fleeting than a dream,
Like breathing at the bottom of the sea,
My favorite seafood restaurant.

[Woman]
What was your favorite dish?
Salmon roe sandwich,
Sea urchin in its shell
Sprinkled with lemon juice,
The chowder bouillabaisse
A specialty from Marseilles,
Lobsters the thermidor style
Not the American style,
I too like
The steamed flatfish Paris style.

For a dress I will choose clothes of black silk.
Don't you like the way my figure looms over the silver wall,
One snowy white rose on my breast,
Pearls for necklace,
A platinum watch on my wrist,
A white diamond ring,
A hat the green color of laver
I will pull down over my eyes coquettishly?
Let me please make my lipstick heavy.
Do you still insist I am princess of the sea?[4]

The Gatekeeper's Son

Antoinette is renting a room
In a house whose gatekeeper's
Only son François,
A handsome lad of fourteen this year,
Honor student in junior high,
Always wins awards—
That is what his straightforward father

Said the other day, chuckling to himself,
Faded pipe in his left hand.

Today, Sunday evening,
When I opened the car door and landed on my feet
Taking Antoinette's hand
On her way back from dancing,
There was François wearing a hat,
Sitting in a chair by the entrance,
François who is fourteen this year,
With an old necktie of mine
Tied on his chest,
Carrying a small Latin grammar.

Oh, François, François,
A handsome lad of fourteen this year,
What whim over came you last night?
Next door you were playing
Earnestly on the harmonica
A dashing sailor's tune,
Singing "The Night of Love of the Beautiful Night"
From "The Tales of Hoffmann."[5]
Who taught you
To entertain us with so much style?

François who is fourteen this year,
Study, study, study
This beautiful Latin—
In the future sometime
A day will come when you will wet your eyes with Virgil,[6]
A day will come when you will pray reading
Augustine's Confessions,[7]
Again a day will come when you will laugh over the gloom
Of the present world grounded in the shape
Of Spinoza's eternity.[8]

Oh, François, François,
A handsome lad of fourteen this year,
Study, study, Latin nouns,
pronouns, adjectives,
Study the conjugation of verbs,

You should not be surprised
That even the old man who loves the dance
Of your friend Antoinette
Speaks the same words
As your junior high teacher![9]

An Autumn Day

Tree lines at Champs-Élysées,
Scattering leaves of horse chestnut trees dyed yellow,
At ten or so this morning you[10] came to my place—
We spoke, we smoked,
We ate lunch, we walked,
We took a rest at a café, we gazed at an exhibit of paintings.
Now it is already dusk,
You and I eccentrics as always.
When we were students, we often spent nights talking till
    dawn,
The next morning you returned home.
The art of overcoming time, denying time,
Looks like an easy art but is not,
An art of which you are a master, genius.
No wonder you do not return even though your term abroad
    has expired.
Even so, have you already picked the ship?
When you return to Japan, I think you must lecture again.
If the topic were the art of the Renaissance
You'd spend one academic year just on the introduction;
If it were the history of Greek sculpture
Would you get as far as the mid-fifth century B.C.?
If it were about French contemporary painting
You'd probably stop at the entrance
With Courbet,[11] Manet,[12] Monet.[13]
Even earlier on, while listening to your comments on the
    exhibit,
Before we saw even a fifth of it,
The closing bell rang—and were we not shown the way out?

Ah, how beautiful! Turn back and look!
The mellow, quiet color of the Arch of Triumph in the purple
    sky,

Always impressive whenever one admires it,
Now that I mention it, what will A[14] be doing at this time?
One year has already gone since he returned to Japan
At the new term after summer vacation,
Is he lecturing on the ethics of Kant?
How rare to find a personality as moral as his,
A man who, even exhausted at night, would say "fulfill your
    duty"
And check the next day's lecture notes while rubbing his
    sleepy eyes.
Have you ever met anyone
Whose categorical imperative[15] is so powerfully alive?
More than ten years have gone
Since the days of high school and university,
The three of us often walking on the Yodo Bridge
    embankment,
A spring day with Chinese milk vetch in bloom, an autumn
    evening with eulalia flowing in the air,
Shinjuku Street on our way back,
The three of us walking in front of the pleasure quarter—
Not once had the three of us
Ever brought up the topic of women!
I yearn for that time,
I was still filled with ambition,
Life was beautiful.

In no time have we come to Place de la Concorde.
The French ask the question,
Why is the Obélisque always standing?
They always reply,
To show one the way to the beautiful Madeleine![16]
A half-tipsy nation with a taste for puns and jokes,
And yet it gave birth to Descartes,[17] gave birth to Pascal,[18]
The chaos that gives birth to stars is a blessing.
Ah, look at the Seine,
The crescent moon hanging in the clear sky,
Those beautiful stars glittering on the clumps of sycamores,
Life emerging from chaos entering chaos,
A flickering, short human life in the midst of eternity,
Both you and I already on the verge of exceeding half of it,

Nel mezzo del cammin di nostra vita...[19]
After all, I am lonesome,
The loneliness of one who follows darkness, the grief of one
  who pursues an invisible shadow,
A philosophy without metaphysics is sad—
I wish for a metaphysics that problematizes human existence
  and death.
Today was a good autumn day,
Let's go somewhere and have supper.[20]

Fragments (From Paris)
[Hahen (Parī Yori)]

The Negative Dimension

In a shadow there is the blessing of a shadow,
It is not just that the shadow is not exposed to sunlight.
Ice has the taste of ice,
It is not the same as cooled hot water.
You can pull out your white hair,
Black hair won't grow.
A eunuch
Cannot become a lady-in-waiting.
Plus and minus—both extremes
Are affirmations second to none.
The law of contradiction regrettably
Is an odd pair, a one-eyed man, a man with one arm.
Glory to yin![21]
Glory to yang!
Good,
Smell the fragrance!
Evil,
Let the flower bloom![22]

Contingency

Could you find a proof to the design
Of parallel straight lines?

That was your aim:
Did you withdraw your fundamental claim?
Did the central issue become
That to the angles of a triangle's sum
Two right angles are equal?
Or was it less than a 180-degree sequel?
In Alexandria the old book was found,
Principles of Geometry two thousand years ago bound,
No matter whether the worms ate it or not,
Euclid[23] is a great man, never forgot,
Who with lines and points the shape of the universe drew!
You and I, I and you,
The secret of a chance encounter I saw,
Of love the anti-law.
This is the geometry of life's retribution,
Won't you bring it for me to some solution?
At the straight line of cause and effect A we look!
The straight line of cause and effect B we took!
The principle that two parallel lines do not intersect,
To the intersection of parallel lines don't you object?
With this, contingency is fulfilled,
With chaos Venus is filled,
Two people a string of pearls detect
Brought by the waves of cause and effect.[24]

The Dialectical Method

Spirit!
Hell, paradise
Sobbing out a counterpoint.
Glaring at each other are clouds of rain,
Not even a canon
Is born!

Living in a field at dawn
Hornets and red starlilies
Entwine to make honey,
Who can explain this?
God and witch
Plight their promise and give birth to humanity.

These are the rules of life,
Thesis, antithesis, synthesis,
The tone of logos,
The singer a priest,
How good, a triple time
Dancing the waltz.[25]

Pure Duration

Falling in love with space
Time,[26] what a shabby illegitimate child!
To give birth was a mistake in the first place,
To repent for it, a good-for-nothing goblin,
The cause of your worries night in and night out.
Hello tortoise, dear tortoise![27]
To lose to a rabbit in a race, isn't that a victory?
A gull floating on the water says,
I will not be outrun by a duck!
You are thirty-something,
Still studying 31-syllable poems?
You say it is a 5/7/5/7/7 syllable poem?
That two stanzas 17/14 is the norm?
That three stanzas 12/12/7 is the poem's original form?
Aren't you rewriting the poem since the caesura splitting
   verses is bad?
Don't mistake "line" for "nine"![28]
A stanza is not made of numbers.
Since homogeneity is the foundation of compromise,
Respect the tune of pure heterogeneity![29]
Recollection of the past as well
Depends on time:
To curl your fingers[30] around moldy possibilities
Is the habit of the loser.[31]
Shout in your heart!
A meteor[32]
A flash of lightning
A melody
A color.[33]

The Human Dance

Destiny!
I dance with you,
Holding you close.
Do you say it's unbecoming to other eyes?
That's of no consequence.
Destiny!
Destiny!
I dance with you.
I am happy,
I am sad.
Oh, beautiful music,
Melody of the celestial spheres
Resounding from the end of the sky,
Night sky of the stars.[34]

Sleep Talking in Paris
[Parī no Negoto]

Self-Questioning

Somehow I wonder
What on earth are you?
Long ears and a tail you have,
Aren't you of the same species as a horse?
And yet you look like a deer.[35]

In the African desert
Lives an odd monster,
Its body no different from that of a beast,
Its head just like a human face,
They call it a sphinx.

In the countryside of America
There is an odd bird,
Face blue like a gourd in the morning,
Becoming ruddy in evening,
They call it a turkey.

Somehow I wonder
What on earth are you?
By rolling yourself backward
Try to unriddle the puzzle
Tangled inside your navel![36]

The Tango

Light!
The soul isn't searching for brightness,
Turn off the dazzling shine
And be darkness!

Moon of the Paris sky!
Entering secretly from the window
Quietly blue,
Lighten the rococo hall!

Yellow rose!
People dreaming of past loves,
Fill with your fragrance
This late autumn night!

White-haired musician!
Take that old violin
From the southern land
And play "Tango of Sorrow"!

Woman of Argentina!
Thrilling together with the string,
Sing in a charming alto
The sadness of nostalgia!

Wandering man from the East!
Loading your tiptoes with grief,
Dance in silence
With a middle-aged actress![37]

Yellow Face

The European:
Your face is so yellow!
Inhabitants of the southern countries of Spain

And Italy,
Unable to stand strong sunlight,
Have a brown face but
Not yellow.
It might be rude to say but
The Chinese and the Japanese have contracted
Something like a chronic jaundice...
This is what we Europeans
Actually think.

The Positivist:[38]
This seems a little harsh.
The place where we find skin pigments and
The layer where the yellow color of jaundice
Is present are different.
It seems that our ancestors
Somehow overate
Pumpkins and tangerines.
Maybe they also drank too much
Of the Yellow River and Yellow Sea.

The Metaphysician:
The distinction between races is inborn.
In a former life we committed mischief,
The gods got terribly upset,
Then the demons came upon us,
Caught us while we were running away,
Forced on our heads the filth of urine and feces.
Our yellow face
Stands as eternal memorial
To the merciless curse
Of just gods.

The Kritik Philosopher:
I am not going to mimic the arguments
Of the birdcatcher in the Magic Flute, but
There are yellow persons
As there are yellow birds.[39]
The issue of becoming is a different complexity,
Reality is given as reality.
In short, we should establish appropriate categories

For the concept of yellow race
And look at it from the standpoint of value.
Well, how can a yellow face become white?
Let's turn this problem from pure reason
To the realm of the practical.[40]

Serenade

Musician!
Play
Once more
That serenade!

Last summer,
The towers of Saint-Germain,[41]
The radiant banquets
Of Parisian gatherings.[42]

The Seine flowing quietly,
The evening moon fragrant in the sky,
Hills far in the distance,
Paris a clump of lights more faint than a dream.

The balustrade of the mansion of Henry IV,[43]
Hand in each other's hand,
The ghostly beautiful Helianne
Donning a robe the color of lilac.

That time, that time
I heard the same melody.
Now a winter night,
Myself all alone.

Musician!
Play
Once more
That serenade![44]

Monte Carlo

Oh, how I want to gamble!
Hurry to the casino.
Oh, I want to see a dance!
Peep in the barroom.

Yearning after what
Did I come to the southern lands?
Wishing for what
Did I come to Monte Carlo?

Let's get intoxicated by the blue expanse of water
In the shadow of a yucca tree!
Let's catch some shrimps,
Smelling the fragrance of seaweed!

Oh, how starved I am for an amorous glance!
Enter a teahouse.
Oh, how I pine for skin!
Go to a brothel.[45]

Ginkgo Leaf

Leaf of the ginkgo tree!
Has one become two?
Leaf of the maidenhair tree!
Have two become one?
Strange form,
Singular shape,
Didn't you whisper
The heart of love
At one time, to a talented poet?
Didn't you tell
The secret of the universe
At one time, to a great philosopher?
And yet why
Do you now
Show
And vividly reflect
Such a pitiful shape
To a soul suffering of fragmentation?

Look!
Chisel on the right, plectrum on the left,
Gray brain, crimson blood,
A contradiction difficult to reconcile,
A constant struggle,
How many souls destroyed like this
Do you think I do not know?
Leaf of the ginkgo tree!
You are split into two.
Leaf of the maidenhair tree!
You are broken in two.[46]

Loneliness

Loneliness!
Too precious reverberation,
Haven't you heard
Its tune?

Go stones!
You are all perfectly round.
No names are attached to you,
Why don't you use numbers?

One, two, three, four
Let's call them meeting stones.
Click, snick, click, snick
Let's call it a friendly chat.

Don't you know
Metaphysical loneliness?
Haven't you seen
The shape of that solemn reality?

True loneliness
Cannot break even for a moment,
True loneliness
Both love and friendship steer clear of it.

Ordinary solitude
Boiling from inside,
Fragility of bitter herb,[47]
Sweetness of honey,

Haven't you
Tasted them in the past?
Go stones!
Curse your perfect round shape.[48]

Pig
(Do not throw your pearls to pigs.)[49]

I remember giving the pig the pearls
Of the fruit of the pearl oyster shell.[50]
The pig swallows the pearls,
Grumbling with her muffled
Creak, squeak, creak,
And trots along here and there
In the mud.
Look in the ordure she dropped!
The pearl as well is the color of dirt.
I remember giving the pig the pearls
Of the fruit of the pearl oyster shell.[51]

Windows of Paris
[Parī no Mado]

Guest

Talk to me
About Japan,
Talk to me in a whisper!

How many buds
Were attached
To the magnolia in that courtyard?

The green ramifications of the evergreens,
Haven't they changed
Over the past five years?

The hair of Father
Celebrating his seventy-seventh birthday
Must have been like snow.

Nuiko,[52] morning and evening,
Does she look sad
Even to a casual observer?

Talk to me
About Japan,
Talk to me in a whisper![53]

A Walk

Spring day smelling of lilac
Faintly in the dark purple,
Without knowing where, I go alone
Through the streets of Paris shining in the sun.

This self yearning after the dark gray color,
The pillars of the church of La Madeleine,
I see the young girl selling flowers,
But for whom would I get flowers?

When I reach the Opéra[54] trudgingly,
My forehead lowered through the avenues of the capital,
A wave of people reverberating, moving forward, returning,
What should I do?

Where should I turn?
Let's go toward the Seine
Whose water slowly flows
Ablaze in the green of chestnut trees.

The lonesome man, what will he seek?
Hiding in Bois de Boulogne
Fragrant with the young leaves of acacia,
I will moan the shimmering spring.[55]

The Russian Song

[Man]
You say, why is your face so sad?
Suzanne, you
Ask repeatedly, worried silly.
Since that Saturday evening!

Since that Saturday evening
When we heard the Russian song together!
Somehow I grew sad in my heart
In a way I cannot say.

[Woman]
That must be why!
That much I noticed—
Your pupils charmed
By the woman who sang the free and easy little song
With an amorous, coquettish voice:
You stared at her steadily.
Her blonde hair,
The looks of a temptress, the shape of her mouth,
Bulging breast, twisted gait,
Her thin legs.
I know, men are all alike,
Fickle, whimsical!
You must be dying for a Slavic girl,
Before even realizing it, you have grown tired
Of a Parisian woman like myself
With a smooth brown cut.
Since that evening, since that evening
You changed completely.
Despite the hot hot kiss
I gave your mouth
You wouldn't return a single lukewarm kiss.

[Man]
Suzanne,
You shouldn't say such silly things!
That was not the love and the song of a young girl,
It was a sailor's song of a man fifty years old.
The dark moan, the dreadful suffocation,
The pitiful lamentation, the sharp anguish
Of the Volga flowing, never coming to an end,
From eternity to eternity,
Through nights of dark in the Russian wilderness,
My heart from its very bottom
Resonated with the same vibration

Of the baritone who sang that song.
Since that evening, turning its back to love
My heart has been sad.[56]

Heine's Tomb

Heine's tomb
On a fine autumn day.
Modest stone pillars,
A simple relief,
A four-string lyre
Symbolizing the lyric poet,
The shape of a butterfly, wings spread,
Showing a man of esprit,
A bust with downcast eyes
Reminiscent of a man of sadness.

Crimson hollyhock
Adorning the grave,
White roses,
Black dahlias,
Yellow chrysanthemums.
Look at the scribblings on the stone pillars!
Countless verses of praise,
Homelands of pilgrims cited,
Signatures of visitors—
I lowered my head in silence.

In the past in my youth
I too was among those who praised him.
Reading his poems
Resembling sad flowers of autumn
There was a time when I wept the night away
To my heart's content.
Laying myself down alone
On the lawn of Mukaigaoka,[57]
While listening to the bell of Ueno,
There was a time when I translated his poems.

Several years later,
When I lived in southern Germany
Near the banks of the Rhein,

A lovely cultured lady
Recited his poems
On a balcony on a moonlit night—
Why did I leave
So bluntly
With the trite reason
That he was a sentimental poet?

A poet who lost his native place
And spent a wandering life,
A poet alone in a foreign land
Who sang a mournful melody—
Now I sympathize with that poet.
How old I must have become
Now that I understand
His jesting and satirical sides
That in my youth I did not like!
Tomorrow I'll go to the bookstore
And buy Heine's collection of poems.

The evening sun has set,
The foliage scattered.
The German with the scanty fortune,
The German resting
Under the maple trees of Montmartre...[58]
The stars of a Paris night.
Soon they will light the lamps.
The Czech student's suicide
Beside this grave
Must have taken place exactly
Last year about this time.[59]

My Heart

When spring comes, although the flowers[60] are fragrant,
Though the foliage swings in the green,
My heart constantly bemoans things,
My thoughts are helpless.

Although I dance with a young girl,
Though I kiss her crimson lips,

My heart constantly bemoans things,
My thoughts are helpless.

Ah, although the spirit is one
And calls itself its own while knowing it,
My heart constantly bemoans things,
My thoughts are helpless.

As long as I live in this changing world,
As long as this human body breathes,
My heart constantly bemoans things,
My thoughts will be helpless.[61]

Vomiting

At times I vomit.
Working alone,
Sitting in a chair in my study,
Suddenly nausea comes.

I bolt up without knowing what I'm doing,
Poke my head out the window onto the street,
Ouch, ouch,
Vomit driven by distress:

Artichokes, asparagus,
Snails, frogs,
Entrails of crabs, jellyfish,
Rabbit's testicles, pigeon's liver.

Divine wrath of gourmandism!
Proof of indigestion!
Ouch, ouch,
It also smells of wine.

Formal wear, pleated skirt, don't get close,
Surplice and priestly robe stay away,
School cap don't come near,
Women, children run!

At times I vomit.
Not a case of appendicitis!
Not a pregnancy!
I must be possessed by an annoying fox.[62]

Short Poems
[Tanka]

Paris Mindscapes
[Parī Shinkei]

1.

Maronie no	When the chestnut trees grow yellowish
Kibamite chireba	And scatter,
Tabi no mi ni	The traveler
Namida moyōsu	Is moved to tears—
Parī naru ka na	This is Paris!

2.

Taoyame to	My life—
Tango o odoru	Dancing the tango
Waga inochi	With a graceful maiden:
Tamayura naredo	Although it lasts only a while,
Waraeru inochi	It is a laughable life.

3.

Vioron o	When the musician takes
Gakushi ga toreba	The violin,
"Samuson to	I ask him to play
Darira" o koinu	"Samson and Delilah"—
Parī no hitoyo	A night in Paris!

4.

Furusato o	Since I think
Parī ni arite	Of my native place
Omou yue	While living in Paris,
Inegataki ka na	How difficult it is to fall asleep—
Tsuki no yo no mado	A window on a moonlit night!

5.

Mata itamu	Again how the heart
Tabi no kokoro yo	Of the traveler hurts!
Itsu shi ka to	When will a sign
Parī ni aki no	Show that autumn in Paris
Tateru shirushi ka	Has come?

6.

Hoshizuki yo	Oh, starlit night!
Yume miru gotoki	In early fall,
Hatsuaki no	On the banks of the Seine,
Sēnu no kishi ni	Lips kissing,
Awasu kuchibiru	As in a dream.

7.

Kuchibiru ni	Putting rouge
Hinageshi no goto	Like red poppies
Beni sashite	On your lips,
Iza odoran to	You stand up
Tachiagaru kimi	Saying "Let's dance now."

8.

Tomoshibi no	The smiling profile
Moto ni Ivonnu ga	Of Yvonne
Emu yokogao wa	Under the light
Doga no e yori ya	Seems to come out more starkly
Idete kiniken	Than from a painting by Degas![1]

9.

Yoishirete	Falling asleep
Fukeshi sakaba ni	In a bar deep in the night
Nemureru mo	Fuddled with drink—
Aoki hitomi no	Must be the blue pupils
Kimi yue to sen	Of your eyes.

10.

Kuchibeni ga	You have dyed
Kara no shiroki o	My white collar
Somekeri na	With lipstick—
Parī no aki ni	This is what makes me marvel
Odoroku wa kore	At autumn in Paris!

11.

Oitamō	Since I awoke
Chichi o yume mishi	Seeing my aging father
Nezame yori	In a dream,
Tabi no makura no	This early fall has been drenching
Nururu hatsuaki	The traveler's pillow.

12.

Puratanu no	One morning in Paris
Ochiba no makie	Ruby shoes
Sono ue ni	Stand on top
Parī no asa no	Of a gold-lacquered box
Kōgyoku no kutsu	With the motif of fallen sycamore
	leaves.

13.

Oshinabete	In the thick hairdos
Parī no bijo no	Of all Paris beauties
Atsugeshō ni	Wearing thick makeup
Kushi to sezaru	I do not see any comb
Yūzukiyo ka na	Shaped like the evening moon!

14.

Hoshi no mure	In the blue sky
Gaisenmon no	Far over the Arch of Triumph
Ochikata no	A group of stars
Aoki sora ni te	Dances—
Odoru jūgatsu	The month of October!

15.

Yamite yaya	Having fallen ill
Hō no hosoriken	Her cheeks will be slightly thinner—
Donīzu ga	When Denise
Emeba koyoi wa	Smiles, how charming
Namamekashikere	This evening will be!

16.

Mata no yo no	Who is that talking
Kinu no iro nado	Of colors of garments and suchlike
Makuai no	Again tonight
Opera no rō ni	During the intermission
Kikaseshi wa dare	In the Opéra lobby?

17.

Hito-yo nete	I spend the whole night
Onna yakusha no	Touching the skin
Hada ni fure	Of an actress;
Parī no aki no	I smell the scent of a rose
Bara no ka o kagu	In the autumn of Paris.

18.

Sakura saki	I hear this is the country
Koi ni hito shinu	Where cherry trees bloom
Kuni nari to	And people die of love—
Furusato o shi mo	Let me talk
Kataritsuru ka na	Of my hometown!

19.

Toki to shite　　　　　　Since, at times,
Koki irodori no　　　　　I pine for
Itaria ga　　　　　　　　The intense colors
Koishiki yue ni　　　　　Of Italy,
Ichijiku o hamu　　　　　I end up eating a fig.

20.

Sabishisa wa　　　　　　Lonesomeness—
Tsubakura no su to　　　No matter how many
Hasu no mi o　　　　　　Swallow nests
Tabi ni kuraedo　　　　　And lotus pips you eat traveling,
Iegataki ka na　　　　　 It is so difficult to recover!

21.

Hatsunatsu ni　　　　　　In early summer
Kimi to fumitsuru　　　　With you I strolled
Namikimichi　　　　　　　Down the tree-lined street;
Ochiba suru hi ni　　　　On the day that the leaves fall
Tada hitori yuku　　　　 Alone I walk.

22.

Bonnō no　　　　　　　　When the blade of desire
Yaiba futatsu ni　　　　Splits me
Mi o saku to　　　　　　In two,
Kimi o nagamete　　　　How sad I become
Kanashimishi ka na　　 To look at you!

23.

Wabishisa to　　　　　　When I look at your letter
Makoto o komeshi　　　Expressing
Fumi o mite　　　　　　The truth of your desolation,
Kokoro ni tohoru　　　A yearning for you
Kimi no koishisa　　　Pierces my heart.

24.

Nuiko yori	Then there are nights
Yokimono nashi to	When I cannot contain my thoughts
Hitamuki ni	Of devotion,
Omoiamareru	Thinking no one is better
Yoi mo koso are	Than Nuiko.

25.

Aki no asa	Even if you hear
Momoiro no fumi	That on an autumn morning
Ukeshi nado	I received
Kikutomo kimi wa	A love letter,
Nikumazaramashi	You probably would not hate me.

26.

Ware inaba	Oh, you told me,
Dare to ka odori	"With whom will I dance
Tamawan to	If you leave?"
Iishi ya karuki	That sounds
Netami nariken	Like a tinge of jealousy!

27.

Burōniu no	On a pale day
Aki no kokage no	In the shade of the autumn trees
Usuki hi ni	Of Boulogne[2]
Ochiba o kikite	I hear the leaves falling
Dōdē o yomu	And read Daudet.[3]

28.

"Usuzumi" no	How did that tune go—
Kano fushimawashi	The melody titled
Ikaga nariken	"Thin India Ink"?
Higashi yori kite	So many years have passed
Toshi hetaru ka na	Since I came from the Orient!

29.

Itsu no hi ka
Furusato o min
Owaretsuru
Ware naranedomo
Inochi hakanashi

When will I see
My native land?
Although it is not I
Who has been pursuing it,
Life is fleeting.

30.

Koyoi shi mo
Roshia no kouta
Shiyo mōshite
Rina ga nuretaru
Me ni zo ikimashi

Saying,
Let's sing the little Russian song
This evening,
If only Rina would live
In the damp pupils of my eyes!

31.

Kushikezuru
Burondo no kami
Tomoshi ni haete
Akashi sachi aru
Neya no kūki yo

Oh, the blessed air
Of the bedchamber
In which I spend the night
In the reflection of the blonde hair
That she combs!

32.

Aki nakaba
Haine ga haka ni
Onore kara
Shinikeri to kiku
Atara wakōdo

I hear he died
By his own hand
Before Heine's tomb
In mid-autumn—
How pitiful the young man!

33.

Utsukushiki
Parī onna no
Tehandan
Tsutsumu koi ni mo
Iioyobu ka na

Will this beautiful
Parisienne
Who reads my hand
Be able to detect
My secret love?

34.

Irimajiri	Night has come
Monmarutoru ni	To Montmartre
Yoru wa kinu	Where people run into each other:
Aoki kokoro to	Blue heart,
Akaki tomoshibi	Red lights.

35.

Torikago ni	A goldfish
Kingyo no oyogi	Swims in the birdcage;
Minazoko ni	A canary chirps
Kanaria no naku	Underwater—
Mariannu ka na	It must be Marianne!

36.

Hitomure no	A group
Hadaka no otome	Of naked maidens
Wa o tsukuri	Forms a circle:
Kūronnu yo to warau	"A crown," she said smiling
Tomoshibi no moto	Under the lamp.

37.

Tawareo to	A profligate and
Asoberu onna	Playful woman,
Kinu naki ka	Was she without clothes?
Kinu wa aredomo	Although the clothes were there
Tokete suberinu	They were untied and slid.

38.

Yukizuri ni	The dark Latin Quarter,[4]
Shiranu onna ga	An autumn night,
Koto kakuru	A woman
Aki no yo naka no	I do not know
Kuraki ratanku	Speaking casually to me.

39.

Ruīzu ga
Ware o mukaete
Yorokobase
Nihon no nui no
Kinu tsukete izu

Louise
Welcomes me
And makes me happy—
She leaves wearing
A garment of Japanese embroidery.

40.

Pansuchiu to
Anrietto ga
Namamekite
Iitsuru kuse mo
Wasuregatakari

How hard to forget even
Henriette's
Charming
Habit of speaking
When she says, "Penses-tu?"⁵

41.

Zensai no
Sunomono mo yoshi
Komayaka ni
Fōku o toreru
Yubitsuki mo yoshi

Vinegar dishes
Are good appetizers, too,
The finger's gesture
In taking the fork delicately
Also is good.

42.

Oriori wa
Sabishiki kao mo
Yuruse kashi
Ko no ha no otsuru
Aki ni arazu ya

Occasionally
Even a sad face
Should be permitted—
After all, aren't we in autumn
When the foliage falls?

43.

Don Juan no
Chi no iku shizuku
Mi no uchi ni
Nagaruru koto o
Hazukashi to sezu

I am not ashamed
Of how many drops of
Don Juan's blood
Flow
Inside my body.

44.

Iwazaru o	Like a monk
Okite to shitaru	Who takes the vow
Sō no goto	Of not speaking,
Parī no aki ni	I keep silent all day long
Modasu hinemosu	During autumn in Paris.

45.

Tobotobo to	Lonesome is the heart
Waga tadoru michi	Gasping after the truth
Hitosuji no	Of the straight
Shinri ni aegu	Road that trudging
Kokoro wa sabishi	I follow.

46.

Yarusenaki	What should I do
Mune no urē o	With this grief
Nani to sen	In my cheerless heart?
Tango ni komete	I will devote it to a tango
Kimi to odoran	And dance with you.

47.

Momoiro no	The day has come to an end
Kutsu o hiruge no	While I was looking at
Taku ni mite	Pink shoes
Hitohi ochiizu	On the lunch table—
Kono kokoro aware	How pitiful this heart of mine!

48.

Namamekeru	I wonder whether you are a witch—
Mami motekushiki	With your beautiful eyes
Wa o kakishi	Drawing
Majo ka aranu ka	A mysterious circle:
Wasureenu kimi	I cannot forget you!

49.

Bosuton o	When we dance together
Tomo ni odoreba	The Boston dance,
Atatakaki	The color of silk gauze
Kumo zo to miyuru	Looks like
Usumono no iro	Warm clouds.

50.

Matsuribi no	Among the people
Būruvuaru no	On the boulevard
Hito naka mo	On a festive day
Arano no gotoku	Who is the girl who moves
Yuku wa ta ga ko zo	As if she were in the desert?

51.

Kosame furu	The avenue in autumn,
Shanzerizē no	Champs-Elysées[6]
Aki no michi	Under a drizzle—
Ihō no hito wa	The foreigner goes
Unadarete yuku	With his head down.

52.

Yoru no machi	The town at night,
Michi ni mayoite	Going astray in the streets
Tsubuyakinu	I murmured:
"Ware no kokoro mo	"My heart too
Onaji yami naru"	Is the same darkness."

53.

Tamashii no	When the soul
Susurinaku toki	Is sobbing,
Mefisuto ga	That is the time
Nagaki shita oba	When Mephisto[7]
Idasu kono toki	Sticks out his long tongue.

54.

Mayoitaru	This is a life
Inochi naredomo	That misses its way,
Shikasuga ni	And yet
Hito o tanomazu	It is the path I came to
Waga kitsuru michi	Relying on no one.

55.

Tokoshie no	A million times
Kokoro no miyai	The palace
Momochitabi	Of the eternal heart
Tatete kobochitsu	Is built and demolished:
Ware munashikari	I am empty!

56.

Sabishisa ni	Because of loneliness
Ochishi ko no mi o	I come and pick up
Kite hirou	The fruits of the trees—
Fuketaru aki no	The Bois de Boulogne
Burōniu no mori	In late autumn.

57.

Kanikaku ni	This and that,
Shibaraku mono o	For a while
Wasuremashi	I shall forget things;
Sarazuba inochi	If I don't,
Shi ni mo koso sure	Life would be death.

58.

Hitomuki no	Only at the times
Kokoro ni ikishi	When I live
Sono kami no	In the heart of single-mindedness
Waga inochi koso	Is my life
Yasukekarikere	Tranquil.

59.

Kagirinaki
Mujun no naka ni
Nayamitsutsu
Shinu hi no kane ya
Kanashikaramashi

Though forever distressed
In the midst of
Infinite contradictions,
How sad the bell will be
On the day of death!

60.

Sēnu gashi
Furuhonmise no
Mae ikeba
Usubi to tomo ni
Nagaretaru aki

When I stroll past
The secondhand bookstalls
On the banks of the Seine,
Autumn drifts away
With the soft beams of sunlight.

61.

"Shimeyaka ni
Koyoi kataran
Urumitaru
Hitomi o motomu"
Kaku iraekeri

"I want your eyes
Moist with tears
And to have a quiet talk
Tonight":
This was my answer.

62.

Yakiguri ga
Parī no tsuji ni
Kaoru yoi
Tachite kuri hamu
Ivonnu, Suzannu

An evening
When roasted chestnuts perfume
The street corners of Paris—
Yvonne, Suzanne
Stand and eat chestnuts.

63.

Aki no machi
Monohoshigenaru
Majimenaru
Kao o ageyuku
Katoriku no sō

The town in autumn—
A Catholic priest
Raising his craving,
Serious-looking
Face.

64.

Mokusei no	On a clear autumn day
Honobono niou	I think longingly
Furusato o	Of my native place
Aki no harureba	Dimly perfumed
Koishi to zo omou	By the fragrance of devilwood.

Sonnets from Paris
[Parī Shōkyoku]

Andantino

65.

Murasaki ni	Rosy garments
Rira no nioeru	Come and go
Burōniu no	Through Bois de Boulogne
Mori o ikikau	Fragrant with lilacs
Momoiro no kinu	Or gromwells.

66.

Magudarena	The rain of spring
Mitera no hashira	Falls dimly
Yawaraka ni	Softly
Honobono to shite	On the pillars of the church
Haru no ame furu	Of Magdalene.[8]

67.

Dobiushī ga	Spring spreads
Yume miru gotoki	In the Paris sky
Neiro yori	From the dreamlike
Parī no sora no	Tunes
Haru no hirogaru	Of Debussy.[9]

68.

Tsubakurame	Swallows—
Wagami mo onaji	I too am like them,
Wataridori	A migratory bird:
Parī no sora ni	How I would like to dance
Mau yoshi mo gana	In the sky of Paris!

69.

Yayoi kinu	Spring has come!
Kesa wa Parī no	This morning
Kiba musha no	Even the sound of hooves—
Hizume no oto mo	The knights galloping through Paris—
Namamekashikere	Is charming.

70.

Sēnugawa	Spring rains
Nōtorudamu mo	Make even Notre-Dame
Hitoiro no	Hazy
Usumurasaki ni	And monochromatic—
Kasumu harusame	Light purple.

71.

Haru to nari	Spring has come!
Sēnu no kishi ni	We went and met
Ikiainu	On the banks of the Seine:
Odori o koishi	You, on a winter night
Fuyu no yo no kimi	When I asked for a dance.

72.

Janīnu ga	Faintly a light rain
Mune naru bara no	Falls dampening
Kurenai o	The crimson
Kosame honoka ni	Of the rose
Nurashitsutsu furu	On Jeannine's chest.

73.

Wakaretsuru	I will send it to you
Kimi ni okuran	From whom I have parted—
Hana hitotsu	This morning I go
Kesa Burōniu no	To Bois de Boulogne
Mori ni kite tsumu	And pluck one flower.

74.

Monsō no	Going
Kōen ni yuki	To Park Monceau[10]
Aoshiba no	I wish I were a pigeon
Ue ni asoberu	Disporting himself
Hato to naramashi	On the green lawn.

75.

Isasaka no	While giving
Zeni o katai ni	A little money
Torasetsutsu	To a beggar,
Kokoro no kate o	I beg for the food of my heart
Waga tame ni kou	For myself.

76.

Kurariji no	The sadness of spring!
Tē dansan[11] *no*	Suddenly I remembered it
Kaerimichi ni	On my way back
Futo oboetsuru	From Claretie's[12]
Haru no kanashimi	Thé dansant.

77.

Ruriiro no	My heart
Na wasuregusa o	Is filled with thoughts
Yukizuri ni	Since I saw
Mishi yori mono o	A forget-me-not[13]
Omou kokoro zo	While passing by.

78.

Haru no asa	A spring morning!
Otogibanashi no	Let's live in a world
Yo ni ikin	Of fairy tales!
Negai mote kinu	This wish I brought
Burōniu no mori	Coming to Bois de Boulogne.

79.

Sugishi toshi	The flowers I saw
Komo no umibe ni	On the shore of Lake Como
Mishi hana no	Last year
Parī ni mo saki	Bloom in Paris as well—
Haru no hi to naru	A spring day has come!

80.

Misa owari	Gracefully
Tera yori idete	They keep their pace
Taoyaka ni	Leaving church
Ayumi o hakobu	At the end of mass—
Sangatsu no hito	People in March.

81.

Usugoromo	While wearing
Shiroki o kitsutsu	A white light dress
Fushime shite	With a downcast look
Hatsu seitai ni	They hurry to First Communion—
Isogu otomera	Virgin girls.

82.

Wabinureba	Since I feel desolate
Sēnu no kashi ni	I come wandering
Mayoi kite	To the banks of the Seine—
Shibaraku miiru	For a while I scrutinize
Wakakusa no iro	The color of young grass.

Nocturne

83.

Sabishisa wa	Lonesomeness
Bara no hanabira	Comes gushing out
Suikuchi ni	From an Abdullah[14] cigarette,
Maku Abudōra no	A rose petal decorating
Tabako yori waku	The mouthpiece.

84.

Odoru ni mo	I make a smile
Sabishiki kao o	Since you scold me
Shitamō to	Saying,
Semeraruru yori	"You look sad
Tsukuru hohoemi	Even when dancing."

85.

Kyarunavaru	"If you ever are in Nice
Nīsu ni arite	Do not miss
Misemeru nado	The Carnival,"
Arisu ga iu wa	Alice says
Hokorinarubeshi	With a proud look.

86.

Hahaue no	I am not at all displeased
Medetamaitsuru	To hear that
Shiracha iro	The pale brown color
Hayari to kiku mo	My mother loved so much
Nikukaranu ka na	Is in fashion!

87.

Furusato no	My heart smells
"Iki" ni niru ka o	A fragrance similar to
Haru no yo no	The "stylishness" of my homeland
Rune ga sugata ni	In the figure of Renée
Kagu kokoro ka na	On a spring night.

88.

Furusato no   I long for
Shinmurasaki no   The Shinmurasaki tune;
Fushi koishi   I long too
Kano utazawa no   For the masters
Shishō mo koishi   Of Japanese popular ballads.

89.

Nihoyaka ni   You,
"Monmarutoru no   Beautifully singing
Akebono" o   "Dawn
Utaishi kimi yo   At Montmartre"!
Hana o mairasu   I'll give you flowers.

90.

Amerika no   People indignant
Hito ni kawareshi   At hearing the rumor
Gekijō no   That the theater
Uwasa o kikite   Was bought
Ikidohoru hito   By an American.

91.

Fukkatsu no   Approaching
Matsuribi chikashi   Is the celebration of the Resurrection—
Maihime mo   The danseuse too
Koyoi zange no   Tonight will speak
Koto o kuchi ni su   Her confession.

92.

Maruseru to   Won't I find consolation
Aniesu to kuu   In the seafood
Puriunie no   Of Prunier,
Sakana ryōri ni mo   Where I eat
Nagusamanu ka na   With Marcel and Agnès?

93.

Utsumukite	An intermission—
Keshō o nahosu	Secretly I steal the profile
Taoyame no	Of a graceful maiden
Yokogao o soto	Fixing her makeup
Nusumu makuai	While lowering her face.

94.

Makishimu no	The endless
Sakaba no odori	Dance at the barroom
Hatenu ma ni	Of Maxim—
Shiroki te o tori	I take the white hand
Yo no machi ni izu	And emerge on the streets at night.

95.

Kimi to nete	Sleeping with you
Bōdorēru no	I recite a verse
Ku o utai	By Baudelaire[15]—
Parī no yayoi	March[16] in Paris grows old
Yo to tomo ni fuku	Together with the night.

Variations

96.

Sasagenan	I sent a letter home
Erizabetto no	In which I quietly wrote
Inori o to	About Elizabeth's
Yasashiku kakeru	Prayer
Furusato no fumi	She wants to address to my family.

97.

Sabishisa no	The evening
Kiwamaru yoi wa	When loneliness peaks
Na o yobite	I call her name
Parī no heya o	And go to her room
To yuki kaku yuku	In Paris.

98.

Utsukushiki   Do not think
Hitomi no koe o   That Parisians
Kikiwakuru   Can recognize
Parībito to wa   The voices
Omoitamō na   Of beautiful eyes!

99.

Butōkai   This evening I will go
Waga shi no hiraku   Neither to the dance party
Opera e mo   Nor to the Opéra
Koyoi wa ikazu   My teacher is opening—
Heya ni fumikaku   I will write a letter in my room.

100.

Shinjitsu no   Crossing the sea
Ai no kotoba o   The winged child
Umi koete   Will tell you
Hane motsu warawa   Words
Kimi ni iekashi   Of true love.

101.

Itsu shika to   Before knowing it
Tomo ni kokoro o   We have become
Sukashimiru   Close relations
Chikaki naka to mo   Holding each other's heart
Narinikeru ka na   To the light.

102.

Kimi o matsu   At seven
Aperitīfu no   The aperitif
Nanatsu doki   Waits for you—
Sakaba no kyūji   Today too the waiter at the bar
Kyō mo seji iu   Passes out compliments.

103.

"Nitsukeru ya"	"Does it suit me?"
Kaku tou kimi no	You ask,
Utsukushiki	Clothed in lilac color
Haru no sugata no	Fashioned to suit
Rirairo no kinu	The beautiful spring season.

104.

Umaretsuki	I am by birth
Kotoba sukunaki	A man of few words—
Saga ni nare	Although I often fall silent,
Waga modasedomo	You know enough
Togamezaru kimi	Not to blame me.

105.

Akashia no	I and someone's wife
Ki o kage to suru	Stepping on
Haru no yo no	Faint beams of moonlight
Usuzuki o fumu	On a spring night
Ware to hitozuma	In the shade of an acacia.

106.

Osoraku wa	Probably
Akashia no ha ga	The acacia leaves
Sasayakan	Are whispering
Futari katarishi	About the spring night
Haru no yo no koto	When the two of us were talking.

107.

Fujiiro no	I first knew you
Kinu kishi kimi o	On the day of the horse race
Ronshan no	At Longchamp—
Keiba no hi yori	You wore a dress
Shirihajimeshi ka na	Colored lavender.

108.

Futo shitaru	When by chance
Kimi ga tetsuki o	I saw how charmingly
En nari to	You moved your hands,
Mishi ni hajimaru	This transitory love
Awaki kono koi	Began.

109.

Wakamidori	Even the freshly green
Maronie no ha mo	Leaves of the chestnut trees
Haru no hi wa	On a day of spring
Parī no ware no	Incited my love
Koi o sosorinu	For Paris.

110.

Sēburu no	More than the lilacs
Kame ni iketaru	Living in a vase
Rira yori mo	Of Sèvres[17]
Kokoro ni ikete	You fragrant
Niou kimi ka na	Live in my heart.

111.

Suzuran no	Never should it happen
Hana o gogatsu no	That I do not present to you
Tsuitachi ni	Lily bells
Kimi ni okurade	On the first day
Arubeku mo nashi	Of May.

112.

Shōsetsu no	Among the people I long for
Naka no Yudaya no	I number
Onna o mo	The Jewish
Koishiki mono ni	Women
Kazoetsuru ka na	Found in novels.

Scherzo

113.

Funsui no	Trying to catch
Hakanaki kiri o	The fleeting mist
Araki te ni	Of the fountain
Toraen to shite	With my rough hands—
Nagekitsuru ka na	How I groan!

114.

Omoikane	Unable to think,
Shirikane sate wa	Unable to know, well,
Haru no yo no	Facing a mirror
Kagami ni mukite	On a spring night
Dōkegao suru	I make a clown face.

115.

Shiru wa dare	Who knows him?
Kigeki yakusha no	That clown
Hitorine no	Lying alone,
Haru no yo fuke ni	Eyes wet,
Me no nururu koto	Late at night in spring!

116.

Tsurezure no	Distress, sadness
Tsutanaki uta no	By far surpass
Atai ni wa	The value
Takaki ni suguru	Of a clumsy poem
Nayami kanashimi	Written in idleness.

117.

Mayaku ni mo	Thinking, "Let's forget
Niru mono o ete	Getting something akin
Wasuren to	To a drug,"
Parī no machi o	I go day and night
Hi mo yoru mo iku	Through the streets of Paris.

118.

Nakitsura to
Shikametsura ni wa
Hima o yari
Hyottoko no men
Kaburite aran

Farewell
To a tearful face
And a grimacing face!
I will wear
The mask of a clown.

119.

Ivetto ga
Mi no uebanashi
Ōuso to
Shiredo soshiranu
Kao o shite kiku

Feigning not to know,
I listen
To Yvette
Boasting about herself,
Though I know it's a big lie.

120.

Ponpei no
Hekiga no sugata
Haru no yo no
Neya ni omou mo
Hakanaki mono o

How short lived
Are my thoughts in the bedroom
On a night of spring!
A scene from the wall paintings
In Pompeii.

121.

Kataware ga
Mataki sugata ni
Kaerinu to
"Enkaihen" no
Kyaku ni tsugemashi

I will inform the patrons
Of the "Symposium"
That the fragment
Has returned
To its complete form.

122.

Yo ni somuku
Kuse o mitsumete
Sabishiku mo
Tsumuji-magari ga
Warau hitotoki

When I look at my habit
Of turning my back to the world,
How lonesome I feel!
It takes an eccentric like me
A moment to laugh!

123.

Kokoro iu	The heart says,
"Konogoro itashi"	"Lately it hurts!"
Yaya arite	After a while
Tamashii no iu	The soul says,
"Kanto ni kaere"	"Go back to Kant."

124.

Fumidana no	Taking in my hands
Ninshikiron o	The epistemology[18]
Te ni torite	From the bookshelf,
Itsushika tsumishi	I wiped off the dust
Chiri o harainu	That had piled up before I knew it.

125.

"Fuhenteki"	Today
"Kyakkanteki" to	Words like "universal"
Iu moji mo	And "objective"
Kyō wa hiniku ni	Bow sarcastically
Mokurei o suru	Before me.

126.

Tsutsumashiku	While reading,
Hi no moto ni ite	Humbly sitting
Yomu hodo ni	Under a lamp,
Waga sabishisa no	My lonesomeness
Yaya usureyuku	Fades a little.

127.

Haiiro no	In order to live
Chūshō no yo ni	In a world
Suman ni wa	Of gray abstraction,
Koki ni sugitaru	The color of earthly desire
Bonnō no iro	Has passed through darkness.

128.

Hanchū ni	How many years have I spent
Toraegatakaru	Lamenting to myself
Onogami o	This body of mine—
Ware to nagekite	As difficult to grasp
Hetsuru ikutose	As a category?

129.

Genjitsu no	Who says
Kaori no yue ni	That the philosophy
Chokkan no	Of intuition
Tetsugaku o yoshi to	Is good
Iu wa tagako zo	Because of the fragrance of reality?

130.

Sorubonnu	I keep silent alone—
Otoko onna no	An old man
Gakusei no	In a group of male and female
Mure ni toshi hetsu	Students
Hitori modashite	At the Sorbonne.[19]

131.

Tamashii no	When my soul
Ureite nakeba	Cries in grief,
Dōmie no	Daumier's[20]
E no warai mote	Paintings
Azakerishi ka na	Laugh with ridicule.

132.

Aoki kao	The "lonesomeness"
Hosoreru kao no	And "desolation"
"Sabishisa" to	Worn by a pale face,
"Wabishisa" mata mo	A thinned face, once again
Ware o torimaku	Enclose me.

133.

Orokasa mo	I say to myself,
Hodo koso are to	"Stupidity too
Mi ni iinu	Has a limit!"
Mata nageku tomo	Again, neither do I grieve
Warau tomo naku	Nor do I laugh.

134.

"Aku no ka" to	"The Flowers of Evil"
"Jissen risei	And "The Critique of
Hihan" to ga	Practical Reason"[21]
Sesera waraeri	Go shoulder to shoulder jeering
Kata o narabete	At each other.

135.

Tamashii o	While staring
Mitsumete nuka ni	At my soul,
Onorekara	I willingly brand
"Jidai sakugo" to	My forehead with the word
Yakijirushi osu	"Anachronism."

136.

Toki ni mata	Sometimes again
Zaratusutora no	The tranquil laughter
Oshietaru	Taught
Nodokeki warai	By Zarathustra[22]
Uchi yori zo waku	Gushes out from inside.

Serenade

137.

Maronie no	A walk in Paris
Hana hono niou	At twilight
Yūgure no	Perfumed by the dim fragrance
Parī no sanpo	Of flowers on chestnut trees—
Nakamahoshikari	I want to cry!

138.

Haru kureba	"Let's sing
Nodokeki uta o	A quiet song
Utawan to	When spring comes!"—
Aishū no ko mo	This must also be the wish
Motsu negai ka na	Of a child of sorrow.

139.

Waga nayami	My distress
Sukoshiku karushi	Is a little light—
Tsumasaki ni	A spring night
Urē o komete	Dancing on tiptoes
Odoru haru no yo	Filled with grief.

140.

Haru no yo no	Although
Kaina no naka ni	On this night of spring
Kimi aredo	You are in my arms,
Parī no tabine	Tears fall from my eyes
Namida koboruru	While spending the night in Paris on my journey abroad.

141.

Tabi ni aru	Do not say it is because
Yue to na ii so	You are on a journey
Onozukara	This lonesomeness
Kono sabishisa wa	Gushes out from inside
Uchi yori zo waku	By itself.

142.

Mado nashi to	Is this grief the result
Monado o iishi	Of knowing about the heart
Wabibito no	Of a man so desolate
Kokoro o shirite	That he calls himself
Etsuru urē ka	A monad without windows?

143.

Sabishisa yo	Oh, lonesomeness!
Tsumetaku tsuyoki	A life that must die
Kuchizuke ni	With a cold,
Inochi shinubeku	Strong kiss—
Ware o dake kashi	Embrace me!

144.

Osanaki hi	The child who wept
Komori no uta ni	At the lullaby
Nakishi ko wa	In his infant days—
Misoji no nochi mo	After age thirty,
Sachi usuki ka na	How thin his blessings become!

145.

Maronie no	While resting in the shade
Kokage ni yoreba	Of the chestnut trees,
Horohoro to	The flowers scatter
Hana no chirikuru	One after the other—
Parī no yūbe	Evening in Paris.

146.

Nioitsutsu	Even the heart
Rira chiru haru ni	Shakes lightly
Kokoro sae	In spring
Karuku furuite	When the lilacs scatter fragrantly—
Kimi o mishi ka na	I saw you!

147.

Koi suru ni	When I am in love
Kokoro wa sukoshi	My heart is a little
Araketari	Wild;
Koi sezaru ni wa	When I am not in love
Urumigachi nari	It fills with desire.

148.

Wakazakari   Oh, I wish to make
Moetsutsu niou   Today that day
Koi o seshi   When I burned
Sono hi o kyō ni   With a fragrant love
Nasu mi tomo gana   In the bloom of youth!

149.

Haru no yo no   The man
Kotowari shiranu   Who does not forget
Akugare ni   The heart's pain
Itamu kokoro o   Of an incomprehensible desire
Wasurezaru hito   On a spring night.

150.

Kane no ne wa   Is the sound of bells
Sakure Kōru ka   Coming from Sacré-Coeur?[23]
Sabishiku mo   How lonesome!
Parī no haru no   Spring in Paris
Owaran to suru   Is going to end.

151.

Katoriku no   Today I wonder,
Ama to narinishi   After so many years,
Koibito mo   How my lover
Toshi hedatarinu   Who became a Catholic nun
Ima ika naran   Is doing.[24]

152.

Puratanu no   When will the color of spring
Konure o tohoshi   Fade?
Ochite yuku   The setting sun falls
Yūhi mo itsu ka   Letting its light though
Yuku haru no iro   The twigs of the sycamores.

153.

Sabishisa ni	Feeling lonesome,
Yubune ni hitari	I enter the bathtub
Omou ka na	And let my thoughts go
Tōki ideyu no	To the mountains of my homeland
Furusato no yama	To the far hot springs.

154.

Haru no kure	The twilight of spring
Aoki Sēnu o	Is suffocating me
Yuku fune no	Even in the far reflections
Tōki kage ni mo	Of the boats going
Museban to suru	Down the blue Seine.

155.

Ā Parī	Oh, Paris!
Sabishiki haru no	Although I did not come
Omoide o	In order to leave
Nokosan to shite	A memory
Koshinaranedomo	Of a lonesome spring.

156.

Ihōbito	The foreign man
Parī no hana no	Bemoans his life
Chiru mama ni	While the flowers of Paris
Inochi o nageku	Scatter—
Haru no kuregata	Twilight of spring.

Winter in Kyoto
[Kyō no Fuyu]

157.

Yukurinaku	By chance
Saigyōan no	I passed the corner
Kado suginu	Of Saigyō's[25] hermitage—
Kyō ni sumu mi ni	For me living in Kyoto
Sachi nashi to sezu	This is not without blessings.

158.

Kamogawa no　　　Cold is the water sound
Mizuoto samushi　　Of the Kamo River—
Kyōdan ni　　　　　Standing in the classroom,
Tachi utsusomi wa　This present body
Horobi yuku nari　　Goes extinct.

159.

Oshiego no　　　　A pupil of mine
Torawarete naki　　Had been taken away and was not
　　　　　　　　　　　　　　　　home—
Uchi toeba　　　　　When I visited him,
Hiei no yama wa　　Clear was the winter sky
Fuyuzora ni sumu　　Of Mt. Hiei where he lived.[26]

160.

Nanitonaku　　　　Drawn somehow
Hi ni akugaruru　　By the lights
Yoiyoi wa　　　　　Every evening
Gion no machi ni　　I scoop up delicious *sake*
Umasake o kumu　　In the streets of Gion.[27]

161.

Kono mune no　　　This is a night
Kasokeki iki o　　　When I desire one beloved girl
Kikiwakuru　　　　Who knows how to listen
Imo no hitori wa　　To the weak breath
Hoshiki yoru ka na　In my chest!

162.

Tatakai ni　　　　　Rousing
Hito shinuran to　　A stern heart that says,
Ogosoka no　　　　"People will die
Kokoro okoshite　　In battle,"
Mizukara o semu　　I blame myself.

Last Poems

The following poems were written as a response to a gift of potted azaleas that Naruse Mukyoku presented during a visit to his sick friend. They are dated 29 April 1941.[28]

Tamawarishi	The azaleas in the pot
Hachi no tsutsuji wa	You gave me
Honobono to	Are now at their peak,
Usuni ni sakite	Dimly blooming
Ima sakari nari	A thin red.

Yamifushite	Lying down sick,
Hito no nasake ni	Receiving
Uruoite	The love of people,
Shimijimi to shi mo	I thoroughly
Namida o otosu	Shed my tears.

Rhyming Poems

Poems Appended to
Rhyme in Japanese Poetry

Thoughts Originating from Herbs

1.

Chinese milk vetch, dandelions, violets
That once my girl plucked apart,
For a long time the early winter rains did not fall into my
    eyelets,
The aching bottom of my heart.

The pampas grass blooms on many an ear,
In autumn fields wandering without aim,
The metaphysics without any cheer
Of the heart fostered in pain.

2.

Ferns, hare's foot ferns, royal ferns, fernbrakes
Shouldering the frost made by dews,
Late in fall the green rust on the front leaves flakes,
Forlorn I am in my love's hues.

Which color should I print
The foliage of my life?
Men weave it with the tint
Of the pitch-black pattern of calamity's strife.[1]

To Ms. D

On the Bois de Boulogne mist rises
Nearby, the path of young grasses surprises,
Bearing sweet dreams of a spring day,
Plucking at my memory a violet on the way,
The pupils of your eyes gently smiling,
You indeed are the wish of my world, charming
To look at, you I do not cease to savor,
When we depart never will my wound recover from your lost
     flavor,
Unknown to people how many drops fall from favor,
My tears, quietly one flower laver
I will put in the old poetry collection, in the leather binding
And leave for a foreign land far away winding,
The purple fragrance will certainly vanish,
And yet it will live in my heart, banished
In the sea of my long voyage far away
Your appearance will always stay.

Envoy

Blooming at the Bois de Boulogne the flower
I plucked at our separation's hour—
To call your name in my heart will it have the power?[2]

A Solitary Life

East of the capital, Yamashina[3] forbidden
Like a remote village looks hidden,
In the ancient era of Engi[4] it occurred
That only the name of Semimaru was heard,
Known as the Fourth Prince, in strings he was very skilled,
Biwa and *koto,* a temporary dwelling he built,
The peak of Mt. Otowa[5] in front of his eyes,
Its sight changing day and night,
When fog rises an India ink drawing appears,

When clouds gather, a pure white curtain coheres,
In springtime the rapes blossom,
In the fall the red cluster-amaryllis is awesome,
In summer the sweet osmanthus is fragrant,
In winter the turning sundial is vagrant,
A body clinging to a solitary life's scars,
People shun streetcars,
How many days spent without a visit to the city,
This life of mine shut in reclusive pity,
Books I read when I grieve,
Inside a thicket of oaks I live.

Envoy

East of the sunny capital forbidden
A thicket of oaks in Yamashina village hidden,
The treetops by beauty ridden![6]

Onogoro and Intercourse

The two pillars Izanagi and Izanami chose
To noisily stir the sacred sea,
From the dripping salt a foamy wave crest rose,
And the island of Onogoro was born free.

When they came around the heavenly pillar wide
They met, exchanged vows, said, "How lovely you are"
    without shame,
The sash of the robe in the hidden chamber was untied,
From their intercourse no misfortune came.[7]

Konohana no Sakuyabime

On the shore of Cape Kasasa cool
A maiden was who I met by chance,
Rouge on a bent *lapis-lazuli* comma-shaped jewel,
Her neck like pure snow at a glance.

Her name of the catalpa bow had the grace,
Konohana no Sakuyabime[8]—a blooming flower in spring,
To a fugitive fragrance an embrace,
Of a fleeting encounter at night a dreamy thing.[9]

Poetry

Cruel are words of betrayal,
Poetry—of a sad flame of love the end,
Without knowing it the cold corpse of a friend,
What title chants its portrayal?

Letters, how many stepping-stones do they mix?
Chinese letters, empty is their sound,
Japanese letters by gray colors are bound,
One, two, three, four, five, six.

Crossing by chance this place,
Who searches for the dead soul's trace
And shouts, "Breathe a breath of life in his face"?

Rarely dances the dead verse in the fog,
Cutting the time of my birth's curse,
Waiting for the blind turtle to stick its head in the hole of a
    floating log.[10]

Journey

On a winter day dimly alone,
Yearning for the blue sky far away,
Following the southern path, how many a day,
Near Cannes protected by the gods to atone.

Of rising plovers on the shore a flight
Their shadows flying beyond the waves vaguely went,
Being on a journey, what do they lament?
Their shelter is the shade of an oak tree site.

When night is gone red is the rose,
Yellow mimosa faintly glows,
Silence, a little puff of breath makes a flower quick.

In my native place my beloved with red cheeks,
In my dreams, even without my consent, speaks,
Oh, the clouds crossing the sky, how homesick![11]

One Night

Rice wine poured in a *sake* cup,
Blue smoke of a cigarette, I recall,
Light reflected on the wall,
All alone in a room shut up.

The passion of a camellia lighting,
The gesture of the watch's hand I see,
At the end, sleep without sex with thee,
Dawn at the window whitening.

Not a cloud in the morning sky,
The native land I reached and cry;
I too will get lost again.

Where did this spider come through?
Silently with you
I will drink *sake,* the two of us, in vain.[12]

Squirrel

Aimlessly he goes through the grove of fresh leaves alone,
Hop hop jumping, a cute squirrel comes out
And, as soon as he sees me, turns back in doubt,
Up an oak tree he runs and looks down at a stone.

The primroses like you in the spring,
On summer nights, he and the stars in the treetops kisses
    consume,
In autumn a tiny, round chair—a mushroom,
In winter snowflakes to his tail cling.

O squirrel, lover of jokes! Squirrel, just keep jumping!
Innocently leaping, up from tree to tree keep running,
Always happily smiling.

Yet I, lowering my head, follow the path of gloom,
Through the darkening grove of fresh leaves in doom,
Of people's afflictions and sadness thinking.[13]

Bookbinder

"Did you check the pages? Paste the cover right again!
The drying of the glue is bad, today is cloudy!"
The boss wearing a short coat, turning toward the apprentice,
     gray,
He is the owner of the bookbinding shop on D'Altois Lane.

The gold letters of the leatherback book—a dimly floating twi-
     light,
Molière,[14] La Fontaine,[15] he has completed,
The political system of Comte,[16] the dictionary of Littré,[17] he
     has greeted,
He works all day seldom going outside.

A nineteen-year-old girl working in a department store,
As soon as she calls out "Father," the working hand stops its
     chore,
With a sweet smile he sits at the dining table.

This summer he lost his jolly wife,
He waits for someone but never again shall see her life,
A night in Paris, the bell of Sacré-Coeur tolls its fable.[18]

Bat

I am a bat,
On an old nest as protector sat.

In the spring twilight stern,
For the world I yearn.

Out I come and fly,
My body flying, I lie.

Thin is my wing,
A distressful thing!

Gray is my face,
Eyes cloudy in space.

Rape blossoms are at their height
In the dim morning light.

Butterflies fly in a stream,
Summoning a dream.

If I pursue them, a phantom afar,
A shooting star.

Trifling it is to moan,
What shall I do on my own?[19]

The Sleepy Inland Sea

Dwellings on the seashore in sight
The windows of night.

Golden stars in the sky,
Phosphorous insects in the water are spry.

The Inland Sea is sleeping,
The lighthouse is watching.

Suddenly clear,
Quickly dark is near.

Early evening in spring,
What thoughts does it bring?

Fragments of the soul depart,
Desires of the heart.

An island far away
I now see gray.

Soft rippling waves, fine,
Cutting the shoreline.

Without a single oh
A meteor draws a bow.[20]

Heart

In the dwelling of my body, come spring,
Although flowers bloom and young leaves are a fragrant
    thing,
My damp heart starts to sink,
Reveries of rain, thin India ink.

Rising to the sound of flutes they dance in crowds,
Only to disappear when they step on each other, glowing clouds,
My damp heart starts to sink,
Reveries of rain, thin India ink.

My dear soul
In my hand I hold, an unsolvable goal,
My damp heart starts to sink,
Reveries of rain, thin India ink.

The taste of the fruit of wisdom you know,
The white mist rises at your gasping blow,
My damp heart starts to sink,
Reveries of rain, thin India ink.[21]

Meeting Bridge

Young leaves,
Of meetings a bridge,
Bright the street lights I perceive
On a popular ridge.

When was the time? So much I grieve!
A stroll
On the riverbank in the early eve,
Catching sight of a soul.

And yet my heart is in pain
When I recall,
My life distressed in vain
When my desires call.

Jazz they played
By chance,
An exit she made,
Never again giving me a glance.[22]

Monte Carlo

Come on a holiday
To Monte Carlo,
An elegant harbor bay,
Come through the water channel's flow!

Here is the casino to play,
The dice to roll,
There is the café,
The sound of coins' soul.

Fresh green is the sea,
The tides pitch black,
The fishing rods of rattan you see
The tunas all in a stack.

Here is the pleasure quarter,
There you'll find the brothels placed,
Only tonight you'll be their supporter,
Have a taste![23]

The Carnival of Nice

A fine carnival today,
Festival music with many large drums, they brag,
Swaggering disguised with false beards, they play,
Clowns, too, walking zigzag.

The fine weather of sunny southern countries,
Dance at the crossroads of the public square!
Youngsters, children, old people, please,
Beat time clapping your hands there!

Tattaa…, tararara…, tattatta…
Dance at the crossroads of the public square,
Tatta…, tararara…, tattatta…
Beat time clapping your hands there!

The paper powder, is it snow, is it hail?
Suddenly they spread it on passing noses,
Like looking at a floral gale,
Spread mimosas, lilies, roses!

Wearing gala dresses more showy than a flower,
Who is that Dancing Miss?
Thinking it is unrestrained for the hour,
Give her a kiss!

Tatta…, tararara…, tattatta…
Who is that Dancing Miss?
Tatta…, tararara…, tattatta…
Give her a kiss![24]

A Wish

Be a highly skilled carpenter, O rhyme!
Strike your jeweled ax!
Rarely does luck to the rafters climb,
When will pagodas become facts?

O rhyme! Which child of the poetry god's of greatest worth?
Stroll in the blue sky!
I, a lump of earth,
The rainbow's color will see in a dream on high.[25]

Wind

Treetops of sycamores, tell,
Autumn wind dancing in the heights
Make me dance as well,
Like wind breathing freedom through the nights.

Without mending
Unsightly forms,
Without hiding
Crooked wheel tracks away from norms.

By chance,
Without agreeing with me,
Just as you are, take a stance,
Without being afraid of people's plea.

Speak frankly
The confession of the flesh,
Sing directly
The scattering flowers for the soul fresh.

Treetops of sycamores, tell,
Autumn wind dancing in the heights
Make me dance as well,
Like wind breathing freedom through the nights.[26]

Farewell to Paris

O Paris, which lodged this wandering body of mine!
Sunsets in early fall when leaves fell on the street,
Bright nights when the round moon was translucent and fine,
Do not forget me now that I leave and greet!

At Champs-Elysées the chestnut trees,
At Bois de Boulogne the acacias and cherry,
Along the river Seine on the houses the breeze,
Of Notre-Dame the Virgin Mary.

The pigeons in the Parc Monceau frolicking,
In the Montmartre bars the yellow shade,
The sparrows in the Jardin de Luxembourg dancing,
The girl selling flowers, her street corner trade.

Of the Sorbonne the rusty door,
Of the professors the thin shapes,
From La Madeleine the beautiful pillars soar,
From the dancers gentle love escapes.

O Paris, which lodged this wandering body of mine, sincere!
What will you say to me now that I leave?
O Paris, O Paris, dear!
In silence I take leave of you and grieve.[27]

Grieving Mr. Iwashita Sōichi

Quietly he passed away,
The hospital director of the Resurrection of the Holy Mount,
To heaven his soul has returned today,
Plaintive cries fill the earth unbound.

Rosary in his cold hands,
Cross on his breathless chest,
Closed eyes that do not open to any demands,
Is there no way to hear his voice blessed?

Lepers coming, forming a line,
Quietly protecting the wake,
A mass gives consolation, divine!
Won't this give grief a break?

The night too cries,
The head nurse, still young,
The winter sunshine at the foot of the mountain's skies,
This morning sadness atop Mt. Fuji hung.[28]

Credo Quia Absurdum

Oh, guts!
Do you curse the pain?
Your declining world is all cuts,
A milepost every three miles in vain.

Recurrent time, a beat,
Going and returning, Being and Nonbeing,
A subjectivity split,
Praises of *sake,* the fragrant thing.

The *epoche*[29] of a prodigal man,
The world of a desolate Being-in-the world,
Giving rise to scandal's (passion's) ban,
Parenthetical comic backchat hurled.

Yet your characteristic deeds
Play the theory of probability with the flute!
Calculate with the abacus beads
Of Hanayagi and Fujima the atomic weight, acute![30]

Drought is drought,
Rain is rain,
A sunshower, a shout,
The awakening of an autumn shower came.

Pathos, ecstasies, sensation,
A talkie of the celestial sphere,
Philosophy dying of starvation,
Fore-throw[31] of throwness[32] to appear.

Getting its wings a mole
Flies upward in the twilight flood,
Arranging its thorns a rose's goal
Is to flirt with people's blood.

The misty moonlight night of contradiction,
Light of the five cardinal colors,
O child with a weak faith of friction!
God is omnipotent honors.

What an agonizing flaw!
Listen to the wisdom of the Fathers' word,
Navel of the antilaw,
Say, "I believe because it is absurd!"[33]

A Stroll

A spring day fragrant with the lilac flowers I stole,
And faintly with the light gromwell,
The peach and scarlet dress of the young belle,
In sunny Paris I stroll.

The columns of the shrine La Madeleine soar,
To see the thin India ink color I come yearning,
At the door of the shrine's colonnade stopping,
Although I push with my hands, it is a heavy door.

Of its avenues the capital brags,
If you go to l'Etoile, the stars,
A square buried by cars,
What might the event be? The three-colored flags.

Where does the heart dwell?
The old bookstores stand in a row,
Letting the fragrance of past wisdom flow,
Isn't that boulevard St. Michel?

For what is the desolate man praying?
Alone, treading on the young grasses,
The Bois de Boulogne he passes,
Is he grieving the shimmering spring?[34]

Renunciation

A soul which to gray turned
Has followed the path of half human life confused,
It seems it says that it has got used
To the renunciation and enlightenment that it learned.

How many times it has stumbled,
Each time faltering and falling,
The forehead wounding,
A face I have seen, that might be my fate, crumbled.

The sound of my clogs is hollow,
A feigned pitter-pat sound,
A faded pipe in his mouth found,
The man vomits words to himself, and swallows.[35]

Cointreau

To the streets of Paris I cling,
A restaurant late at night,
Small bottle of Cointreau, a bite,
The blessing of a fleeting spring.

The shell of the cinnamon—the color of thin India ink—creeps,
The stem of a clove on the sausage looms,
The branch of lilac flowers blooms,
The water of the river Seine sleeps.

An uncalled for wall clock curves,
Ding-dong, two in the morning,
A dream of emotions, rainbow of the senses—a warning,
A dancing heart, sharpened nerves.[36]

Luxor

Africa, where camels neigh,
Spring in Luxor, March,
They excavate a golden dream in the sand, an arch,
The whereabouts of Tutankhamen, I say.[37]

Twinkling stars in the sky,
Evening through the flower gardens flying,
The fiery hot wind faintly sighing
Casts shadows on the Nile's water, I cry.

The perfume of the heliotropes blown,
Of bougainvilleas a fragrant smell,
Of pitcher plants a bushy swell,
Egyptian hollyhock standing alone.

Lizards embroider the twilight,
To love beautiful things I came,
Intoxicated with Cleopatra's name,
The crimson petals I breathe of light.[38]

Fontainebleau

Of the forest of Fontainebleau I sing,
The palace of François I ablaze,
Swans floating on the pond reflecting spring,
The border where Cupid plays.

While my soul grieves dumb,
The autumn sunset when the chestnut trees turn a yellow
      spray.
If to feed the red carps you come,
In a whisper, say:

Looking back at the vestiges I left
Of a rococo pavilion buried in the flowers of May, bereft.[39]

The Geometry of Gray

A perfect circle wrapping a dream's tips,
How many days going round and round,
The orbit an ellipse,
A fire burning in the focal point is found.

Waking up a triangle,
A theory born of the angle,
The chart a rectangle,
How many names for stars dangle?

A round square
= contradiction,
The awakening of the soul's glare?
∞ opposition's fiction.

The geometry of gray,
Is that the spirit solving human play?[40]

Arabesque

Osiris,[41] Apis,[42] bull god on earth,
Teeth of a crocodile, eyes of a snake, hair of a lion's mirth,
Waves of transmigration, rebirth.

The Ptolemaic digest, principles of geometry's sets,
Vivisection, blood spurting in jets,
A mummy that does not rot, imperial garden's regrets.

Tutankhamen, the pyramid I see,
A papyrus scroll, the Sphinx, free,
Unlimited curios, treasures' spree.

A veil of black silk gauze, a hood, alarms,
Earrings, love charms,
Cleopatra sells love in her arms.

Sun and moon, stars, palm trees,
The Red Sea, deserts, reeds of the Nile's breeze,
Nothing has changed in the past or now with ease.[43]

Tango

The soul for glory is not yearning,
Blow out! Many lights burning,
Desire is darkness that makes a gem sprouting.

The moon in Paris a willowy circle's guise,
Do you see the rococo world in front of your eyes?
The goddess of beauty, flowers worn on her head, appears
floating.

Come spring! The fragrant early eve,
Fishing fires without traps is love, I believe,
Half body in distress falling.

The owner of the violin with four strings,
The melody of a tango plays and sings,
Sweet tears to the cheeks transmitting.

The singing voice is a good mezzo-soprano, grand,
Mignon thinks of her native land,
A distant south in a dream seeing.

Together with a girl smelling lilac flowers,
The traveler dances his lonely hours,
The end of life is water flowing.[44]

Mediterranean Sunset

From the forest of silvery olives,
The south wind fragrantly blowing,
The sea on the other side of the agaves.

Even the shadow of the Apennine range is thinning,
The evening sun falls into the Mediterranean Sea,
In the mist dimly dissolving.

It reminds me of the beach of Awa's existence,
The shivering waves of the shore, the color of a rose,
Purple Mt. Fuji in the distance.

A bitter taste mixed with beautiful things blows,
Signs of grief encroaching on my life, persistence,
A faint anguish attacking me flows.

That was still I in the days of my youth,
When I had finally come to know love's pain,
Twenty years ago, without realizing the truth.

Now I feel the same
As my heart did in the moment of ruth,
The only difference being time and place to blame.

After all I am the I of before—how uncouth![45]

Repentance

Eve:

The red, red
Apple, entrapping, inviting,
Why, why, know its dread!
The argot of a serpent badly joking,
The protection of a god not returning.

Persephone:

The sweet, sweet taste to blame
Of a pomegranate well ripe to swallow,

Apology is eternal shame,
A loathsome hollow,
An ugly dwelling that does not see sunlight follow.

Izanami:

Just one bite, just one bite,
Eating the food of the dreadful yellow springs,
Now, now, a grumble in the night,
A repentance that does not precede her deadly strings,
The retribution of a pledge due to offensive things.[46]

Evening in the Alps

Listen, listen to the sound of bells on the way!
Jingling, tinkling, jingling,
A ridge where cows play,
Tinkling, jingling,
Tinkling, jingling.

Look! The goats are under our noses
Near the black rocks,
The deep-red flowers are alpine roses,
A girl alone stops,
Kneels down, the Angelus drops.

Standing by are shepherds, shy,
Looking perhaps at places
In the evening sky,
Simple, honest faces,
Glory of the god of mountainous spaces.

The sun has set from view,
Look at the skin of the snow now!
Pink has become its hue,
The piled-up peaks of the Jungfrau,[47]
Cradle of the Alpine brow.

The penetrating clear blue sky for its sake
Gives shelter to many shadowy scars,
Look in the middle of the lake,
How many blinking stars!
Oh, this beautiful vision of ours!

Listen, listen to the sound of bells on the way!
Jingling, tinkling, jingling,
A ridge where cows play,
Tinkling, jingling,
Tinkling, jingling.[48]

Dialectic

Hell, paradise—they disappoint,
Sobbing out a counterpoint,
A journey is a fellow traveler's grime,
Glaring at each other are clouds of rain,
Even a canon in vain
Misses the time.

Hornets and red starlilies
Entwining to make honey with smiles,
Bless the fields in early summer wild,
Benevolent god and witch,
Embrace each other, become one twitch,
Give birth to a human child!

The tone of life,
Thesis, antithesis, synthesis' strife,
Well now, call the tune,
Blind priest,
How grand, a triple feast,
Dance the waltz soon![49]

The Ruins of Karnak

Crossing the clear night sky, this evening the moon is fully cast,
Alone is the traveler wandering without a sign,
He keeps going, yet the desert is endlessly vast,
The famous Amon[50] is near the shrine,
Beside him attendants' statues with body of lion and head of
      sheep,
Black shadows, how many wretched figures creep!
The upper currents of the river El, Karnak of Egypt, flow,
Listen, what bird is that? What a strange sound!
The soul bird, the soul bird,[51] crying, hoh, hoh,
To become the soul bird that flies deep into the night is bound.

Large square gate, conical pillars nod,
Buried foundation stones, the rising obelisk soars,
Broken, crooked head of the bull god,
This desolation, this tragedy, what for?
Did I once see a dream of eternal life profound?
How moving! Now dead bodies rest beneath the ground,
Low reliefs silently adorning the walls' word,
Speak the glory of the ancient Ramses' days,
The hieroglyphs of lion, ostrich, crocodile, tiny bird,
Sing, bringing your voices together, and Thebes praise!

I too in the past, wandering in grief alone,
Built an eternal shrine in my heart.
The dream I saw on that day is now entirely gone,
The dazzling vision too all fallen apart,
What is barely left? Traces of a ruined land,
Dwelling of flesh buried in sand,
Look up at Africa's high night sky!
The moon makes it translucent, the color of silver girds it up
    blue,
Listen to the voice of the soul, to the soul bird's cry,
Calling mysteriously, the calling bodies of a dead crew.[52]

Flower Picking

The Alpine mountains,
Of snow the mountains,
Of evening glow the mountains,
Of flowers the mountains,
Rouge trefoils I pick,
Turquoise azaleas, thick,
The double blossom alpine rose,
The gingili plant, vines, dark purples' rows,
The white chrysanthemum speaks,
The red wild pink from high peaks,
The one-leaf plover, the bellflower,
The blue and grayish blue gentians tower,
The yellow buttercup on the peaks is seen,
The round sengreen,
The valley lily, short,
The violet like bladderwort,

The willow orchid in bloom, fire red,
The mountain peonies shining saffron spread,
The Alpine mountains,
Of snow the mountains,
Of evening glow the mountains,
Of flowers the mountains.[53]

Three Comma-Shaped Figures in a Circle

Rolling to a point where together it comes,
A figure I draw of a rope's sums,
The crest the three comma-shaped figures in a circle gaining,
An old painting,
One in three,
Three in one I see,
The amulet of the almighty god
On the body of a warrior's nod,
The loud ring is the sound of the archer's arm protector,
The reversed movement of a flying arrow, a specter,
An attacking vision,
Far from love's decision,
An unfulfilled heart,
An eternally unraveling thread apart,
Think of the inner form!
The three-comma-shaped circle is a pitiful norm,
Without stopping the tear flow,
Flowing they whirl and go.[54]

[The poems "Contingency" (Gūzensei) and "The Negative Dimension" (Fugōryō) are the same as those that appeared earlier in *Paris Mindscapes*.]

Destiny

Destiny!
Thus you sing your song,
With you I dance,
Dance, embracing strong
Your stance,
Do you say that other eyes will find it unfit?
No matter what they say, it's up to my wit.
Destiny!

Destiny!
With you I dance,
Dance with you while singing in trance,
With happiness I am mad,
And I am sad,
This feeling's knife,
This is my life,
A beautiful music it was,
The melody a circle draws,
The harmony played in cheer
By many a celestial sphere
Of the stars in the sky at night,
A wreath of diamonds bright,
Destiny!
With you I dance,
With you I dance my chance.[55]

Essays on Poetry

The Genealogy of Feelings

A Guide to Poetry

1

I want to try to follow the path of the genealogy of feelings *(jōcho)*, which I will do as a guide to poetry *(uta)*. The word "guide" might be a little overstated. It might be more appropriate to say that I will provide concrete examples taken from poetry. We must say that since poetry is a manifestation of emotions *(kanjō)*, it is a splendid document for investigating its genealogical connections with different levels of emotions. There is no tool more convenient than poetry to get a full picture of certain set emotions, especially because of poetry's small format and the fact that it is filled in its entirety with emotions.

When I ask which is more convenient to this purpose, whether the 17-syllable *haiku* or the 31-syllable *tanka*, I believe that *tanka* serves the purpose better. From the perspective of the literary arts, the 5/7/5 syllable structure of *haiku* looks like a point, whereas I feel a flow of time in the 5/7/5/7/7 syllable pattern of *tanka*. If I may overstate the specific characteristics of each poetic form, I might perhaps say that *haiku* is spatial and pictorial while *tanka* is timely and musical. As a result, I can also say that *haiku* is suited to objective descriptions of scenery while *tanka* is more fit for subjective lyrical expression. The formal structure of *tanka* entrusts the reverberation of emotions to the closing 7/7 verses after singing those emotions in the first 5/7/5 verses.

If we want to make the object of our investigation the feelings felt by moderns, we must turn to contemporary poetry. Since the *New Ten*

Thousand Leaves (Shin Man'yōshū) is in the process of being published, I will use it as my source. For the sake of convenience I will limit myself to the second volume alone, which by itself includes 2,870 poems by 756 poets. Both in terms of the number of poets and the number of poems, the volume is quite sufficient for my purpose.[1]

2

We can say that the most important feelings are the feeling of happiness *(ureshii)* and the feeling of sadness *(kanashii)*. According to Descartes, when good and evil are represented as something belonging to us, the consciousness of current good engenders happiness in us whereas the consciousness of current evil produces sadness.[2] To use an expression by Spinoza, happiness is the passage of the spirit from a lesser to a greater perfection whereas sadness is the movement of the spirit from a greater to a lesser perfection.[3]

> *Miinochi ni*　　　　　The happiness of being able
> *Aeru ureshisa*　　　　To meet with her life:
> *Otoroeshi*　　　　　　I, sitting
> *Haha ga mi chikaku*　　Next to my emaciated
> *Ware wa suwaru mo*　　Mother.
>
> 　　　　　　　　　　　EZURESHI ROCHŌ[4]

> *Karete ishi*　　　　　　How happy
> *Ta ni naminami to*　　　To keep on seeing,
> *Sosogu mizu*　　　　　Holding up a lamp,
> *Ranpu sashiyose*　　　The water flowing to the full
> *Mitsutsu ureshi mo*　　In the dried-up rice field.
>
> 　　　　　　　　　　　KATAGIRI RYŌ[5]

> *To no sukima*　　　　Although the crack
> *Imada kurakedo*　　　In the door is still dark,
> *Suzumego no*　　　　How happy I am to hear
> *Saezuru kikoyu*　　　The chirping of baby sparrows—
> *Ureshi ya asa nari*　　It is morning.
>
> 　　　　　　　　　　　KAWABATA CHIE[6]

In the first instance we see the happiness of someone who, having heard that his mother is seriously ill, returns to his native place, worried whether he will make it in time, and is able to meet with his mother while she is still alive. The second poem sings the happiness of the moment when water pours into the rice field at a time of drought. The third example relates the happiness of the time when a sick person realizes that dawn has come after a sleepless night. Therefore, we can say that happiness is the transition from a lesser to a greater perfection. Moreover, we can also say that it is the consciousness of current good. Sadness *(kanashimi)*, by contrast, is as follows:

Kan no kuni no	By word of mouth
Owari no kimi to	I will transmit to the ten thousand worlds
Yorozu yo ni	Today's sadness:
Kanashiki kyō o	The last king
Iitsugi ni semu	Of the Korean country.

KAWADA JUN[7]

Dairen no	The sadness
Eki ni kyō furu	Of spring rains
Haru no ame	Falling today
Kanashiki koto wa	On the station of Dairen—
Iwade wakaremu	Without a word I will part.

OKUYAMA SHŪHO[8]

Kono kurashi ni	The sadness of a heart
Nazumi kinitsutsu	That has become attached
Kokoro kanashi	To this way of life—
Asaasa haha no	My mother polishing my shoes
Waga kutsu o migaku	Morning after morning.

KAWANAKA YŪKŌ[9]

Since the first poem was sung at the time of the funeral of His Majesty King Yi,[10] the passage from life to death is the transition from a greater to a lesser perfection. The reality of separation in the case of the second poem, and the fact that in the third poem the mother, rather than a servant, polishes the shoes, correspond to lesser perfections. We can say that "sad" is the consciousness of current evil. Ribot distinguishes three types of sadness: a positive, a negative, and a mixture of the two.[11] He regards positive sadness a consumption of movement; he considers negative sadness a stopping of movement. In other words, the representation of a hard task and a new labor is a "positive sadness." This would be the case, for example, when one has to take an exam again after failing the first time. The consciousness of loss and forfeiture is a "negative sadness," as in the case, for example, of the death of someone we love. A "mixed sadness" would be for a man of wealth who has gone bankrupt to try to recover his wealth once again. But in all the cases described here, no matter whether we face a positive consumption or a negative stopping, we feel them as current evil and a smaller perfection.

The feelings of being happy *(ureshii)* and lonesome *(sabishii)* are emotions deeply felt in the innermost part of the heart. Once they are directed toward the outside, however, they take on the modalities of joy *(yorokobi)* and sorrow *(nageki),* as we can see from the following examples:

Tsutome osoku	Raising their voices
Kaerishi ware o	When I return late
Koe tatete	From work
Yorokobu made ni	The children grow up
Ko wa oitachinu	To my joy.

KABUKI FUMI[12]

Nisshoku no	Do you see
Owareri to miru ya	That the solar eclipse has ended?
Ainura wa	The Ainu people
Uenkamui sareri to	Dance to their joy
Yorokobi odoru	Saying the demons have left.

ŌE TAKEO[13]

Kuni kozoru	A great joy
Ōki yorokobi wa	Filling the country
Shinbun ni	Overflows
Rajio ni afure	In the newspapers and the radio—
Kokoro niginigishi	The heart is merry!

KANBARA KATSUSHIGE[14]

To take a direction that overflows in voices, dances, newspapers, and radio is a characteristic of the modality of joy. Similarly, sorrow also denotes a centrifugal direction:

Ima ni shite	"If now
Kono ie uraba	We sell our house
Oi no yo ni	Where shall I go
Izuchi yukamu to	In my old age?"
Haha no nagekasu	So my mother grieves.

ŌNO TAMOTSU[15]

Nebusoku o	The diary lamenting
Nagekeru niki wa	Lack of sleep—
Yamaguni ni	The same will be
Kaeritamaishi	After I return
Nochi mo onajiki	To the mountainous country.

ŌMURA GORŌ[16]

Hahatoji ga	The grieving words
Nagekasu koto wa	Which I once heard
Sanagara ni	Of a mother
Katsute shiritaru	Are just like
Waga omoi naru	My own thoughts.

KAWAI TAKAKO[17]

The second poem is by the editor of *The Collected Works of Nakamura Kenkichi*.[18] The third poem was sung by a woman who had listened to the grieving words of a mother whose son had been killed—a woman who had experienced the death of her own son. Joy *(yorokobi)* and sorrow *(nageki)* possess the modality of an outward direction. It goes without saying that they are not completely different from happiness *(ureshisa)* and sadness *(kanashimi)*.

Here we must pay attention to the fact that what happiness *(ureshisa)* is to joy *(yorokobi)* is not necessarily the same as what sadness *(kanashimi)* is to sorrow *(nageki)*. Since happiness is an exciting feeling, it has, from the outset, a strong tendency to develop into joy. The passivity of happiness necessarily has to go through the activity of joy. Since, contrary to this, sadness is a depressive feeling, it is not necessarily required to go through the activity of sorrow. The passivity of sadness does not necessarily go through the activity of sorrow. Unlike a profound happiness that necessarily shifts into joy, a deep sadness tries to shut itself in itself without opening into a sorrow. As a result, it becomes rather easy to distinguish between sadness and sorrow, whereas in fact it is remarkably difficult to differentiate happiness from joy. Georges Dumas argues, moreover, that it is not difficult to distinguish what is passive from what is active in *tristesse* (sorrow), something that is actually difficult to accomplish with regard to *joie* (joy).[19] Among these four elements, joy and sadness exhibit their specific characteristics in the best possible way. Compared to joy, happiness lacks something; compared to sadness, sorrow is somehow excessive. Ordinarily, rather than using the antonyms "happiness" and "sadness," we employ the pair "joy" and "sadness."

With regard to these relationships, and focusing especially on them, I will now turn to the fact that happiness shows itself on the face as a smile *(emi)*, while sadness invites tears *(namida)*:

Monoiu to	When you speak
Mikawasu me sae	Even my eyes smile
Onozukara	By themselves
Emi to nariyuku	While exchanging glances—
Ureshisa ni ori	I am truly happy!

KATŌ SUGIE[20]

Ikite yuku	Just when I was writing a letter
Koto toburawamu	Inquiring
Tegami kaki	How you were doing
Masa ni kanashiku	I wept
Namida otoshikeri	Sad tears.

KAWASAKI TOGAI[21]

Moreover, there are cases when the feelings of happy *(ureshii)* and sad *(kanashii)* are made minor and superficial and form special feelings indicating an area of the heart that has come into contact with the outside. The minor form of happy is the feeling of pleasant *(tanoshii)*. Since pleasure *(tanoshimi)* is original and sensorial, it brings in its density traces that change into something spiritual:

Ura hata ni	In the back field
Kemuri no gotoku	It rains on and off
Shigure suru	Like smoke—
Kesa o tanoshiku	I delight in this morning
Na o nite taburu	Boiling and eating vegetables.

KATŌ TŌRI[22]

Kangiku o	Beside the vase
Iketaru bin no	In which winter chrysanthemums
Katawara ni	Are arranged
Ringo o okite	I place an apple
Hitori tanoshimu	And take pleasure alone.

KAITATSU YOSHIFUMI[23]

Chichi to nari	Being a father,
Ko to narite	Being a son—
Aiidakitsutsu	The pleasure
Shizuka ni yo o	Of sleeping the night away
Nemuru tanoshisa	Embracing each other.

KANEKO KUN'EN[24]

The word "pleasant" *(tanoshi)* comes from the song of joy sung by all deities who "reached for" *(tanoshite)* Amaterasu Ōmikami when she emerged from the heavenly cave.[25] "To reach for" (*te o nobasu;* literally "to stretch one's hand") has a temporal meaning in addition to a spatial one; it is a reaching for the future in time. There are cases in which the expression "pleasant" brings with it a clear view of the future:

Kago ni kau	The pleasure
Chiisaki tori sura ni	Of seeing even
Umare kite	Small birds
Sodachiyuku mono wa	Kept in a cage
Miru ni tanoshi mo	Being born and growing up.

KAWASAKI TOGAI

Soine seru	Lying asleep with my child
Ware no oyobi o	Who keeps clenching
Nigiritsutsu	My finger,
Iyuru sono hi o	Pleasantly waiting for the day
Tanoshimi machitsu	When he will recover.

KAWATANI TOSE[26]

Shitazumi no	For a long time
Tazuki wa nagashi	I have been making a living in a lowly
	position—
Nenkin no	I take pleasure alone
Nebumi o shitsutsu	While estimating
Hitori tanoshimu	My pension.

KANASAWA CHŌZABURŌ[27]

The equivalent of "pleasant," as the minor form of what is sad, is "painful" *(kurushii)*. Even in the cases of the three or five sensations *(ju),*[28] the sensation of pain *(kūju)* is set in opposition to the sensation of pleasure *(rakuju)*. According to the *Doctrine of Consciousness Only,*[29] the discriminatory sensations facing the border of orderly emotions are joyful sensations *(kiju),* while the discriminatory sensations facing the border of evil emotions are grieving sensations *(yūju)*. Moreover, the indiscriminate sensations facing the border of orderly emotions are pleasant sensations *(rakuju),* while indiscriminate sensations facing the border of evil emotions are painful sensations *(kūju)*. We might also say that happiness *(ureshisa)* and joy *(yorokobi)* nearly correspond to joyful sensations, while sadness *(kanashimi)* and sorrow *(nageki)* correspond to grieving sensations. Pleasure *(tanoshimi)* corresponds to pleasant sensations; pain *(kurushimi)* amounts to painful sensations:

Nengetsu o	Years and months
Shitashiku kikishi	I have heard
Sono koe wa	That familiar voice—
Ima rinjū no	Now it reveals the pain
Kurushimi morasu	Of the dying hour.

KAWABATA CHIE

Negai naki	When you will know me
Mi to shi shiru toki	As someone without desire
Shizuka nare	Be silent!
Yasashiki koto o	It is painful to hear
Kiku wa kurushiki	Your gentle words.

KANEDA CHIZU[30]

Yukizumaru	I have reached
Yo no moto sue o	The beginning and end of a world
Kiwametsutsu	Which has come to its limits—

> *Mura o osamuru*   I am in pain
> *Koto ni kurushimu*   At managing my village.
>
>   KARAKITA RISON[31]

It goes without saying that since pain is something sensorial, it changes into something spiritual.

If we translate into a diagram the six feelings that I have so far introduced—happiness, sadness, joy, sorrow, pleasure, and pain—happiness and sadness occupy a position at the center of a circle. Joy and sorrow are like radiuses drawn from the circle's center toward the circumference. They are like the opening of a closed umbrella whose center is the beginning and whose radius is nothing but an emanation from the center. The umbrella of happiness wants to be opened, whereas the umbrella of sadness is satisfied with being closed. Pleasure and pain are located close to the circumference, far from the center. The part painted in black on the periphery of an umbrella with a bull's-eye design is the space of pleasure and pain.

Usually when happiness emanates in great measure, it exceeds a smile and explodes into laughter *(warai)*:

> *Nese okedo*   Whether I lay him down to sleep
> *Nese okikanete*   Or cannot lay him down to sleep,
> *Kao daseba*   As soon as I show my face
> *Koboruru bakari*   He breaks into big smiles,
> *Warau ako ka na*   My dear child!
>
>   KATŌ MICHIKO[32]

> *Tawamurete*   When I heard
> *Umi ni waraeru*   A playful voice
> *Koe kikeba*   Laughing at the sea,
> *Tengusadori wa*   The agar-agar picker
> *Wakaki ominago*   Was a young girl.
>
>   KAWABATA CHIE

Once sadness is repressed, it accumulates into gloom *(urei)*:

> *Imo ga urei*   Unable to console
> *Nagusame kanete*   The gloom of my dear girl
> *Amatsuhi no*   I stand until the end

Hikari no moto ni   In the light
Tachitsukushitari   Of the heavenly sun.

                                                KATSUTA MOTOBUMI[33]

  Magirezaru   When possessed
Urei o moteba   By unmistakable gloom
  Cha o tatsuru   I make tea
Waga sanmai no   And fall
Toki ni kuzururu   Into a state of samādhi.

                                                KAMIYOSHI TAEKO[34]

Zarathustra's clear laughter and Christ's "gloom of mere death"
stand at both extremities. Next, moods are what we should call the lin-
gering tones of feelings. A happy mood is sung in the following poems:

   A o omou   I tell myself
Tarachine no haha   Cheerfully
   Yo ni masu to   That in this world
Kokoro hogara ni   I have a mother—the woman of the
                                      drooping breast—
Dokugen shitari   Who loves me.

                                                KAWANAKA YŪKŌ

   A ga inochi   Days also come
Nodoka naru hi mo   When my life
   Arinikeri   Is peaceful—
Kōen ni kite   I come to the park
Tsuru o mite ori   And look at the cranes.

                                                KAWADA JUN

A sad mood is sung in the following poems:

  Murasaki no   There is shade
Hana ni kage ari   On the gromwell flowers,
  Hikari ari   There is light—
Mitsumete itari   I stand staring at them
Kuraki kokoro ni   In a dark heart.

                                                ŌTA FUJIKO[35]

Amemoyoi	Face to face
Omoki kokoro ni	With my heavy heart
Mamukau ya	Under a threatening sky—
Hikari shizumuru	The color of mustard flowers
Na no hana no iro	In the sinking light.

KAWAGUCHI REI[36]

Now at the root of all these feelings and moods, there are the emotions of delight *(kai)* and displeasure *(fukai)*, which possess a primary meaning. It goes without saying that happiness, joy, and pleasure are feelings of delight, whereas sadness, sorrow, and pain are feelings of displeasure.

3

All the feelings that I have presented up to this point have been purely subjective. There is a group of feelings, however, which take as their main content the intentionality toward their objects. We might perhaps call the latter objective feelings in contradistinction to subjective feelings.

If the object engenders happiness in us, we feel love *(ai)* for that object; if the object brings sadness to us, we feel hatred *(zō)* for that object. To borrow Spinoza's words, love is happiness accompanying the concept of external cause; hatred is sadness accompanying the concept of external cause.[37] On the whole, happiness and love are deeply connected even at a semantic level: The Japanese word *"ureshi"* (happy) comes from a transformation of *"uruwashi"* (lovely), and *"uruwashi"* is nothing but "heart's love" *(ura-hashi):*

Me o toraba	I thought,
Me o aisamu to	"If you take a wife,
Omoikeri	You love that wife"—
Aware sono koro no	That pitiful childish mind of mine
Kodomogokoro ni	At that time!

KANEKO KUN'EN

Sono morote	He looks at me,
Konata ni mukete	Both arms
Idakaru to	Stretched out
A o mite suru yo	While I embrace him—
Ko wa hashiki ka mo	How lovely this child!

Kaneto Sōshi[38]

Isarai ni	To see from behind
Ke naki ko no tori	A chick with no feathers
Su ni iru to	On his rear
Ushiromi sureba	Entering the nest—
Hashiki yō nari	What a lovely view!

Kawasaki Togai

The reading *"niku"* for the Chinese character indicating "hatred" *(zō)* is an abbreviation of *"nigaaku"* (bitterly weary). We feel a distaste for those objects that bring sadness:

Kataku na ni	Concealed
Omoihisomete	In stubborn thoughts
Hitasura naru	An earnest rage
Ikari wa hito o	Has begun to make my heart
Nikumi sometsu mo	Hate people.

Kanazawa Hisako[39]

Nikumaruru	To be hated—
Sore mo hitotsu no	Shall we consider it
Seikatsu no	One of life's
Hariai to sen ka	Goals,
Kotonaku orite	And keep living as if nothing has
	happened?

Kawabata Chie

Yoki koto wa	I no longer hate
Makoto sukunaki	The knowledge that good things
Yo zo to shiri	In this world
Nikumazu nareru	Are few indeed—
Waga wasureguse	This is my habit of forgetting!

Kawashima Sonoko[40]

The two feelings of love and hatred have different modalities from which various feelings are born. The intensional emotion of familiarity *(shitashii)* is born when negotiations on the side of love with its object reach in its temporal being a peak that departs from a beginning:

Heigoshi ni	Exchanging words
Asaasa mono o	Over the fence
Iikawashi	Morning after morning
Shitashiku narite	People become familiar
Hito sariyukeri	And depart.

KASHIWAHARA TOSHIRŌ[41]

Sumitsukite	Familiar to me
Yamaga wa shitashi	Is the mountain hut where I have
	settled—
Yoiyoi ni	The time has come
Karigane wataru	When every evening
Koro to narinishi	The wild geese cross over.

EBIHARA HAMATOSHI[42]

Habusō wa	Silently in the evening
Yūbe shizuka ni	The senna
Ha o tojinu	Shuts its leaves—
Ikizuku mono no	I feel a familiarity
Shitashimi o omou	With something that makes me sigh.

ŌI HIDEKO[43]

In the continuation of their temporal existence, negotiations with an object of love are always accompanied by the extensional emotion of insatiability *(akitaranai)* so long as they have an end in view:

Ware ni niru to	Everybody says
Hito mina ieri	That she looks like me—
Hahaue no	No matter how much I look at
Wakaki sugata wa	My mother's young shape
Miredo akanu mo	I never get tired.

ŌTSUJI MIEKO[44]

Shinkyū no	Old and new
Karon sōzentari	Poetic commentaries are noisy—
Ningen no	I never get tired

Uta o utaite	Of singing
Ware akanaku ni	People's songs.

ŌHASHI MATSUHEI[45]

Furthermore, the disappearance of the object of love brings with it the critical emotion of having regret *(oshii)* over a temporal nonbeing:

Usubeni no	How regrettable to cut
Chisaki kaigara o	The nails of my child
Omowasuru	Which are suggestive of
Ako no tsume ka mo	Small, light crimson
Kirioshimaruru	Seashells!

KŌMURA KASUMI[46]

Makurabe no	I regret the vase
Bin ni shi oshimu	At my bedside
Hana sura mo	When I think that even flowers
Todomaranaku ni	Do not linger…
Ware wa nagayamu	Sick, I lie for a long time.

ŌKUMA CHŌJIRŌ[47]

Love is always a reluctance to separate. Semantically speaking as well, to regret *(oshi)* is to love *(oshi)*:

Oshimarete	A warm window
Ikuru o mina no	On the day when I think
Saiwai o	That to live
Omoiiru hi no	While being loved
Atatakaki mado	Is the blessing of everything.

KATŌ TOSHIKO[48]

Mi o oshimu	I regret myself,
Kokorogire nari	My heart filled with heartrending
	sorrow—
Machi o kite	I come to town
Kōkū hyōshikitō	And look up for a while
Shibashi aoginu	At the beacons.

ŌTSUKA GORŌ[49]

As a reluctance to separate, so long as it foresees its demise against the background of loving, love is not a pure, happy emotion; it is a variety of absolute emotion mixed with a seasoning of sad emotions. The subsidiary emotion of sad *(kanashi)* is included within the absolute emotion of darling *(kanashi):*

Nagaraemu	I came to know
Nozomi munashiki	The hope of living a long life
Ko to shiritsu	To be an empty child—
Iyoiyo kanashiku	Is it becoming
Nariyuku mono ka	Increasingly darling?

KAWASAKI ISHIMATSU[50]

Hoozuki o	Here they are
Kuchi ni fukumite	Blowing a whistle,
Narashiori	Holding it in their mouths—
Kanashi to omou	I think they are darling,
Yama no koro ka mo	The little girls of the mountain!

KANEYA SHŌJI[51]

The nonbeing of the temporal existence of the object from which one is reluctant to separate produces an autonomous ontological emotion known as frailty *(hakanasa):*

Tsutsuoto no	It is frail
Hibiku toki no ma	The fall
Utaretaru	Of a hit bird
Tori no otsuru wa	At the sound
Hakanakarikeri	Of the gunshot.

ŌKOSHI KŌCHŌ[52]

Kaibōdai ni	It is frail
Yokotawaru hō ni	To see faint traces
Oshiroi no	Of face powder
Kasuka ni nokoru o	On the cheek lying
Miru wa hakanashi	On the dissecting table.

ŌTSUKA TAKESHI[53]

The emotions mentioned earlier—"familiar," "insatiable," "regrettable," and "frail"—are contemporary emotions that directly feel, in the object of love before one's eyes, its intensional, extensional, critical, and ontological nature. But there are also special emotions that love the object while recollecting the past. To be yearning for something *(natsu-kashii)* is such an emotion directed toward the past. This emotion takes as its main moment the reality, or at least the assumption, of recollection or new recognition:

Hinageshi no　　　　A person I yearn for
Saku hi to narite　　As much as the gentle breeze
Sono ue no　　　　　Blowing on
Soyokaze hodo ni　　The poppies
Natsukashiki hito　　On the day of their bloom.

KAKEGAI YOSHIO[54]

Wakaki hi no　　　　The tree I used to climb
Kinobori no ki wa　　In my youth
Imada ari　　　　　Is still there—
Haha ni augoto　　　I yearn for it
Natsukashiki ka na　Each time I see my mother.

ŌTSUKA TORAO[55]

There is also a future-oriented emotion springing from love. The emotion of sighing for something *(koishii)* is tinged with futurality. Familiarity is stipulated by the present nature of the object. In opposition to "yearning for," whose moment derives from the past nature of the object, "sighing for" has the inclination of supplementing the object's lack in the future. In love *(kou)* there is a search in the future that goes through an asking *(kou):*

Yama ikeba　　　　　When I go to the mountain
Wakaba no nioi　　　A fragrance of young leaves
Tadayoeri　　　　　Drifts about—
Kono yamamichi ni　I sigh for someone to be here
Hito no koishisa　　On this mountain path.

ŌKUBO HITŌ[56]

Nantonaku　　　　　Somehow
Hito no kohoshiku　I sigh for people—
Zawamekeru　　　　In the evening
Yoi no chimata o　　I wander around
Waga samayoeru　　The busy town.

KAWAKAMI ICHIRŌ[57]

Koigokoro	My sighing for you
Setsunaku narite	Having become melancholic
Ima no ima	I wrote a letter
Aitashi to kimi ni	To you saying I want to meet you
Fumi kakinikeri	Now, right now.

ŌMURA TSURUKO[58]

The formation of Plato's *erōs* by way of recollection *(anamnesis)* is nothing but a "sighing for" *(koishisa)* mediated by a "yearning for" *(natsukashisa)*. The characteristic of *eros* is not simply a desire as reminiscence of the past. It takes its true meaning for the first time as a desire for an idea that demands realization in the future. In his explanation of the reality of the psychological futurality of sighing for something *(koishisa)*, Plato introduces the assumption of a metaphysical past dimension. When sighing for something is simply a desire for the past, the anticipation of love becomes nothing more than an image reflected on the background.

The fact that sighing for something establishes itself on the ground of a lack of the object has a great meaning for the genealogy of feelings: the emotion of lonesomeness *(sabishii)* is always behind the emotion known as sighing for *(koishii)*. Sighing for something is an emotion in which a fragment searches for other fragments in order to become a whole; lonesomeness is an emotion in which the fragment realizes itself as fragment:

Yamazato no	Winter
Fuyu wa sabishi mo	In a mountain village is lonesome—
Tamago kai	One person only
Hitori kishi mama	Came to buy eggs
Kuru hito mo nashi	And no one else.

ŌMORI HIROMU[59]

Inishie no	Even if I turn to
Hijiri no fumi ni	The writings of learned men
Mukaite mo	Of the past,
Kimo o shi mineba	Since I do not see you,
Sabishikarikeri	I am lonesome.

ŌNISHI HAJIME[60]

Sabishikereba	So lonesome
Nagisa ni tachite	I stand on the shore
Asa o miru	And look at the morning—
Kono aoumi wa	This blue sea
Kimi ni tsuzukeri	Continues in you.

KAMIYA MASAE[61]

We must pay attention to the fact that on the underside of sighing for something as an objective emotion there is a subjective emotion known as lonesomeness *(sabishisa)*. Moreover, there is a subjective emotion known as desolation *(wabishii)*, which is analogous to the emotion of lonesomeness. It would be correct to say that once we add sadness *(kanashisa)* to lonesomeness *(wabishisa)*, by and large we have desolation *(wabishisa)*:

Ikiwaburu	When I turn
Kanashimi ni hitato	Close to the sadness
Mukau toki	Of the lonesomeness of life
Nakite sugaramu	I hold onto tears,
Haha o shi zo omou	Thinking of my mother.

KAWASHIMA FUMIKO[62]

Michinobe no	I passed by
Kojiki ni zeni o	Throwing a coin to a beggar
Nagetesugi	By the roadside—
Nao wabishisa o	All the more I walk
Mochitsutsu ayumeri	With my desolation.

ŌKAWA SUMIE[63]

Hito no yo ni	Since I live a desolate life
Wabite sumaeba	Away from the world of men,
Inishie mo	I realize
Nasake ni ikite	How much we grieved too in the past
Nageki ainishi	Over this pitiful life!

EBIHARA HAMATOSHI

The fact that the spiritual life of Japan values *sabi* (lonesomeness) and *wabi* (desolation) depends on the training people receive to the point that they actually take pleasure in the wanting nature of lonesomeness *(sabishisa)* and desolation *(wabishisa)*. Even the paradox that the shade of India ink is richer than actual colors derives from the same mental attitude and absurdity according to which lonesomeness *(sabishisa)* is pleasant *(tanoshii)*:

Sabishisa o	Me, in the field
Tanoshi to omou	Where wild birds
Yachōra no	Play hiding,
Asobi kakururu	Thinking that lonesomeness
No no naka ni ware wa	Is pleasant.

KATAYAMA HIROKO[64]

Kono yama ni	Like a monk
Chikazuku fuyu no	Of the Rinzai school
Sabishisa o	Who takes pleasure
Rinzai no sō	In the lonesomeness of winter
Tanoshimu gotoshi	Getting closer to this mountain.

KAWADA JUN

So far I have spoken about emotions directed toward the present, past, and future on the side of love *(ai)*. Now I will turn to the corresponding emotions on the side of hatred *(zō)*. Dislike *(en)* is a present emotion that is felt intensionally for an object which is in front of our eyes:

Hito itou	I seclude myself
Kokoro idakite	Bearing a heart
Komori ori	That dislikes people—
Itsu ka aki sari	Lonesome is the sky
Sora sabinikeri	When fall comes.

KAWASAKI TOGAI

Niwasaki wa	Hot is the garden
Hi no teri atsushi	Under the shining sun—
Abura uku	Disliking
Kitanaki kao o	My dirty face on which oil surfaces
Itoite komoru	I hide myself from view.

KANBARA KATSUSHIGE

There is an extensional emotion of weariness *(aki)* on the side of hatred that corresponds to insatiability *(akitaranai)* on the side of love:

Tsurezure ni	How many folded cranes
Ori tsuru ikutsu	I have made
Tsukuru koto zo	While lying idle
Nomiakitarishi	With the wrapper of the medicine
	powder
Kogusuri no kami ni	That I am too weary to drink!

KAWABATA CHIE

Gikai bōchō	Weary of attending
Akite idekishi	The National Diet
Hyakushō no	I left—
Ware wa tsukarete	Me, a tired farmer,
Asakusa ni kitsu	Ending up in Asakusa.

KAWAI ICHIRO[65]

While on the side of love there was a critical emotion of regretting *(oshii)* for disappearance, on the side of hatred there is a fin-de-siècle emotion of being vexing *(wazurawashii)* in response to duration:

Furitsuma wa	My old wife
Iyoiyo furite	Getting increasingly old—
Iu koto no	Oh, how vexing
Ana wazurawashi	What she says,
Ashita yūbe ni	Morning and evening!

KAWASAKI TOGAI

Next, on the side of hatred there is an emotion directed toward the past—repentance *(kai)*—which corresponds to yearning for something on the side of love. Repentance similarly takes the recollection of the past as an important moment, but it is a recollection related especially to one's faults and sins:

Isogashisa ni	Having been seized
Shimijimi dakishi	By busyness
Hi mo marera	The days were few—
Ako o shinasete	After my child has died
Nochi kuinikeri	I repent.

KANEKO FUKYŪ[66]

Ura wakaki	Since I was overcome
Hito no kokoro no	By the single motive
Ichizusa ni	Of the young person,
Hodasare mo seba	How many times
Kui o kasanemu	Will I repent!

KAWABATA CHIE

The emotion directed toward the future on the side of hatred, corresponding to sighing for something on the side of love, is fear *(kyō)*. Fear is the feeling of hate for occurrences taking place in the future of things and phenomena:

Mazushisa ni	Secretly I fear
Tsumako no kokoro	That in poverty
Ijigitanaku	The heart of mother and son
Nari wa senu ka to	Might become
Hisoka ni osoru	Greedy.

ŌSAWA ISAMU[67]

Tanazoko ni	The coins
Kazoe ozuozu to	That people take out nervously
Dasu hito no	Counting them on the palm
Zeni wa yakuka no	Are not enough to pay
Nakaba ni tarazu	Half the medical bill.

ŌTSUKA ETSUYO[68]

Iegataki	Fearing inside my heart
Tsui no yamai ka	That this illness difficult to cure
Kokoro osore	Might be my last one,
Ishi ni shitagai	I follow the doctor's instructions
Tokage ni tateri	And stand in the shade of the door.

KAWABATA YASUTO[69]

Thus have I provided the modalities of love and hatred colored by a temporal dimension.

4

In what follows I will talk about three aspects of love and hatred separate from temporal stipulations: first, things stipulated by the general character of being of the object; second, things stipulated by special operations of the object; third, things stipulated by the character of ownership of the object.

With regard to the first stipulation, the modality of love regulated by the disposition of the object itself, love produces a change in such modalities according to the greatness or smallness of the character of the loved object in comparison to the self. When the object of love is smaller than the self, the emotion of care *(itawari)* occurs:

Setonabe o	She rejoiced
Yasuku kai kite	At buying cut-price
Yorokoberi	A Seto pot—
Mazushiki tsuma wa	I should show more care
Itawari yaramu	For my poor wife!

KAWABATA SHUNPO[70]

Ominako wa	The little daughters
Tada itawarare	All understand
Iki yo to iu	Their mother's words
Haha no kotoba o	To live
Kikiwakete ori	Taking care of each other.

ŌTA TOSHIKO[71]

On the underside of the objective emotion of being careful, we find the subjective emotion of gentleness *(yasashisa):*

Saewataru	The waning moon
Tsuki no shitabi ni	Brightly crosses the sky—
Ito semete	I will tell my wife
Tsuma ni yasashiku	As many gentle words
Mono o iwaba ya	As possible!

ŌHASHI MATSUHEI

Harisakuru	Tears fill up
Mune ippai no	My chest
Namida nari	To the point that it breaks—
Yasashiki koto wa	The dream of hearing him
Notamau na yume	Saying a gentle word.

KAMIYA MASAE

Gentleness is the subjective side of careful. It is normal, however, for the object of care to in turn possess gentleness as subjectivity. Things that do not have gentleness as subjectivity are unworthy of being the object of care by gentle subjects. To give care to something unworthy of care is a matter that exceeds human nature. In other words, care *(itawari)* is the same as sympathy *(awaremi)*, which I will treat later. It is the same because the smallness of the being of the object of love is the same smallness for which the possessor of the object must hate it. I think that here we also have primarily the genealogical position of the so-called *agape* as a special characteristic of love. There are many cases in which *agape* takes the form of compassion *(airen)*, which is care for all people:

Junrei no	There are also
Ko o yobitomete	People
Mono megumu	Who stop pilgrims
Hito mo arikeri	And give them offerings—
Aki no yūgure	Autumn evening.

OCHIAI NAOBUMI[72]

Ainureba	When I meet her
Haha to yobubeki	I should call her mother—
Chichi no tsuma	My father's wife
Nasake komorishi	Speaks words
Koto o norashinu	Filled with compassion.

KAMIZAWA HIROSHI[73]

When the object of love's character is remarkably larger than the self, the emotion of awe *(osore)* occurs:

Kashikosa ni	I look up with respect
Namida tamarite	Collecting my tears
Augitari	In awe—
Waga ōkimi wa	My Lord granted me
Kyoshu o tamaeri	His lifted hand.

KŌSAKA NOBUKATSU[74]

Hachijūyon sai	I jotted down the note
Aki no mifude to	That my beloved father
Kakisoete	Wrote this

Chichi ga mifumi o	When he was eighty-four years old,
Tebako ni shimaeri	And put the precious letter in the box.

KAWASHIMA SONOKO

In such circumstances, when the feeling of love is deep, the emotion of love dependence *(amae)* is liable to take place:

Akago daku	I hold the baby in my arms.
Ware ni amaete	Depending on my love,
Nakiyoru ko	The child draws near to me crying—
Ani to wa iedo	Although you are the eldest brother
Nare mo osanashi	You are such an infant!

KABUKI FUMI

The taste of sweetness implies the presence of both the giver and the recipient of dependence *(amae)*. As the taste of love, the sweetness of this dependence seems to stand in opposition to the bitter taste of hatred. In other words, we can also say that the sweet addiction to the mysticism of emotions is the natural manner that feelings have of doing things.

Once we move to the side of hatred, when the ontological character of the object of hate is smaller than the self, the emotion of contempt *(sagesumi)* occurs, often accompanied by a sneer:

Mizukara o	Turning my eyes
Neraeru tsutsu ni	To the gun
Me o yarite	Aimed at me
Tsumetaku emishi	I was hit
Toki ka utareshi	While smiling coldly.

OKUMURA OKUEMON[75]

Ita shiaguru	While planing away
Kanna kezuri mo	To finish the board
Araki mama	I had to stop
Yameneba naranu	Before it was done—
Tema yasuki shigoto	Bad piece of work!

OKUDA KAZUO[76]

When the object of hatred is remarkably bigger than the self, the emotion of resignation *(akirame)* occurs:

Akirame yo	While vomiting blood
Akirame yo to haha ga	I agree to follow
Iu koe o	The voice of my mother
Chi o hakinagara	Saying, "Give up,
Ware wa ubenau	Give up!"

ŌNO TORAJI[77]

Hito to umareshi	I stand
Sabishisa ni sae	The lonesomeness
Taete ari	Of being born as a human being—
Sono yo no koto wa	Will I endure
Shinobazarame ya	The rest?

OKIMOTO SHIGETORA[78]

When the object of love and hatred is ontologically big, we see that a mixed emotion of devotion and submission occurs in religious sentiment in which awe *(osore)* and resignation *(akirame)* merge.

With regard to the second stipulation—that is, the modality of love and hatred regulated by special operations of the object—when we come in contact with lovable things our response to them, which accompanies love, is obligation *(on)*, namely, the emotion of appreciation:

Itawaritsutsu	When I start to think
Katsu hagemashishi	Of the obligation and love
On'ai ni	For your care
Omoiitareba	And your encouragement,
Araki namida ari	Violent tears come to my eyes.

ŌTA SEIKYŪ[79]

Hei no soto o	Whose voice
Kakeyuku ware no	Is warning my child
Osanago ni	Who is running
Ki o tsukekururu	Outside the fence
Donata no koe ka	To be careful?

ŌHASHI MOYO[80]

Opposed to this, when we come in contact with hateful things our response to them, which accompanies hatred, is anger *(ikari)*:

Kono shigonichi	This past four, five days
Hito ni kakawaru	I was in a rage
Ikari arite	About people—
Kazeare no nodo ni	An unsavory meal I swallow
Mazuki meshi kuu	Down my throat, rough because of a cold.

KANEKO SHINSABURŌ[81]

Haradachite	My wife has begun
Hayane seshi waga	To sew some clothing
Makurabe ni	At my bedside
Tsuma wa kimono o	Where I went to sleep early
Nuihajimetari	In anger.

KAWABATA SHUNPO

When the anger becomes depressive and continuous, we have a grudge *(urami)*. Since anger is usually accompanied by excitement and out-breaks, the emotion on the side of hatred corresponding to obligation on the side of love is not anger but grudge:

Haha wa dare mo	Without begrudging,
Uramazu semezu	Without blaming anybody,
Me o tojinu	My mother
Waga jūichi no	Closed her eyes
Aki samuki yo ni	In my eleventh fall, on a cold night.

KANEKO KUN'EN

Omoitsukushi	While exhausting my thoughts,
Uramitsukushite	While exhausting my grudge,
Nagaki yo no	The moon has come out
Akatsuki kuraku	In the dark dawn
Idete ishi tsuki	Of a long night.

ŌTA MIZUHO[82]

When anger is rooted in a sense of justice and takes a moral aspect, it becomes indignation *(ikidōri)*:

Kono kuni no	While being indignant
Jānarisuto no	At the lethargy
Mukiryoku o	Of journalists

Ikidōritsutsu   In this country,
Shika mo ubenau   Nevertheless I agree with them.

                      EMURA JŌKEN[83]

Itsuwari ōki   While thinking
Yo to omoitsutsu   This is a world filled with lies,
Arinarete   I get used to it,
Ikidōru koto mo   And without indignation
Nakute sugikishi   Have come to this point in my life.

                      KAWABE MORIHEI[84]

With regard to the third stipulation, I will raise the issue of the modality of love and hatred regulated by the character of ownership of the object. If one's property is lovable, the emotion of pride *(hokori)* comes about:

Jōbafuku   While being praised
Tazuna sabaki o   For my way of handling the reins
Homeraretsutsu   In my riding habit,
Mishi hi ni nitaru   Today's sky looks like
Kyō no sora ka na   The day I saw you.

                      KAWAGUCHI KOZUE[85]

Itten no   O Father, O Mother,
Kimi owashimasu   Wheeling up
Miaraka ni   To the palace
Maunobori kitsu   Where the lord of the firmament
Waga chichi yo haha yo   Resides!

                      OKUMURA OKUEMON

When it continues and degenerates, pride becomes the emotion of arrogance *(kōman)*:

Mioboe no   Although I do not recognize
Nakitsura naredo   The face,
Keiki yoku   Nonetheless
Ware mo bōshi ni   I tip my hat
Te o kakeshi ka na   Spiritedly.

                      EBATO HAKUKA[86]

If one's property is detestable, the emotion of shame *(haji)* comes about:

Hazukashiki	I am not hungry
Hodo ni wa uezu	To the point of being ashamed—
Mazushi tou	The word
Kotoba wa imada	"Poor" is still
Harukekarurashi	Far away.

ŌHASHI MATSUHEI

Tsukitsumete	The girls of this village
Ikin to negau	Who want to squeeze out
Kono mura no	A living
Musumera wa kami no	Are not ashamed
Odoro o hajizu	Of their disheveled hair.

KARAKITA RISON

When it continues and degenerates, shame becomes the emotion of servility *(hikutsu):*

Hito no mae ni	The habit of sitting down
Kata o otoshite	Dropping the shoulder—
Suwaru kuse wa	Did that begin
Mise o tozashishi	When you shut down
Koro yori no koto ka	The store?

KAWACHI EISŌ[87]

Next, if the property of others is lovable, the emotion of envy *(ura-yami)* occurs:

Onkyū ni	My friend,
Yasukeku kurasu	Who lives peacefully
Tomo wa waga	On a pension,
Uuru shirota o	Passes by, looking at the field
Mite tōritari	Where I plant rice.

KANAOKA MASAO[88]

Omou mama	Doing everything
Shitaizanmai	That he wanted to do
Shitsuku shite	As it pleased him—

| *Shi ni yukishi chichi wa* | How envious I am of my father |
| *Urayamubekari* | Who now is dead! |

KANAZAWA TANETOMI[89]

Once a competitive spirit is added that tries to possess for the self the lovable things possessed by others, envy becomes jealousy *(netami)*. While with envy the other is an object of love, with jealousy it is clearly an object of hatred. In the following two poems jealousy is somehow hidden:

Tokkahin	I was defeated
Arakenaku eru	After I mingled
Ominara ni	With women
Majirite wa ore	Violently choosing
Kokoro okuretsu	Bargain-priced items!

KAGAMI MASAKO[90]

Kōshigoshi ni	Pale is the moon
Miyuru koyoi no	This evening
Tsuki awashi	As I see it across the lattice—
Tsuma wa kaeraji to	Desolation at the thought
Omou wabishisa	That my husband will not come back!

KAWAZU TERUKO[91]

If, by secretly harboring a competitive spirit against the women who snatch up bargains at a sale, one hates her competitors—or if, by attributing the fact that one's husband does not come home to the presence of a competitor in the possession of the husband, one hates this competitor—then we have jealousy.

When the other is the object of hatred since the property of the other is hateful, the emotion of ease *(iikimi)* occurs:

Kōbun shiken ni	My heart
Ochitaru tomo o	Consoles the friend
Nagusame iru	Who has failed
Ware no kokoro wa	The higher civil service examination—
Tanoshimite wa inu ka	Is that not taking pleasure?

ŌSHITA MITSUO[92]

When the other's possession is hateful, however, in most instances the other is the object of love rather than hatred. In this case the emotion of sympathy *(awaremi)* takes place:

Kuesomeshi	While looking
Repura kanja no	At the ruined face
Kao mitsutsu	Of a leprosy patient,
Renbin no kokoro	A compassionate feeling
Shibashi okorazu	Arises in me for some time.

ŌYA ICHIZŌ[93]

Aihanare	When you separate from the other
Oreba katami ni	You feel sympathy
Awaremite	For the mementos—
Ikiyuku koto o	You mourn
Toburaitamaeri	Going on living.

KAWASAKI TOGAI

Sympathy is necessarily care *(itawari)*. Moreover, since the feeling of compassion is based, on the one hand, on the fact that everything confronts the self as other and, on the other hand, on the fact that everything is stamped with the seal of finiteness, compassion fills everything:

Tazukare no	Feeling sympathy
Uma no neiki o	For the breathing of a horse asleep
Awaremitsu	After tiring work in the field—
Osoki yūge no	I took up the chopsticks
Hashi torinikeri	Of a late supper.

KATAGISHI YOSHIKUMI[94]

Okinagusa no	Feeling sympathy
Hana o awaremi	For the pasqueflowers,
Tamoto horu	I keep walking
Kusafu no michi wa	On the path of a grassy field
Sunahama ni tsuku	Which ends at a sandy beach.

ŌKURO TOMIJI[95]

At the same time, moreover, everything melts together with the self, becoming one with it. Everything is a finite other and also a finite self. This is what is called the moving power of things *(mono no aware)*. The "moving power of things" is nothing but the inner mournful melody of the self that springs forth by itself from the finiteness of everything. The sympathy *(awaremi)* of objective emotions and the moving power *(aware)* of subjective emotions mutually limit each other. Both components of the word *"aware"*—*"a"* and *"hare"*—are exclamations. But the self, facing the finiteness of the other and turning toward its own finiteness through the other, calls out "ah!" *(a)*; it hails "oh!" *(hare)*. Further, I mentioned earlier that there is a minor pain *(kurushimi)* confronting sadness *(kanashimi)*. "Moving power" also occupies a minor position with regard to sadness. As the moving power of things, the power of things has a strict materiality:

Uma o uru	The talk of selling the horse
Hanashi matomari	Is settled—
Iroribe ni	The sound of settling the bargain
Teuchi no oto wa	Next to the sunken hearth
Aware narikeri	Is moving.

KATŌ MEIJI[96]

Kane narite	I, standing at the riverside,
Segakibune yuku	Looking at
Awaresa o	The moving scene
Kawabe ni tachite	Of hungry ghost ships going
Ware wa mite ori	At the sound of the bell.

EBISAWA KINZŌ[97]

Seitō jidai no	The moving power
Toki no hito aware	Of times of political activism—
Ikishi ni mo	Now I have come to the point
Ima wa shirarezu	Where I do not know whether
Narinikeru ka mo	Those people are alive or dead.

KAWAMURA SENSHŪ[98]

5

Previously I stated that the purely subjective emotions of happiness *(ureshisa)*, joy *(yorokobi)*, pleasure *(tanoshisa)*, sadness *(kanashimi)*, sorrow *(nageki)*, and pain *(kurushimi)* are either agreeable *(kaikan)* or disagreeable *(fukaikan)* feelings. Agreeable or disagreeable emotions are also found at the root of objective feelings, and they have a primary meaning. Love and its modalities—for example, familiarity *(shitashisa)*, a yearning for something *(natsukashisa)*, a sighing for something *(koishisa)*, obligation *(on)*, pride *(hokori)*, and the like—belong to agreeable feelings. On the opposite side, hatred and its modalities—for example, dislike *(en)*, repentance *(kai)*, fear *(kyō)*, anger *(ikari)*, shame *(haji)*, and the like—belong to disagreeable feelings. But anger is also accompanied by feelings of pleasure. Contempt *(sagesumi)* occurs in response to hateful objects; but since it is accompanied by an awareness of the greatness of the self that looks down upon undersized objects, it is rather a feeling of pleasure. So-called romantic irony is based on a prodigious sense of superiority toward the dwarfishness and nothingness of all creation. Therefore, we can say that in the genealogy of feelings, while being rooted in contempt, romantic irony is also an artistic feeling of pleasure blooming in the fragrance of amusing *(okashii)* and beautiful *(utsukushii)* emotions, which I discuss later. Resignation *(akirame)* also takes place in response to objects of hatred; but by sinking the small self in the majesty of the object, it secures a feeling of pleasure. Its opposite, awe *(osore)*, which occurs in response to the majesty of a lovable object, is not a pure feeling of pleasure so long as it is accompanied by an awareness of the dwarfishness of the self. As a response to the possession of a hateful thing by an other that is the object of hatred, poetic justice *(iikimi)* belongs to feelings of pleasure by being a negation of a negation. Envy *(urayami)*, which occurs when the other possesses something lovable, is rather a disagreeable feeling. Sympathy *(awaremi)* is a response to the object of love possessing a hateful thing; but so long as the ontological character of the object of love is small, sympathy gets blended with the self's sense of superiority, thus becoming a mixed feeling of pleasure and displeasure. Moving power *(aware)* is not an aspect of pure sadness *(kanashimi)* because, as a feeling mutually limited by sympathy *(awaremi)*, it is a subsidiary emotion incorporating both the agreeable feeling of the sympathizing person and the agreeable feeling of the one who has been sympathized with.

In short, all the emotions that I have discussed so far, both subjective and objective emotions, are guided by feelings of pleasure and displeasure. In opposition to these emotions, there is a group of feelings guided by the emotions of tension and relaxation. Undoubtedly, emotions of tension and relaxation were blended in various forms in the emotions I have been discussing. In particular, tension was greatly involved in sighing for something *(koishisa)* and fear *(kyō)* as futural emotions. Notwithstanding, we can conclude that agreeable and disagreeable feelings have a primary meaning. Even the group of emotions that I will be discussing from now on is vividly tinged by agreeable and disagreeable feelings. Their primary meaning, however, shifts toward tension and relaxation. This group is made of futural emotions in the truest sense of the word. I will divide this group into three subgroups.

The first subgroup is made of feelings of desire *(yoku)* or feelings accompanied by desire. Since the object of desire is always located in the sphere of the future, the feeling of desire takes tension as its essence. Whether we look at desire in the ancient categorizations of the five emotions (happiness, pleasure, desire, anger, pity) or the seven emotions (happiness, anger, pity, pleasure, love, evil, desire), desire has always been counted among the main emotions:

> *Zeni hoshi to*
> *Omou kokoro o*
> *Shikaritsutsu*
> *Mukaeba shiroki*
> *Iwakine no yuki*
>
> While rebuking
> The mind's thinking
> "I want money,"
> I look out:
> White snow on the peak of Mt. Iwaki!
>
> KATŌ TŌRI

> *Ōkata no*
> *Mono wa shōka o*
> *Sezu narishi*
> *Hara ni iki yoki*
> *Sakana o kuitashi*
>
> I want to put
> Fresh fish
> In a stomach
> Which now cannot digest
> Most things!
>
> ŌNO TORAJI

> *Hana kaite*
> *Kaeru kokoro to*
> *Narinikeri*
> *Kono shizukesa ya*
> *Ikuka horiseshi*
>
> I bought flowers
> And I have decided
> To leave—
> Oh, this tranquillity,
> How many days might it continue!
>
> KANEKO KUN'EN

The fact that desire feels tension toward a possible object is grounded in the lack of the object in actual reality. The subjective emotion toward lack is lonesomeness *(sabishisa)*. It is self-evident that a human being, so long as one exists as an individual, brings as primordial feelings the desire of the continuation of existence as well as the lonesomeness of individuality. We can say that the individual is where desire and lonesomeness are. Moreover lonesomeness, on the one hand, radiates toward the moving power in self-denial and toward sympathy *(agape)* while, on the other, it concentrates itself on the support of sighing for something in self-affirmation *(erōs)*. The life of lonesomeness is found where an emanation of benevolence and a concentration of love breathe at the same time. How does desire develop? Once desire is fulfilled, tension relaxes and the feeling of satisfaction *(manzoku)* arises. Satisfaction is a loose feeling of pleasure:

Futari ite	I am silent,
Tarau kokoro ni	Content
Modashiori	Being with another person—
Kaze watari kite	The breeze comes
Matsuba o furasu	And scatters the pine needles.

OKUNUKI NOBUMITSU[99]

Tōka amari o	Being content
Asobi taraite	With their more than ten day excursion,
Chichi haha wa	Father and mother
Yuki furu sato ni	Return again
Mata kaerimasu	To their snow-covered village.

ŌISHI ISSAKU[100]

When desire is not fulfilled, the feeling of dissatisfaction *(fuman)* arises. Dissatisfaction does not have as much relaxation as satisfaction. It is a half-loose, half-strained feeling of displeasure.

Taru koto naku	The wishes of my mother
Sugishi hitoyo o	Who has been talking
Iiizuru	Of a life
Haha no negai wa	Spent without satisfaction
Ware ni kakareri	Hang on me.

KATŌ TŌRYŌ[101]

Musaborite	Unsatisfied
Yomu naga fumi no	By the brevity
Mijikaki o	Of your letter
Monotarazu omoi	That I craved to read,
Kurikaeshi yomu	I keep reading it over and over.

ŌNO KAZUO[102]

While satisfaction branches out in happiness *(ureshisa)* and pleasure *(tanoshisa)*, dissatisfaction ramifies in sadness *(kanashimi)* and pain *(kurushimi)*.

The second subgroup is made of the feelings of doubt *(utagai)* and delusion *(madoi)*. In desire the object is fixed, generally speaking, and the relationship with such a fixed object is a feeling of tension. But doubt and delusion are products of a tension where the object is not fixed, a tension that switches from object to object like a pendulum. In other words, they are feelings of tension produced by an object of intention rolling on the horizon of the future. Moreover, when the ground of determination left in the future is thought to be on the side of the object, we have the feeling of doubt:

Te ni oenu	While admonishing
Ko o satoshitsutsu	My unruly child
Kyōiku no	I keep thinking to exhaustion,
Chikara utagaite	Doubting the power
Omoitsukaruru	Of education.

KANAMORI HIROSHI[103]

Utagai no	Softening
Kokoro no yuragi mo	The heart's fluctuations
Nagomite wa	Of doubt
Sara ni sabishiku	I sink again
Omoishizumeri	In lonesome thoughts.

ŌYA ICHIZŌ

When the ground of determination left in the future is perceived as depending on the subject's will, we have the feeling of perplexity *(madoi):*

Tōku mite	I am surprised
Arieshi mono no	And perplexed
Mi ni chikaku	To find next to me

Aru ni odoroki	Something that I thought
Kokoro madoeri	Existed so far away!

KAWASAKI TOGAI

In the third subgroup we find hope *(kibō)* and concern *(shinpai)*, which occur when there is doubt about the attainment of the object of desire. Hope brings a lovable object onto the temporal horizon of the future; it is a feeling that responds to the possibility of attaining this object at some point in time. Hope is a feeling of pleasure in full tension:

Kōfuku no	Sunflowers
Ware ni megurite	Have begun to bloom
Kuru gotoku	As if
Sakihajimetaru	They came
Himawari no hana	To surround me with bliss!

KAITATSU YOSHIFUMI

Kenarabete	For some days
Netsu idenu mi no	I have not had any fever—
Sawayakeshi	I will eat
Mono ōku kuite	Many refreshing things
Ware wa futoramu	And get fat!

KATŌ TŌRYŌ

The counterpart to this, the feeling of concern *(shinpai)*, brings a hateful object on the temporal horizon of the future; it is a feeling that takes place when there is the possibility for the attainment of this object at some point in time. Concern is a feeling of displeasure in full tension:

Kusushitachi	Doctors gather
Yorite hisohiso	To speak
Hanashiori	In hushed tones—
Waga chichi ni kakawaru	I wonder whether
Koto naramu ka	It concerns my father!

KAWACHI EISŌ

Naki hito ga	What will become
Nagaku hirakite	Of the dictionary
Tezuretaru	Worn by the hands

Gensen wa ika ni	Of a person, now gone, who
Nariyukuramu ka	Opened it for many years?

KATŌ ISAMI[104]

Concern is included in hope, and hope is included in concern. When the probability for hope is extremely high, the emotion of promising *(tanomoshii)* occurs. This is a tense feeling of pleasure:

Akatoki to	Clouds
Shirami sometaru	Faintly burning
Himugashi ni	In the east
Honoka ni yakuru	Dyed in white at dawn
Kumo wa tanomoshi	Are promising.

ŌTSUKA TAIJI[105]

When the probability for hope reaches certainty, the emotion known as certain *(tashika)* occurs. This is the result of a fulfilled hope and a relaxed feeling of pleasure:

Karamatsu no	A downward path
Hayashi nakaba no	In the heart of a forest
Kudarizaka	Of larch—
Yokan masashiku	A sure premonition
Mizuumi ga miyu	That the lake is visible!

KAWABATA CHIE

When the probability is small, by contrast, the emotion of uncertain *(obotsukanai)* occurs. In this emotion the tension leans toward relaxation; it is a feeling of displeasure:

Wasure yo to	Although your messages
Kakitamō ni wa	Do not tell me
Aranedomo	To forget,
Obotsukanashi ya	Your recent letters
Konogoro no fumi	Are so uncertain!

KAKEGAI YOSHIO

When the probability gradually decreases and becomes zero, the emotion of despair *(zetsubō)* takes place. This is a relaxed feeling of displeasure. This emotion of despair is felt as the limit of decrease on the side of hope; seen from the side of concern, however, it is the result of the fulfillment of that concern:

Nagaraemu	I came to know
Nozomi munashiki	The emptiness of the child's hope
Ko to shiritsu	To live a long life—
Iyoiyo kanashiku	Will this increase
Nariyuku mono ka	My love for her?

KAWASAKI ISHIMATSU

Moreover, when the hope suddenly turns into its opposite, a special feeling of disappointment *(shitsubō)* occurs. Disappointment is a relaxed feeling of displeasure:

Atatakaku	I delight in the thought
Naraba iemu to	That when it warms up
Tanoshimishi o	I will recover—
Sakura no hana mo	They say that even the cherry blossoms
Chiru to iu nari	Scatter.

KAWABATA CHIE

Furthermore, when we see the opposite result of our concern take place, the emotion of relief *(anshin)* occurs. Relief is a relaxed feeling of pleasure:

Yubikirite	When you pledge
Chikaeba yasuku	By hooking little fingers
Oru ko nari	The child becomes quiet—
Sono osanasa yo	Such childishness,
Okashigatashi mo	Difficult to violate!

KAWABATA CHIE

The feeling of anxiety *(fuan)* is an absolute tension in which a subjective delusion combines with the moment of objective doubt *(utagai)* within the relation hope / concern:

Hi ni ikudo	In the toilet
Kayou kawaya ni	Where I go how many times a day
Shinbun no	I read

Sōba no kiji o	The stock market news
Ware wa yomitsugu	In the paper.

ŌNO TORAJI

In other words, the emotion of crisis filling this or that decision is anxiety. Anxiety is not limited to disagreeable feelings. As a concrete absolute of the sense of tension, anxiety is a mood essentially conditioned by the tensions of human desire, an emotion whose essence is pregnant with the possibility of the future. The "philosophy of anxiety" after World War I is rooted in this feeling.

6

We find feelings with a primary meaning among emotions of excitement and tranquillity. There is no doubt that even in anger, fear, disappointment, and the like, a high degree of excitement is reached. In anger and fear, however, emotions of pleasure and displeasure assume control; in disappointment the emotions of tension and relaxation predominate. In contrast, surprise *(odoroki)* is the feeling in which excitement and tranquillity manifest a primary meaning:

Inagara ni	I looked
Nemureru hito no	At their surprise—
Tokiori ni	Those faces dozing off
Odoroku kao o	At times
Mite itarikeri	As they sit.

KAMATA KEISHI[106]

Utsusamu to	I was surprised
Idaki agetaru	By the weight of my child
Utatane no	Napping in my arms
Ako no omoki ni	When I lifted him up
Odorokinikeri	To shift him.

EBARA SEICHŌ[107]

Yubiorite	Counting on my fingers
Odorokasaruru	I am surprised
Toshitsuki no	By the years and months that have passed—

> *Haru wa futatabi*   Spring is again
> *Me no mae ni ari*   In front of my eyes.
>
>   Okuda Tomio[108]

Surprise does not belong to either agreeable or disagreeable feelings; in other words, it is a neutral, indifferent emotion. It is a sensation of no pain, no pleasure. In a sense, we must say that Descartes understood correctly when he considered the first among all emotions this uncommon sense that does not partake of either pleasure or displeasure. Aristotle too considered wonder to be the starting point of philosophy. Surprise is an ontological emotion accompanied by contingency. (See the chapter "Contingency and the Emotion of Wonder" in my *Problem of Contingency;*[109] see also "The Feeling of Surprise and Contingency" in my *Man and Existence.*)[110] It is interesting to notice that Spinoza, who rejected all contingencies from the standpoint of determinism, did not acknowledge surprise as an emotion. There are three dispositions in contingency. In the first, the possibility of both Being and Not-being is contingent. In the second, the meeting of something with something else is contingent. In the third, what comes into being only rarely is contingent. Accordingly, the emotion of surprise indicates these three directions:

> *Koto areba*   When a thing is
> *Arite odoroki*   I am surprised by its being;
> *Koto nakuba*   When it is not
> *Koto naki mama ni*   My heart gets tired
> *Tsukaruru kokoro*   At its not being.
>
>   Kawaguchi Kozue

When the contingency of the possibility of Being and Not-being exists, we are surprised:

> *Odoroki wa*   Surprise is
> *Shukuchokushitsu no*   To open the door
> *To o akete*   Of the night watchman's room
> *Kaku mo yosetaru*   And find a curtain of fog
> *Ichimen no kiri*   Come so close to me.
>
>   Ōki Yūji[111]

When the poet opened the door, a meeting took place between the eyes and the fog, and he was surprised at the fortuity of such an encounter.

Mono o mochite	I get startled
Hito o hedatsuru	When, at times, I discover
Shūsei o	In me
Toki ni waga ue ni	A habit of alienating people
Miidete odoroku	When I hold something.

ŌYA JŪEI[112]

The surprise follows the contingency of discovering something occasionally, rarely, something that usually is not seen. The reason why the ancient word for waking from sleep is "to be surprised" *(odoroku)* is probably due to the fact that some accident unexpectedly surprises our subconsciousness, becoming an opportunity for waking up.

There are cases in which what is rare (the third disposition of contingency) develops into an autonomous feeling known as strange *(mezurashii)*:

Aota no naka o	The path
Basu yuku michi wa	Taken by the bus
Heibon ni te	Through the green rice fields
Mezurashiki gotoshi	Is ordinary and yet it looks strange—
Rihatsuten aru wa	There is a barber shop.

ŌTSUKA TAIJI

Momiji aseshi	On top of the mountain
Arayama no ue ni	Where the maple's flaming foliage has faded,
Asunarō no	I look up at
Aoki hitomoto	A green, solitary cedar
Aogi tomoshimu	And feel that something is missing.

KAGOSHIMA JUZŌ[113]

The feeling of strange has already shifted from indifference to a feeling of pleasure. This is why the word *"tomoshi"* has shifted its meaning from "uncommon" *(toboshi)* to "strange" *(mezurashii)* to "darling" *(airashi)*.

When what is strange is at the same time a small thing and comes to the surface all of a sudden, a kind of surprise occurs, known as the emotion of amusement *(okashii)*:

Kobashiri ni	The chest of a dog
Waga mae o yuku	Hurrying along with small steps
Inu no chibusa	In front of me,
Akaku harikirite	Red, stretched to the full,
Yusayusa ugoku	Moves swaying.

KAMADA KICHISABURŌ[114]

Why do we laugh when it is "amusing"? A taut, red chest is usually hidden from view—or is something that should be hidden. The fact that, contrary to the idea of purpose known as "should," the chest appears swaying is a failure of the actualization of such an idea of purpose. Poetic justice *(iikimi)*, which is related to the blunder of the other, invites laughter as joy *(yorokobi)* of the self; or at least this takes place at the outset. To realize that what is actually given contradicts the idea of purpose is a highly intellectual action; "amusing" is therefore a remarkably intellectual, logical emotion.

To feel amusement is entirely a small thing; accordingly, we rejoice in a light frame of mind and laugh. On the opposite side, a surprise related to a big thing causes the emotion known as solemnity *(ogosoka)*:

Haroharo to	To think
Ame ni mukaite	Turning toward the sky
Omou koto	Far away—
Hateshi mo arazu	The flow
Ginga no nagare	Of an endless Milky Way!

KANBAYASHI FUMIKO[115]

A great solemnity is found, not just in the external world, but also inside:

Mono manabi	August
Ōku o shiranu	Is the Yamato soul
Waga haha no	Of my mother
Yamato o gokoro	Whose learning
Tōtoku arikeri	Is not very great.

KAGEYAMA MASAHARU[116]

Kant says that a starry sky above us and the moral law inside us fill our heart with wonder and reverence.[117] Solemnity is an emotion abundant in moral color. In opposition to amusement, which is almost always an agreeable feeling, solemnity, like awe *(osore)*, is in many circumstances a mixed emotion of agreeable and disagreeable feelings.

Contrary to surprise for small things—which is funniness *(okashisa)*—and surprise for big things—which is solemnity *(ogosoka)*—surprise directed at the consolidation of various things is the emotion known as beautiful *(utsukushii)*:

Yane no sori	The arches of the roof,
Ryōyoku no nobi	Two extended wings—
Kono dō no	The stillness
Totonoeru bi no	Of this temple
Moteru seijaku	Ordered with beauty.

KAWAI CHIOKO[118]

It goes without saying that the emotion of the beautiful is an artistic emotion.

When an object of surprise's reason for being cannot be determined by the intellect, doubt intervenes and the emotion of suspicion *(ayashii)* occurs:

Motoyui no	With the cord for tying the hair cut,
Kirete kurameru	The morning mirror
Asa kagami	In the dark,
Magamagashisa wa	We should not think
Omoubekarazu	Of misfortune.

KAWAZOE YUKIKO[119]

The emotion of surprise known as suspicion is indispensable to the formation of religion; it is what scholars of religion call the path to mana.

I think the feeling of surprise may suggest a genealogical meaning that must develop into an intellectual, moral, aesthetic, and religious sentiment. In any case, we can say that, as a feeling of excitement and tranquillity, surprise is essentially a feeling of contingency. And yet, since all tense and relaxed feelings are related to future possibilities, we can say that it is a feeling of possibility. Moreover, in opposition to both sets of feelings mentioned earlier, I might also be allowed to call "the feeling of necessity" the agreeable and disagreeable feelings on which one theory of the extension of emotions is based. (See my *Man and Existence*, pp. 22–28.)[120]

7

I have pursued the path of the genealogy of feelings. The most apparent among the numerous feelings are, first of all, surprise and desire, which are related to being and existence; in second place are fear and anger, which are related especially to self-preservation; in third place is love, which is related to the preservation of the species and its reverse, loneliness; in fourth place are the subjective emotions of joy and sadness, as indexes of fulfillment and unfulfillment of being, as well as the objective emotions of love, hatred, and so forth. Since it functions within a solipsistic self, self-preservation pours its main force into hatred for others, taking the forms of the defensive negativity of fear and the offensive positivity of anger. While having at its foundation lonesomeness *(sabi)* as awareness of lack since it operates within a mutually compensatory intersubjectivity, the preservation of the species emphasizes sighing for something *(koi)* as a compensatory demand on the horizon of love for others.

If we count the number of times that the ten kinds of feelings appear concretely in the form of words in the 2,870 poems of the second volume of the *New Ten Thousand Leaves* from which I took my examples, we find surprise *(odoroki)* in twenty poems, desire *(yoku)* in three poems, fear *(kyō)* in nine poems, anger *(ikari)* in thirteen poems, sighing for something *(koi)* in twelve poems, lonesomeness *(sabi)* in one hundred and five poems, happiness *(ureshisa)* in sixteen poems, sadness *(kanashimi)* in forty-eight poems, love *(ai)* in fourteen poems, and hatred *(zō)* in five poems. The fact that lonesomeness *(sabi)* appears in the absolutely largest number of instances indicates that *sabi* is acknowledged as the emotional self-reflection of the individuality of individual existence. Moreover, if we add to the sixteen poems on happiness *(ureshisa)* the twenty poems on joy *(yorokobi)* and the thirty-three poems on pleasure *(tanoshimi),* the total comes to sixty-nine poems. If we add to the forty-eight poems on sadness *(kanashimi)* the twenty-four poems on sorrow *(nageki)* and the eight poems on pain *(kuru-*

shimi), the total comes to eighty poems. Again, if we further add the thirty-eight poems on moving power *(aware)* to the latter group, we have one hundred and eighteen poems. Among subjective emotions it is agreed that sorrow *(kanashimi)* and its modalities dominate over happiness *(ureshisa)* and its conditions. Among objective emotions we might think that the ratio between love *(ai)* and hatred *(zō)* is only natural. There is nothing more to add with regard to the number of times that surprise *(odoroki)*, fear *(kyō)*, and anger *(ikari)* appear. As for the comparatively few instances of sighing for something *(koi)*, I think we should not overlook the fact that sighing for something is concealed behind the disguise of lonesomeness *(sabi)*. The fact that desire *(yoku)* is the less represented emotion must be mainly due to a reason to which I must now turn my attention.

Properly speaking, several restrictions apply to the figures I have given. First of all, the feelings filling the poems are not limited to the actual words indicating these feelings. The numbers I provided are not the same as the number of poems that sing set emotions. For example, the term "sighing for" *(koi)* does not appear more than twelve times in the poems, yet there are dozens of poems on the subject of sighing for something. Second, it goes without saying that there is a considerably different proportion between singing about a feeling in a poem and actually feeling it. There are many instances in which lonesomeness *(sabi)*, sadness *(kanashimi)*, and the like are expressed as poems; however, there are exceedingly few cases in which desire *(yoku)*, hatred *(zō)*, and the like become the motivating force of a poem. This must be why desire has the smallest number of poems, immediately followed by hatred. Third, we might also think that the taste and aim of those who decided on the selections for this anthology are reflected and that there was a tendency to exclude—either consciously or unconsciously—poems filled with certain feelings. I believe that here we find the main reason why among the 2,870 poems only a few dozen are love poems. (See my *Essays on the Literary Arts*, p. 121.)[121] With all their limitations, numbers are valuable as research materials.

Next I will quote from the ancient *Ten Thousand Leaves (Man'yōshū)* ten examples of surprise, desire, fear, anger, sighing for something, loneliness, happiness, sadness, love, and hatred as primary emotions:

Yume no ai wa	The encounter in a dream
Kurushikarikeri	Was painful—
Odorokite	When I awakened
Kakitoredomo	I grasped you,
Te ni mo fureneba	And yet could not touch you even with my hand.

ŌTOMO NO YAKAMOCHI[122]

Inishie no	Apparently
Nana no sakashiki	What the seven wise men
Hitodomo mo	Of the past
Horiseshi mono wa	Desired
Sake ni shiarurashi	Was rice wine.

ŌTOMO NO TABITO[123]

Kasugano no	It was the time
Yamabe no michi o	When I did not see you
Osorinaku	Coming,
Kayoishi kimi ga	You, unafraid of the path
Mienu koro ka mo	Along the mountain of the Kasuga Plain.

ISHIKAWA NO IRATSUME[124]

Uretaki ya	How hateful
Shiko hototogisu	That ugly cuckoo bird—
Ima koso wa	Now
Koe no karuga ni	It makes its coarse voice
Kinaki toyomame	Reverberate!

ANONYMOUS[125]

Takakura no	When the crying birds
Mikasa no yama ni	Of Mt. Mikasa—
Naku tori no	The high abode—
Yameba tsugaruru	Stop singing,
Koi mo suru ka mo	I will resume my sighing for you!

YAMABE NO AKAHITO[126]

Sazanami no	It is lonesome to look at
Shigatsu no kora ga	The path of the rapids
Makariji no	Where the funerals
Kawase no michi o	Of the young girls
Mireba sabushi mo	Of Shiga Bay by the small waves go by.

KAKINOMOTO NO HITOMARO[127]

Wagaseko to
Futari mimaseba
Ikubaku ka
Kono furu yuki no
Ureshikaramashi

How happy I would be
To look
At the falling snow
Together with my husband,
The two of us!

THE FUJIWARA EMPRESS[128]

Mei no no no
Susuki oshinabe
Furu yuki ni
Yado karu kyō shi
Kanashiku oboyu

Sadly I think
Today of my borrowed quarters
Under the snow falling
On the fluttering eulalia
Of Mei field.

TAKECHI NO KUROHITO[129]

Hashiki yoshi
Kaku nomi kara ni
Shitaikoshi
Imo ga kokoro no
Sube mo subenasa

The poor darling,
My beloved who yearned
In such a brief space of time—
All her anguish
Came to nothing.

YAMANOUE NO OKURA[130]

Ware koso wa
Nikuku mo arame
Waga yado no
Hana tachibana o
Mi ni wa koji to ya

How hateful
I must be to you!
Won't you come see
The blooming orange flowers
Of my house?

ANONYMOUS[131]

8

I can illustrate what I have said on the genealogy of feelings in the accompanying chart. To make it as concise as possible I have omitted feelings that are excessively derivative. Big circles indicate the ten main feelings. The circle with dotted lines encasing desire *(yoku)* and lonesomeness *(sabi)* indicates the nucleus of a human being as individual existence. Tense and relaxed emotions take their place immediately above and below this circle. Moreover, the formative elements of so-called sentiments and noble emotions constitute a group in the upper part of the chart, on the periphery of surprise *(odoroki)*, which is an emotion of excitement and calm. In the lower part, emotions of pleasure and

displeasure develop in a variety of ways, forming the four centers of hap-
piness *(ureshisa)*, sadness *(kanashisa)*, love *(ai)*, and hatred *(zō)*. We may
call fear *(kyō)* and anger *(ikari)* instinctual feelings, which are meaning-
ful in the line of animal evolution. We should not overlook the expressly
anthropological importance of the line connecting lonesomeness *(sabi)*,
moving power *(aware)*, sympathy *(awaremi)*, love *(ai)*, and sighing for
(koi). The following points should be self-evident from the chart: the
logical relationship between the lonesomeness *(sabi)* of individuality and
the moving power *(aware)* of finiteness; the mutual limitation of subjec-
tive moving power *(aware)* and objective sympathy *(awaremi)*; the fact
that love *(ai)* implies dialectically the two directions of self-denying sym-
pathy *(awaremi)*, or *agape*, and self-affirming sighing for something
(koi), or *eros*; and the fact that negative lonesomeness *(sabi)* is always
grounded in the underside of positive sighing for something *(koi)*.

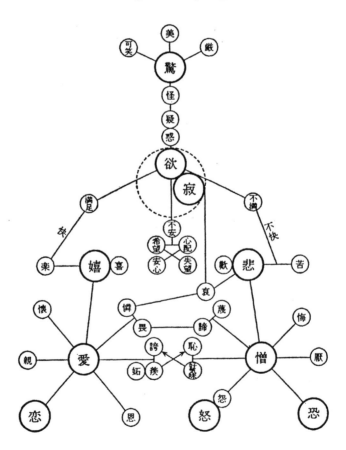

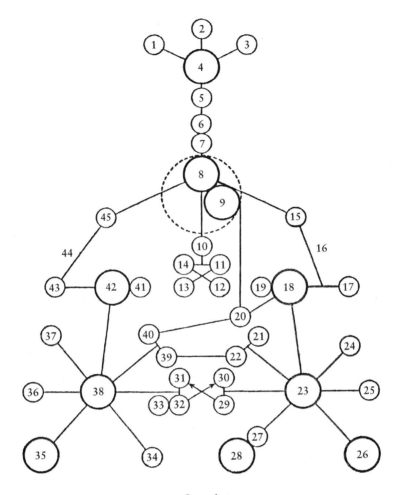

Legend

1. funniness *(okashisa)*
2. beauty *(bi)*
3. solemnity *(ogosoka)*
4. surprise *(odoroki)*
5. suspicion *(ayashii)*
6. doubt *(utagai)*
7. perplexity *(madoi)*
8. desire *(yoku)*
9. lonesomeness *(sabi)*
10. anxiety *(fuan)*
11. concern *(shinpai)*
12. despair *(shitsubō)*
13. relief *(anshin)*
14. hope *(kibō)*
15. dissatisfaction *(fuman)*

16. disagreeable *(fukai)*
17. pain *(kurushimi)*
18. sadness *(kanashisa)*
19. sorrow *(nageki)*
20. moving power *(aware)*
21. contempt *(sagesumi)*
22. resignation *(akirame)*
23. hatred *(zō)*
24. repentance *(kai)*
25. dislike *(en)*
26. fear *(kyō)*
27. grudge *(urami)*
28. anger *(ikari)*
29. poetic justice *(iikimi)*
30. shame *(haji)*

31. pride *(hokori)*
32. envy *(urayami)*
33. jealousy *(netami)*
34. obligation *(on)*
35. sighing for *(koi)*
36. familiarity *(shitashimi)*
37. yearning *(natsukashisa)*
38. love *(ai)*
39. awe *(osore)*
40. sympathy *(awaremi)*
41. joy *(yorokobi)*
42. happiness *(ureshisa)*
43. pleasure *(tanoshimi)*
44. agreeable *(kai)*
45. satisfaction *(manzoku)*

The Metaphysics of Literature

1

If we view literature as *a totality expressed by language,* literature comes to encompass an extremely broad subject. Hōnen's *Letter on Climbing the Mountain (Tozanjō),*[1] Kaibara Ekiken's *Ten Precepts (Jikkun),*[2] Nishikawa Joken's *Essays on Astronomy (Tenmon Giron),*[3] and Satō Nobuhiro's *Digest of Economy (Keizai Yōroku)*[4] would all belong to the category of literature. Thus the metaphysics of literature becomes the metaphysics of language. Here I do not intend to deal with the metaphysics of language. In other words, taking literature in a narrow sense, I will look at it as an art expressed by words and take as my subject the metaphysics of literature as a linguistic art. Moreover, by metaphysics I mean nothing more than general philosophy as opposed to aesthetics; I will attempt a philosophical investigation of literature.

The essence of literature is, in short, temporal art depending on language. Therefore, I think that to explicate literature in relation to the horizon of time is the major issue of a metaphysics of literature. There is no need for me here to restate the philosophical relevance of the issue of time: we might think, for example, of Bergson's statement on time, according to which in time "we find the major key of all philosophical problems";[5] or we might remember Heidegger's expression, "all central problems of ontology are rooted in the phenomenon of time correctly observed and correctly explained."[6] The fact that literature is

one of the temporal arts suggests by itself how we must deal method-
ologically with a philosophical analysis of literature.

2

Before examining literature from the perspective of time, we must pon-
der over the temporality of art in general. Human history is grounded in
the fact that human existence is temporal existence (strictly speaking,
spatio-temporal existence). History becomes history in the truest sense
when it gives birth to culture; within the process of its formation, cul-
ture includes art as one of its moments. When we ask what kind of tem-
poral quality art possesses, we can say that so long as it takes intuition
as its specific character, art holds a temporal place in the present. A pre-
requisite of intuition is to see with one's own eyes. To see with one's
own eyes is possible in the present. Somehow history moves in a set di-
rection, but here we may think of a surface on which two lines cross at
a right angle, that is, the present. Moreover, history throws the self onto
the surface of the present; in a sense, what reflects the self is art. All the
statues in the Dharma Hall of Tōdaiji, as well as the *Collection of Ten
Thousand Words (Man'yōshū)*, are nothing but a projection on the sur-
face of the present of the movements of a history centered around the
Nara court. *The Love-Tinted Plum Calendar (Shunshoku Umegoyomi)*
by Tamenaga Shunsui[7] and the Kiyomoto tunes by Enju Daiyū I[8] are
images of the Bunka and Bunsei periods (1804–1829) reflected on the
surface of the present. Art is the maturation and the completion of his-
tory on the surface of the present—the reaching of the pinnacle of ripe-
ness and height of perfection. Art is intuited and produced in the form
of ripeness and perfection and this, in turn, is intuited and appreciated.
People speak of the microcosmic structure of art, but art is something
completed as a macrocosm. The Golden Hall of the Hōryūji, *The Tale
of Genji (Genji Monogatari)*, Unkei's statue of Muchaku,[9] the land-
scapes of Sesshū,[10] the *haiku* of Bashō,[11] the puppet theater *(jōruri)* of
Chikamatsu,[12] the ditties of Ryūtatsu,[13] and so forth all possess a
microcosmic structure. Moreover, microcosmic structure means the
largest limit of inner fullness. In such a form of inner fullness and com-
pletion, art becomes visible to our own eyes. In other words, art

possesses the temporality known as the present. The essence of art is the expression in the face of the present, "Linger still, you are so beautiful!,"[14] and the lament, "I shall halt for a moment the shape of this maiden."

When we consider the temporal nature of knowledge and morality in contrast to art, we see, first of all, that knowledge possesses a basic structure which proceeds rationally from cause to conclusion. The conclusion is deduced from the cause. All scientific understanding is simply rooted in the condition that stipulates one truth as truth. Scientific knowledge comes into existence when a new thing is explained according to something old that already existed. When water is explained scientifically as the chemical compound of hydrogen and oxygen, for example, we think of the compound "water," which is the object of our new explanation, in terms of its reduction to old things that we call the elements of hydrogen and oxygen. The scientific understanding of Newton's theory of universal gravitation also was rooted within the bounds of a reduction of the movements of the whole universe to the earth's laws of physics, which were already known at the time.[15] With regard to the moon's movement around the earth, although by the law of inertia the moon should move toward the tangent of the circle, Newton thought that the moon actually moved away from the line, as the law of inertia would have required, solely based on the law of falling resulting from the given distance between the moon and the earth. In other words, he reduced the truth of the moon's movement, for which he had to provide a new explanation, to the well-known law of falling movement based on the experience of seeing an apple fall. The structure of knowledge proceeds from the old to the new, from cause to conclusion. Cause has a definite meaning as a starting point. We can say that so long as the old provides a basic horizon as ground, the temporal nature of knowledge is the past. A past cause becomes a starting point leading to a future conclusion. Old things of the past become ground, and on top of this base new things develop. In this sense I may say that the temporal structure of knowledge lays emphasis on the past.

Once we turn to morality, we see that the realm of morality is the domain where a conscious purpose rules. The fact that morality is the law of *müssen* (have to), or of what should be, as opposed to nature, which is the law of *sollen* (ought to), anticipates the rule of conscious purpose. Morality takes the form of an imperative mandating the actualization of a purpose. Although the purpose that must be actualized is nothing but the content of a hypothetical imperative, and although it is a self-purpose unconditionally valid within a categorical imperative, in any event, moral consciousness does not come into being without the consciousness of purpose. Moral phenomena develop where the purpose of action is consciously grasped beforehand in the future; where the distance toward the future possesses a tension as obligation; and where such an obligation is carried out by effort. I believe that Kant's comparison of the moral law to shining stars in the sky does not simply express the sublimity of the starry heavens as an object of contemplation.[16] The starry heavens are realized as a purpose "above me"; the distance between me and the starry heavens carries a tension as obligation; elimination of the gap is demanded in the future. We can see that the starry heavens are compared to the moral law in their nature as a question that must be realized in the future, not as an object of art that is appreciated in the present. The notion of personality also must have as its major moment the possibility of future formation. If we think along these lines, we can argue that the temporal nature of morality is futural. I believe that, in addressing the question whether in history emphasis is put in the past or in the future, there is a tendency to lay emphasis on the past if we look at the question from the standpoint of scientific knowledge and to lay emphasis on the future if we look from the perspective of moral formation.

If the temporal nature of art is the present, of knowledge the past, and of morality the future, we might ask what happens to religion. In religion eternity becomes central. Whether we set up the category of *"sempiternitas,"* thinking of infinity as potential, or we use the category of *"aeternitas,"* thinking of it as actuality, there is, after all, no wide difference between the two. In religion the eternal now brings reality with it. We may think that the present now has an infinite depth. We can say that, while the temporal nature of art is a phenomenological present, the temporal nature of religion is a metaphysical present. Moreover, here we find the similarity between religion and art.

In any case, we can say that the temporal nature of art is the present. But when I say "present" in this instance, I do not mean present as a point; I mean a present possessing a definite duration whose contours are made by intuition. In his famous essay on time Augustine says that the present lacks extension, since it goes by in one point; but he argues that "the presence of all present objects" *(praesens de praesentibus)* has a duration as intuition.[17] The difference between a present as a point and a present that continues in intuition is very important. We might say that the abstract time with which the natural sciences deal is a present counted as a point; the present which is the site that makes art come into being is a present which continues in intuition. There is an interesting example that clarifies this difference. At the Louvre museum in Paris there is a painting of a horse race by Théodore Géricault.[18] All the horses extend their legs before and behind. But when I looked at a snapshot of a running horse, I realized that horses never take that posture. In recent times people have gradually stopped portraying horses in this posture. And yet Rodin[19] defends Géricault and says: "Pictures are lies. Such an instant in reality does not exist. Géricault has portrayed a posture that appears through a sequence of instants. The painting has more truth than the picture. The horse painted by Géricault looks as if it were really running." The snapshot has photographed a present as a point that lacks extension. Yet Géricault portrays the presence of all present objects thanks to a continuing intuition. So long as it is limited by the mechanism of the natural sciences, the snapshot conforms to the present of abstract time. The painter Géricault grasped by intuition a continuing present, and there he made art come into being.

3

I have tried to think about the temporality of art. Now we can understand the temporality of literature from this point of view and should be able to bring literature onto the philosophical or metaphysical horizon. So long as we consider literature one kind of art, we can say that, generally speaking, the temporality of literature is the present. However, I will need to return to this point in more detail later. I have said that the present in which art comes into being is not the abstract present of the natural sciences but the concrete present of duration in intuition. In connection to this we can clarify the temporal nature of literature.

It is common to differentiate between quantitative and qualitative time in the phenomenon of time. Quantitative time is the time that can be counted as one, two, three, and four, like the time of the clock. The characteristic of measurable time lies in the fact that its units are homogeneous and, at the same time, detached. Each unit can be added to the other as numbers exactly because, by being the same, they become separated from each other. So long as it can be treated mathematically, quantitative time is the foundation of the temporal concept of the natural sciences. On the opposite side, qualitative time is a flux and a duration characterized by heterogeneity and mutual penetration. The indivisible variety of qualitative time is often compared to the flow of the melody of music. While the musical bar always ends, the whole bar ceaselessly changes by adding a new note. The flow of the melody is one whole; its variety is not divided. Qualitative time is also compared to a succession of colors appearing in the spectrum of light. Imperceptibly red turns into yellow passing through orange; yellow becomes blue via green; blue changes into violet after becoming indigo. When we look at orange we see that it is mixed with both red and yellow. We find the flow of colors in the one entering the other as an indivisible variety. Qualitative time is flow and transition. We might think that quantitative time comes into being by ordering the flow to stand still and counting that point of stillness as simultaneity.

When we ask whether the temporality of literature belongs to quantitative time or to qualitative time, the answer is that, as in the case of music, it definitely belongs to the latter. The rhythm of poetry is the closest thing to quantitative time in literature. In Japanese poetry, both the 5/7 and 7/5 syllable meters have 12 syllables. If we follow the expression of quantitative time, time is cut into twelve. Poetic form comes into being through the repetition of that pattern as one verse of the poem. The rhythm of poetry, however, is based on people's breathing rhythm. In other words, a verse is formed on condition that it can be recited in one breath. And since the rhythm of human breath is basically fixed, the length of a verse of a poem is about the same in any language. As in Japan where a verse is made of 12 syllables in the 5/7 and 7/5 syllable meter, the alexandrine line, the most characteristic poetic form in France, is also made of 12 syllables.

Although we might think poetic time to be quantitative when we look at poetry from the viewpoint of a count of syllables, this is not a correct assumption: poetic time is qualitative. The time of poetry is pure duration and flow, as we can clearly see from the 5/7 and 7/5 syllable meter. The fact that the 12 syllables are cut into fixed patterns of 5/7 and 7/5 syllables is already evidence of the qualitative rather than quantitative nature of time.

> *Komoro naru / kojō no hotori*
> The vicinity of the ancient castle / in Komoro[20]

> *Mizu shizukanaru / Edogawa no*
> The quietly flowing water / of the Edo River[21]

Although we are dealing with 12 syllables, by being cut in the 5/7, 7/5 syllable pattern, the measure of duration takes on a completely different feeling: here we find the flow of qualitative time. In the French alexandrine verse the 12 syllables are equally divided in two sets of 6 syllables each. In other words, it performs a cut on the sixth syllable:

> *L'amour n'a plus de goût, non plus que la dispute.*
> There is no more pleasure in loving, than in dispute.[22]

Here the verse is very different from the 12 syllables that form it. One verse is divided equally in two parts by the tension of duration: here we see a qualitative thing. In other words, we are in the presence of qualitative time. With regard to the qualitative difference, despite the same 12 syllables that we feel when looking at an alexandrine verse and a verse in the 5/7, 7/5 syllable pattern, we can say that it is similar to the qualitative difference we experience when we look at a woman tying her sash *(obi)* in the middle, upper, or lower part of her body. Even when we think of the rhythm of a short poem *(tanka)*, we cannot simply reduce it to the quantitative number of 31 syllables. If we divide it into an upper and lower verse, then we have a combination of 17 and 14 syllables. But since the original form of *tanka* corresponds to the end of a long poem *(chōka)* in the 5/7, 5/7, 7/7 syllable pattern, we have a combination of 12, 12, and 7 syllables:

Akiyama ni otsuru momijiba
shimashiku wa na chirimidare so
imo ga atari mimu[23]

O yellow leaves, falling on the autumn hills,
just for a moment do not scatter so wildly—
I would see the homeland of my love.[24]

Karakoromo kitsutsu narenishi tsuma shi areba
harubaru kinuru tabi o shi zo omou[25]

Since this Chinese robe I am accustomed to wearing is as dear to me
    as my beloved wife,
I feel the pain of travel, having come to a place so far away.

Although these two poems share the same foundation of 31 syllables, we feel in the different ways they are cut the same qualitative difference that we perceive when we listen to a koto or a flute. Even when we turn to the 17-syllable *haiku,* no matter whether we read it as one 17-syllable verse, or as three verses of 5, 7, and 5 syllables, or as two sets of 12 and 5 syllables or 5 and 12 syllables, the temporal nature of rhythm is certainly qualitative in the *haiku,* showing a variety of tensions of duration:

Tsurigane ni tomarite nemuru kochō kana[26]

Temple bell—perched on it and asleep, a butterfly.[27]

Na no hana ya
tsuki wa higashi ni
hi wa nishi ni[28]

Mustard flowers
with the moon in the east,
the sun in the west.[29]

Daimon no omoki tobira ya
haru no kure[30]

The heavy door of the front gate—
spring evening.

Yuku haru ya
omotaki biwa no dakigokoro[31]

Spring departs—
a heart embracing a heavy lute.

Besides the way verses are cut, we find other characteristics of qualitative time in poetry—in the length or shortness of the syllables and in the strength or weakness of the accent. The strength or weakness of the accent limits from the outset differences in qualitative impressions. Even the meaning of the length or shortness of syllables in poetry is not a quantitative relationship, however, but a relationship based on the degree of tension. In Greek and Latin poetry the length or shortness of syllables characterizes the qualitative time of poetry; in English and German poetry the accent indicates qualitative time. Even when we consider that the length and shortness of syllables of ancient languages such as Greek and Latin have been replaced by the strength or weakness of the accent in the modern languages of English and German, we know that the length or shortness of syllables possesses a qualitative meaning. The long/short, short/long, long/short/short, short/short/long, and long/long measures in the meter of syllables, as well as the high/low, low/high, high/low/low, and low/low/high measures of accent, indicate the structure of poetry's qualitative time. We might consider the rules of tones in Chinese poetry *(kanshi)* a kind of accent. Japanese and French poetry do not give proper consideration to accent. Whether it is a hendecasyllable, or a dactyl,[32] or a trochee,[33] the fact that in Italian poetry the accent always falls on the tenth syllable indicates that the accent is a formative moment of qualitative time.

As I mentioned earlier, we come to understand that poetic time is qualitative time from the cuts in the poem, the length or shortness of syllables, and the strength or weakness of the accent. The qualitative nature of time becomes even clearer, however, when we take rhyme into consideration. Rhymes are possible because one variety of qualitative time enters into and permeates another variety. For example, when we ask from the viewpoint of the structure of temporality why rhymes come into being as alliteration in the poem that says,

*Nitsutsuji no **ni**howamu toki no*
*sakurabana **sa**kinamu toki ni*[34]

When the red azalea disperses its perfume,
when the cherry blossoms come into bloom.[35]

we find a reason in the reciprocal permeation of the *"ni"* of the word *"nitsutsuji"* (red azalea) entering the *"ni"* of the verb *"nihowamu"* (to perfume) as a result of the poem's qualitative time characterized by the reciprocal interpenetration of varieties. Moreover, we find another reason in the mutual permeation of the sound *"sa"* from the word *"sakurabana"* (cherry blossoms) and the *"sa"* of the verb *"sakinamu"* (to bloom) lingering in the reader's memory. Even if the corresponding rhymes are homophonous, as in the case of the repetition of *"ni"* and *"sa"* in the previous poem, they show a qualitative difference in their concreteness by receiving the embellishment of duration. It is the same difference that we see when we look at Shizuka expressing regret at parting on Mt. Yoshino or Shizuka dancing at the Tsuruoka Hachimangū.[36] We can say the same thing with regard to end rhymes:

> *Ch'u wang kung pei cheng huang hun*
> *Pai ti ch'eng hsi kuo yü hen*[37]
>
> North of the King of Ch'u's palace is just dusk,
> West of the White King's citadel are traces of the passing rain.

The rhyming even tones of "dusk" *(hun/kon)* and "signs" *(hen/kon)* reverberate exactly because the interpenetration of elements as qualitative time comes into being in the form of qualitative time.

So far I have chosen poems that I thought were the closest ones to quantitative time in literature, and I have clarified that their temporality is not quantitative. It is safe to say that the temporality structuring literature is qualitative time. Moreover, qualitative time is a characteristic shared by literature and music, which are temporal arts. It is the foundation of the inner relationships of both and an indication, especially in poetry, of the original weakness of poetic treatises that exclude the dimension of musicality.

4

Next I would like to examine the temporal nature differentiating literature as a linguistic art from music as an acoustic art. While music comes into being in the perception of sound, literature makes its domain the imagination grounded in language. Moreover, generally speaking, while music belongs to the expressive arts, literature belongs to the representational arts. Differences in the temporality of both arts are found in the fact that music is an expressive art based on sound while literature is a representational art based on language.

The duration of music's qualitative time is time perceived as sound, which is only the duration of time that the music actually fills. I do not know how long it would take to perform a piece in "six parts," but if we assume it would take five or ten minutes, these five or ten minutes would be the total temporal duration of a six-part musical composition. In the case of literature, however, we can say that, in addition to filling its own time, literature suggests to the self the duration of a different time. This results from the fact that language has the function of bringing the unreal to intuition; thus it seems that the time of literature is characterized by a multilayeredness. Probably it will not take more than five, six, or ten seconds to hum a 17-syllable *haiku* or a 31-syllable *tanka*. The temporal duration filled by one *haiku* or one *tanka* is only about five, six, or ten seconds. But we can argue that the time of perception during those five, six, or ten seconds contains within itself the duration of a much larger conceptual time. Because of the perception of sound on the one hand and the imagination through language on the other, the phenomenon of time presents a multilayeredness. Strictly speaking, multilayered time appears by means of the double nature of the sensorial and the conceptual aspects of language.

In the poem

> *Chiru yanagi aruji mo ware mo kane o kiku*
> The scattering willow, both my host and myself listen to the bell.

the time during which the reverberation of the bell continues appears conceptually as the temporality of the upper layer. In the poem

> *Nagaki hi o saezuri taranu hibari kana*[38]
> All this long day and yet wanting to sing more, a skylark.[39]

the time of at least one day is implied. In the poem

> *Kokoro ni wa wasurenu mono o tamatama mo minu hi samaneku tsuki zo henikeru*[40]
>
> Though in my heart I have not forgotten you, so many days have slipped away without my seeing you, and now a month has passed.[41]

the time of one month has passed, according to the imagination. In the poem

> *Hitotose ni hitotabi kimasu kimi mateba yado kasu hito mo araji to zo omou*[42]
>
> Since she is waiting for her lord to come once a year, I do not think she will lend her place to us.

one year is contained inside the poem. In the poem

> *Inishie no furuki tsutsumi wa toshi fukami ike no nagisa ni mikusa oinikeri*[43]
>
> The years have deepened on the ancient, crumbling embankment, and waterweeds have spread over the rims of the pond.[44]

the months and years of a long past flow. In the poem

> *Miredo akanu Yoshino no kawa no tokoname no tayuru koto naku mata kaerimimu*[45]
>
> Like the eternal moss slick by the Yoshino River, on which I do not tire to gaze, may I never cease to return and gaze on it again.[46]

a view over the future opens boundlessly. In the poem

> *Tachibana ya itsu no nonaka no hototogisu*[47]
>
> Mandarin orange—when did I hear the cuckoo in the field?

in the very moment when the poet actually smells the perfume of a mandarin orange, the earlier instant when he had heard the cuckoo's song while sniffing the same scent comes back to life. Here we find two presents that are absolutely the same, a present with a boundless depth. We can say that time takes on the character of recurrence by repeating itself. We might also say that the eternal now exists in the present. The examples I have given so far have a multilayered temporality. The conceptual time of the upper layer of these examples has a longer duration than the time of perception of the lower layers. Yet we also have examples in which this relationship is reversed—namely, there are many cases, especially in novels, in which in order to conceptualize an event that lasts one instant a perceptual time with a long duration is used. It is not strange at all to find novels dedicating many pages to the description of a single moment in which two trains pass each other.

We can almost say that the multilayeredness of time is practically the life of literature. When we look at the beginning of Natsume Sōseki's *Kokoro*,[48] the first words meeting the reader's eyes are the following:

> I always called him "Sensei." I shall therefore refer to him simply as "Sensei," and not by his real name. It is not because I consider it more discreet, but it is because I find it more natural that I do so. Whenever the memory of him comes back to me now, I find that I think of him as "Sensei" still. And with pen in hand, I cannot bring myself to write of him in any other way. It was at Kamakura, during the summer holidays, that I first met Sensei. I was then a very young student.[49]

The same thing can be said with regard to the opening page of Nagai Kafū's *Bokutō Kidan* (A strange tale from east of the river):[50]

> I almost never go to see a moving picture. If vague memories are to be trusted, it was toward the end of the last century that I saw, at the Kanda theater, a moving picture of a San Francisco street scene. I suppose it must have been about then, too, that the expression "moving picture" was invented. Today it has almost been discarded.[51]

The opening paragraph of the *Taketori Monogatari* (Tale of the bamboo cutter) says:[52]

> It is now an event of the past, when there was an old bamboo cutter who went into the mountains and fields, cut bamboo, and put the stalks to all kinds of uses. His name was Sanuki no Miyakkomaro. Now it happened that one stalk of bamboo shone at the base. Puzzled, the old man went up

to it and found that the light was coming from its interior. When he examined it, he saw a dainty little girl, just three inches tall, sitting inside.[53]

Even when we look at the *Genji Monogatari* (Tale of Genji), we find the following opening:[54]

In a certain reign (whose can it have been?) someone of no very great rank, among all His Majesty's Consorts and Intimates, enjoyed exceptional favor. Those others who had always assumed that pride of place was properly theirs despised her as a dreadful woman, while the lesser Intimates were unhappier still.[55]

The multilayeredness of time takes as its lower layer the time of perception of music and takes as its upper layer the conceptual time forming meaning. But we can also argue that the upper layer piles up several layers of time one on top of the other. The "past" *(mukashi)* in the sentence "it is now a past event" *(ima wa mukashi)* from the *Taketori Monogatari,* quoted earlier, constitutes the foundation of conceptual time, but a secondary conceptual time flows on top of this primary conceptual time:

"Because she is here in this bamboo I cut every morning and evening, I can tell that she is destined to be my child," the old man said. He put her in his hand and took her home....The child shot up swiftly while they cared for her. By the time she was only three months old, she was as big as an adult, so they put up her hair and dressed her in a train.[56]

"Every morning and evening" and "only three months old" stand for the secondary conceptual time. Moreover, we can also say that this secondary conceptual time builds up higher dimensions of time, such as a tertiary dimension, on the horizon of the imagination. In the *Genji Monogatari* the phrase "in a certain reign (whose can it have been?)" indicates the primary conceptual time of the story, but the flow of a secondary and a tertiary time piles up in layers:

The way she waited on him day after day only stirred up feeling against her, and perhaps this growing burden of resentment was what affected

her health and obliged her often to withdraw in misery to her home; but
His Majesty, who could less and less do without her, ignored his critics
until his behavior seemed bound to be the talk of all. From this sad spec-
tacle the senior nobles and privy gentlemen could only avert their eyes.
Such things had led to disorder and ruin even in China, they said, and as
discontent spread through the realm, the example of Yōkihi came more
and more to mind, with many a painful consequence for the lady herself;
yet she trusted in his gracious and unexampled affection and remained at
court. The grand Counselor, her father, was gone, and it was her mother,
a lady from an old family, who saw to it that she should give no less to
court events than others whose parents were both alive and who enjoyed
general esteem; but lacking anyone influential to support her, she often
had reason when the time came to lament the weakness of her position.
His Majesty must have had a deep bond with her in past lives as well, for
she gave him a wonderfully handsome son.[57]

"The way she waited on him day after day" forms the secondary layer
of conceptual time, while "such things had led to disorder and ruin
even in China," "from an old family," and "in past lives" make the
third layer of conceptual time. Moreover, the layers of conceptual time
bring with them the possibility of carrying on indefinitely the so-called
phenomenon of iteration—as in the case of an image reflected in a mir-
ror that is further reflected in a second, third, and fourth mirror or as in
the case of a nest of boxes in which a box is inserted into a series of
larger boxes.

We can say that the philosophical characteristic differentiating lit-
erature from music is the multilayeredness of time, although here a
question could arise. In Beethoven's Sixth Symphony, for example, the
temporal layers of a morning in the countryside, the surroundings of a
creek, the feast of farmers, the storm, and the happiness after the storm
are created conceptually on the horizon of the imagination. Moreover,
in descriptive music we also have representations of watchmaker's
stores in which a clock announces three o'clock and a bell rings four
o'clock. To have a multilayeredness of time set forth in music is not a
special characteristic of music, however; this rather belongs to the ama-
teurish aspect of music. The special characteristic of music is its being
to the last an expressive art. We must consider a music that departs

from its expressiveness, and tends toward representation, a literalization of music. In this case a simple sound is a proxy functioning as language; this is never the regular path of music. So long as music is an acoustic art and literature a linguistic one, temporal single-layeredness is a characteristic of music, while multilayeredness is a characteristic of literature. Furthermore, it goes without saying that vocal music is a mixed form of music and literature. Now we must pay attention to the fact that unlike music—which, when it tries to express a temporal multilayeredness with sounds, makes itself into literature by denying its own original single-layeredness—literature, and especially poetry, when it stresses its musicality, thanks to its original multilayeredness, does not deny the conceptual time of the upper layer and shows the musicality of perceptive time of the lower layer. While the literalization of music in the form of descriptive music transforms music into something other than what it actually is, the musicalization of literature is simply a display of literature's essential inner self. Literature cannot exist without including music in some form. Poetry especially, including its shortest form, namely *haiku,* which comes into being in a 5/7/5 syllable pattern, possesses the tripartite structure of music, which is made up of contrasting themes in the beginning and middle part of a musical piece and whose ending is a repetition of the beginning.

Now we can make a comparison between literature and painting from the viewpoint of multilayeredness. Literature's relationship with time is similar to painting's relation with space. Spatial arts come into being by filling a set space. But those arts that take shape in a three-dimensional space such as sculpture and architecture only possess the extent of space they actually fill. As a representational art, sculpture creates the image of an object; as an expressive art, architecture takes inner space as its material. But they share the fact that both arts do not include any other space aside from the space they actually fill. Contrary to these arts, painting that comes into being in a two-dimensional space, besides possessing the meaning of a two-dimensionality that includes the third dimension as conceptual space, piles up conceptually a layer of a larger spatial expanse within the very space it actually fills. This phenomenon is particularly remarkable in landscape paintings, although we can see it in almost all other types of paintings. Instances of a multilayeredness composed of more than two layers are not rare. The motif of the "Hikone Screen," which stands within painting as a landscape screen, is just one example.[58] When it tries to express a multilayeredness of time, sculpture is nothing but a kind of pictorialization departing from its own characteristics. The tableaux in the five-storied pagoda of the Hōryūji[59] and "the bodhisattva holding a memorial service in the clouds" in the Phoenix Hall of the Byōdōin[60] are fitting examples. Moreover, if sculpture tries to create a multilayeredness of meaning inside its inner space, in special cases not only will it require special pictorial techniques but it will also go one step further and borrow the help of painting itself. The inside of the Forbidden Palace in Beijing is an example of architecture skillfully incorporating the spatial multilayeredness of painting. At the end of the corridor there is a scene painted according to the law of perspective; but when we step back a little, no matter where we turn our eyes, we have the optical illusion that this is actually an extension of the corridor. In any case painting, unlike sculpture and architecture, is characterized by spatial multilayeredness. Moreover, literature and painting have an affinity with regard to setting forth a multilayeredness, although literature is temporal and painting is spatial. This explains why one way to catalog the arts is to consider music, architecture, and sculpture in one category and to put painting and literature in another category. Music, architecture, and sculpture are tied to the real present. With regard to painting and literature and the extent of their relationship with the structure of their upper layer, however, the intuition of something unreal contains the moving present. Painting and literature lead to the illusion of perception and representation. Painting does it through colors; literature does it through language. By so doing, they gain a large spatial and temporal view. The fact that painting and literature possess a spatial and temporal multilayeredness is based on the perception and representation of the unreal through color and language.

Now it is a fact that literature possesses a conceptual space in addition to a conceptual time and, moreover, that painting possesses a conceptual time in addition to a conceptual space. Space becomes a formal condition of literature in drama, which formalizes dialogue. Drama is not only a spectacle in which characters come on the stage; it also has the possibility of being played out in a real space as a play. In novels as well there are almost no cases in which space does not appear as content. The beginning of Sōseki's *Kusamakura* (The grass pillow) is just one example.[61] Spatial representation also enters poetry easily. The following examples take as their content purely temporal representations exclusively:

> *Itsu wa shimo koinu toki to wa aranedomo yū katamakete koi wa subenashi*[62]
>
> Be it when it may, I have never a moment free from this longing, but when evening comes upon me I am helpless in my love.[63]

> *Fumizuki ya muika mo tsune no yo ni wa nizu*[64]
>
> The Seventh Month—the night of the sixth day is not like any other night.

The following examples include spatial representations:

> *Tago no urayu uchiidete mireba mashiro ni so Fuji no takane ni yuki wa furikeru*[65]
>
> Coming out from Tago's nestled cove, I gaze: white, pure white the snow has fallen on Fuji's lofty peak.[66]

> *Botan chirite uchikasanarinu ni san pen*[67]
>
> The peony has fallen—laying upon one another, two or three petals.[68]

The more space enters literature, the closer literature gets to painting. Drama becomes play, eventually turning into a picture by going through pantomime and living picture. Yet we cannot deny that painting as well in a sense includes the flow of time. The more a painting contains time, however, the closer it gets to literature. We can say that paintings which express all movements contain a time grounded in spatio-temporality. *Amida and the Twenty-Five Bodhisattvas Descending from the Sky,* Sesshū's *Landscape of Wind and Rain, Mountains and Waters,* and Hiroshige's paintings of Yokkaichi and Shōno in the *Fifty-Three Stations of the Tōkaidō*[69] are good examples. When it comes to things such as picture scrolls, time becomes remarkably present. I would like to say that in works such as *The Origin of Dōjōji*

(Dōjōji Engi) time flows like a wave. Yet we must ponder over the fact that the temporality of picture scrolls is grounded mainly in the real time during which one actually unfolds the scroll; the distance between a picture scroll seen as a temporal art, and a moving picture seen as a spatial art, is a short one. Moreover, it is not only literature and movies, especially sound pictures, that are closely related. Picture scrolls are also essentially close to literature—to the point of being called an art that synthesizes literature and painting. This is clearly demonstrated, even in a genetic sense, by works such as *The Scroll on the Sūtra of Past and Present Causations (Kako Genzai Ingakyō Emaki)* and *The Illustrated Words of "The Tale of Genji" (Genji Monogatari E-kotoba).* Thus we might think that although painting implies the presence of conceptual time, it is also characterized by conceptual space; although literature implies the presence of conceptual space, it is also characterized by conceptual time.

Based on the preceding discussion, I should be able to conclude that the multilayeredness of time is the philosophical essence of literature seen as a temporal art based on language. Even for Marcel Proust the novel comes into being by "searching for lost time."[70] Near the end of *The Past Recaptured* we read the sentence: "It was this conception of time as incarnate, of past years as still close held within us, which I was now determined to bring out into such bold relief in my book."[71]

5

So far I have clarified the following points with regard to the temporality of literature: first, so long as literature is a type of art, the temporality of literature, generally speaking, is the present; second, as a temporal art such a temporality is *qualitative;* third, as a linguistic art the time of literature possesses a *multilayeredness.* In short, the temporal essence of literature is a *qualitative present with multilayeredness.* Here I have provided a general clarification of the temporality of literature. I must now examine, however, how these general characteristics are further differentiated according to different types of literature. As I proceed along these lines, the temporal nature of literature will become clear in its concreteness. In other words, whereas such a nature is the

present time in general, remarkable differences come to light in litera-
ture depending on whether we emphasize the *past,* the *future,* or the
present as its basic aspect. We can say that the *novel* emphasizes the
past in the temporal structure of literature, *drama* emphasizes the fu-
ture, and *poetry* emphasizes the present.

I begin by briefly addressing the meaning of concentrating on either
the past, future, or present with regard to the phenomenon of time.
First of all, there is a view related to time that considers time to be a
flow proceeding from the past toward the future. Time is a progression
that has its origin in the past—a continuity of the past flowing into the
future. Accordingly, memory is considered to be the essence of time;
emphasis is put on the continuation from the past. Without memory as
continuation from the past, two moments are simply one or the other,
without a before and an after. Time as continuation is nothing but
memory. Since it does not matter if memory is not necessarily a clear
consciousness, memory fulfills its task by simply connecting a before
and an after. In this sense, a seedling has the memory of a seed; a flower
has the memory of a seedling; a fruit has the memory of a flower. This
way of thinking is found in theories of time that place emphasis on the
past. A second view tries to put the temporal accent on the future. This
view grasps time by making the future its starting point. It does not
simply imply that a time without future does not exist; the fact of pos-
sessing a future is the main characteristic distinguishing time from
other things. There is a goal that needs to be reached; the distance to-
ward that goal comes into being first as time. Time is simply will or ef-
fort. Accordingly, the essence of time is anticipation. The meaning of
time is not memory but anticipation. Time is born in the future and
flows in reverse back to the present and the past. The third view is a
theory of time that locates the main point of time in the present. Past
and future do not exist in actuality. The past does not exist since it has
already gone; the future does not exist since it has not yet come. What
exists is only the present. The past is not; only the memory of the past
is. The future is not; only the anticipation of the future is. Moreover,
the place where the memory of the past and the anticipation of the fu-
ture are formed is the present. The starting point of time is the present.
The one spring known as "now" gushes forth as original impression.
Now, now, now, now, now…is time. The past is a now that has sunk;

the future is a now that has not yet risen to the surface. When we think of now as strictly a point, it looks as if now does not exist; and yet if we grasp and anticipate—just a little—the now that has appeared then the present appears in front of our eyes as intuition. The present as intuition must be the essence of time. Time flows extending from the present to the past and future.

Roughly speaking, then, we have these three views on the essence of time; however, we can add a fourth theory of time. The past is not simply something that has already gone. The future is not simply something that has not yet come. The past comes again in the future; the future has already come in the past. If we follow the past for a long way, we return to the future; if we follow the future for a long way, we return to the past. Time forms a circle; it is recurrent. If we locate time in the present, we can say that this present possesses, as present, an infinite past and an infinite future and, as well, that it is the identity of countless presents. The present is the eternal present with an infinite depth; in short, time is nothing but the infinite present, the eternal now.

When we compare the first theory of time emphasizing the past with the second theory, emphasizing the future, we can say that the first theory is biological while the second is ethical. The irreversibility of time is imprinted in organisms, so that living beings become old. The trunks of trees become thicker year by year. The time imprinted in living beings is the continuity of the past. For this reason we can say that the theory of time that emphasizes the past is biological. The theory of time laying emphasis on the future, by contrast, is ethical. The fact that the future can contain the present and has the power of determination is due to the fact that consciousness anticipates the future. Properly speaking, everything is preceded by a cause and followed by an effect. Consciousness, however, anticipates a set effect as a goal in the realm of the future; consciousness can draw, in reverse, the means for achieving such a goal. Since here we can see the activity of the will at work, the theory of time that locates the essence of time in the future contains an ethical coloration. Next we can say that the third theory of time is a psychological theory since it is based on the original impression within the present of the phenomenon of time. In contrast to the latter theory, we might say that the fourth theory of time emphasizing a thinkable eternal present is a metaphysical theory.

To be more precise, there are differences among the various ways of looking at the fundamental nature of time as past, future, or present. When the self tries to flow together with the flow of time, emphasis is sometimes naturally put on the past, sometimes on the future. Moreover, it appears as if the present does not exist. When, instead, we try to stare at the flow of time, temporal emphasis spontaneously falls on the present. Like Confucius, who said in the vicinity of a river, "Is it like this to pass away without resting day or night?" we can compare time to the flow of a river. To emphasize the past is like sailing on a ship. The ship flows downstream from the upper stream. To emphasize the future is like going upstream by having the boat towed. The characteristic of the river is located in the point where we can go back upstream after departing from downstream. To emphasize the present is like facing the river and looking straight ahead. Here what is newly born dies, and what dies is born. The fountainhead is the present known as "now." Moreover, looking at the river, we can also think that the water enters the sea, becomes vapor rising to the sky, and then becomes rain falling on earth and wetting the mountain, so that the water gradually flows from the valley into the river. In other words, the water of the river that I observe now is a water circulating eternally. Accordingly, we can think that the water I observe now has an infinitely deep background. Thus the water of the river comes to be seen as a symbol of the eternal present.

I have pointed out that several theories of time are possible which locate the center of time in the past, future, and present. Even with regard to the temporal structure of literature we can argue that the novel emphasizes the past, drama accentuates the future, and poetry centers on the present. Next I will be examining in some detail these distinctions in the temporality of literature.

6

The novel is one kind of tale *(monogatari),* with one subject and a telling of that subject. "To tell" *(noberu)* is "to stretch" *(noberu),* which is to say the same thing. To tell with words is like stretching things. It is to tell things with words gradually, like stretching and unrolling by hand something that was rolled up. Accordingly, in terms of time, the past is the point of departure developing toward a future. The compositional form of a novel is to tell by pursuing memory. This is a matter of course for novels based on personal experience; but the same thing is true for novels centered on the observation of the life of others. In all novels someone's life is portrayed and recorded according to memory. No matter whether the existence revived by memory is one's own experience or somebody else's life, the novelist takes the position of a third person quietly observing and telling the story. The fact that the novel is realistic or idealistic, naturalistic or symbolistic, materialistic or expressionistic, does not bring any change to the way it proceeds by unfolding the deposits of the past, taking the past as its point of departure. It goes without saying that the novelist freely bestows selectivity, variation, and arrangement on the memory of the reality he observes. He does not need to determine beforehand the plan of his composition and go into details, however; he usually unfolds the beginning plot toward the future, following his interest. This is why we hear of "plotless" novels and the "purposelessness" of novels. Accordingly, the flow of life that runs from the past to the future enters the novel in the form which is most true to itself. As a result, compared to other literary works, the novel is the most inclusive form. When we think of the works of Natsume Sōseki, the meaning of "inclusive" comes naturally to mind. We can say the same thing with regard to the length of the novel, no matter how long it is: *The Tale of Genji* is a good example. Life simply keeps flowing under the pressure of the past. The real time of perception filling the reality of the language spoken in the novel, and the conceptual time of the imagination that is included in the novel, are an extension of each other; they are comparatively close. The basic structure of the novel, in which the past develops as the realm of memory, makes possible the properties of purposelessness, inclusiveness, and length.

The conceptual time of the novel moves within the freedom of the concept. The form of historical account known as "annals" presents, to a great extent, features close to quantitative time, although it is not quantitative time. In the novel, however, the writer freely transforms the proportion of event and time following his own personal views. He can consume tens of pages in order to follow the memory of an event that has taken place in ten minutes, or he can dedicate only half a page to a memory of many years in the background of the story. A reversed arrangement of time is also possible. In the short novel *Recollection (Tsuioku)* by Hayashi Fumiko,[72] the title already refers to the temporal structure of the novel; but using the way that memory arranges it, she goes back, in the middle of the story, to a memory of an event two years earlier. This is not in conflict with the general temporal structure of novels that make the past their point of departure. A fine example of the freedom of conceptual time in a novel is Tanizaki Jun'ichirō's *The Reed Cutter (Ashikari)*.[73] Although the author describes the memories of a certain September day in a certain year, half of the story recounts the events that took place between a little after 3:00 P.M. and 6:00 P.M. Taking as pretext the Minase detached palace, the memory calls back the age of Retired Emperor Go-Toba during the early Kamakura period.[74] The memory of the age of Murasaki Shikibu[75] during the early Fujiwara regency piles up on top of the temporal layer of Emperor Go-Toba. In connection with Yamazaki station, the age of Nobunaga,[76] the year before the expansion of the city of Kyoto, the age of the loyal retainers,[77] and the age of Sugawara no Michizane[78] are all remembered one after the other. With regard to the Yodo River, both shores of the Sumida River occur to the author's mind as a memory of his childhood. Retired Emperor Go-Toba and the Edo connoisseur are tied together in terms of time. When the emperor recollects his visit to Minase in his place of exile in Oki, the clock indicates six o'clock. The second half of the novel develops under the moonlight from after supper until midnight. Taking as pretext the ferryboat, the memory first of all reveals the time of childhood. Then, in relationship with Mt. Otoko, it turns to the Edo of Kageki[79] and Kikaku.[80] While looking at the extensive river width, it shifts to the Tang dynasty of Tu Fu[81] and Po Chü-i.[82] Moreover, in relation to essays on courtesans, the memory moves from the Heian court of Ōe no Masahira[83] and Ōe no Masafusa[84] to the age of Saigyō.[85] Then, suddenly, a man by the name of Kinkyō appears who, by enjoying the view of the moon every year, remembers when his father was taking him to moonlight parties. He then tells the long love story of his dead father that had taken place several decades earlier. The peak of this love story is the scene when Seribashi as a child remembers his father absorbed in memories of the past, taking out the long underwear that once enveloped the body of his lover. Although this love story was narrated in less than an hour and must have lasted one-fifth the time of basic recollection from after three o'clock until midnight, it occupies more than two-thirds of the pages of the entire novel. In addition to clearly indicating the phenomenon of the freedom of conceptual time, *The Reed Cutter* makes us easily understand that the novel's temporality emphasizes the past.

The development of the novel as a kind of tale from past to future following the path of memory is analogous to the development in scholarship of new things grounded in old things of the past. The temporal structure of scholarship accents the past in the same way the novel does. We can say that this proves the predominance in novels of the intellectual moment. As in scholarship where things are deduced quietly and coldly from reason to conclusion, causes and effects of human experience in novels are coldly analyzed and narrated from the perspective of a third person. Tokuda Shūsei[86] says the following with regard to the composition of novels: "We can begin writing a novel when we feel like seeing and portraying. By becoming old and accumulating experiences, the light of the intellect shines in reverse proportion to the weakening emotions....At this point, for the first time, we become able to clearly represent to the eyes reality as it is. We feel like looking and portraying. If we reach this point, we can write a novel. For people who have not yet reached this feeling, it is too early to write a novel. Of course, there is a slight difference of being late or early between emotional and intellectual people....Generally speaking, however, compared to people from other ages, modern men are quicker to see and portray in proportion to their age. The modern spirit, to say it simply, has taken a way in which naturalistic thought coldly awakens to scientific and intellectual reason more than it gets excited by passions. People who, without realizing it, have been transformed by the spirit of this age cannot sit still dreaming and singing forever like people in the past. Songs are becoming excessively intellectual. People look intently and quietly and, after looking, they judge....It is natural that today's youth do not turn to poetry, do not familiarize themselves with lyrical writings, and try to write novels straight away." When we look at the reality of the predominance of the intellectual mode moving from reason to conclusion and shifting from cause to effect, in the novel we see that literature and scholarship are remarkably close in form. We can say that, compared to poetry and drama, novels are the form of literature possessing intellectual characteristics closest to those of scholarship. This is why we also have the view that novels are one form of thinking. It is in this view that we ground the belief that—just as scholarship possesses a temporality oriented toward the past—the temporality of novels is also the past. But so long as the novel is art, no matter how much its temporal configuration is past-oriented, we cannot deny that at its root there is a present intuition. In this respect, novels are strictly different from scholarship. In a word, we can say that the temporality of novels is a *past present.*

7

The novel has one subject and tells of an event; in this sense the novel is monistic. Drama, by contrast, has a pluralistic structure: the whole is presented by several subjects in the form of a dialogue. We find the essential relationship between the several subjects, however, in the action. Accordingly action is the essential meaning of drama. Since action is the essence of drama, the possibility of putting it on stage arises. Furthermore, drama as a temporal art changes into a play as a spatiotemporal art. Additionally, since play is genetically prior to text, the formation of drama as literature should be thought of as a later development. The formative elements of a play are acting and speech. Since the setting up of speech independently from acting became drama, the language of drama is directly related to action. Generally speaking, *drama* shows *drontas* (people acting); gestural dances *(wazaogi)* are also nothing but an act *(waza),* which is to say, a type of action. And since human behavior is the externalization of the will, we can safely conclude that a play, and consequently the content of drama, is a personal conflict played out by the human will against destiny and circumstances—a characteristic dissension between will and will. Someone also says that drama is a negotiation between souls in the form of a dialogue. Since the negotiation between souls—that is, the primary phenomenon of intersubjectivity—is an operation of the will, however, no matter how little movement there is in a drama, no drama exists that does not reveal action as a path to the will.

The temporal character of drama becomes self-evident when we look at its essence, which is made of will and action. So long as human will and action show themselves in the realm of purposiveness, drama moves, making the future its point of departure; as a result, the temporality of drama emphasizes the future. In addition to being regulated by the future in each of its parts, drama as a whole also begins in and develops from the future. In drama there must necessarily be a clear plot. Moreover, the plot is constructed backward starting from the finale. In classical theater the determination of whether a play is a tragedy or a comedy is based on the conclusion, which ends in either hopeless catastrophe or harmonious resolution. Tragedy, which is characterized by a catastrophic conclusion, requires, prior to a catastrophe, the presence of a crisis leading to the catastrophe; prior to the crisis there must be a progression toward a crisis. To say it simply, the plot of a tragedy is made of three steps: progression, crisis, and catastrophe. Generally speaking, we have a line rising in the first half of the play and moving toward a suddenly descending line, as in the case of a mountain or an electric commutator. Comedy, which is characterized by a resolution, requires, prior to the solution, the presence of an imbroglio that must be solved; prior to the imbroglio there must be a progression that develops into an imbroglio. The following steps are the essence of a comedy's plot: progression, imbroglio, and resolution. Usually a descending line in the first half moves gradually toward a rising line passing through the bottom as in an electric commutator. Tragedy is organized in its entirety to bring something great and beautiful into a future of destruction and ruin. Comedy as a whole is structured with the aim of eliciting the laughter of a happy ending. We must say that the starting point of drama is located in the future: in tragedy we find it in a wretched catastrophe; in comedy we see it in a joyful resolution. By pushing the whole drama into a unitary, future phase known as catastrophe or resolution, a dramatic effect is achieved.

In Chikamatsu's *Love Suicides at Sonezaki (Sonezaki Shinjū)*,[87] the fact that Ohatsu and Tokubei commit a double suicide, their bodies tied together under the twin trees of a pine and a hemp palm in the grove of Sonezaki, is anticipated beforehand as the play's conclusion. The breach of faith on the part of the friend Kuheiji has brought the crisis to a catastrophe. The relationships of love and obligation between Tokubei, Ohatsu, and the niece of the master's wife form the progression of the first part of the play. In Soga no Yagorō's *Handclasp of Treasures (Takara no Hakushu)*,[88] the enormous profit of four hundred *ryō* gained by the stonemason Tomizō is the comical resolution of the play. The imbroglio introduced as a premise for the final resolution is the scene where people discover that he has made a huge speculation on the rice market because he confused one *shō* of rice with one thousand *koku* of rice. He is told that this is a felony and feels great distress— "Such a deep sadness…I never imagined—not even in my dreams—that I would have stirred such a riot." Up to this point the entire event was simply a progression toward the imbroglio. In Okamoto Kidō's *Story of Shuzenji (Shuzenji Monogatari)*,[89] the starting point of the entire play, the apex of the rising line, is the cheerful laughter of the maker of masks, Yashaō: "Man's destiny that cannot be ruled without deities.…First of all my work shows the response of nature, the mystery of nature.…This is what it means to enter into the deity of art! Yashaō of Izu, if I can say so about myself, is the best in the whole splendid world!" The scene in which he feels that Yoriie's return of his mask is a source of eternal shame—and decides never again to take up the hammer—is the electric commutator to which the falling line has arrived. The death of Yoriie and Katsura, by contrast, aims at a dramatic effect that is the end of the falling line. The love scene at the edge of the Kokei bridge near the Katsura River forms the rising line of a mountain. The nature of the craftsman represented by Yashaō and Kaede, and the disposition of the aristocrat typified by Yoriie and Katsura, indicate the dramatic sign of two conflicts. Both signs, however, become the decisive drives of the whole drama whose future is anticipated beforehand. In Kurata Hyakuzō's *A Monk and His Disciples (Shukke to Sono Deshi)*,[90] the scene in which Shinran dies peacefully saying, "This is good! Everybody is saved!" is the essential point of departure for the dramatic composition. Instead the corrupt life of his only child Zenran and the love of his favorite pupil Yuien are deduced inversely.

Since the temporality of drama has an inner relationship based on an emphasis on the future, drama is characterized by the necessity of not being too long. Although we may think that this rule is due to drama's relationship with the actual performance on the stage at the theater, in fact it is the original nature at the foundation of drama. Since the whole drama is formed by making the future its starting point, separately from the issue of actual performance on stage, drama must show the future within a set amount of time. Accordingly, even when drama is performed on stage it can be shown to the audience within a set amount of time. Whereas it does not matter how long the narration of a novel is deferred—since novels make the past the point of their departure—drama, which makes the future its departing point, demands a set limit with regard to the passage of time.

Like the novel, which is close to scholarship in terms of a temporality oriented toward the past, drama is contiguous with morality in that they share a future temporality. This explains why Aristotle said that drama, especially tragedy, has the function of purging the emotions. Although we can interpret Aristotle's words in a variety of ways, no one can deny that after we see a tragedy, the mind, purified of all passions, becomes clean and lucid. Tragedy shocks the whole moral personality of the spectator. The audience feels through its own morality that everything is the emptiness of emptiness. When an outstanding personality plays the leading role in a tragedy, the tragedy's moral effect becomes increasingly deep and large. When we witness the sudden ruin of a beautiful, noble, and mighty person, we are left with the anguish of disillusionment that nothing can be trusted. Furthermore, at that moment, everyone returns to his own original self and becomes the special owner of a pure and innocent spirit. It is also common for comedy to bring about an analogous moral effect. In order to receive a comedy, the spirit must be calm; the passions, which rise like waves, are purified of their own accord. Ugly feelings such as anger, hatred, and jealousy disappear from the spirit of a spectator watching a comedy.

In a word, the essence of drama is will and action based on a pluralistic structure; with regard to temporality, drama emphasizes the future. As a result, drama assumes an ethical structure. However, we can say that, so long as drama is art, the futurality of drama floats on the basis of the present and that the temporality of drama is a *futural present*.

8

Contrary to the novel and drama, which are objective, poetry is subjective. When I say "poetry," of course I mean lyrical poetry. We only have poetry, however, when feelings that cannot be restrained overflow. This is also what Motoori Norinaga meant when he said: "The composition of poetry is an action that takes place when we cannot endure the 'pathos of things' *(mono no aware)*."[91] We must savor the following statement that Ishikawa Takuboku made with regard to poetry: "Poetry must be an exact report, an honest diary, of the changes in a man's emotional life. Accordingly, it must be fragmentary; it must not have organization. (Poetry with organization, i.e., philosophy in literature, is the novel deductively, and the drama inductively. The relationship between them and poetry is what exists between a daily balance of accounts and a monthly or yearly settlement.)"[92]

When excitement and intuition are in the present, poetry comes into being. Poetry must directly express the excitement and the intuition of the present. Hitomaro's poem written "when he passed the ruined capital at Ōmi" is a good example:

> Since the reign of the Master of the Sun
> at Kashiwara by Unebi Mountain,
> where the maidens
> wear strands of jewels,
> all gods who have been born
> have ruled the realm under heaven,
> each following each
> like generations of the spruce,
> in Yamato
> that spreads to the sky.
>
> What was in his mind
> that he would leave it
> and cross beyond the hills of Nara,
> beautiful in blue earth?
> Though a barbarous place
> at the far reach of the heavens,
> here in the land of Ōmi
> where the waters race on stone,
> at the Ōtsu Palace
> in Sasanami
> by the rippling waves,
> the Emperor, divine Prince,
> ruled the realm under heaven.

Though I hear
this was the great palace,
though they tell me
here were the mighty halls,
now it is rank with spring grasses.
Mist rises, and the spring sun is dimmed.
Gazing on the ruins of the great palace,
its walls once thick with wood and stone,
I am filled with sorrow.[93]

We can say that, with regard to time, poetry focuses on one point in the present. Poetry comes into being by having everything gathering in a center known as the present—like outspread casting nets that close on one point of the stem when you pull them up:

Sora kazou Ōtsu no ko ga aishi hi ni ō ni mishikaba ima zo kuyashiki[94]

When I met the girl of Ōtsu—like the sky in its vastness—I saw her only faintly. Now, now I regret it![95]

Naru kami no oto nomi kikishi Makimuku no Hibara no yama o kyō mitsuru kamo[96]

Today I saw Mt. Hibara in Makimuku of which I only heard from the sound of the thunder god.

Mukashi mishi kisa no ogawa o ima mireba iyoyo sayakeku narini-keru kamo[97]

Gazing now on the stream at Kisa that I gazed on in the past, I see how, more and more, it has become bright and clear.[98]

Koishikeba katami ni semu to waga yado ni ueshi fujinami ima sakinikeri[99]

The wisteria I planted in my garden as a memento when I was in love is now blooming.

Okurara wa ima wa makaramu ko nakuramu sono ko no haha mo wa o matsuramu zo[100]

Okura shall take his leave now. My child must be crying and its mother, who bears it on her back, must be waiting for me.[101]

> *Aoniyoshi Nara no miyako wa saku hana no niou ga gotoku ima
> sakarinari*[102]

> The capital at Nara, beautiful in blue earth, flourishes now like the
> brilliant fragrance of the flowers in bloom.[103]

In these poems the excitement and the intuition of the present are
shown in such words as "now" and "today," but it goes without say-
ing that there is no absolute need for these words to be mentioned.

> *Ōmi no umi yūnamichidori na ga nakeba kokoro mo shinuni inishie
> oboyu*[104]

> Plover skimming evening waves on the Ōmi Sea, when you cry so my
> heart trails like dwarf bamboo down to the past.[105]

> *Kozo miteshi aki no tsukuyo wa terasedomo aimishi imo wa iya
> toshi sakaru*[106]

> The autumn moon shines as it did when I watched last year, but my
> wife, who watched with me—the drift of the year has taken her.[107]

> *Miyoshino no kisayama no ma no konure ni wa kokoda mo sawagu
> tori no koe kamo*[108]

> In fair Yoshino, in the vale that lies between the mountains of Kisa,
> from every treetop rise the voices of the gaily singing birds.[109]

The foregoing poems clearly focus on the present. The emotions ex-
pressed in poetry come gushing out burning, irrepressible, from the in-
stant of the present. Furthermore, since poetry focuses on one point of
the present, poems cannot be too long. This explains why a short form
such as *haiku* came beautifully into being as poetry from *tanka:*

> *Furuike ya kawazu tobikomu mizu no oto*[110]
> The old pond—a frog jumps in, water's sound.[111]

> *Hana no kumo kane wa Ueno ka Asakusa ka*[112]
> Clouds of blossoms…that temple bell, is it Ueno or Asakusa?[113]

> *Samidare o atsumete hayashi Mogamigawa*[114]
> Gathering the rains of the wet season, how swiftly flows the Mogami
> River![115]

Sanshaku no koi kugurikeri yanagikage

A three-foot carp moves around—the shade of a willow.

Shigonin ni tsuki ochikakaru odori ka na[116]

A dance—the moonlight falling on four or five people.

In all the preceding poems we see the intuition and the excitement of the present.

We are justified in saying that the temporal nature of poetry is the present; yet we can also say that the present of poetry is the "eternal now." The present with the depth of eternity appears in the formal stipulation of poetry. The repetition of poetic rhythm is the eternal reiteration of the present. For example:

5/7 syllables, 5/7 syllables, 5/7 syllables,…>

The unlimited repetition of the present means that the present possesses the depth of eternity. Not only poetic rhythm, but also rhyme, has the same function:

> *Ch'iu feng hsiao se t'ien ch'i **liang***
> *ts'ao mu yao lo lou wei **shuang***
> *ch'ün yen tz'u kuei yen nan **hsiang***
> *nien chün k'o yu ssu tuan **yang***
> *ch'ien ch'ien ssu kuei lien ku **hsiang***
>
> Chilly is the autumn wind, cold is the weather,
> Grass and trees shake and fall, dew has turned into frost,
> A group of swallows has left as they return home, wild geese soar to
>   the south,
> I think of you, a traveler with a broken heart,
> So disconsolate that I think of returning as I yearn for my
>   hometown.[117]

This poem is a repetition of rhymed *"yang"* in the even tone. It is also a repetition of verse created by dividing a poem into lines. This repetition is like scattering and separating something that has become one thick body, something that is the result of piling up several lines. We can see this, for example, in the following poem by Miyoshi Tatsuji:[118]

Nagisa ni idete
*ami o tsukurou hitokage **ari***

Kabe shiroki shōgakkō no kōtei ni
*mari naguru dōji **ari***

Nami wa
*iso ni **kudaku***

*Ware wa **kiku***
*ware wa mimi **katamuku***

*Saredo waga kiku wa kano nami no hibiki ni **arazu***
*karekusa no hazue o suguru kaze uta ni mo **arazu**.*

Going out to the shore
there is the shade of a person repairing nets,

in the backyard of an elementary school by the white walls
there is a child throwing a ball.

The waves
break on the seashore.

I hear,
turn my ears.

But what I hear is not the sound of those waves,
not the song of the wind passing through the leaf tips of withered
   grasses.

In this instance we have a repetition in two lines. Similarly, the refrain used in poetry also uses the principle of repetition. Take, for example, the following poem by Hagiwara Sakutarō:[119]

Shizuka ni kishire yorin basha.
Honoka ni umi wa akarumite
Mugi wa tōki ni nagaretari
shizuka ni kireshi yorin basha.
Hikaru gyochō no tenkei o
mata mado aoki kenchiku o
shizuka ni kishire yorin basha.

Squeak quietly, four-wheeled horse cab!
Faintly the sea becomes clear,
the wheat has been washed away in the distance.

Squeak quietly, four-wheeled horse cab!
The sky of shining birds and fishes
and the building with blue windows.
Squeak quietly, four-wheeled horse cab!

We might also think that the envoy at the end of a long poem
(*chōka*) performs the same task—a reiteration at the level of content:

Ashihara no mizuho no kuni wa kami nagara kotoage senu kuni
shikaredomo kotoage zo wa ga suru kotosakiku masakiku maseto
tsutsumi naku sakiku imasaba arisonami arite mo mimu to momoe-
nami chienami ni shiki kotoagesu ware wa

Henka

Shikishima no Yamato no kuni wa kotodama no tasukuru kuni zo
masakiku ari koso[120]

The rice-abounding Land of Reed Plains,
Is a land where things fall out
As will the gods, without lifted words of men,
Yet must I lift up words:
"Be fortunate, and travel safe and sound!"
If you be free from evils,
Then shall we meet once more;
So I lift up words over and over again
As the waves roll a hundredfold,
A thousandfold!

Envoy

The Land of Yamato is a land
Where the word-soul gives us aid;
Be happy, fare you well![121]

A repetition takes place as if the present possessed a depth. Even if
the poetic form is slightly long, a repetition is persistently employed
either by rhythmic skill, or by rhyme, or by lines, or by refrain, or by
envoy—as if everything concentrates on the point of the present. All
these devices reduce a lengthy poetic form. These formal poetic tech-
niques bring the poem to a halt in the place of the same present; they
make the poem concentrate on the limitless instant of the eternal present.

Of the literary genres, poetry is the one in which the present is especially prominent. The poetic present is further added to the general present of art. We can say that the temporality of poetry is a *present present*. Furthermore, it is safe to conclude that whereas the novel, which emphasizes the past, is close to scholarship, and whereas drama, which emphasizes the future, comes close to morality, poetry, which emphasizes the present, is the most artistically oriented form of literature.

9

To summarize what I have been saying so far, if we look at literature philosophically from the perspective of temporality, literature is a microcosm of qualitative time with a multilayered structure. Moreover, so long as it is a microcosmic art, literature, generally speaking, possesses a nature oriented toward the present. When, through a process of diversification, literature becomes novel, drama, or poetry, it receives a further coloring of past, future, or present.

A literary work cannot necessarily be confined to the meaning of one of the three organizational boxes, however, thus simply being reduced to either novel, drama, or poetry. Novel, drama, and poetry have been compared to chemical elements. Elements rarely exist autonomously in a pure state; most of them are found in the natural world as compounds. We see an analogous phenomenon in literary works. In this sense we can speak of poetic elements in a novel, dramatic elements in poetry, and novelistic elements in drama. With regard to temporal structure, moreover, all three genres carry all sorts of complexities. As an example of the presence of poetic elements in a novel, we may think of Kawabata Yasunari's *Snow Country (Yukiguni)*.[122] At the level of content we can already see that this novel is poetic when we look at the nature of the character Shimamura, who delights in the unrealistic world of visions. And yet, even at the level of content, an intensely realistic everydayness comes to the front that almost destroys the visionary. I believe that we actually find the poetic side of this novel at the level of form. By employing devices corresponding to the rhythm, rhyme, and refrain of poetry, the whole novel acquires a tenor that is intuited as a present possessing depth. The same scene of the hot spring village in the northern country is repeated, creating the three rhythms of fresh verdure in early summer, end of the year in winter, and maple leaves in autumn. The same simile of Komako's lips looking smooth as a beautiful ring of leeches, which returns three times in early summer, winter, and fall, plays the role of three end rhymes corresponding to the three rhythms. The merging of the reflection in the train's window glass of the night scenery outside with Yōko's beautiful figure inside the car; the coming of Komako's crimson cheeks to the surface of the mirror reflecting the white snow of the mountains; Komako's face blazing up in the shining glass of the waiting room; the reflection of the mountains' maple leaves and the sunlight of autumn on the dressing table that Komako has carried to the window's side; the reflection in the mirror of the cold petals of large snowflakes, which make a white line float around Komako's neck: all these same unreal sensations are repeated at suitable intervals like a poetic refrain. Moreover, even the theme of Komako's reverberating voice, beautifully clear to the point of being sad, is repeated three or four times, vibrating like a variation. The same locution comes up here and there like an alliteration, emphasizing the unreality of reality, as in the following instances: "so many stars that it looked incredible!"; "thinking that the thickness of the ice was incredible"; "I felt it was incredible…to shoulder the samisen box of paulownia wood until she reached the drawing room"; "it was so disappointing that I could not believe it"; "it was like a quiet lie." Komako repeats the same words—"You do not even believe it! I don't like people from Tokyo: they are liars!"—at the end of the year and in the fall of the following year. Through such repetitions, narration in the novel takes the form of intuition and, with regard to temporality, the present is emphasized with a particularly remarkable strength.

Next, as an example of dramatic elements in poetry, I will quote a poetic dialogue from the *Man'yōshū*:[123]

[Question]

On sodden nights when rain comes gusting on the wind,
On freezing nights when snow falls mingled with the rain,
Shivering helplessly in the all-pervading cold,
I take a lump of hardened salt and nibble on it

While I sip diluted lees of *sake* from my cup.
Clearing my throat, sniffling as my nose begins to run,
Stroking the few hairs of my meager, scraggly beard,
I puff myself up: "What do people matter anyway,
Aside from me?" But still I'm cold, and so I take
My hempen quilt and pull it up around my shoulders.
I put on every sleeveless homespun frock I own,
Layer upon layer, but the night is cold. And he,
The man more destitute than even I, on such a night
His father and mother must be starving, bodies chill and numb;
His wife and children moaning softly in the dark:
Yes, you—at times like this how do you manage to go on,
How do you get through your life?

[Answer]

Although men say that heaven and earth are vast,
Have they not dwindled to a narrow frame for me?
Although men say that the sun and moon are bright,
Have they not refused to grant their shining unto me?
Are all men thus, or am I alone deprived?
Though by rare chance I was born into the world of men,
And as any man I toil to make my living on the land,
Yet must I throw rags about my shoulders, mere rotten
Shreds of a sleeveless frock, hemp with no padding,
Dangling like branches of sea pine over my bones;
And in this crazy hut, this flimsy, tumbling hovel,
Flat on the ground I spread my bedding of loose straw.
By my pillowside my father and my mother crouch,
And at my feet my wife and children; thus am I
Surrounded by grief and hungry, piteous cries.
But on the hearth no kettle sends up clouds of steam,
And in our pot a spider spins its web.
We have forgotten the very way of cooking rice;
Then where we huddle, faintly whimpering like *nue* birds,
Deliberately, as the saying goes, to cut
The end of what was short enough before,
There comes the voice of the village chief with his whip,
Standing, shouting for me, there outside the place we sleep.
Does it come to this—Is it such a helpless thing,
The path of man in this world?[124]

In this "Dialogue on Poverty" by Okura, the sign of a futural action is postulated in a potential form as an appeal to public authorities by setting up a dialogue between an inquirer and a respondent. Even in the following *sedōka* (head-repeated poem), the dramatic dialogue between Isukeyorihime and Ōkume no Mikoto anticipates the close future in which the princess will follow the emperor's messenger:[125]

> (Mon) Ame tsutsu chidori mashitoto nado sakeru tome
> (Kotae) Otome ni tada ni awamu to waga sakeru tome[126]
>
> (Question) Rain swallow, wagtail, plover, and meadow bunting:
>   why the sharp, wide-open eyes?
> (Answer) To find a maiden who will meet me face to face are my
>   sharp, wide-open eyes.[127]

In these ancient poems in the form of dialogues we can see the original form of dramatic poetry, so we can say that poetic elements and dramatic elements are equally distributed. Accordingly, the temporal nature of these poems is also equally endowed with present and future. Furthermore, novelistic elements in drama can be seen in all explanatory passages; here we see the past even at the level of temporal structure that determines a change of the whole temporal structure. To differentiate between the literary genres of the novel, drama, and poetry is not an easy task—this has become clear from the preceding analysis. Consequently, distinguishing among temporalities in literature has remarkably complicated aspects. Furthermore, we may say that, as a basic form including distinctions, the general essence of literature's temporality is a *multilayered qualitative present*.

History is the concreteness of time. The descriptive and scholarly attitude is the one that sees time departing from the past and flowing toward the future and tries to explain new things according to old ones. In this instance, the relationships of cause and effect, reason and conclusion, are dominant. In other words, this is the realm appropriate to necessity: the necessity that is grasped possesses the characteristic known as "truth." Contrary to this, the active or moral attitude is the one that, taking the future as the point from which time departs, thinks of time as something that is brought about from the future and ponders over the fact that the emphasis of the past is actually in the future. This is a field dominated by purposiveness, a realm in which freedom is demanded for a teleological reality. What must be actualized through reason takes the characteristic known as "good." In a sense we can say that both the scholarly attitude, which pursues the truth under the guidance of necessity, and the moral attitude, which aims at practicing good under the concept of freedom, are active attitudes. The artistic attitude tries to savor and scrutinize a cross section of the movements of history; it intuits time in the present and aims at penetrating its flavor. Here necessity takes the form of freedom, and freedom dons the shape of necessity: the form of necessary freedom is called "beauty." Although there are instances in which an artist takes the scholarly attitude of searching for causes and effects in the creative process, and although the possession of a moral attitude with regard to the demand of a tireless effort in order to complete his work is an inevitable condition for the artist, the coming into being of a work of art as a work of art takes place in the intuition of the present. Without an intuition of the present, no matter how much one searches for causes and effects and how much effort of the will one makes, the beauty of art cannot be created. This is what I mean when I say that the temporal characteristic of art is the present.

The fact that art is a cross section of history and the intuition of the present means that the temporality of art is a qualitative present. The qualitative present possesses a certain duration as intuition; it is a present that implies the interpenetration of heterogeneity. It is different from quantitative time inasmuch as the latter comes into being in the form of a mathematical point. When we ask why quantitative time comes into being, we see that it can materialize within the bounds of the scholarly attitude which takes necessity as its guiding principle. The scholarly attitude understands the future according to a past that is dominated by reason and tries to explain new things according to old ones. To understand the future according to the past is to erase the future from its bounds; to explain new things according to old ones takes as its ideal the extinction of new things. In this case, past and old things are simply fixed as present—like a point. In other words, the present comes to take a quantitative meaning as the simultaneity of all points. Quantitative time, in the sense of simultaneity counted as such points, is the place where mathematical natural sciences come into being. The so-called nature of mathematical natural sciences is like the lump sum of the quantitative present. Physical and abstract time and space possess the same qualities.

So long as they are art, so-called spatial arts such as painting, sculpture, and architecture are not devoid of qualitative temporal elements based on intuition. In terms of materials, however, they only possess coexistent spatial elements. Consequently, it is possible for works of spatial art to be treated like natural objects. We can say that spatial arts come into being as natural objects in the quantitative present and as objects of art in the qualitative present. The fact that there are people who emphasize records of measurement as standards to judge the authenticity of paintings and sculptures indicates that they are trying to deal with works of spatial art as one kind of natural object. Temporal arts, such as music and literature, can come into being purely in qualitative time. To dissolve music with the measure of simultaneity by making its essence a succession of sounds is nothing less than to silence music. Music comes into being for the first time in the perception of the duration of sounds as interpenetration of heterogeneity. Literature also comes into existence in qualitative time. Unlike music, moreover, which as perception of sounds shows a temporal one-layeredness, literature constructs a multilayeredness of time by having language produce a conceptual time. Temporal multilayeredness is the point that distinguishes literature as a linguistic art from music as an acoustic art. Moreover, we can also say that unlike music, which expresses the form of the duration of life and spirit through temporal one-layeredness and consequently is the most directly sensuous art in terms of impression, literature expresses life and spirit in its entirety of form and content through temporal multilayeredness and consequently is the most deeply human art, showing the life and the soul of people as they are. In sum, I will conclude my philosophical examination of literature by clarifying its temporal nature, which works as a foreground of the temporality of history, and saying that the temporal characteristic of literature is the multilayered, qualitative present.

SELECTED ESSAYS

My Family Name

1

People often ask me about my family name. It does not make any impression on me since I got accustomed to using it from the day I was born. But apparently it makes a strange impression on others. When I think about it, I see there is a reason for that—it is a strange name! I feel something dark, something uncanny. Westerners often ask the meaning of my name and when I tell them that it means "nine devils,"[1] they are surprised without exception. A Catholic missionary priest told me that my name is blasphemy since *novem diaboli circulum faciunt* (nine devils make a circle) and said that I should change *"diaboli"* (devils) into *"angeli"* (angels). During an afternoon tea in Freiburg Professor Husserl offered a friendly interpretation of my name, saying that since it appeared to be the name of a samurai family, it came from the fact that its members threatened the enemy by attaching the figure of devils to their helmets during the turbulent age of wars.

Originally the Western word "devil" seems to go back to the Greek *"diabolos."* Coming from the verbs "to throw through," "to sever," "to slander," it means "slanderer." It seems that after going to Palestine, the devil became remarkably horrific. "You are of your father the devil, and the lusts of your father ye will do. He was a murderer from the beginning" (from the Gospel according to St. John 8:44). "Have not I chosen you twelve; and one of you is a devil?" (John 6:70). "Depart from me, you cursed, into everlasting fire which was prepared for the devil and his angels" (Matthew 25:41). It is quite natural that Westerners shout with surprise when they hear that my name means "nine devils." Germany too has the family name Teufel (devil).

The Sanskrit word *"preta"* comes from "departed," "gone," "dead." Passing through the meanings of "deceased," "dead," and "ghost," it eventually came to mean "devil." In China they are often called "spirits." The "Commentary on the Appended Judgments" of the *Book of Changes* says: "The union of seed and power produces all things; the escape of the soul brings about change. Through this we come to know the conditions of outgoing and returning spirits."[2] Chang Heng-ch'ü[3] wrote in the section on "Transformation of Spirits" of his *Cheng-meng* (Correcting youthful ignorance): "Spirits (heavenly and earthly) mean to come and go, to extend and contract. Therefore, when they are in the sky, they are called heavenly spirits; when they are on earth, they are called signs; when they are in man, they are called earthly spirits." In the section on "Animals" he says that heavenly spirits "proceed," earthly spirits "return." From "stretching" (Ch. *shen,* Jpn. *shin* 伸/to stretch = *shen, shin* 神/heavenly spirit or god) comes the word "heavenly spirit"; from "returning" (Ch. *kuei.* Jpn. *ki* 帰/to return = *kuei, ki* 鬼/earthly spirit or demon) comes the word "earthly spirit." In the "Treatise on Death" from *The Balanced Inquiries* Wang Ch'ung[4] says: "When a man dies, his spirit ascends to heaven and his flesh and bones return *(kuei)* to earth, and that is why an earthly spiritual being *(kuei)* [and a heavenly spiritual being *(shen)*] are so called. To be an earthly spiritual being *(kuei)* means to return *(kuei).*"[5]

In Japan the word "devil" *(oni)* seems to be a corruption of the word *"onu"* (to be hidden). Demons are hidden; they do not show their form. Therefore demons came to be called *"oni"* (*Wamyōshō* 2:21). In Takuan Zenshi's *Tōkai Yawa* (Night talks at the Tōkai temple)[6] we find this sentence: "I remember with great interest that, among the many things that came to my mind when waking from sleep during the autumn nights, I kept reading the Chinese character 'devil' as *oni.*" However, in no time 'devil' *(oni)* came to mean "hungry ghost" *(gaki),* as the *Myōgishō* (Dictionary of Japanese names) confirms: "Searching for became '*oni.*' A hungry ghost always follows other people, searching for food and drink." Then Hiraga Gennai[7] said: "Devils in different forms and colors—red devils, black devils, dappled devils, brown devils, grass green devils, checkerboard-like devils. They come in different varieties and shapes—with one horn or two horns; with one eye or two eyes; with the head of a cow or the head of a horse; giant monsters devouring beasts and men *(rāksasa).* They gather in one place—hell's tormenting devils!" *(Nenashigusa,* pt. 2, vol. 1). Fuse Shōō,[8] a member of Shingaku (Studies of the Human Spirit), said: "Devils are not far from you. You can find some of them in front of your nose. Your parents telling you what to do, your son with his puffy face, your mother saying something strange again, your daughter who never changes—they all become half devils." He wrote the following poem: "Although they do not go as far as Adachigahara,[9] in their hearts a devil is hidden" *(Shōō Dōwa,* pt. 3, bk. 2).

2

What is the meaning of *"ku"* in the name Kuki? In elementary school I was teased because the character *"ku* 九" (nine) was attached to my name: they called me "bergamot" (*kunenbo* 九年母). Nine is considered an unlucky number since it closes the series of numbers from one to nine and therefore indicates death. The Pythagorean school, however, considered it a righteous number since it shows equality by maintaining balance, as we see in three times three. Generally speaking, in Greece odd numbers were thought to be better than even numbers. The *Book of Changes* also contrasts odd numbers as yang to even numbers as yin, and, based on the fact that it considers nine to be representative of odd numbers, it calls the line of yang "nine." In any event, nine is used in several contexts, such the nine springs (Hades), the nine-level Pure Land, the nine heavens, and the ninefold (imperial palace). Nine cannot be simply dismissed as a sign of bad or good luck.

The essential thing about nine is that it has a deep relationship with dialectics as the square of three. The mystic Raimundus Lullus[10] proposed three groups of three so-called absolute predicates and divine participations, for a total of nine. The number nine had a particular meaning for Jakob Böhme[11] and Hegel as well. Three is inadequate to symbolize dialectics with numbers; it must be three times three: nine. In the science of studying personal names there are eighty-one numbers indicating good and bad luck in the creation of names. The reason is that eighty-one is the square of nine. Nine has become a mystical kernel. Even the Indian philosophy of the Vaiśesika school distinguishes nine realities forming the basic elements of all things: earth, water, fire, air, ether, time, space, soul, and mind.

Whether we look at the meaning of *"ku"* or the meaning of *"ki,"* the name Kuki is undoubtedly charged with a metaphysical coloring. Objectively speaking, the biggest probability is that when three groups of three devils gather—three red, three blue, and three black—a Kuki (nine devils) is born. Buddhist scriptures again give us dogmatic answers to the question of how "the geometry of devils" developed.

In the section on "Hungry Ghosts" of the first volume of the *Treatise on the Ten Abodes of the Mind (Jūjūshinron)* we read: "There are three species of devils: those with no, little, or great talents. Since each of the three species is further divided into three, we actually have nine types of devils." We find the most detailed description of devils in the "Hell" chapter of the thirty-first volume of the *Treatise on Following the Right Principles (Junseiriron)*: "There are three species of devils: those with no, little, or great talents. There are three types of devils with no talents: the devil with the torch mouth, the needle mouth, and the stinky mouth. There are also three types of devils with little talents: the devil with the needle hair, the stinky hair, and the devil with the lump. Furthermore, the devils with great talents are also divided into three: the shrine beseeching devil, the trash beseeching devil, and the prosperous devil." The devils with no talents belonging to the first species are the devils that cannot find any food. Among this type of devils, the devil with the torch mouth is the one continuously spewing flames from his mouth. The devil with the needle mouth cannot eat anything, even if he sees something delicious, because his mouth is as small as the hole of a needle. The devil with the stinky mouth cannot eat anything because he vomits everything he puts in his mouth as a result of the stench filling his mouth. The devils with little talents, which belong to the second species, somehow appease their hunger and thirst by eating impure things. Among them, the devil with the needle hair stings himself and others with his body covered with needles. The devil with the stinky hair is the one whose dirty fur emanates a terrible stench. The devil with a lump is the one with a big boil in his throat. The devils with great talents, which form the third species of devils, are devils without any problem related to eating. Among them, the shrine beseeching devil eats the offering left by people inside the tutelary shrines. The trash beseeching devil eats the leftovers that people discard and he picks up. The prosperous devil is a powerful figure whose blessings are said to be as big as those found in heaven. Since each of the three species of devils is divided into three types each, three times three means that we have a "Kuki"—"nine types of devils."

If devils were like Socrates' *daimōn,* we would not be too concerned about nine devils getting together. They appear to be a group of *diaboli,* however, as the Catholic priest had realized.

3

When I come to consider the sound of "Kuki," I realize that it does not reverberate too well. Both sounds *"ku"* and *"ki"* are jammed, making it impossible to pronounce them clearly. The fact that I usually have a hard time making my name understood on the phone is not only because my name is so rare that others apprehend it with great difficulty. The sounds *"ku"* and *"ki"* do not ride electric waves unless they are chanted with a rhythm, as in the case of those cuckoo clocks produced in the Schwarzwald area of Germany. Once I was unable to hear that my name was called in a meeting and I realized it only afterward.

If I stretch the word and make it longer so as to say Kukī in an attempt to pronounce it clearly, then I encounter other embarrassing results. During the Russo-Japanese War apparently someone in a neutral country was unable to tell who was Russian and who was Japanese between General Kuropatkin[12] and General Kurokī[13]—a quite justifiable mistake. When I was in Heidelberg Mr. Miki Kiyoshi[14] was also there. One day Professor Rickert[15] turned to me and said that in Japan there seemed to be many names ending in "kī," as in "Kukī" and "Mikī." He said the same thing happened in Russia and it seemed to be a common phenomenon in the East. Rickert made words such as Kukī, Mikī, Ugakī, Gorky, Trotsky, and Kandinsky phonetically universal and homogeneous.

During a trip to Brittany in France, I had to leave my name to be put on some purchase that needed to be delivered to my hotel. The shop clerk wrote "Quequi" without hesitation. Since I thought it was funny, I asked him, "Qu'est-ce que Qui" (Who is he?). On another occasion, in a café in Kyoto I was recommended some kind of sweets that looked like biscuits and were called cookies. Being little acquainted with these things, I remember my perplexity. Maybe, if I went to an American pastry shop, they would write my name "Cookie."

In Japan, too, whenever I shop at a store for the first time, they write my name on the delivery tag with the characters 久木 (red oak). This name would be better pronounced Hisagi.

> *Nubatama no/yo no fukeyukeba/hisagi ofuru/kiyoki kawara ni/chidori shiba naku*
>
> YAMABE NO AKAHITO
>
> As the night grows deep/in darkness black as beads of jet,/ where the red oak grow/along the clean-swept river beach/the plovers keep endlessly crying.[16]
>
> *Kozo sakishi/hisagi ima saku/itazura ni/tsuchi ni ka ochimu/ miru hito nashi ni*
>
> ANONYMOUS[17]
>
> The red oak that last year bloomed/now blooms./To no purpose/it will scatter to the ground/while no one comes to see it.

Occasionally there is a kind store clerk who writes my name with the characters 久喜 (long-lasting gladness). Meaning "eternal joy," it reminds me of Spinoza's *Ethics* and Beethoven's Ninth Symphony—is this too presumptuous?

A gardener once wrote my name with the characters 久貴 (eternally precious). At a hot-spring hotel someone wrote 久城 (eternal castle) on my bill. *Ewiges Schloss* (eternal castle) feels like a Wagnerian opera. Kuki, written with the characters 苦喜 (bitter joy), would make the science of names argue that it is half good and half bad fortune. I have yet to meet someone cynical enough who would compare me to the owner of complicated feelings of the "painful pleasure" and "sweet sadness" type. But a Frenchman living in Japan once wrote me a letter with Kuki 茎 (stalk) written on the envelope. He was an expert in Japanese literature who could write Japanese limericks, but in this case he clearly did not know what to do. Even stranger, if someone were to write Kuki with the character 豉 (fermented soybean), the post office might have difficulties delivering the letter, although it would be a nice joke: this *"kuki"* is an ancient word indicating a kind of *nattō*.

There is also a river fish called *kuki,* although I do not know the characters used to write it. *Kuki* is another name for dace.[18] When I was a student, I received a postcard from Kojima Kikuo[19] who had climbed Mt. Akagi.[20] He had pasted the skin of a white birch on the card. He wrote that he had eaten a fish called *kuki*. That was the first time I heard of the existence of this fish. Later I tried this fish when I went to Mt. Akagi myself, but I no longer remember its taste. In the summer of the year before last, while I was passing by Akagi after going to the town of Ikaho, I ordered *kuki* for lunch, but since I was told that in the past few days they were unable to catch any, I was given a char[21] instead. After lunch I laid down to take a nap, but I could not sleep; there were too many horseflies, maybe because of the proximity of farms. While staring at the ceiling I kept on thinking about the possible etymology of *kuki*. Given the fact that in classical language the word *"kuki"* 岫 indicates a grotto in a mountain, the *kuki* of Akagi probably comes from the fact that this fish lives in the water flowing in the recesses of these grottoes. If we go one step further in our etymological search, we reach the noun form *"kuki"* 漏き from the verb *"kuku"* 漏く, which means "to pass through." The fish might be called *kuki* because it passes through the clefts in the rocks with the water.

I tried to compose a couple of poems:

> *Ashihiki no/yama no ogawa o/uguiko no/iwama tobikuki/sa hashireru ka mo*
>
> The baby dace/sailing across/the mountain brook,/foot-stretching mountain,/indeed he runs.
>
> *Kusamakura/tabi no susabi ni/kuki naniga/shikuu ki ni nari/kiku no yakimono*
>
> As a pastime on my journey,/grass as my pillow,/I ask what a *kuki* might be./I am in the mood to eat one:/a broiled dace.

4

There is a factual relationship between *kuki* 岫 (mountain grotto) and *kuki* 九鬼 (nine devils) that goes beyond a simple case of homophony. A fishing village in the Kitamuro district of the Kishū area is called Kuki 九鬼. This Kuki village is located deep in the bay. Surrounded by mountains on three sides, it looks like a grotto. The theory according to which the village was called Kuki because it is located in a grotto appears to be correct. The fact that the spelling of the village's name changed from "mountain grotto" to "nine devils" points to the negotiations between geography and history. The surroundings of Kuki village are filled with devils: Mt. Yaki (mountain of the eight devils), Mikizaki (cape three devils), Onigajō (devil's castle).

One October morning on a fine autumn day, the steamboat that I boarded at Owase entered the port of Kuki after about an hour. The waves were quiet. The green on the mountains was fresh, and the color of the sea was darker than the indigo plant. The village was climbing the mountain's slope from bottom to top. The tangerines had just begun to turn yellow. The pale red early-flowering cherry trees and the second-bloom peach trees were blooming beautifully, together with the golden sweet osmanthus. On the shore many fishing boats were tied up, and on the roadside dried horse mackerels were spread out all over the place. The season was still a little too early for the renowned yellowtails.

Apparently it was a man by the name of Yakushimaru, who lived at the beginning of the Ashikaga period, who called this village Kuki for the first time. But the history of this place goes back to the time of the Genpei wars. In any event, in the past there was a fortress here. Now the castle ruins are wide open and an imposing house stands in the middle—the house of those newly rich thanks to yellowtails. The village shrine, known as the Kuki Shrine 九木 (nine trees), was located in a dense forest. The fact that "tree" (*ki* 木) rather than "devil" (*ki* 鬼) was used in the name of the shrine might indicate a process of Shintoification of the type "original ground, manifest trace."[22] The temple—the Shinganji of the Sōtō school—looked over the entire village of Kuki from a high place. While I was climbing the stone steps I noticed that a naked man wearing a simple loincloth was reclining in front of the main hall. My guide told me that he was the abbot. When I bowed, the abbot apologized, saying that he was basking in the sun because of his weak body. At present there are several families with the name of Kuki who live in this area. The Kuki Umanosuke family and the Kuki Samanosuke family are fighting over who should be the head family. Umanosuke changed his name to Moritaka and went to Tokyo, where he became the founder of some religion. Samanosuke practices medicine in Sakhalin. Relatives of both families still live in this village. The present village headman is Samanosuke's younger brother. The abbot told me all this not knowing that my name was Kuki too. I listened to him as if I were listening to a fairy tale or something like that. I was planning to leave when the abbot took a pocket watch that was lying by his side and stopped me saying that he was going to stay in the sun for thirty minutes and still had fifteen minutes left.

During the Genroku period[23] in this village there were one hundred families. A song written at that time says:

> A thousand families in Owase, ninety-nine are Kuki,
> If the temple adds one, one hundred families, one hundred families.

Prostitution had taken place since ancient times for the seamen. In the past there were brothels and more than a hundred prostitutes. This was a kind of pleasure quarter for seamen. An old song says:

> Thirty days at Toba, twenty days at Matoya,
> One simple night at pretty Kuki Bay.

When I was walking on the seashore, looking around, I noticed several bars and cafés, lined up on the street facing the port, that reminded one of the past:

> How can you forget the place of yellowtails,
> Kuki port at the foot of Mt. Yaki?
> Well, oshashanoshan,
> Oh, oshashanoshan.
>
> Waves breaking on Kuki Cape
> Bloom as flowers after smashing on the rocks.
> Well, oshashanoshan,
> Oh, oshashanoshan.

While looking at the quiet evening sea, I listened to women with heavy makeup taking a samisen and singing the Kuki tunes with high-pitched voices. A steamboat entered the bay leaving waves behind, tugging several fishing boats. The fishermen had returned to the port.

A long, long time ago, the port of Kuki was a den of pirates from Kumano. The spoils of pillage—people and goods—were hidden deep in this port. Mt. Yaki was a renowned place for robbers. This place was widely known for the murder of pilgrims going to Kumano. On a moonlit evening I went to Onigajō. Several ghastly caves stood in a row in front of the sea. There was a rock called Devils Lookout where devils are said to keep on the watch for wayfarers on the Mihama highway. A legend says that Sakanoue no Tamuramaro,[24] thanks to the miraculous power of Kannon, conquered the devils and subjugated the pirates. I felt as if I were looking at a scene from a Buddhist scripture: "West of the Senbu region there are five hundred beaches. Among them two stand out. One, however, is populated by devils. On each beach there are two hundred and fifty castles. In one castle live the devils with virtue and power; in another castle live the devils without virtue and power" (*Junseiriron,* vol. 31). The ceilings of the caves hung over my head, completely dark. Reflecting the moonbeams, Kumano Bay in front of me was shiny like the devil's mirror. When I turned to the right, the pine, the sand, the street, and the hills of Shichirimihama had all disappeared in the distance, melting in a bewitching silver color.

In the *Kokon Chomonjū* (Stories heard from writers old and new),[25] there is a suggestive story. "On the eighth day of the Seventh Month, 1171, a boat reached the beach of Yoshima in Izu province. The islanders thought the boat had been blown by a strong wind. When they turned to look at it, they saw it had stopped seven or eight steps away from the land. After tying the four sides of the boat with a rope to rocks at the bottom of the sea, eight devils descended from the boat, entered the sea, and landed on shore. The islanders gave them *sake* made with millet, and the demons drank it like horses without saying a single word. They were eight or nine feet tall, and their hair was like that of a demon. Their bodies were dark red, and their eyes were round like the eyes of monkeys. They were all naked. There was no hair on their bodies. They braided some bulrush and tied it around their waist. Their bodies were tattooed with different patterns. Ornamental rims were hanging around their bodies. Each of them had a stick six or seven feet long. The islanders came with bows and arrows. The devils asked for the weapons. Since the islanders were reluctant to give them away, the devils took their sticks and raised their voices, killing first the islanders who had the arrows. Of the nine people who were hit, five died. Four survived, although they were wounded. Then the devils emitted fire from their armpits. Fearing they would all be killed, the islanders brought out the bows and arrows offered to the gods in the shrine and turned toward the devils. At that point the devils entered the sea, returned to their boat, and boarded it. They left immediately, drawn by the winds" (Book 17). Although we do not know whether these devils came from the port of Kuki, there is no doubt they were some kind of pirates. Later the Kuki family transferred from Kuki village to Toba in Shima.[26] The largest ship during the attack on Korea of 1592 was called "Oniyado" (dwelling of devils).

In *Shōō Dōwa* we read: "Places named Kuki (nine devils), Yaki (eight devils), Sanki (three devils), Goki (five devils) were all inhabited by robbers" (pt. 3, vol. 2). Undoubtedly the forces of darkness transformed the "devils" *(oni)* of Kuki village into "nine devils" *(kuki)*.

5

Although, of course, I love quiet mountains, I cannot refrain from loving that blue sea. Furthermore, in my blood there is also the habit of liking the whole gamut of adventure and the bizarre. To this day, I cannot break it. Maybe, after all, I cannot cut my blood relationship with pirates.

From ancient times my house has followed the custom of saying, "fortune in, demons in" at the bean-scattering ceremony at the beginning of the year.[27] It is an invitation to fortune and demons to come together. Hiraga Gennai called for "fortune in, demons out," but I was prohibited from doing so by nature. Faust's lamentation, "Oh, two spirits live in my heart," never leaves me. My wish is to dance with the Nine Muses in a golden haze, but nine devils tie my hands and feet to the ground of hell. Nine devils! A name is not always just "voice and smoke." The name is also inseparable from the body and is one's own nature. To me my name is my prehistory, my mythology, my destiny.

Negishi

In a normal year the seventeenth of July would have been scorching, but this year it had already cooled off during the preceding four or five days, as if autumn had already come. For some time I had had the idea of visiting Negishi, but it was on that early evening that, all of a sudden, I decided to go. I once lived in Negishi when I was seven or eight years old. At that time my father lived in Sannen-chō, Kōjimachi. My mother lived separately, in Naka-Negishi's Ogyō no Matsu, together with my brother, who was three years older than I, and myself. That was forty years ago, and until that day I had never returned to Negishi. During the last several years I had been mainly in Kyoto, and before that I lived nine years in Europe. Earlier on I was mostly in Tokyo, but I was still in the bloom of my youth and did not have the time to look back on my past. Thus I visited my beloved Negishi for the first time in forty years.

It was probably a little before five in the afternoon when I stepped out of the car at Ueno's Uguisudani, a place with a sweeping view. Under the gloomy sky I could look across as far as Asakusa and Honjō. This is the part of Tokyo with which I am particularly familiar. As I was going down the asphalted slope of Uguisudani reminiscing on the past, on the left my eyes stopped on restaurants such as "Ikaho" and "Shihobara." These names were there in old times, when they were impressed in my memory. Eventually I reached the street that divides Naka-Negishi on the left and Tansumachi on the right—a street popularly known as "Negishi Grand Avenue." If you keep going a little further you find the Kakinomoto Hospital on the left and, further down, the Senjuin temple. At the time when I was living in Negishi, Professor Okakura Tenshin[1] lived just around this area. I searched for his house, wondering whether it might still be there, but I was unable to find it. Since then something else must have been built in its place.

After a while the street narrowed. Although on the left side there is the Shimotani Hospital, an imposing Western-style building, I was surprised to find so many old houses that preserved the elegance of the past. My brother and I used to pass this street on a ricksha every day on our way from Negishi to the elementary school attached to the building for high school teachers in Kanda Hitotsubashi. I remember that a stupa with Sanskrit letters could be seen from the street. Wondering what might have happened after so many years, I kept on walking until I reached a temple by the name of Seizōin. I could see the head of the stupa with the Sanskrit letters flickering on top of the zinc fence. I was truly filled with joy. There was a street that turns to the left following the fence. I remembered that Negishi's elementary school was around here. When I inquired I was told that, yes, it was still there. I approached the school, expecting to see a building made of concrete, but I found an old wooden structure instead. I asked the clerk of a stationery store, a lady forty-five, forty-six, years of age—a store located in front of the school where I bought a pocket notebook and a pencil—if this area had not burned down after the big earthquake.[2] She said the fire had burned down everything up to the street at the foot of the slope, but this area had been spared. Then I asked her whether the elementary school was just as it used to be a long time ago, to which question she answered with a face expressing nostalgic thoughts, "It sure is! It is exactly the same!" When I was living in Negishi this woman might have been a girl two or three years younger than me who lived in the same area. I remember that my mother had asked the principal of this Negishi normal elementary school, Professor Ōtomo Hyōma, to tutor both my brother and me, and that he used to come to our house several times a week. The instruction was held in a detached house at the edge of the garden. Apparently, being a man of science, Professor Ōtomo was good at making scientific experiments with the chemicals and glass tubes he brought with him. Although he was a quiet old man of around fifty who did not talk much and never scolded us, I was always afraid of him. I was once on the garden's pine tree with my brother when he suddenly showed up and, feeling that I was doing something awfully bad, I fell out of the tree while trying hurriedly to come down. At that time I had come to the Negishi elementary school once or twice to meet Professor Ōtomo. I peeped into the playground of the school but did not remember anything about it. But since it was certainly a wooden building, and considering the fact that I was now facing an old structure, it was probably the same building as in the past. Near the windows of the schoolhouse there was a drawing of someone doing physical exercise, accompanied by the sentence "Radio exercises for thirty minutes every morning at six." Who would have ever imagined something like "radio exercises" forty years ago? Professor Ōtomo, who liked physics, would have been really excited had he known that something like a radio existed! When I walked back to where the stupa in the Seizōin temple could be seen, I heard the sound of a radio coming from the front of a little shop. It was such a strange feeling for someone like myself who was coming back to this place after forty years.

Retracing my steps from there, I came to a place called the "Negishi Club" and from there the street continued in three different directions. This area was exactly as I remembered it. How happy I was to see that it had escaped the earthquake! If I turned to the right there, and then again to the left, I should find a house with a gate, a little off the street. I wandered around the area for quite a while before I finally saw the house. The old entrance was somewhat familiar to me; it was probably the original entrance. I stood still in front of the gate, feeling an unutterable longing.

If I remember well, I lived in this house for one or two years. I think I was seven when we moved in, and eight or nine when we moved out. We were my mother, my brother, and I. We had at least three maids. We also had a houseboy and a ricksha man outside. My mother spent her time reading or playing the koto. My elder sister lived in Sannen-chō with my father, but she used to come to Negishi every Sunday and practice the tea ceremony with my mother on the second floor. My brother and I sometimes went to our father's place. When the time came to return home, he would inquire about my mother saying, "How is Mom?" and he would give us fruit or something as a present for her. My parents were separated and they never visited each other.

I was a first or second grade student at the normal elementary school at that time, and I used to play in the yard when I got back from school. At the front of the yard there were one or two big pine trees. There were also Japanese and Chinese quinces that sometimes bloomed and sometimes bore fruit. On the side of the mezzanine, at the back of the house there was a gigantic old tree that looked like a hackberry or something of the sort, and also a big banana tree. I loved to make bamboo *katana* swords, hang them from my waist, and run up the little hills pretending to be a soldier. I remember that one day I was severely scolded by my mother and taken to the hospital because I had stabbed myself on the side with one of these bamboo sticks and was bleeding. She also scolded me once after our neighbor had complained to her about me. The reason was that I had climbed on the roof, torn off pieces of plaster from it, and thrown them down onto our neighbor's house. Sometimes I also played soldier with my brother; I was naughtier than he, and a bad loser. I was pretty much spoiled by my mother, who always bathed me. Once she pointed at my navel and said I was born from that part of her body. It seems that I was a lonesome boy in my early childhood, for I liked to go to bed early, when everybody was lively, talking by my bed.

Professor Okakura Tenshin came to visit my mother quite often. This was when he was still the director of the School of Fine Arts in Ueno. At that time my mother was probably thirty-six or thirty-seven years old. It happened that, when my father was an ambassador to the United States, he entrusted my mother to Mr. Okakura, sending her back to Japan before him. Since then a close relationship had developed between my mother and Mr. Okakura. There were days when he would have dinner with my mother in the back room on the mezzanine, and I would listen to him while I leaned on my mother's lap. Mr. Okakura used to tell us about how he had met a tiger in Korea and stories of that sort. One night he had seen two eyes that were glittering in the darkness and, according to him, those were the eyes of a tiger. He also told of his glorious and shocking deeds, like the one about how he had swaggered at the view of his two Korean guides, who were a pair of rascals and wore guns. Moreover, apparently Mr. Okakura used to tell my mother many things about the School of Fine Arts. Once my childish heart was amused when he said that he had reprimanded one of his students because the young man had chosen "a moon over a graveyard" as the theme for his work, which was not interesting at all. Mr. Okakura also took me once to the School of Fine Arts. Scattered in a large tatami-floor room, many students were drawing and painting while sitting here and there on the floor. To my young eyes all the students looked like adults. The artist Hashimoto Gahō[3] made a sketch painting of me, making me wear a three-cornered hat with a red tuft. I kept that portrait for quite a while but then—I don't know when—I gave it away to a school friend. Now that I think about it, I regret it. Gahō drew a book of samples for me and, although I think it was a little bit after the Negishi period, Kawabata Gyokushō[4] also drew a sample book for me once. When we were children, we often went to Kamakura for the summer vacation. At that time, the seashore promenade was still surrounded by fields. My father used to make me paint paintings there. He was always very glad to see that I liked painting, and I think he wanted me to become a painter. He sent me to study painting with Kawabata Gyokushō who was trying to escape the summer heat in a villa nearby. I hated the idea of becoming a painter, but it was no use saying it. When he asked me what I wanted to be in life, I answered that I wanted to become an army general. That was during the Sino-Japanese War. When my father heard me, he laughed. To think that I did not become a painter, despite the love that both my father and Mr. Okakura had for the fine arts, indicates how unrelated human destinies are in this world. Mr. Okakura once drew me a portrait of a Chinese man on a donkey. To this day, that painting remains clearly lodged in my memory.

Speaking of donkeys, that reminds me that Mr. Okakura once told me he was going to ask my father, who lived in Sannen-chō, to buy me a donkey so that I could ride it to school. I waited and waited for the donkey, wondering when it would come. But the donkey never came. Most probably my father, who hated extravagance, resisted the idea of the donkey. There was another occasion, however, on which I benefited from Mr. Okakura's intercession. He said children needed a swing or something similar and told me he would ask my father to order one for me. Shortly after that a swing was built in the middle of the yard.

I also once went hunting to Mt. Tsukuba with Mr. Okakura. I think we went with Mr. Okakura's eldest son, Kazuo, and my brother—a group of four people. I also remember that we went astray for a while in the mountains, and that at the foot of the mountain we rode a horse. While we were resting at a teahouse, an old lady grasped me and said with an air of flattery, "This little boy looks just like his dad!" Mr. Okakura laughed without saying a word.

The impression I have of Mr. Okakura is that of a good uncle. Once I caught a cold and lay in bed looking at a picture book. There was a picture of Renba and Rinshōjo.[5] Mr. Okakura explained their story to me and, grasping my arm strongly, he said, "Wouldn't you pledge eternal friendship to me?" I also went, though rarely, to Mr. Okakura's house. He loved dogs. He had a big dog that once cut his iron chain with his teeth. As a result, he called the dog "Iron Eater." I also remember that when I told him my father used to make me tell visitors that he was absent, even if he was at home, Mr. Okakura said, "I don't like using such excuses." On the side of the mezzanine a banana tree bore lots of small fruits. Mr. Okakura taught me that those fruits were edible when they became bigger. We can find bananas in the shop windows on the wayside now, but at that time there was no way for children to know about the existence of such a fruit. Now that I think about it, it sounds like an old story.

In a sense, I cannot think about Negishi without relating it to Professor Okakura Tenshin. I tried to have a look inside, over the wall, wondering in my recollection of the past whether the big pine tree or the banana tree would still be there, but I saw nothing.

From there I went to Ogyō no Matsu. Although I had heard that Ogyō no Matsu had already disappeared, I could not help being strongly moved by the knowledge of the past, thinking of the luxuriant vegetation. But at least it was a relief to find that a thick stump five or six feet tall had been left there. I was also happy to see posted a picture of the pine tree in its original splendor at the rear of the house. On the side there was a stone monument with the following inscription carved on the back: "This tree withered in the third year of the Shōwa era (1928). It was cut down in the fifth year (1930), and its memory was preserved by erecting this stone monument in order to commemorate its remains. May of the fifth year of the Shōwa era (1930)." I regretted that I had not visited the place right after I came back from Europe. As this was in the fourth year of Shōwa (1929), I would have been able to see the pine tree, even though it would have already been dead. My mother used to bring me here quite often. When there was some festival, stalls would occupy the whole area under the tree. After walking around for a while, I was surprised to see that there was a bewitching geisha district. I wondered whether it had been there during my childhood, but in any event I was still too young to have had the slightest hint of its existence. As I found it strange, I inquired about it, and the answer was that the quarter was created one year before the earthquake. There were posters everywhere announcing Negishi's Bon dance festival. When I came to a square originally called "the remains of the Odaka estate," the Bon dance turrets and the dance platform were beautifully decorated with paper lanterns and curtains. Men and women gathered, both young and old, although they were not dancing yet, for the dance was supposed to start at seven o'clock. Then I was attracted by a notice that said "Fly-Catching Day[6]—July 20th." I felt that it was rather ridiculous to use the English word "day" at a time of extreme nationalism when the Bon dance was being revived. I recalled that my colleague, Professor Omodaka Hisataka, once joked saying, *"Nandē, nandē, nandei, nandei, nani o itteyagarundei,"*[7] and I wondered why we had to make such an effort and use dummy words like "day," which come from the country of the red-haired Europeans, having in our native language such beautiful words as *"hi,"* which refers to the Sun Goddess. With these thoughts lingering in my mind, I came out again to Negishi Grand Avenue, and I remembered the old place where Professor Okakura Tenshin, an extreme nationalist of his times, had lived. While I was in Europe I was absorbed in reading his *Book of Tea* and *The Ideal of the Far East.* Then I climbed the slope of Uguisudani and arrived at the Ryōdaishi temple in Ueno. On both sides of the street dozens of garden lanterns were aligned, just as they used to be forty years ago. ——— [17 July 1934]

Remembering
Mr. Okakura Kakuzō

When I was eight or nine years old and a first or second grade elementary student, my father lived in Kōjimachi's Sannen-chō, while my mother lived separately in Shimotani's Naka-Negishi, near Ogyō no Matsu, together with my elder brother and myself. Mr. Okakura lived in Kami-Negishi at that time, and he used to come and visit my mother. That was the period when he was the director of the School of Fine Arts in Ueno. My mother was thirty-six or thirty-seven years old, one or two years older than Mr. Okakura. Since I am talking about a time when my father lived in Washington as ambassador plenipotentiary to the United States, and when the future prime minister Saitō[1] was a navy lieutenant and a military officer at the legation, I am referring to a very long time ago. For some reason my father entrusted my mother to Mr. Okakura and made them return to Japan on the same ship. I was still in my mother's womb and was born after she came back to Japan. My mother's close relationship with Mr. Okakura started in those days, and we used to call him "uncle."

I have heard that, maybe because it was the era of the Rokumeikan,[2] my mother liked to dance when she was in America, but when we were in Negishi she devoted her time to calligraphy, koto playing, the tea ceremony, and flower arranging. Except for Mr. Okakura, very few people came to visit my mother; only some female relatives visited us occasionally. Mr. Okakura used to come in the evenings. Often he had supper with my mother in the flickering light of a small paper-covered lantern, in an inner room of the mezzanine. I always noticed *sake* bottles on the table. I also witnessed his red face sometimes. I leaned on my mother's lap and listened to Mr. Okakura's stories. I also remember him telling a story about how he had met a tiger in Korea. He said he was in the road at night when he saw two eyes glittering in the darkness. According to him, that was a tiger. He also told of his glorious and shocking deeds, like the time he exaggerated his own strength and courage, which stunned his two Korean guides, a pair of rascals wearing guns. He also shared with my mother many stories about the School of Fine Arts. Being still a child, I used to be amused by the things he said, such as when he reprimanded a student because he had painted the moon rising over a graveyard, which he considered pretty dull.

Mr. Okakura once took me with him to the School of Fine Arts. In an extremely large tatami-floored hall, students seated all over the place were painting. Being a child, to me they all seemed adults. Mr. Okakura mentioned my father's name to Hashimoto Gahō, introducing me to him. Gahō made a sketch of me wearing a three-cornered hat with a red tuft used in the affiliated elementary school. I remember the sketch's form and colors very well, for I had it with me for a year or half a year. I gave it away, however, maybe to a maidservant who wanted it. Whomever I gave it to, I regret it now. Later on, Gahō sent me a sketchbook with samples of paintings. I gave that book away as well, maybe to a school friend.

Also at that time Mr. Okakura himself drew a painting of a Chinese person on a donkey and gave it to me. I remember that painting very well, too. He also said it would be good to ask my father for a donkey so that I could ride to school. I waited and waited for the donkey to come from Sannen-chō, but the donkey never came. Furthermore, Mr. Okakura said that children needed something like a swing, and he assured me he would ask my father to order one for me. Soon after that a swing was built in the middle of the yard.

Mr. Okakura also took me with him to do some hunting on Mt. Tsukuba. We went together with Mr. Okakura's eldest son, Kazuo, and my brother—a group of four people. I remember that we got lost in the mountains, and also that we rode horses through the fields at the foot of the mountain. While we were resting at a teahouse, the old lady of the house flattered us by comparing Mr. Okakura and myself, saying, "The little boy looks just like his father!" Mr. Okakura simply laughed without saying a word.

Once, having caught a cold, I lay in bed looking at a picture book. There was a picture of Renba and Rinshōjo promising eternal friendship to each other. Mr. Okakura explained the story to me and, grasping my arm strongly, asked whether I would pledge eternal friendship to him. That was the only time I felt he was a frightening uncle. At the side of the mezzanine there was a tall banana tree that had once borne many fruits. Mr. Okakura explained to me that the bananas could be eaten when they got bigger. We can find bananas in the shop windows on the wayside now, but at that time children did not know what a banana was.

Once in a while I also went to Mr. Okakura's house. I remember that his Japanese-style studio had plenty of light and was very pleasant to visit. Looking back in my vague memory of his room, I think the decoration consisted mainly of Chinese motifs. Mr. Okakura loved dogs. He had a big dog that once cut his iron chain with his teeth. As a result, he called the dog "Iron Eater." The yard was not very large, but there were dumpling and sushi stands all over it, and my mother took me sometimes to those stands. Mr. Okakura must have invited people related to the School of Fine Arts and must have held parties in the garden. Taikan, Kanzan, and Shunsō[3] would have been there too. I do not remember the occasion, but once I naively told Mr. Okakura that when I was at my father's house in Sannen-chō, he used to make me say that he was absent even if he was at home. Mr. Okakura just smiled and said, "I don't like using such excuses."

Mr. Okakura's younger brother, Yoshisaburō,[4] lived near him. I also remember going there. He showed me his collection of stamps and coins. Mr. Kakuzō and Mr. Yoshisaburō made totally different impressions on me. I did not know the word "genius" at that time, but Mr. Kakuzō was deeply impressed in my young mind as being one. Recently when I heard that an anonymous lady who was listening to my radio program had commented that I talked pretty much like Mr. Okakura Yoshisaburō, I could not help smiling grimly.

Suddenly my mother had to go to Kyoto alone. One night I was lying on my mother's lap when Mr. Okakura, looking at me, said solemnly, "Poor kid!" Apparently my father had sent my mother to Kyoto in order to keep her apart from Mr. Okakura. Later on I heard that Mrs. Okakura was jealous of her husband's acquaintance with my mother. In any event, my mother finally went to Kyoto, and my brother and I were sent to stay for a while at the house of Mr. Kubota Kanae, the director of the Ueno museum at the time. Afterwards my mother came back from Kyoto and lived again apart from my father. When I was fourteen or fifteen years old and in the first or second grade of junior high school, I stayed at the private school of Mr. Sakai Saisui, spending the weekends from Saturday to Sunday at either my father's or my mother's place. I was playing alone in the yard of my mother's house one Sunday, early in the morning, when suddenly I exchanged a glance with Mr. Okakura who was exiting the house and proceeding toward the gate. I have a very clear picture in my mind of that concrete scene, but I cannot bear to talk about it. Soon afterward my mother got divorced from my father....

With regard to Mr. Okakura, my father used to say that he had been of great help in public affairs but had caused many troubles to our family. Sometimes, after Mr. Okakura went to the Boston museum, Americans would visit my father with a letter of introduction from him. Typically the letters were written in India ink on rolled paper and came inside a Japanese envelope. During my college years, and until my graduation, I was in charge of our family relations with Western people, so I more or less knew, though indirectly, about Mr. Okakura's movements. According to my father, the Americans said that if there were in the world of Japanese politics such people as Mr. Okakura was in the world of the fine arts, things would be great. Mr. Okakura was constantly traveling between the United States and Japan. Sometimes he would come home to pay a visit to my father and have supper together with many other people, but I never met him. The houseboy told me that when Mr. Okakura got drunk, he would urinate at the entrance, a fact that was confirmed by my father's mistress, who spoke ill of him.

At that time, for six months during his stay in Japan, Mr. Okakura lectured on the history of oriental art at the Imperial University in Hongō.[5] One day I was going through the Red Gate on my way to the classroom when I saw him coming from the opposite direction. He was wearing a blue, Chinese-style suit. Although I had not seen him for about ten years, I recognized him immediately. There was no way that he could recognize me, for I was but a little boy the last time he saw me. I kept my eyes lowered when we passed each other, and let him go away without bowing at him. That was in part because I am somewhat reserved, but also because I had mixed feelings for him since I thought he was responsible for my mother's fall into a wretched destiny. That was the last time I saw Mr. Okakura. He died at the Akakura hot spring in 1914. The funeral was held in Yanaka, and I went on my father's behalf.

I heard that Mr. Okakura was an extraordinary person, and that his lectures on oriental art were truly outstanding, but at that time I was governed by personal feelings toward him and never attended his lectures. Now that I think about it, I truly regret it. During my stay in the West I was deeply moved reading the original versions of *Cha no Hon* (The book of tea) and *Tōhō no Risō* (The ideal of the fat East). Sometimes I gave these books to Westerners as presents. Before long, both my father and my mother died. Now I feel only an almost undiluted respect for Mr. Okakura. All my memories of him are beautiful, both the bright and the dark aspects. No one is bad. Everything is as beautiful as a poem.

I still keep with great care several letters that Mr. Okakura sent to my father. I framed one and hung it in the tearoom of my house in Kyoto. There is a special beauty in his characteristic penmanship:

> Dear Sir, I am pleased to hear about your increasing prosperity. I went to Tokyo last night and I will travel West tomorrow evening. It is my intention to stay without fail at the Ōsaka Hotel until the night of the seventh. First of all, I would like to thank you for all the consideration and support that you bestow on me. The title of my lecture on the eighth will be "On the Preservation of National Treasures." You will forgive my enumerating trite matters in front of Your Excellency. However, I would like to attempt to give an exposition of the current preservation techniques that are used in other nations of the world. I rely on your approval, as I would like to raise our people's awareness. I am aware that many things will encounter your criticism. My words are given in expectation of a great future.
>
> In haste, sincerely yours,
>
> October 4th

Mr. Okakura wrote this letter during his stay in Izura; he addressed it to my father who had gone to the Kansai area in western Japan. I am glad to see that the letter vividly shows how my father and Mr. Okakura maintained their friendship until the end, regardless of their complicated relation at the family level.

I remember one more thing about Mr. Okakura. Shortly after my graduation from college, the viscount Hamao Harata[6] told me that Mr. Okakura had recently been to Paris attending Bergson's lectures. It is not without interest for me to imagine Mr. Okakura listening to Bergson's lectures in the auditorium of the Collège de France.

Remembering
Mr. Iwashita Sōichi

I have so many recollections of Mr. Iwashita that I almost do not know what to write. Moreover, I was so close to him that I feel it is difficult for me to write about him. I became very familiar with Mr. Iwashita when I first came to know him at the First High School, although he took English as his first language and I took German. I should say that we truly became friends in 1909, when we entered the philosophy department of Tokyo Imperial University together. I believe our friendship reached its peak after Mr. Iwashita left graduate school in 1915, during the several years of his appointment to the Seventh High School in Kagoshima. In other words, this was the time when I was an undergraduate and a graduate student at the university.

That was a budding time for Iwashita. He had no worries about external matters; in a sense, that must have been the happiest time of his life. He was an extremely brilliant man whose talent was unrivaled. Because of his diligence and seriousness in his studies, he was a model student in the truest sense of the word. He was not as erratic as I was, and he was particularly loved by Professor Koeber.[1]

At that time Iwashita lived in Kioichō, Kōjimachi ward, and I lived in Nagatachō. We almost always came back together from the university in Hongō. From Hongō Avenue we crossed the Ochanomizu Bridge; from Takebashi we passed in front of the headquarters of the Imperial Guards Division; and after going through Hanzōmon and Miyakezaka, we parted company in the surrounding of today's Imperial Diet. Since not many people were around and the place was relatively quiet, we could talk about many things. Our houses were in the center of Akasaka Mitsuke, separated only by Shimizudani and Hoshigaoka parks; therefore, we often visited each other. Furthermore, during vacations both Iwashita and I generally went to Kamakura, so that we kept close company almost all year long.

We both felt that at the university the lectures of Professor Koeber were delightful. In addition to lecturing on the outlines of philosophy and the general history of Western philosophy, Koeber gave specialized courses on medieval philosophy, the philosophy of Kant, the phenomenology of Hegel, the French philosophy of the nineteenth century, and more. Iwashita was interested in Hegel. In parallel with the lectures, he apparently read the book on Hegel by Kuno Fischer,[2] a book that he savored in depth since he said it was too good to read quickly. In terms of his approach to the study of the history of philosophy, he benefited from *Studies of the History of Philosophy* by Boutroux.[3] Since he was a devotee of the Catholic faith, Iwashita was deeply interested in the New Scholasticism of Mercier[4] and de Wulf[5] from the time he was a student. This explains why he went to Europe later on to study at the University of Louvain in Belgium. This is also the fundamental origin of his article "The Philosophy of New Scholasticism," which appeared in the book *Philosophy* of the Iwanami series. He also admired Cardinal Newman[6] but did not write about him. This must have been a motive for his studies in England. To think about it now, I feel the strangeness of the changing times to the point that it sounds funny: one day, on the way back from school, Iwashita told me that a Frenchman laughed at him because he had never heard of Bergson even though he was studying philosophy. That was the first time I ever heard the name of Bergson. For his graduation thesis Iwashita wrote on "Augustine's Philosophy of History" in French. I chose the title "The Interrelationship of Matter and Mind," but Professor Koeber expressed his dissatisfaction by saying that the topic was too modern; I remember that even Iwashita looked displeased. With regard to the philosophy of history, Mr. Iwashita consulted Eucken's chapter "The Philosophy of History," which appears in the section on "Systematic Philosophy" of *Die Kultur der Gegenwart* (The culture of the present).[7] He often spoke with me about Augustine's *City of God*. The essay "The City of God" that Iwashita wrote for Iwanami's series on great thinkers, which he dedicated to the late Professor Koeber, has a long history. When he graduated he received a silver watch as a gift from the professor. I remember that Iwashita's research topic in graduate school was Greek philosophy. At that time Dr. Tanaka Hidenaka had just graduated from the university and begun his career as a lecturer of Greek at Tōdai: Iwashita and I were the only students studying Xenophon's *Memorabilia* with him. Iwashita's translucent pronunciation of Greek, as beautiful as a jewel, which I heard during his readings, still remains in my ears. Later on Iwashita wrote the article "Medieval Currents of Thought" for Iwanami's *World Currents of Thought.* In it there is a section titled "Greek Philosophy as an Essential Element of the World Currents of Thought," which shows his deep knowledge of Greek philosophy as well.

At that time Iwashita and I did not talk only about learning; we also discussed the indistinct movements of our hearts. I remember being absorbed in reading *The Autobiography of Saint Theresa of the Child Jesus* that I had received from Iwashita.[8] Knowing that I was looking for Gibbons's *Faith of Our Fathers,*[9] Iwashita told me it was published by Sansaisha or some other press and gave me a copy as a present. In the book he inserted a dark gray ribbon with a pattern of pyrographic flowering plants on it instead of the usual bookmark. He wrote in India ink, "Lord, abide in us," and signed it "Sōichi." Mr. Iwashita was the one who introduced me to Father Ligneul.[10] Since Iwashita's family and my family had originally known each other to a certain degree, our acquaintance extended directly to our families. I remember that I received as a present a beautiful fountain pen from his father who had traveled to the West and that we joined his mother and their son-in-law, the late Mr. Yamamoto and his wife, for a happy family supper. My father often asked me about Mr. Iwashita. I was somehow reserved when talking with Mr. Iwashita, yet I managed to talk about women with him. We ended up talking three times or so about the issue of marriage. The first two times Iwashita introduced the topic; in our later discussion I brought it up myself. Maybe Iwashita and I could have become closer with regard to appearances as well. He once told me of how, out of concern, his mother kept him away from an attractive maid. To think about it now, this is nothing but a minor, smile-provoking episode. At that time Mr. Iwashita played the organ and practiced calligraphy.

That was the time when we were still in our twenties. Later on Mr. Iwashita was appointed to the Seventh High School in Kagoshima and subsequently went to study abroad in Europe. I left for Europe two years later. During my stay in Nice on the Mediterranean shore of France, I received a letter from Iwashita, who was in London. We never had a chance to meet in Europe, but I missed him when in Paris I read the lines, "according to the explanation I received from Mr. Iwashita in Tokyo," following the names of Sylvain Lévi[11] and Meyer, regarding a philosophical and comparative linguistic analysis of the word *"pensée"* in a book collecting conversations by Maurice Blondel.[12]

I returned from the West in 1929 and finally met Mr. Iwashita again after ten years. The first time I saw him wearing a black priest robe I felt a lump in my throat—I don't know why. Since then I would meet him occasionally either at the house of Professor Iwamoto Tei[13] in Yotsuya, together with Tatsuzawa Tsuyoshi, Mitani Takamasa, and Tanaka Kōtarō, or at my house. Since I lived in Kyoto ordinarily, Mr. Iwashita visited me every time he came to the Kansai area. Sometimes he came with Amano Teiyū;[14] at other times there were only the two of us. Iwashita smoked and was fond of a little *sake.* Since we spoke to each other without any barrier, I never felt that I was talking to a priest. I spoke freely and Iwashita was in the mood of his student days—they looked like truly cheerful meetings.

When I heard that he had become director of the Leprosarium of Mt. Kamiyama I was quite surprised. When I asked him why he did it, he only answered that he was asked, but I immediately felt something truly deep behind his words. When I met him after his appointment to the hospital he talked about the leprosarium. I could read between his words the trust and affection that the patients felt for their director, and I also clearly understood Iwashita's total dedication and love for his patients. Undoubtedly Iwashita's life at Kamiyama was as pious as the life of a saint, as strict as the life of a monk, an exposure of the self to the most deeply wretched aspects of life. A third party can hardly imagine the hard work and strife day and night, and yet it seems that he had ample leeway in other respects. I remember that Iwashita was reading Shakespeare at that time, and he told me how he was educating a nurse, saying, "You have an admirer of your *Structure of Iki.*" He often invited me to visit the hospital, reminding me of the beauty of the scenery of Mt. Fuji, but in the end I missed the opportunity to visit while he was alive. I remember that once he told me how happy he was to build a cistern immediately after receiving a large sum of money from Mr. Iwanami Shigeo.[15] He told me about the visit he received from Professor Nishida Kitarō, his wife, and his daughter during their trip to the five lakes of Mt. Fuji, and he even sent me a picture of that meeting. After I indicated to him my interest in the literary works of lepers, he occasionally sent me journals with printed *tanka* and *haiku* written by patients. At the news of his death I went to Kamiyama and was given a tour of the hospital by the present director Chiba. He told me how Mr. Iwashita changed the old facilities in the kitchen and other places into modern equipment. I also heard for the first time that every year Mr. Iwashita disbursed more than ten thousand yen of his own money in order to surmount the hospital's economic difficulties. I was deeply moved when I saw Iwashita's extremely small and simple study room, which he also used as a bedroom, on the second floor of the hospital, the floor reserved for the most critically ill patients.

This might be a minor point, but there is something about which I feel the need to apologize to Mr. Iwashita. When, a few years ago, he came to visit me in Kyoto in the fall, he remarked how beautiful the maple leaves of Takao must be. On that day the weather was fine and, had I offered to go, Iwashita would have immediately followed me with joy. Instead I did not say anything because I was thinking about the lecture I had to deliver the following day and could not feel calm and collected. It would have been proper of me to forget about the lecture and invite him to join me in viewing the maple leaves. I deeply regret my lack of sympathy for someone who had come to visit an old friend, because of my feeling momentarily down as a result of an occasional social responsibility. For that I want to sincerely apologize to Mr. Iwashita. He did not show any sign of disappointment; he talked with me, and then he left.

I lived alone in Kyoto for my official duties and left the members of my family behind in Tokyo. Since things were not going too well in my family—and, of course, I had myself to blame—after much thinking, I ultimately asked Mr. Iwashita to provide my wife with spiritual guidance. I thought I could feel at ease by entrusting this matter to him. Thereupon at that time she must have visited Mr. Iwashita in

Yotsuya once every week to listen to his words. If I am allowed to use some harsh words, I would say that Mr. Iwashita did not lack a mundane, worldly side; I could say that he did not possess the affectation of the religious person. He maintained the balance of an individual carrying a great weight between strong faith and wide education, high morality and deep knowledge. I have met many people so far in my life, but very few are those whom I can trust from the bottom of my heart as Mr. Iwashita. Above all things, he engendered the fragrance of warmheartedness and a serene personality, thus fascinating those who came in contact with him.

When in May of last year I boarded a train bound for Kyoto at Shinbashi station, by chance Mr. Iwashita was sitting together with his mother on the opposite side, and he called me. Noticing the tag of the First Hotel on my luggage, he gave me a cynical smile and said, "That's not a place for you to stay! You shouldn't go there!" He strongly showed his ill feelings for the popular level of that hotel. An acquaintance of Iwashita who was chief of the Educational Bureau of the Shizuoka Prefectural Office, or something like that, sat beside us, and while we were talking about different matters the train reached Odawara. There I got off the train. With one of my bags hanging from his hand Iwashita accompanied me all the way to the exit. When I informed him that my marriage had ended in failure, he kept silent, a dark look on his face. That was the last time I met Iwashita. When I saw his cold face in the coffin at Kamiyama, I could only think that everything was but a dream.

Two or three years ago, while having a quiet supper with him, hoping that he would pay more attention to learning, I encouraged him to write his doctoral dissertation, although I realized I was making an uncalled-for interference. He replied that in the midst of all the chores that were part of his daily job, he would have been unable to do the quiet study required to write a dissertation. After his death, however, I heard that last year he resigned his position as director of the hospital and decided to steep himself in scholarship. This was exactly what I had hoped for; to see him die before he could accomplish this task is beyond regret. In recent years Mr. Iwashita had seriously turned his attention to the issue of Japan; apparently he had felt an earnest concern for Japan even at the level of hobby. He once told me that he thought of selling the family collection of Japanese paintings in order to meet the hospital's expenses, but he could not resolve himself to dispose of it. From the bottom of his heart, he savored the small parlor and the food of the Hyōtei restaurant of Nanzenji. He even wrote me a letter praising my essay "The Japanese Character."

It is truly interesting to notice that, having being entrusted with the development of Asian hospitals, he went to China as a church inspector of northern China, became sick on his way back, and eventually collapsed at Kamiyama. As a man of religion and as a social businessman Iwashita brought with him a great deal of knowledge that would have benefited the construction of the new order in East Asia. There is no doubt that his understanding of Japanese and oriental things would have definitely proved useful in this regard as well. Japan's academia never stopped longing for Iwashita's return as a scholar. Some time ago a person who happened to come to Kamiyama said that Father Iwashita accomplished things that no one else would have been able to do in one hundred years of life. Indeed, that might well be the case. But I would have liked him to live twenty more years. I had great expectations for what he would have done for the justice and the truth of the Japanese land, whether he decided to be active in society as a practical man or in academia as a scholar. ———[January 1941]

A Recollection of
Henri Bergson

I only met twice with Bergson. The first meeting took place after he re-
tired on account of poor health from the presidency of the committee
on international cooperation of the League of Nations, which was
formed after World War I. At that time he only met with very close
friends. I was able to meet him thanks to the good offices of Mr. Ishii
Kikujirō, Japan's ambassador to France, who had connections with
the League of Nations.[1] Mr. Ishii knew Bergson quite well. I am talk-
ing about a meeting that took place fourteen or fifteen years ago.

Bergson's house was located in rue Vital, a quiet street whose name
sounded as if it was related to his philosophy.[2] Not far from the Troca-
dero, this area could be considered Paris's uptown. It was a cold winter
day. After waiting a moment in the reception room, I was shown to his
study on the second floor. He was sitting in a chair, but he stood up
using a stick, and he greeted me with that special French courtesy. The
walls in his study had become bookshelves. In the middle of the room
there was a big desk with many books piled on it. He looked exactly as
I had seen him in a picture—an elegant old man with Parisian style.

He began by asking me where I studied philosophy, which philoso-
phers and which philosophy I specialized in, and he mentioned that
there had been a good philosophy teacher from the United States in To-
kyo. Bergson must have heard about Fenollosa from someone.[3] He
asked about the topic of my graduation thesis at the university, and I an-
swered that I had discussed the interrelationship of matter and mind.
He said this was an issue in which he had been particularly interested.

Then he mentioned that the starting point of his research was Kant's transcendental aesthetics and the mutual confrontation of space and time. He also voiced his skepticism for the same position taken by Spencer,[4] who was widely studied at the time. Although a product of his youth, written when he was still in his twenties, his first book on the notion of pure duration was an answer to this skepticism.[5] Later his interest was taken by the problem of the interrelationship of matter and mind. He dedicated five years to studying the illnesses of memory exclusively and, finally, after seven years of work, he published his second book, *Matière et Mémoire* (Matter and memory). He then turned his scholarly attention to the issue of "life" and produced his third book, *L'Évolution Creatrice* (Creative evolution). After that, his thought went in the direction of society and ethics.

Bergson spoke very clearly, cutting his words short, one by one. People say that he used the same style during his lectures at the Collège de France. He talked in great detail of the course of his studies up to that time. Suddenly I noticed a volume on the history of religions on a small stand next to me. I had heard that at the time he was studying Spanish in order to do research on Spain's mystic Saint Theresa.[6] It would be difficult to equal his dedication in studying a foreign language at the age of almost seventy, and despite his illness, in order to read the original texts.

When I mentioned *Durée et Simultaneité* (Duration and simultaneity), he showed his antagonism to Einsteinian physical time and emphasized with great vigor that true time in philosophy is pure duration. He mentioned that Einstein would have not have approved his thought. Einstein was a physicist, not a philosopher. In order to understand *Duration and Simultaneity,* he said, one should be physicist and philosopher at the same time.

When I alluded to the criticism of mysticism that was leveled against him, his face showed disapproval and he immediately rebutted. One can say so only if he gives an arbitrary meaning to the word "mysticism." First of all, mysticism usually meant the rejection of positive science. In this sense, his philosophy could not be called mysticism at all. Moreover, mysticism implied a relationship with God or the divine. In this sense, too, his philosophy could not be called mysticism. When I reminded him of a sentence from his *Introduction à la Metaphysique* —

"philosophy is nothing but an effort to overcome the human condition"—he answered that he meant intuition, which is independent from the understanding used by people every day; it had nothing to do with the divine. Bergson strongly refuted the interpretation of mysticism along the reductive lines of Christian mysticism. He acknowledged, however, that his philosophy had a tendency toward mysticism.

After talking about Hamelin,[7] I was about to take my leave when he said it was difficult for him to sit in the chair since his fever was still quite high. He invited me to continue this discussion after he had recovered a little more. He asked me to give his best to ambassador Ishii and his wife. He said that Mr. Ishii was very much respected and loved in Paris. He would have liked to show me out but, unfortunately, was unable to do so. He stood up from the chair with the help of his stick.

One or two years later I submitted to a print shop in Paris some work based on my lectures at the philosophical meeting of Pontigny. Jacques Chevalier,[8] a favorite student of Bergson, read my work and paid me a visit. He invited me to meet once again with Bergson, saying that he would arrange it. As a result, I was able to meet with Bergson a second time. This time his wife accompanied me to a room on the second floor that looked like a living room. Since this was our second meeting, Bergson chatted in familiar tones and talked about many things. I had heard that his illness was related to his bones. He said that most of the day was taken by medical treatments, and the little time left in the day he dedicated to his work.

Bergson's daughter came into the room. She was about thirty years old. She was deaf and mute, and Bergson talked to her using hand signals. Only a slight sound emerged from her mouth, and I truly felt sad. This was Bergson's only child. Someone said that this event bears an intimate relationship to Bergson's later thought. This girl was a student of the sculptor Bourdelle[9] and she was also a painter. In the parlor downstairs there were many paintings by Bergson's daughter. Several of her paintings depicting dances and other scenes were exhibited at the Salon d'Automne in Paris under the title "Mouvement." I wanted to get one for myself as a memento. I thought these paintings were related to the philosophical thought of her father.

Mr. Lefevre,[10] editor in chief of the journal *Les Nouvelles Litteraires,* came to the room. Since at that time Bergson had just received the

Nobel Prize, Lefevre had come to consult with him in order to prepare a commemorative issue for *Les Nouvelles Litteraires*. He also said that he wanted to borrow several pictures of Bergson. On that occasion Lefevre asked me to write something for the issue, and this is how I came to write a piece titled "Bergson au Japon" (Bergson in Japan), in which I introduced the state of research on Bergson in Japan.[11]

Later the discussion continued with Bergson addressing Lefevre and myself on the topic of agnosia. To listen to a philosopher whose daughter was deaf and mute talking about an illness of speech made me feel an indescribably strange sensation.

My article in *Les Nouvelles Litteraires* became an opportunity for receiving letters from Bergson from time to time. Since I was planning to go back to Japan, he told me that he wanted to see me once again before my departure. Due to his illness, however, which had not taken a favorable turn, and to the fact that I was very busy with preparations for my return to Japan, in the end I left France without seeing him. Before my departure he sent me a picture with his signature and asked me to let him know about my movements after my return to Japan. Since writing was bothersome, however, I never wrote him a letter after my return.

At the end of last year I read in the newspaper that the French deputy prime minister, Laval,[12] had resigned and that at the same time Jacques Chevalier had become minister of education. I am sure it was the same Chevalier who was a student of Bergson. A very active person (one can see it from the fact that he even came to see me), Chevalier had been a professor of philosophy at the University of Grenoble. A man with pro-English tendencies, he had lectured at English universities and, like Bergson, respected English thought. The newspaper reported that in France the pro-German atmosphere was becoming weaker, and I think this episode was related to it.

According to the newspaper, the Vichy government did not apply the anti-Semitic laws to Bergson, as I think it was proper of that government to do. But the paper also reported that Bergson had refused this special treatment, as I think it was only proper for him to do.

I cannot bear the grief at the thought of this old philosopher dying in Paris under German occupation in the midst of the expulsion of so many Jews. What I feel to be a joyful occasion for Bergson was that he managed to complete *Les Deux Sources de la Moral et de la Religion*

(The two sources of morality and religion) after many years of research and to see it published several years before his death. With this book the Bergsonian system—although Bergson disliked the word "system"—was complete.

In the English and American philosophical world William James[13] and Whitehead[14] are particularly related to Bergson. It goes without saying that James's "flow of consciousness" shares several common features with Bergson's thought. Whitehead's organic view of nature was made possible by the influence of Bergson. In his own writings, Bergson paid his tribute of praise to both philosophers. Bergson stated that among contemporary German philosophers he esteemed Freud and Husserl the most. I see why we can accept this assessment. There are similarities between Bergson and these two thinkers: Freud brought an irrational topic such as the unconscious into the sphere of research; Husserl held intuition in great account, although Bergson's notion of intuition was different.

Bergson's philosophy has become the target of several criticisms. His pupil Péguy[15] made the following pertinent statement: "A philosopher without at least one antagonist voice is not a great philosopher. Great is the philosophy that says something." We cannot deny that since the time of the Greeks there have been philosophies with a tendency similar to Bergson's. The names of Heracleitus and Plotinus usually come to mind. Asked what he thought about the philosophy of Bergson, Tagore[16] answered that in India this philosophy existed long before in remote antiquity. The Germans would probably mention Schelling and Schopenhauer. Yet I think we can say that no one in the past articulated his philosophy as well as Bergson did. Moreover, even if I do not know whether it can be said about the second half of the twentieth century, I believe that anyone would probably agree with me when I say that Bergson was the world's greatest philosopher of the first half of the twentieth century.

Tokyo and Kyoto

I was born and raised in Tokyo. For thirty years from the day I was born I never lived anywhere other than Tokyo. Then, upon my return to Japan after a while spent in the West, I happened to get a position in Kyoto. When I went to Kyoto I visited an acquaintance. The host came out to the entrance and said to me, smiling, "Until now in Paris, from now on in Kyoto?" I knew Kyoto only as a tourist, and I felt sad to go and live in a place so far from the capital. I thought that, if I disliked it, I would return to Tokyo after one or two years. Since then eight years have gone by.

Recently people from Tokyo often qualify my name by adding "from Kyoto" to it. The editor of Iwanami's *Philosophy* series made a mistake by introducing me as a graduate of Kyoto Imperial University. It appears that, lately, many people think I am from Kyoto. Since I left my family in Tokyo, I always go back there during the spring, summer, and winter breaks. The letter from the publisher of *Bungei Shunjū* asking me to write this essay was forwarded to me from Kyoto to Tokyo, and I am now writing this essay in the study of my home in Tokyo. People from Tokyo, especially those I have known for many years, treat me as a Kyoto person. In Kyoto, of course, people from that city treat me as a Tokyo person. I think it is only natural for Kyoto people to treat me as someone from Tokyo, but I object to being treated in Tokyo as someone from Kyoto. Since, according to the rules, it does not really matter where one pays his taxes, I chose to pay them in Tokyo for convenience's sake. I stopped doing so, however, after the tax office in Tokyo had avoided dealing with me for the past year or two, and I decided to pay my taxes in Kyoto. I do not know how many more years I will be living in Kyoto, but the longer I live there the more I will be treated as a Kyoto person. As a result, I will find myself in the situation of having several native places.

At this point I feel attached to both Tokyo and Kyoto. Whenever I go out for a walk in Kyoto, I always end up at some famous historic site. I always stop at the signboards set up by the city tourist bureau. I feel a strong tie with history simply by reading these signs—"In this mound Emperor Kanmu buried his armor and helmet after having chosen this capital, and the capital was pacified"; "Saigyō wrote his famous poem, 'I pray that I might die in spring under the cherry blossoms,' under this cherry tree." In Tokyo, with the exception of the riverside shrouded in night fog and the Kannon Hall in Asakusa, which remind me of Hiroshige's prints, I am usually unaware of any clear tie with history. Furthermore, Kyoto is blessed with nature. If I walk about fifteen minutes from my house in Nanzenji, I am already in the midst of the mountains. In spring the azaleas bloom with a pale purple color; in autumn I feel I am walking in a new territory, close to mushrooms. In Tokyo, even if I keep going half a day as far as Kōnodai and Tamagawa, I do not feel any closeness with nature. History and nature have made my life in Kyoto happy.

When it comes to modern life, however, everything is in Tokyo. Ginza and Shijō Avenue cannot be compared. When I go to the section on foreign books in Maruzen and Mitsukoshi, I feel irritated by Kyoto's meagerness. Even when I go to the used-book stores in Kanda, I realize Tokyo's greatness. If you go to Prunier at the Tokyo Assembly Hall or the grill at the Imperial Hotel, you understand Tokyo's side of modernity.

When comparing Tokyo and Kyoto, it is quite commonplace to refer to the Sumida and Kamo Rivers. The Kamogawa with its scarce pure water is truly representative of Kyoto, while the muddy and rushing water of the Sumidagawa symbolizes Tokyo well. I like to observe Mt. Hiei quietly from Sanjō Bridge; at the same time, I also like to entrust my heart to the colors of the neon signs while standing on the riverbank at Ryōgoku. For me Kyoto is a tranquil and pure thing. Tokyo means a complicated relentlessness. Since I always go to Kyoto alone, I am almost free from worldly concerns and can steep myself in a quiet life of scholarship. My colleagues, of course, are many men, many minds. Basically, however, they are all sincere, good, and wise people. I really feel amazement that, as someone coming from the outside, I joined the highest seat of learning. For someone like myself who is absorbed in learning together with such distinguished colleagues, Kyoto is truly a quiet city. When I go back to Tokyo, however, I become a family man. By being in the midst of complex family relationships, troubles and worries arise unexpectedly. In this context I cannot necessarily rely on sincerity, goodness, and wisdom. Moreover, since occasions arise when I come into contact with people from different fields, I learn about real society. Frequently I see mean things, petty things, cruel things, silly things around me. Usually I get upset and suppress my feelings in Tokyo. When I am in Tokyo I am clearly aware of the rough waves of the world. Moreover, I feel that I want to apply the following verse from Goethe's *Tasso* to my life in Kyoto and in Tokyo:

> *Es bildet ein Talent sich in der Stille,*
> *Sich ein Charakter in der Strom der Welt.*
>
> [Talent is built in quietness,
> Character is built in the currents of the world.]

With regard to "talent," life in Kyoto is desirable; but for "character," life in Tokyo is something not to be missed—this is my truth.

Once my teacher at Tokyo Imperial University, Dr. Koeber, told me that you can do philosophy even in Kamchatka. Undoubtedly there is an element of truth in that. But it is not the whole truth. The place where a philosopher lives is automatically reflected in his philosophy. This becomes clear when we look at Bergson's and Heidegger's philosophies. Bergson's philosophy is intimately the philosophy of a Parisian. Such stylishness in terms of content and the form of enunciation could only be the product of someone born and raised in Paris. Heidegger, by contrast, is a philosopher raised in the shade of the dark forest of Schwarzwald in southern Germany. When he was a professor at the University of Marburg, the problem of the invitation to the University of Berlin arose and he stayed a couple of nights in Berlin. After coming back to Marburg, he told me that the only time he had passed through the city of Berlin was as a soldier during World War I. The first time he saw Berlin, he was astonished by its modern life. I could not refrain from smiling secretly at the idea of being astonished by something as little as Berlin. Heidegger's gloomy philosophy took on the character of the land of the Schwarzwald and the black tinge of *Tanne* (silver fir).

Tokyo and Kyoto—I would be very fortunate if my thought could naturally reflect in content the richness of Tokyo and in form the quietness of Kyoto.

Contingency and Destiny

The issue of contingency was a popular topic in the press the year before last, but this is an issue that has existed in the world of intellectual history for more than two thousand years; it is by no means a momentary fad. Contingency is the possibility of becoming on the part of what is not, the coming into reality by accident of something that, if rarely occurring, becomes particularly conspicuous. The contingency that gives an enormous meaning to human life is called "destiny." Today in my lecture, after explaining contingency by mentioning its three modalities, I will also discuss the meaning of destiny.

I want to talk about the issue of "contingency and destiny," but first I must begin by explaining the meaning of *contingency*. The issue of contingency became such a frequent topic in Japanese newspapers and magazines two years ago that no one seems willing to revisit this issue today. The problem of contingency is by no means a temporary fad, however, as one can see from the fact that in India in the fifth century B.C. Makkhali Gosāla[1] raised the question of contingency, in China Wang Ch'ung of the Eastern Han[2] addressed this problem, and in Greece Aristotle too brought up this issue. From the ancient past to the present, contingency has always become the object of either direct or indirect speculation. It is not an issue that can be easily discarded after one brief moment of popularity. In order to talk about contingency I should start by looking at what I think to be its three modalities. The first is the chance that both what is and what is not might become. The second is the chance encounter between two entities. The third is the chance that something rare happens.

Let's begin with the first modality—the possibility that both what is and what is not might become. Although this is not something that must necessarily happen, it is not absolutely impossible for it to happen. Therefore, the possibility that something that does not exist comes into being must be contingent. If you toss a die in an inkpot, every side will become completely dark. If a side of the die comes up black when you cast it, it will not be the result of chance. In this case it would be impossible for one face to turn out white and, therefore, contingency cannot take place. If in the next scenario a regular die is tossed without being put in an inkpot and a 3 is produced, we can think of that as contingency. There is no necessity *necessarily* requiring the 3 to come up. Moreover, it is not impossible that the 3 will *never* come up. It is possible that the 3 will either come up or will not. If what either could come out or could not come out did indeed come out, then we have contingency. But since the die has six sides, the certitude that a 3 will come up is one possibility out of six. Although it feels as if contingency has lessened, in actuality it does not diminish. The certitude of one out of six simply means that if the die is rolled six times, it is likely that a 3 will come up once. If one were to roll the die an extremely high number of times, such as a hundred or a thousand, the number of times that 3 comes up is likely to be one-sixth of the time. If the number of the times the die is rolled diminishes, the outcome will also necessarily diminish in proportion. I think everybody knows it is quite possible that if you roll the die six times, the number 3 will not come up even once, and that out of six times the same number 3 might come up three times. Certitude—in other words the quantitative relationship based on the theory of probability—in actuality holds good for the sum total of many instances; what number will come up in each instance is a matter of pure contingency. This is true but, in a sense, we can say that this is not contingent. We should also think that each time we roll the die, the face that appears each time is necessarily determined by physical elements such as the die itself, the surface on which the die is thrown, the way it is thrown, and the resistance of the air. If the number 3 comes up, this means there is a physical reason that makes the side with the number 3 come up. Accordingly, we should not think this to be the result of contingency. But if we think from a viewpoint one step higher, we find again as before an element of contingency. Even if the 3 has actually come up as a result of a necessity determined by the law of cause and effect, there is no reason why such a law of cause and effect should necessarily exist. A 5 could well have come up, determined by a different order of cause and effect. The fact that one particular order of cause and effect has materialized out of a series of six orders with logically equal value indicates that, as before, we are confronted with a case of contingency. A logical, metaphysical contingency hides behind a physical necessity. It is important to recognize this fact clearly. The possibility that, when rolling the die, a 1, or 2, or 3, or 4, or 5, or 6 might appear is grounded in a logical, metaphysical contingency. In other words, that something which is (and which is not) can become is contingent. There is an expression, "the force of circumstances," but "circumstances" is a word expressing chance in the sense of flying here and there bound by the moment, of showing this side or that side without knowing. Moreover, since the fact that the possibility that both being and nonbeing have to become lacks the absolute reason that they must necessarily become, there are also times when we can call contingency what is born *without* a reason, *without* a cause. Words such as *"unexpected" (yukurinaku, hashitanaku mo)* indicate the lack *(nai)* of reason and cause through the negative particle "un" *(naku)*.

There is still some ambiguity about what I have been saying so far. That what is and is not can become simply has the quality of possibility; it is *necessary* for the formation of *contingency,* but it is not yet sufficient. A condition for the formation of contingency is the *materialization* of possibility *as* possibility, a coming into being as a possibility that does not turn into necessity. Here we come to the meaning of the second modality of contingency—the chance encounter between two entities. In the moment when I meet someone, the possibility materializes and becomes contingency. The way of encountering someone is important, however. The first modality of contingency prescribes that this way of encountering someone must be open to the possibility that the encounter either does or does not take place. A way of meeting in which the encounter is necessarily established is not contingency. If one goes to meet someone on purpose, that is not a chance encounter. Going to visit a sick man is not contingency, for example, since we went to meet someone on purpose. But to meet someone unexpectedly who happens to have come to visit this sick man is contingency. There is no necessity in the meeting with that person. Indeed by going to the hospital there was undoubtedly the possibility of meeting him, but there was also the possibility of not meeting him at all. If we meet with him, it is by chance. In other words, it is *not* settled that we will necessarily meet that person; the openness of the way of the encounter to the possibility of either meeting or not meeting is what makes the meeting contingent. If a meteorite flying through the sky falls onto the earth in its incandescent state, igniting a source of oil, the way the meteorite and the oil meet is contingent. The encounter of the blind Kiyuki at the inn at Shimada who happens to meet the traveler Komazawa by chance— as presented in *Asagao Nikki* (Diary of a morning glory; a libretto by Umata Ryūrō that is staged in *jōruri* and *kabuki* and performed occasionally; published in 1810)—is contingent. If the number 3 comes up when I roll the die, the encounter between my eyes and the sign "3" is contingent. When the necessity that something must come into a meeting does not enter the space of the meeting, which maintains possibility as possibility, then we have contingency. The left-side radical of the character "*gū* 偶" in the word "*gūzen* 偶然" (contingence, chance) is "man," but the word "*gūzen*" has the same meaning as the character "*au* 偶う" (to meet) written with the left-side radical of "advancing," a character which means that two things meet. It is the same "*gū*" found in the word "*haigū* 配偶" (combination).The fact that you and I happen to meet is the essential meaning of "*gūzen*" (by chance). Words related to "*gūzen*," such as "*yukiatari battari*" (haphazard), "*meguriawase*" (a turn of fortune's wheel), "*shiawase*" (good fortune), and "*magureatari*" (a fluke), all in some way express the idea of two things coming together and becoming one.

So far I have considered the first two modalities of contingency. The third modality—the coming into being of something that happens only rarely—remains to be analyzed. Since this modality is limited again by the first modality, we might say that it sharpens the contingency of contingency, defines the direction of contingency, so that, through the process, contingency stands out prominently. It is a modality that is integral to the cognition of contingency. If people who work in the same factory meet in the building of that factory without any particular intention of meeting, we are faced with contingency. This tends to happen occasionally, however, and, although it is undoubtedly something that happens by chance, it is a chance facing the direction of necessity and, as a result, a chance that is not too conspicuous. But if the two people meet unexpectedly in some town far away from the site of the factory, in this case contingency comes to stand out in all its sharpness. The reason is that something has come into being which rarely occurs. If something happens rarely, it means that it is unusual to encounter it. If it is by chance that 3 comes up when I roll the die, it is an even greater chance if 3 comes up six times after rolling the die six times, since this is something that happens only rarely. It is truly by chance that each 3 meets face to face six times in succession. There is an ancient term that indicates "by chance" in the *Man'yōshū* (Ten thousand leaves): *"wakuraba ni."* *"Wakuraba"* refers to the leaves of trees that are already red and yellow in summer and wither very early—an event which is extremely rare and explains why the word was chosen to mean "by chance." There is another word that indicates "by chance": *"tamatama."* This word too has the meaning of "rare." *"Tamatama"* is the repetition of the word *"tama,"* and *"tama"* is written with the characters *"te no ma* 手の間" (between hands); *"ma"* (between) is the center of the word's meaning. *"Ma"* indicates spatial and temporary distance. We now finally understand the meaning of the Japanese word *"mare"* (rare). *"Mare"* is a contraction of *"ma are* 間有れ" (being between). In any event, there is no beginning or end to *"ma."* Since it was a rare event, *"ma"* came to mean "by chance." *"Ma ga warui"* (unlucky) means that the fortuitous circumstances that have presented themselves to me lack fittingness. The expression *"konna ma ni natta"* (things came to this end) means that things turned out fortuitously. There are instances in which *"ma"* takes an additional *"n"* for euphonic reasons, thus becoming *"man."* *"Man"* (fortune) is a remarkable word expressing "chance." When an interesting hue of color comes out, potters say this is the fortune *(man)* of the kiln. *"Man"* indicates that something has come into being by chance without even knowing it. While the last few words we have examined all represent contingency, as can be observed by the expression "only rarely," contingency comes up and catches our attention in unusual cases. Unusual cases are those with few possibilities. When things that are close to impossible (although they are possible) come into being by mere chance, contingency stands out in all its sharpness, thus making itself easily recognized. We can say that contingency turns its back on *necessity* while facing toward *impossibility*.

I have examined the three modalities of contingency. To sum it up I would say that contingency is the possibility of Being and Nonbeing; it is a sudden turn of the wheel of fortune, which is all the more conspicuous if it happens all the more rarely. Next I would like to address the issue of destiny. Destiny is something you understand immediately once you understand the meaning of contingency. A contingency that drastically affects human existence is *destiny*. Human existence can be affected by either internal or external factors, but since it is internal matters that decide the direction of human life, destiny is usually interpreted as internalized contingency. An example of destiny would be if a person were walking along a road under a cliff. If this person were to die from being buried under the cliff when it caved in, that would be this person's destiny. This, however, is a rather externalized example. Another example would be Miyuki's destiny when he met Komazawa Jirōzaemon while catching fireflies in Uji. This event had a lasting effect on Miyuki's entire life. In this case, the internal color of destiny comes out very strongly. In another case, the person known as Saigō Takamori[3] could have been born in Edo, or Kyoto, or Ise, or Tosa. Instead he was born in Satsuma, and that was Saigō's destiny. We could have been born American, French, Ethiopian, Indian, Chinese, or as a people from any other country. It was our destiny that made us Japanese. It was our destiny to be born as human beings rather than as insects, birds, or any other beasts. By chance the side of the die came up that said that we were born Japanese. By chance someone's die showed a side saying they were born with a harelip or a hunchback.

In Nietzsche's *Thus Spoke Zarathustra* we find the following story.[4] One day Zarathustra was crossing a great bridge when he found himself surrounded by cripples and beggars. In the crowd a hunchback turned to Zarathustra and said: "A great number of people have come to believe in your teachings, but not everybody yet. There is still one important thing left for you to do. You must first persuade us cripples." Zarathustra responded with the doctrine that "will brings salvation." Being born a hunchback is destiny; but will rescues one from destiny.

Zarathustra taught that "the will to reverse the will" in the form that "one wants to be born a hunchback" is the path to one's salvation. Zarathustra taught the secret of putting contingency and destiny in parentheses. Men must love their destiny and become one with it. This, I think, is the first step to be taken in life. You all listen to radio nowadays. There are many different broadcasting stations that broadcast their waves at different frequencies. By turning the dial of the receiver you find many different frequencies and you can choose the frequency that you prefer. You can choose freely and listen to a specific station. Destiny is like a broadcast we are forced to listen to whether we like it or not. Although there are many broadcasts happening at the same time, for some reason we are forced to listen to *this* broadcast. Although things could have been different, *this* specific thing has become my own destiny. What one can do at this point is to reverse one's will and to will it—to make it the same as if we were freely choosing our own destiny. Yamaga Sokō[5] taught that warriors must feel at ease with their life; in other words, they must feel at ease with their destiny. I think we should learn not simply to feel at ease, but to become one with our destiny and love it deeply. I end my lecture with the wish that by loving your own destiny from the bottom of your heart you might also build a new and fresh destiny for yourself.

Contingency and Surprise

I want to write about "contingency and surprise." Someone might think that, at such a time of political pressure, this subject is too far removed from the present reality. Yet one could also think it is exactly because we find ourselves in the present circumstances that it might be a good idea to discuss deeply and calmly the topic of my title. When one makes a boisterous sound by beating a drum, a deaf person recognizes a small, low voice better. I believe it is possible to read in a composed manner about a valuable topic such as "contingency and surprise" that is spoken in the lowest possible tone in the midst of the upheavals which have thrown our nation into a deep crisis. Timeless issues are not always discussed at the highest pitch.

The Meaning of Contingency and Surprise

I would define contingent as something deprived of necessity. To give a common example, when a statue of the Buddha is found during construction of the subway, the primary aim in the necessary building plan is to dig deeply in the ground in order to build the passage for the railway. The discovery of an ancient statue is not included in the plan. If an old statue surfaces, this should be considered a result of contingency. Another example would be to say that the entire biological world is made of the necessary sum total of its members—insects, birds, other animals, and human beings. But the fact of being born as a human being, rather than an insect, a bird, or some other animal, is purely contingent.

I would define surprise as something unexpected, which is unrelated to us by any form of necessity, arousing the emotion of surprise. Far from being necessary, surprise is an emotion that arises toward something fortuitous. A laborer in the subway is surprised when he digs up an ancient, beautiful statue of the Buddha, because this act is the result of contingency. I am surprised at being born as a human being and not as an insect, a bird, or some other animal, precisely because of the contingency of the event.

Moreover, as an emotion based on the realization of contingency as contingency, surprise is a particularly intellectual emotion. Accordingly, we can also say that it is preeminently a human emotion and that, unless they are of an advanced species, animals cannot distinguish clearly between surprise and fear. In the daily life of human beings several complex and accidental phenomena are the cause of surprise. I will take an example from the current war with China. It was reported that a commanding officer was wounded by an enemy bullet and admitted to the field hospital. In the next room he heard there was a soldier on the verge of death because of a hemorrhage. When the officer went to visit the soldier with the intention of conveying his last words of encouragement, he was surprised to see that the soldier was actually his younger brother. The two brothers had departed for the front at different times and belonged to different units. They did not know they were fighting on the same front. The last meeting of the two brothers was entirely fortuitous and, as a result, they were truly surprised. When some event has the character of contingency, it becomes a reason for surprise. Since the reason for surprise is often a complicated, intellectual phenomenon, we can say that surprise is a particularly intellectual feeling.

Experience and Surprise

We can also say, however, that surprise is a feeling which occurs to someone with little experience. If one has enough knowledge about different things and knows how to grasp things in their context, his sense of surprise should necessarily disappear. When we accumulate experience and can put the event into the proper context, what we originally thought to be contingent loses its contingency and, proportionately, surprise also gradually disappears. While walking on a mountain trail, for example, if a snake appears by chance in the middle of the path, anyone would feel some degree of surprise. If the snake were a two-headed snake—a snake with one body and two heads—anyone would undoubtedly be greatly surprised. We think that a snake with two heads is the result of contingency because we have a general notion of the snake. There must be a reason why this snake has two heads. According to experiments by biologists, it is possible to create a snake with two heads artificially through surgical intervention. Since the snake that we see in nature with two heads is undoubtedly the result of an event at the time of the birth of the snake's eggs, when the part which is destined to become the snake's head was cut in two, we see a moment of necessity present in the process. Then, when coming face to face with a snake on a mountain trail, the ordinary person will be immensely surprised; the biologist, on the other hand, should not be surprised at all. I am not saying that contingency has totally vanished. Contingency is found in the meeting between the snake's eggs and the cause that produced the two-headed snake: a wound deriving from some external object, or the activity of bacteria, or some other reason. We can say that two different orders of cause and effect have met by chance.

Absolute Contingency

Even if, in order for the two orders of cause and effect to be able to meet, there is temporarily a necessary cause shared by both orders, if we go back ad infinitum searching for such a cause we should think that eventually we will find an absolute contingency that has no necessary cause. In other words, no matter how much surprise we eliminate, in the end some surprise is bound to remain, something that urges us to be surprised. This is the world as totality that forces us to be surprised. We cannot ban the emotion of surprise toward the actual world. The actual world as a whole is a contingent being in which things that are and things that are not have the possibility of becoming, and in which things can come into being with a different form. This is why we feel surprise for contingency, and here a big, deep problem is cast in a form that has no solution.

History and Contingency

The Greek philosopher Heracleitus[1] compared the world to children playing chess. Here he was clearly grasping the contingency of the world. Heracleitus is usually called a fatalist, and fate is nothing but contingency, which plays such a large role in people's life.

Epicurus[2] also discussed fortuity from the point of view of atomism. He argued that the original movement of atoms was a perpendicular movement with the same speed from top to bottom and said there were atoms that deviated a little from this perpendicular line by total chance without any predetermined reason. As a result, atoms crashed into each other, a vortex arose, and the world came into being.

In modern times Leibniz[3] argued that the present world is not the only possible world, and he acknowledged the existence of a great number of possible worlds. In Roman history there is a person by the name of Sextus Tarquinius.[4] He was the son of Tarquinius Superbus, the last king of the Roman period of kings. Sextus raped the married woman Lucretia, thus causing Lucretia to commit suicide. This became the motive for the ruin of the Roman system of kings and the establishment of the republic. The Tarquinius family was exiled. This is a given historical reality, but Leibniz argued that beside the world in which Sextus Tarquinius appeared as a citizen of Rome, the rapist of Lucretia, and an exile, another world was possible—he could have been a citizen of Thrace and a truly blessed man revered by the whole people; or he could have been part of a world in which he was born a Corinthian citizen, living a normal life until old age, loved by the townspeople. Many other worlds were possible that included different types and shapes of Sextus Tarquinius. In other words, Leibniz thought that since many worlds are possible, the actual world is simply a contingent thing, one among many. Not only Leibniz but Schelling[5] too was sensitive to the issue of the contingency of the world, arguing that the world's beginning derived from primeval contingency. He thought that the beginning of the world was original contingency. Since this primeval contingency was realized by the will as destiny, the will was surprised to see such a realization.

Fortuitism in India and China

In India, too, the doctrine of no-causation and no-relation of the Six Masters of the Outside Way[6] is actually a version of fortuitism. According to this doctrine, there is no cause and there is no effect in the present condition of things; all elements simply meet each other by chance. They say it is like throwing a skein. To the question of why a self-sufficing and perfect Brahma creates the world—and why a free deity, who is within the bounds of perfect enlightenment, changes—the theories of Sānkhya-Yoga and Vedānta philosophy answer that "it is for play's sake." This is a thought that must be savored deeply.

In Buddhism we find the concepts of chief cause[7] and karma. In thinking about it briefly, one might think these concepts are actually against fortuitism. If we go back into the history of cause and karma, however, we end up reaching contingency. There are eight troubles, known as the eight calamities, in which a person has no chance to meet with Buddha's world or to listen to the Buddhist law: hell, hungry ghosts, animals, paradise, the paradise of long life, deafness and muteness, attachment to worldly wisdom, and birth before or after the appearance of the Buddha in the world. This scheme shows the contingency of life—in what environments a person can be born. The metaphor of the blind turtle sticking its head in the hole of a floating log expresses the surprise at contingency.[8]

In China also, the ground of the principles of divination is found within the realm of contingency, in which the dual cosmic forces of yin and yang meet. Which one of the eight trigrams—the creative, the receptive, the arousing, the abysmal, the static, the gentle, the clinging, and the joyous—will appear depends on the contingency of the combination of these divination signs. Moreover, divination comes about exactly because its principles are grounded in contingency. When the fortune-teller practices divination, he takes fifty sticks of bamboo and takes one away, dividing with his thumb the remaining forty-nine into two groups at random. Then, after counting according to a fixed pattern the divining rods he has divided, he combines the number of remaining divining rods (a contingent reality) with the eight trigrams. The combination of the chance number of rods with the trigrams is made possible by the fact that the trigrams are structured by contingency. In China Wang Ch'ung too has expounded a philosophy of contingency. In this regard he used a clever metaphor—saying that in order to become a public servant the conditions required by the sovereign must be successfully and fortuitously met by the conditions provided by the retainer.

Japanese Mythology and Contingency

Even when we look at Japanese mythology we see that in the beginning there was movement, and from that movement primeval contingency was born. The expression "the time when the land drifted like a jellyfish" that we find in the *Kojiki* (Records of ancient matters) symbolizes movement. Izanagi no Mikoto and Izanami no Mikoto's act of standing on the Heavenly Floating Bridge and stirring the sea water with the jeweled spear is another image of movement. Moreover the "churning-churning sound" *(korokoro)* resulting from the stirring of the sea is actually the same as the sound of the rolling *(korogasu)* die. The coming into being of Onokoro Island (Onokoroshima)[9] from the piling up of the brine dripping from the tip of the spear symbolizes the same contingency we see in the appearance of one of the die's sides. The name "Onokoroshima" indicates the primeval contingency that has already come into being. The "ono" part of the word "Onokoro" is usually interpreted to mean "by itself" *(onozukara);* "koro" is thought to be "*koru* 凝る " (to solidify), that is, "to coagulate." If we look for the etymology of "*koru,*" however, the word is probably a variation of "*korokoro.*" The island was called "Onokoro" because it tumbled down *(korobu)* by itself, coming into being by chance. The passage that says, "Only Onokoro Island was not born," tells us that although Izanagi and Izanami gave birth to many islands and deities, only Onokoro Island was not born from a relationship of cause and effect; this island came into being by chance. The word "Onokoroshima" means that reality came into being fortuitously from within the movement of infinite possibilities.

Actuality and Surprise

To think about something that is given to us in terms of necessity is quite an abstract, partial, and plain way of thinking. To see that it is contingent—one out of many possibilities—is a concrete, wholesome, solid way of seeing—active rather than passive. We can think that the birth of someone who is blind, deaf, and mute is determined necessarily by specific embryological and pathological causes. Despite this truth, whether a man is only blind, or only deaf and mute, or whether he is a perfectly healthy person with clear sight and the ability to speak, everybody possesses equal logical possibilities. To be deaf and mute in addition to being blind is simply one of four possibilities that I have sketched out. In this sense, this reality is contingent, not necessary. The side on the die with blindness, deafness, and muteness has just come up, although any other side filled with different possibilities could have come up. This way of thinking is concrete, wholesome, versatile, and active.

In short, we are greatly surprised when we face the contingent being that is the actual world given to us. Even the person who never marvels at anything should be surprised by this reality. If he is not surprised, it means that such a person is deaf to, and has no ear for, primeval contingency. Surprise has been seen from ancient times as the departing point of philosophy. There is a saying: "A great thought comes from the heart." I think that whatever makes the heart throb with regard to the contingency of the actual world is the moving force of philosophical speculation and religious sentiment. Today in the sky of East Asia the cannons roar loudly and trumpets give strong blasts. I put down my pen while harboring doubts that this essay I have written in such a low tone will ever reverberate even faintly in your hearts.

A Joke Born from Contingency

The inner life of a person who either feigns ignorance or raises his eyebrows when he hears a joke is surprisingly empty. A light laughter casts a bright light on a serious, gloomy daily life. One day I was having a haircut in Paris when the hairdresser turned to me and said that apparently *"de japonè"* (the Japanese) did not need horsemen. When I asked why, he answered: "Because they are *'deja'* (already) *'ponè'* (ponies)." This joke that was meant to make fun of me actually consoled the lonesomeness of someone journeying in a foreign land. Such lonesomeness also pounces upon life's journey. Sometimes a light joke is not bad. Paul Valéry compared two homophonous words to the smiles exchanged between two twins. No one will blame me if I introduce two sets of jokes born by pure chance like triplets.

The first joke might already be old news since it has already appeared in the newspaper. This took place when Mr. Watsuji Tetsurō[1] was still in Kyoto. I invited Professor Nishida Kitarō to an excursion to Kibune[2] to eat *amago*[3] (trout). Mr. Amano Teiyū went to Professor Nishida's house and asked him whether he would come to Kibune to eat *anago*[4] (sea eels). Professor Nishida answered that he did not like fatty food like sea eels. When Amano conveyed Nishida's message to Mr. Watsuji, Watsuji explained that they were going to have *amago*, not *anago*. Professor Nishida said he did not have any problem with eating *amago*, and, therefore, the plan to go to Kibune materialized happily. This is the story in which *Amano* mistook *anago* for *amago*. Mr. Amano, the translator of Kant's *Critique of Pure Reason*, was brought up in the Kantō area: he knew what *anago* was, but he did not have the slightest idea what *amago* meant.

At the end of this year, on a cold evening, I went to drink tea at a teahouse on Shijō Avenue together with Mr. Amano and Mr. Ochiai Tarō.[5] I said to the waitress that Kuki wanted tea and *"bisuketto"* (biscuits). The waitress asked me: "What is *'bisuketto'*? Is it the same as *'kukkī'* (cookies)?" Kuki said laughing: "If it is *'kukkī'* I don't need to get one; I'll give it to you!" I felt a throb *(gukitto)* in my chest. For the first time I realized that the old word *"bisuketto"* had been replaced by the new expression *"kukkī,"* and I felt a light dizziness in the space between the old world in which I was living and the new one in which the waitress lived. This is the story of *Kuki* who had a throb of the heart *(gukitto)* over a cookie *(kukkī)*.

Whereas the sentence is smooth in the case of the Kuki joke *("Kuki ga kukkī de gukitto shita"),* the Amano joke *("Amano ga amago to anago o machigaeta")* requires a slight effort of the tongue to get it out. Whereas the first case can be reduced to a quantitative relationship based on identity, the latter presupposes a qualitative relationship based on similarity. ———[December 1936]

Sound and Smell

The Sound of Contingency and the Smell of Possibility

When I was a boy, one summer morning I heard the sound of the lotus flower blooming in the garden of the Hachimangū shrine in Kamakura. One autumn evening I also listened to the sound of the opening primrose in the dry riverside field of the Tamagawa River. It is nothing but a remembrance—a dream, an old dream. This longing for a faint sound does not abandon me even today. Now I am trying to listen to the birth of contingency. I can hear a "slam" *(pishari)*, "a snap" *(pokkuri)*, "a pop" *(hyokkori)*, and "a maybe" *(hyotto)*. There are also times when I hear "a puff" *(futto)*. The word "suddenly" *(futo)* might well come from the latter. Occasionally I also hear a sound of something "slipping through" *(sururi)*. Contingency stimulates wonder. There is no doubt that the word "thrill"[1] is also related to *"sururi."* Once I tried to express the birth of contingency by creating a chain made of the sound *"su"*—as when I called it "a disjunction, the speed of change sliding and slipping through toward reality" *(genjitsu e sururi to subette kuru suii no supīdo).*

   Smell is another yearning of mine. I am going to make a confession. When I was young I felt an irresistible fascination for the faint smell of face powder. When I was in Paris I liked Guerlain's *L'Heure Bleu* and Lanvin's *Quelque Fleurs* out of the perfumes available for ladies. It also happened that I sprinkled the inside of my vest with Guerlain's *Bouquet de Faunes,* since they said its fragrance was masculine. Today everything has sunk into the past. Moreover, I have come to like smelling from the window of my library the garden's sweet osmanthus on quiet autumn days. I sniff the fragrance fully, all alone. Then I am carried to a far, far place, a place that is even further away than my birthplace—to a place where possibility remains a possibility.

A Record of Short Songs

Madame Hayashi Fumiko[1] came to visit me in Kyoto on her way back from her trip to Peking. It was an autumn night. She came to my house together with Naruse Mukyoku. She expressed her opinions about Japan's foreign policies with China and about issues related to anti-Japanese sentiments. She admired the English and American cultural activities vis-à-vis China and, too, the contemporary awakening of Chinese women. We also spoke about Chinese pottery. Since by chance Madame Hayashi mentioned that she liked short songs *(kouta),* I put on a record and the three of us listened.

"Whenever I listen to short songs I feel that I cease to worry about things," she said. These words resonated at the bottom of my heart, and I said:

"I totally agree with you. When I listen to music like this nothing matters any more!"

Then Mr. Mukyoku showed joy all over his face, and said to me with an air of rebuke:

"Until now you've never said a thing like this!"

At that moment I felt that the eyelids of each of us became warm, and tears oozed out from our eyes. Madame Hayashi had expressed honestly what a man would never admit. Mr. Mukyoku said:

"We are accustomed to worrying too much about truly insignificant matters."

He began walking in circles inside the room, as if he could not contain his deep emotions. Madame Hayashi kept her gaze low without saying a word. I felt as if the three of us were living in a temporary hut ready to fall to ruin, on top of an abyss of nothingness.

Whenever I listen to regional songs *(hauta)* and short songs I often feel a pressure that fills my entire person from the ground up with trembling. When I hear the live human voice, human pains come together and my heart ends up being engrossed in them. Records, however, create with their melodies a pure realm into which the soul can jump in all its nudity. Whenever I hear popular songs and short songs I do not feel regret for anything I thought had value for me, even if these things were to disappear altogether. I only feel that I want to live in a world of emotions.

> "After all this world is a flow of water, clouds crossing the sky…"
>
> *Avalanche, veux-tu m'emporter dans ta chute?*[2]

My Thoughts on Loanwords

This happened quite recently. Somewhere I used the word *"koyomi"* to indicate "calendar," saying that I wanted to see the calendar. Then the shopkeeper said, *"Koyomi* does not sound like you. Are you going to check your fortune?" When I answered that I wanted to check on what day of the week a certain date in the next month would fall, he replied: "Well, in that case a *karendā* (calendar) would do, right?" "Indeed," I thought, *"karendā* is what I need!" Somehow I was dumbfounded. Now I have reached a point where I hesitate a moment before deciding which expression would be clearer to the driver when I mail a letter: should I ask him to *"tomeru"* (stop) at the *"yūbinbako"* (mailbox), or should I say he should *"stoppu"* (stop) at the *"posuto"* (mailbox)?

I do not intend to revisit the argument over whether we should stop using the words *"papa"* (dad) and *"mama"* (mom), but when loanwords start to proliferate you begin to think more deeply about the matter. The following took place seven years ago now, in the spring of 1929, after my return from Europe: a journalist asked me to talk about my impressions upon seeing Japan after such a long time. I told him I had the feeling of being in a colony such as Singapore or Colombo. No matter where I walked, the signboards were all in English. I felt a sense of shame: you read a few lines in the newspaper and foreign words start sprouting everywhere. The journalist took notes while his face showed that he was not too taken with my ideas. Since this took place after a full nine years' absence from Japan, however, I believe that my impressions about the culture of my homeland were quite fresh. Since then I have tried to refrain from using loanwords from foreign languages unless it becomes truly unavoidable.

The following happened in the summer of the year before last. I was walking in the evening from Ueno Park to Negishi when I saw an announcement pasted here and there advertising the Bon dance of Negishi. When I finally reached the square, the platform of the musicians and the dance space around were beautifully decorated with paper lanterns and curtains. The dance had not yet started but a good number of old and young people, male and female, had gathered. I thought with great nostalgia of the Bon dance I saw in the neighboring village of Arima hot spring when I was a child accompanied by my father. Then I caught sight of a notice that said, "Fly-Catching *dē* (Day)—July 20th." This simple sticker entirely destroyed the mood of the occasion. *Dē* is truly an ugly expression. Dr. Omodaka Hisataka had every reason to resent what he felt to be the use of dummy words like *"dē"* (day) from the country of the red-haired Europeans, while we had a beautiful word for "day": the word *"hi"* found in the name of the Sun Goddess (Hi no Kami). He used to make the following joke: *"Nandē, nandē, nandei, nandei, nani o itteyagarundei."* (what, what, what on earth, what on earth, what on earth are you saying?).[1] Loanwords have even invaded the purple mountains and clear waters of the ancient capital without restraint. When a dancer *(maiko)* in whose obi are languidly embroidered one thousand years of tradition since the time of the Heian court says, "Would the honorable customer like to have a *duraibu* (drive) in an *ōpun* (open) cart?"[2] one feels tickling to the very bottom of his belly.

The following words have already entered the vocabulary of common usage: *nyūsu* (news), *sensēshon* (sensation), *sābisu* (service), *sabotāju* (sabotage), *kamufurāju* (camouflage), *interi* (intelligentsia), *sararīman* (salaryman), *runpen* (Lumpen),[3] *birudingu* (building), *depāto* (department store), *apāto* (apartment), *hyutte* (Hütte),[4] *supōtsu* (sport), *haikingu* (hiking), *pikunikku* (picnic), *gyangu* (gang), *anaunsā* (announcer), *menbā* (member), *masutā* (master), *fuan* (fan), *shīzun* (season), *chansu* (chance), *sutētomento* (statement), *messēji* (message), *rīdo* (lead), *matchi* (match), *surōgan* (slogan), *burokku* (bloc), and more.

Recently dictionaries of loanwords have begun to appear little by little in Japan as well, but in Germany dozens of similar dictionaries have been published from much earlier times, since there are so many loanwords there. I went to Germany immediately after the Great War and this was a time when the entire German people were striving to reject foreign words. Even in the Baedecker guide of Heidelberg, the inn that became the Grand Hotel was renamed Heidelberg Hof. In the food menu the word "sauce" was written *"Tunke."* Even the Germans had difficulties understanding the word *"Tunke."* The telephone was called *"Fernsprecher,"* and the radio was referred to as *"Rundfunk."* Wouldn't it be difficult to expect to find the entire Japanese people similarly interested in the regulation of loanwords, unless we go through a bloody war with Europe and America?

There are, as well, opposing opinions on the regulation and control of loanwords. The first reason for such an opposition is that since most words in current usage are of foreign origin, it would be better if we avoid excluding loanwords today. This argument makes sense, but I think that unless we consider the levels of cultural difference between the present age and the age when Chinese and Sanskrit words were imported, we cannot apply the same standards to different situations. The theory according to which contemporary Japan should follow the principle of nonresistance with regard to loanwords, because in primordial times Japan imported foreign words, does not stand to reason. This theory ignores the enormous cultural differences between East and West. Don't you feel that to act indifferent—saying that in any event most of our daily words are imported at a time when the system of the Japanese language is so remarkably troubled by the penetration of English and American words we see happening today—lacks solid judgment?

The second reason for opposing the control of loanwords is that there are times when particular shades of meaning do not come out in Japanese. For example, they argue that the feeling coming out from the word *"dē"* (day) is much stronger and more effective than the one achieved with the word *"hi"; "gō"* (go!) and *"stoppu"* (stop!) are more effective than the Japanese expressions *"susume"* (go!) and *"tomare"* (stop!). According to this theory, the feeling of *"tero"* (terrorism) is not properly expressed by the word *"kyōfu shudan,"* and *"gyangu"* (gang) is much more effective than *"satsujin gōdattai."* *"Iroke tappuri"* (sexy) lacks the tint of modernity found in *"ero hyaku pāsento"* (100 percent erotic). People defending this reason argue that it is only logical for the

recent penetration of foreign cultures to be accompanied by the arrival
of foreign words. They say that after having opened its doors wide to
Western civilization, Japan cannot possibly reject foreign words in the
contemporary situation. This reason is quite a strong argument for the
opposition—especially the idea that there is no way out but accepting
specific loanwords expressing particular emotions. I myself am opposed
to the radical conclusion that we should completely reject all loan-
words. No matter what one says, this will never happen.

Since there is plenty of room for us to learn from Western civiliza-
tion, we should be tolerant and to a certain degree overlook loanwords
as an indispensable evil. This, however, is a problem of degree. I
strongly believe we should not allow the alleged strength or weakness
of linguistic emotions to become the standard for the adoption of loan-
words. Compared to Japanese, the feelings expressed in English and
German words are, generally speaking, much stronger. If the Japanese
people of today are delighted by a language with a strong linguistic feel,
they can discard the Japanese language and use English and German in-
stead. The emotional value of an exam finds a much clearer expression
in the word *"ekuzāmen"* than in the simple Japanese word *"shiken."*
"Main fātārando" (mein Vaterland) reverberates with greater solem-
nity than the Japanese *"waga sokoku"* (our homeland).

The third reason for the opposition to the control of loanwords is the
idea that a natural selection of the survival of the fittest takes place even
in the linguistic world. The supporters of this view argue that the reorga-
nization of language is difficult by artificial coercion. Haven't we grown
accustomed to using words such as *"garasu"* (glass), *"beru"* (bell), and
"koppu" (cup) in daily life? Words such as *"juban"* (underwear),[5] being
totally prescribed by long usage, do not even have the smell any longer of
their foreign origin. We do not even know of their Portuguese origin un-
less someone tells us. These people say that the bottom line is the word's
handiness, and that by letting it be, it gets perfectly assimilated into the
language. Moreover, they say that since the social masses are wise, use-
less loanwords decay with time. To a certain point I agree with this lin-
guistic reality, but I cannot approve taking such a liberalistic view against
the control of loanwords based on this reality alone.

I would like to think that the defense of the Japanese language from
the invasion of Europe and America is an important topic for the con-

temporary Japanese person. To send troops to Manchuria is not the only national defense. We should protect the national character of the Japanese language by supporting national unity. The cause of the rejection of loanwords promoted by the late minister of education, Matsuda, was certainly a farsighted move on the part of the head of education. But we should not feel reassured by entrusting the matter to the inquiries and deliberations of the Ministry of Education. The problem of the regulation and control of loanwords is not an issue that requires particular inquiries and deliberations; it only needs implementation. It is a mistake to feel relieved by entrusting this matter to the arbitrariness of social masses. The people are wise, but they can also be benighted. We cannot deny that people have a childish side which makes them want to use loanwords indiscriminately, even when they are not needed; and we cannot deny that people like to show off their knowledge of foreign languages recklessly.

We often see in the newspaper the advertisement of *"eiga ābento"*[6] (evening at the movies). I think the word *"ābento"* was used for the first time at the end of the Meiji or beginning of the Taishō period when the Philosophy Society established "Kant Evenings" (Kanto Ābento) at the Sanjō Conference Hall of Tokyo Imperial University. Although the expression "Kant Evening" makes reasonable sense, once we get to "movie evening" the expression becomes quite laughable. Before long it may well be that the wind is blowing from France and we will say "movie *soarē*" *(soirée)*. We can already see signs that the *"kissaten"* (tearoom) is on the verge of becoming a *"saron do tē"* *(salon de thé)*. I feel that one cannot simply laugh listening to the voice of Yajiuma calling Kamiya Jihei stepping onto the passageway of the kabuki stage, *"modan bōi"* (modern boy). I do not blame someone whose name is Nagako (Long Girl) taking pleasure in calling herself "Rongu" (Long), or Omon (Gate) calling himself "Gēto," or Koeiryū (Small Prosperous Dragon) calling himself "Sumōru Purosuperasu Doragon," but I am disgusted to the point of anger when I see newspapers carrying in a dignified manner advertisements such as *"satadē sābisu"* (Saturday service), *"hina ningyō setto"* (a set of dolls), *"gofuku sorudo ichi"*[7] (bargain sale of clothes), *"kon-shīzun daiichi no meiga"* (the best film classics of the season), *"ai to yūmoa no akarui hishochi"* (a cheerful summer resort of love and humor), *"kono chansu o nogasazu honjitsu tadaima mōshikomare yo*" (reserve it immediately today without missing the chance). I have a feeling that they are laughing at us, thinking we are fools. To whom are those advertisements addressed, I wonder? Aren't we all Japanese? It is a total mystery to me how someone can establish a column in a newspaper called *"bukku revyū"* (book reviews) or *"hōmu sekushon"* (home section).

The following example alone from a recent newspaper article indicates how much people like to use loanwords: *"suramu no burujoa, runpen gunchū no kuīn"* (the bourgeois of the slum, the queen in a group of vagrants). In the May issue of *Bungei Shunjū* a minister and a person with the rank of a minister say, "It is not a problem with workers; it is that there are too many *'mentaru'* (mental) workers. As a result, advanced education and the situation of our country do not *'matchi'* (match)." And: "The unselfishness of Mr. Takahashi, which is the virtue of his character, *'supūrurōsu ferurōren'*[8] (disappeared without leaving a trace)! Indeed he was an unusually impressive person." I have a hard time understanding the need to use loanwords in these sentences.

What should we do to control society's frivolous curiosity for European and American languages, which is so widespread, and to awaken people's respect for the Yamato language and other oriental languages? It goes without saying that the foundation for this movement is to advocate the Japanese spirit far and wide. Once we establish a foundation, loanwords will thin out by themselves. Without such a foundation we will not be able to accomplish anything. While premising our argument on this foundation, as a way to control language—a service that must be rendered for the construction of this foundation—people dealing with writing must strengthen their resolute determination to avoid using unnecessary loanwords; whenever a new foreign word happens to enter the vocabulary, they should restrain their curiosity and immediately create a suitable translation; moreover, whenever a loanword has become a current word, they should strive to find a translation quickly and expel the original word from the threshold of social consciousness.

Whenever a foreign word has become part of the popular consciousness and moved into common understanding, anybody will use it since it has become a handy word. As a result, we must concentrate our energies on arresting the process of letting these words circulate at large before they become part of people's common understanding. And if, unfortunately, the word has already become linguistic currency, we should address all our efforts to eradicate the counterfeit money. We need not despair. The word *"ōrudūvuru" (hors d'oeuvre)* has been almost completely ousted by the Japanese word *"zensai." "Bēsubōru"* (baseball) has been totally replaced by *"yakyū."* These examples give us courage and hope. Of course, the easiest way would be to use loanwords to indicate new linguistic meaning. Moreover, this would also satisfy our curiosity. But this attitude would be extremely lacking in love for our mother tongue and in ethnic duty.

Most technical terms of Western philosophy have been translated since the Meiji period thanks to the efforts of all my predecessors. Today, difficult words such as *"hanchū"* (*Kategorie* or category), *"tōi"* (*Sollen* or ought), *"shiyō"* (*Aufheben* or supercession), *"datō"* (*Gelten* or valid), and others have entered our daily language. In a sense, since words related to philosophy are conceptual and abstract, it is easier to translate them and circulate them. It is a proven fact that when the linguistic content is objective and intellectual, a translation easily materializes; when it is subjective and emotional, translations are less successful.

Words with a close and concrete relation to life do justice to the emotions of the ambience, and they are undoubtedly difficult to translate into other languages. This is also a question of degree, however, and efforts must be made to find, as far as possible, native translations of foreign words. I believe that if the intellectual class makes sincere and extensive efforts in this direction, the social masses will necessarily agree and we will find that new, fresh translations are being used by everybody.

The Japanese people should thoroughly eradicate their worship for the West as soon as possible. Above all, scholars who are in a position of leading the people with their writings, as well as men of letters and journalists, should strongly awaken the ethnic consciousness; they should make efforts to refine our national language; they should fight desperately for the rejection of loanwords; and they should aim at guiding the tastes of society toward lofty destinations.

Tradition and Progressivism

Recently I have been criticized as being someone who is happy smelling only of the traditional past. It would be too easy to dismiss these opinions as simply foolish criticisms. Instead, since it gives me the opportunity to do so, I would like to analyze myself objectively and see whether this criticism is justified.

The criticism includes two issues. One is that I smell of the traditional past; the other is that I am satisfied with it. I will begin by addressing the second issue. To me it is absolutely clear that I am not satisfied with keeping to the old customs of tradition. I firmly believe there are many things we should learn from the West, as one can see from the fact that I have dedicated half of my life to studying Western cultures. The culture of my native land must increasingly gain weight. To this end it must adopt the new and strong points of foreign countries. This is such an obvious and banal point that it is almost ludicrous to reiterate it at this point in time. I believe profoundly that we should learn all sorts of things from the West—not only things related to science and technology but also matters of art and morality. I believe it is absolutely wrong for the Japanese people to think they are by no means inferior to the world in any field because of their overconfidence. On many scores we should proceed by taking in new things. I am not at all someone who is satisfied with keeping the old customs of tradition.

With regard to the first point, what should I say about giving the impression that I have a strong smell of tradition? I am in total agreement with the impression I give. I wrote *Iki no Kōzō* (The structure of *iki*) at a time when Marxism was at its height and I felt I had the whole world against me. A few years later, when I wrote "My Thoughts on Loanwords" (Gairaigo Shokan), the context had become totally opposite, and I probably gave some readers the impression that I was flattering the Japanese nationalism that was quite popular at the time. The same flow of convictions sustained me from the time I wrote *The Structure of Iki* to the time I wrote "My Thoughts on Loanwords." What has changed are the surrounding circumstances.

I indeed have the smell of the traditional past. My love for tradition, however, is not as faint as a scent.

Notes

Introduction

1. Two versions of this work are currently available in English: John Clark's *Reflections on Japanese Taste: The Structure of Iki* (Sydney: Power Publications, 1997) and Hiroshi Nara's *The Structure of Detachment: The Aesthetic Vision of Kuki Shūzō* (Honolulu: University of Hawai'i Press, 2004).

2. The essay is translated in this book in the section "Selected Essays." I am indebted to the editors of Kuki's *Collected Works* for providing dates for each essay, especially the essays that Kuki did not publish in his lifetime. See "Kaidai" (Explanatory notes) in *Kuki Shūzō Zenshū* (hereafter *KSZ*), 5 (Tokyo: Iwanami Shoten, 1981), pp. 471–477.

3. *Iki no Kōzō* appeared in the January and February 1930 issues of *Shisō* (nos. 92 and 93). The book was published by Iwanami in October 1930.

4. The journal *Shisō* dedicated half of its February 1980 issue to "Kuki Shūzō: Poetry and Philosophy." See *Shisō* 2 (1980): 65–140. The two major monographs on Kuki in Japanese, Sakabe Megumi's *Fuzai no Uta: Kuki Shūzō no Sekai* (Songs of absence: The world of Kuki Shūzō) and Tanaka Kyūbun's *Kuki Shūzō: Gūzen to Shizen* (Kuki Shūzō: Chance and nature), were published in 1990 and 1992 respectively. Daitō Shun'ichi's *Kuki Shūzō to Nihon Bunkaron* (Kuki Shūzō and Japan's culturalism) appeared in 1996.

5. Several English translations of works by the major members of the Kyoto school, such as Nishida Kitarō, Tanabe Hajime, and Nishitani Keiji, have appeared since 1970. David A. Dilworth has been writing on Nishida since the late 1960s. Evaluations of the school as a whole, however, have taken place only during the past two decades. See Thomas P. Kasulis's review article, "The Kyoto School and the West: Review and Evaluation," *Eastern Buddhist* 15(2) (Autumn 1982): 125–144. The major accounts of issues related to the Kyoto school and nationalism are the articles included in James

W. Heisig and John C. Maraldo, eds., *Rude Awakenings: Zen, the Kyoto School, and the Question of Nationalism* (Honolulu: University of Hawai'i Press, 1994). In that book the only reference to Kuki Shūzō comes in the article by Andrew Feenberg (p. 151), who mentions Kuki together with Tanabe Hajime and Watsuji Tetsurō as one of Japan's major thinkers who "defended Japanese imperialism." Feenberg's authority for this statement is Peter Dale, *The Myth of Japanese Uniqueness* (New York: St. Martin's Press, 1986). For a recent account of the school see James W. Heisig, *Philosophers of Nothingness: An Essay on the Kyoto School* (Honolulu: University of Hawai'i Press, 2001).The only relevant reference to Kuki in Heisig's book comes in a note on p. 276 in which the author mentions the entry on the Kyoto school in the 1998 version of Iwanami's *Dictionary of Philosophy and Ideas:* "Watsuji Tetsurō and Kuki Shūzō, both of whom had taught philosophy and ethics at Kyoto for a time during the period of Nishida and Tanabe, are properly listed as peripheral." For an account of the postcolonial critique of Nishida Kitarō (although Kuki is not mentioned) see Yoko Arisaka, "Beyond 'East and West': Nishida's Universalism and Postcolonial Critique," in Fred Dallymayr, ed., *Border Crossings: Towards a Comparative Political Theory* (Lexington, Mass.: Lexington, 1999), pp. 236–252.

6. See Karatani Kōjin, "One Spirit, Two Nineteenth Centuries," translated by Alan Wolfe, in Masao Miyoshi and H.D.Harootunian, eds., *Postmodernism and Japan* (Durham: Duke University Press, 1989), p. 267.

7. Leslie Pincus, *Authenticating Culture in Imperial Japan: Kuki Shūzō and the Rise of National Aesthetics* (Berkeley: University of California Press, 1996), p. 142.

8. "But it was only after the encounter with hermeneutics, particularly in its Heideggerian form, that Kuki was able to pull this diverse assortment of lists and notes into the tight symbolic weave of collective meaning and value." See Pincus, *Authenticating Culture*, p. 53.

9. Ibid., p. 121.

10. "In the final analysis, the logic of organicism—a logic that Kuki first articulated in *Iki no Kōzō* and simply presumed in the later essays—underwrote the Japanese invasion of China in particular, and the excesses of national aestheticism in general." See Pincus, *Authenticating Culture*, p. 231.

11. Ibid., p. 210.

12. Consider, for example, the following statement: "This concept of Asia as a unified field of culture or spirit reflects, of course, the various political discourses mobilized to justify Japan's military expansion throughout Asia and Southeast Asia, including the 'Greater East Asia Co-Prosperity Sphere,' or 'East Asian Cooperative Community,' which was advocated by intellectuals such as Kuki Shūzō and Rōyama Masamichi." See Seiji M. Lippit, *Topographies of Japanese Modernism* (New York: Columbia University Press, 2002), p. 226.

13. The philosopher Graham Parkes has written a brilliant critique of the conspiracy theory of which Kuki has become a target. See his article, "The Putative Fascism of the Kyoto School and the Political Correctness of the Modern Academy," in *Philosophy East and West* 47(3) (July 1997): 305–336, in which he writes: "One must again protest this practice of condemning a Japanese thinker, even at second hand, on the basis of his association with Heidegger. When evaluating philosophical ideas or the integrity of philosophers, assigning 'guilt by association' is as questionable a tactic as it is in the real world of law" (p. 325). See also Parkes's review of *Authenticating Culture in Imperial Japan*, in *Chanoyu Quarterly* 86 (1997): 63–69, in which he writes: "Since Kuki's writings provide so little in the way of evidence for his alleged fascist proclivities, Pincus tries to establish some guilt by association through invoking his relations with Heidegger, whose credentials in the area of political incorrectness apparently need no establishing" (p. 66).

14. We find this trend in the essays by Hiroshi Nara, J. Thomas Rimer, and J. Mark Mikkelsen in Nara, trans. and ed., *The Structure of Detachment*. In "Capturing Shudders and Palpitations: Kuki's Quest for a Philosophy of Life," Nara states: "Ultimately, Kuki's thinking about *iki* aligned itself with Bergson's thinking. Like his mentor, he thought that conceptual analysis—the mainstay of Neo-Kantian thought—failed to connect its findings....In general, one might say that Kuki's debt to Bergson was real and warm and human. The same cannot be said about his debt to Heidegger." He also points out: "As Tom Rimer shows elsewhere in this volume, Kuki's colleagues at Kyoto thought of him as a Francophile. That can't have done his standing much good in a department committed to German idealism, a school of thought he had turned away from in the late 1920s. His chronology (in this volume) shows how often he lectured on French philosophy. Though he divided his time fairly equally between German and French schools of thought, Kuki's lecture schedule attests to special interests in, for example, Bergsonian vitalism. In fact, his contemporary Amano Teiyū characterizes Kuki as a scholar working in French philosophy." On Kuki's French connections see also the excellent book by Stephen Light, *Shūzō Kuki and Jean-Paul Sartre: Influence and Counter-Influence in the Early History of Existential Phenomenology* (Carbondale: Southern Illinois University Press, 1987).

15. See, for example, Mikkelsen's article "Reading Kuki Shūzō's *The Structure of Iki* in the Shadow of *Le Affaire Heidegger*," in Nara, trans. and ed., *The Structure of Detachment*. Mikkelsen states: "I suggest that this linkage [between Heidegger and Kuki] should not be taken for granted, that the common practice of highlighting Kuki's relationship to Heidegger has not generally served Kuki well, and that the practice of linking the name of Kuki with that of Heidegger has actually distorted efforts to appreciate fully Kuki's work and its significance. To suggest that the names of Kuki and Heidegger should, in effect, be de-linked is not, however, the same as claiming that there

are no grounds for linking them." This statement is followed by an analysis of problems related to attempts to "make Kuki into a Heidegger."

16. The essay is translated in this book in the section "Selected Essays."

17. Japanese scholars, sponsored by the Japanese government, would usually spend a couple of years in Europe studying Western learning in European universities. Kuki's independent wealth, however, afforded him the privilege of spending eight years in France, Germany, Switzerland, and Italy, from 1921 to 1928, while engaging in conversation with Nobel Prize winners, diplomats, and the leading intellectual voices of Europe.

18. These efforts immediately become clear to readers of my *Modern Japanese Aesthetics: A Reader* (Honolulu: University of Hawai'i Press, 1999) and *A History of Modern Japanese Aesthetics* (Honolulu: University of Hawai'i Press, 2001). For further information on the complex negotiations between Japanese thinkers and Western thought in the realms of philosophy, aesthetics, and literature, see also Michael F. Marra, ed., *Japanese Hermeneutics: Current Debates on Aesthetics and Interpretation* (Honolulu: University of Hawai'i Press, 2002).

19. David A. Dilworth, Valdo H. Viglielmo, and Augustin Jacinto Zavala, eds., *Sourcebook for Modern Japanese Philosophy: Selected Documents* (Westport: Greenwood Press, 1998), pp. xiii–xiv.

Worlds in Tension

1. Tanaka Kyūbun, *Kuki Shūzō: Gūzen to Shizen,* pp. 15–28. For Kuki's account of the deep impression Okakura made on his young imagination see Kuki's essays "Negishi" and "Remembering Mr. Okakura Kakuzō" translated in this book.

2. English translation by Nara, *The Structure of Detachment,* which I have modified slightly in light of John Clark's *Reflections on Japanese Taste,* pp. 38–39. The original text appears in *KSZ* 1 (Tokyo: Iwanami Shoten, 1981), p. 17.

3. In 1931 Kuki divorced Nakahashi Nuiko, the widow of his brother Ichizō, whom Kuki married in 1918, one year after the death of his brother.

4. Kuki made this point in "Shosai Manpitsu" (Jotting of my library), which is collected in *Ori ni Furete* (Occasions). See *KSZ* 5, pp. 40–57.

5. See Yasuda Takeshi and Tada Michitarō, *"'Iki' no Kōzō" o Yomu* (Tokyo: Asahi Shinbunsha, 1979).

6. Sakabe Megumi, *Fuzai no Uta: Kuki Shūzō no Sekai.* For Tanaka's quotation of Sakabe's argument on tension see Tanaka Kyūbun, "Kuki Shūzō and the Phenomenology of *Iki,*" in Marra, *History of Modern Japanese Aesthetics,* pp. 341–342.

7. Heidegger here refers to a fragment by the pre-Socratic philosopher

Heraclitus; English translation by Gregory Fried and Richard Polt, in Martin Heidegger, *Introduction to Metaphysics* (New Haven: Yale University Press, 2000), pp. 141–142.

8. See Stephen Light, *Shūzō Kuki and Jean-Paul Sartre: Influence and Counter-Influence in the Early History of Existential Phenomenology* (Carbondale: Southern Illinois University Press, 1987), pp. 99–141, in which the author includes a notebook by Kuki titled "Monsieur Sartre."

9. Kuki was familiar with Boutroux's *La Nature et l'Esprit* (Nature and the spirit) and *De la Contingence des Lois de la Nature* (The contingency of the laws of nature). Of the latter we find the French, English, and German versions in Kuki's library. See Amano Teiyū, ed., *Kuki Shūzō Bunko Mokuroku* (Kobe: Kōnan Daigaku Tetsugaku Kenkyūshitsu, 1976), pp. 30–31. For Sartre's development of the notion of contingency see his *L'Être et le Néant* (Being and nothingness), especially pt. 4 on "Having, Doing, and Being."

10. See Kuki's explanation of Bergson's philosophy in his *Gendai Furansu Tetsugaku Kōgi* (Course on contemporary French philosophy) in *KSZ* 8 (Tokyo: Iwanami Shoten, 1981), pp. 294–354, especially the section on "freedom," pp. 319–322.

11. In the preface to the *Course on Contemporary French Philosophy* Kuki criticizes Rickert on the ground that his abstract notion of "cultural value" (*Kulturwert*) does not do justice to the drives of the flesh, of "life value" (*Lebenswert*), the latter being a value fully developed by Bergson in his philosophy. See *KSZ* 8, pp. 7–8.

12. "A 'Conservative Revolution' in Philosophy" is the title of chap. 3 of Pierre Bourdieu's *Political Ontology of Martin Heidegger* (Cambridge: Polity Press, 1991).

13. This is the title of chap. 7 of Philippe Lacoue-Labarthe's *Heidegger, Art, and Politics: The Fiction of the Political* (Oxford: Blackwell, 1990).

14. "Heidegger the Neoconservative" is the subtitle of chap. 3 in Luc Ferry and Alain Renaut's *Heidegger and Modernity* (Chicago: University of Chicago Press, 1990), an outstanding summary of French criticisms of Heidegger and critical contextualizations of those criticisms.

15. Kuki published several poems in the Japanese journal *Myōjō:* the collections *Parī Shinkei* (Paris mindscapes) in April 1925 and January 1926, *Parī Shōkyoku* (Sonnets from Paris) in September 1925, and *Parī no Mado* (Windows of Paris) in December 1925. All poems were published under the initials S. K. In October 1926 Kuki published in the same journal *Parī no Negoto* (Sleep talking in Paris) under the pseudonym of Komori Rokuzō. Kuki used the name Komori when he published *Hahen* (Fragments) in April 1927. All poems are translated in the present book.

16. The main sources for a study of temporality in art are the two lectures that Kuki delivered in Pontigny on 11 August and 17 August 1928 following the invitation by the French writer and scholar Paul Desjardins to participate in

a philosophical *décade* on "Man and Time. Repetition in Time. Immortality or Eternity" (8–18 August 1928). Kuki titled the first lecture "La Notion du Temps et la Reprise sur le Temps en Orient" (The notion of time and repetition in oriental time); the second was titled "L'Expression de l'Infini dans l'Art Japonais" (The expression of the infinite in Japanese art). There are two English translations of these lectures: Steven Light includes his translation in *Shūzō Kuki and Jean-Paul Sartre*, pp. 43–67; V.H. Viglielmo's translation appears in David A. Dilworth et al., eds., *Sourcebook for Modern Japanese Philosophy: Selected Documents* (Westport: Greenwood Press, 1998), pp. 199–219. Another important source on the temporality of art is Kuki's essay "Bungaku no Keijijōgaku" (The metaphysics of literature; 1940), which Kuki included in his last book, *Bungeiron* (Essays on the literary arts; 1941), and which I have included in this book in English translation.

17. *KSZ* 1, pp. 131–133.

18. *KSZ* 4, pp. 223–513.

19. Kuki contended that since it would be difficult to return to the 5/7 poetic pattern of traditional poetry, emphasis on rhyme might well compensate for the lack of rhythm. To those who argued that Japanese language was not suited to rhyming, Kuki responded by tracing a history of rhyme in premodern Japanese poetry. He found examples of rhymes in the techniques of alliteration, pillow words *(makura kotoba)*, and tautologies. Kuki also found in *karon* (essays on poetry) such as Fujiwara Hamanari's *Kakyō Hyōshiki* and Fujiwara Kiyosuke's *Okugishō* discussions of the need for using rhymes in Japanese poetry. Japanese poetry should strive to reproduce the form of the Italian *sonetto*, which became very popular all over Europe. According to Kuki, the lack of symmetry in the *haiku* (5/7/7) and *tanka* (5/7/5/7/7) forms hindered the development of rhymes in Japan. The possibility of rhyming could be found in poetic forms such as *chōka*, *sendōka*, and *imayō*, which never fully developed in Japan.

20. Ishimatsu Keizō, "Haideruberuku no Kuki Shūzō," in *Kuki Shūzō Zenshū Geppō*, 1, vol. 2 (Tokyo: Iwanami Shoten, 1981), p. 4. On the meaning of the name "Kuki" see the essay "My Family Name" in this book.

21. *KSZ* 1, pp. 143–146.

22. *KSZ* 1, pp. 133–135.

23. Henri Bergson, *The Creative Mind: An Introduction to Metaphysics* (New York: Philosophical Library, 1946), pp. 207–217.

24. *KSZ* 1, p. 190, n. 128.

25. The first chapter of Heidegger's *Introduction to Metaphysics*, titled "The Fundamental Question of Metaphysics," begins with the formulation of this question. See Heidegger, *Introduction to Metaphysics*, p. 1.

26. Kant classified nothing as follows: "(1) an object of a conception, to which no intuition can be found to correspond (empty conception without object). That is, it is a conception without an object *(ens rationis)*, like *noumena*, which cannot be considered possible in the sphere of reality, though they must

not therefore be held to be impossible....(2) Reality is *something;* negation is *nothing,* that is, a conception of the absence of an object, as cold, a shadow *(nihil privativum)* (empty object of a conception). (3) The mere form of intuition, without substance, is in itself no object, but the merely formal condition of an object (as phenomenon), as pure space and pure time. These are certainly something, as forms of intuition, but are not themselves objects which are intuited *(ens imaginarium)* (empty intuition without object). (4) The object of conception which is self-contradictory, is nothing, because the conception is nothing— is impossible, as a figure composed of two straight lines *(nihil negativum)* (empty object without conception). We see that the *ens rationis* is distinguished from the *nihil negativum* or pure nothing by the consideration that the former must not be reckoned among possibilities, because it is a mere fiction—though not self-contradictory—while the latter is completely opposed to all possibility, inasmuch as the conception annihilates itself. Both, however, are empty conceptions. On the other hand, the *nihil privativum* and *ens imaginarium* are empty *data* for conceptions. If light be not given to the senses, we cannot represent to ourselves darkness, and if extended objects are not perceived, we cannot represent space. Neither the negation nor the mere form of intuition can, without something real, be an object." See Immanuel Kant, *Critique of Pure Reason,* trans. J.M.D.Meiklejohn (New York: Prometheus Books, 1990), p. 185.

27. Kant developed this argument in *Versuch den Begriff der negativen Grössen* (Experiment: The concept of the negative dimension in the sphere of the world). For a French translation of Kant's essay see Immanuel Kant, *Essai pour Introduire en Philosophie le Concept de Grandeur Négative,* trans. Roger Kempf (Paris: J.Vrin, 1949).

28. See, for example, the following famous passage from the *Chuang Tzu:* "Once Chuang Chou dreamt he was a butterfly, a butterfly flitting and fluttering around, happy with himself and doing as he pleased. He didn't know he was Chuang Chou. Suddenly he woke up and there he was, solid and unmistakable Chuang Chou. But he didn't know if he was Chuang Chou who had dreamt he was a butterfly, or a butterfly dreaming he was Chuang Chou. Between Chuang Chou and a butterfly there must be *some* distinction! This is called the Transformation of Things." English translation by Burton Watson, *The Complete Works of Chuang Tzu* (New York: Columbia University Press, 1968), p. 49.

29. *Kokinshū* 8:942; English translation by Helen Craig McCullough, *Kokin Wakashū: The First Imperial Anthology of Japanese Poetry* (Stanford: Stanford University Press, 1985), p. 207.

30. Kuki quotes Seneca, "Never was there a great mind without a mixture of insanity" *(nullum magnum ingenium sine mixtura dementiae fuit),* and Horace's "lovable insanity" *(amabilis insania).*

31. See the section "Sekkyokuteki Mu (Nihil Positivum)," in *Bungaku no Gairon, KSZ* 11 (Tokyo: Iwanami Shoten, 1980), pp. 45–73.

32. English translation by W.Hamilton Fyfe and W.Rhys Roberts, in Aristotle, *The Poetics* (Cambridge, Mass.: Harvard University Press, 1927), p. 103.

33. For a recent discussion of Chikamatsu's concept see Ōhashi Ryōsuke, "The Hermeneutic Approach to Japanese Modernity: 'Art-Way,' '*Iki*,' and 'Cut-Continuance,'" in Marra, *Japanese Hermeneutics*, pp. 27–29.

34. See the section "Shōkyokuteki Mu (Nihil Negativum)," in *Bungaku no Gairon*, pp. 74–82.

35. See the section "Sonzai no Bunrui (Sonzai to Bungaku)," in *Bungaku no Gairon*, pp. 125–126.

36. *KSZ* 1, pp. 130–131.

37. Explaining the "basic colors" *(Grundfarben)* yellow and blue, Goethe pointed out that while yellow was the color of the positive side *(Farbe von der Plusseite)*, blue was the result of the negative side *(Farbe von der Minusseite)*. The eye perceives the color yellow when the light penetrates a muddy medium; if the muddiness increases, yellow becomes orange and ruby. The eye sees the blue color when darkness passes through a bright medium with little muddiness; if the muddiness further decreases, blue becomes violet.

38. See the section "Kesseiteki Mu (Nihil Privativum)," in *Bungaku no Gairon*, pp. 28–44.

39. English translation by F.L.Pogson in Henri Bergson, *Time and Free Will: An Essay on the Immediate Data of Consciousness* (London: Allen & Unwin, 1971), pp. 53–54. For the original text see Henri Bergson, *Essai sur les Données Immédiates de la Conscience* (Paris: Presses Universitaires de France, 1946), pp. 40–41.

40. Bergson, *Time and Free Will*, p. 100.

41. Ibid.

42. Ibid., p. 106.

43. Henri Bergson, *Duration and Simultaneity: Bergson and the Einsteinian Universe*, trans. Mark Lewis and Robin Durie (Manchester: Clinamen, 1999), p. 42.

44. Bergson, *Time and Free Will*, p. 95.

45. *KSZ* 1, pp. 135–137.

46. "Line" in Japanese is *ku*; "nine" is *kū*.

47. It means "to count."

48. This refers to the regrets that a person has once he starts thinking, "Oh, if only I had done this, or if only I had done that." Such a regret is an indication that the person is still imprisoned in quantitative time.

49. Bergson, *Time and Free Will*, p. 99.

50. Ibid., p. 104.

51. Ibid., p. 84.

52. The song by Ishihara Wasaburō appears in Horiuchi Keizō and Inoue Takeshi, eds., *Nihon Shōkashū* (Tokyo: Iwanami Shoten, 1958), p. 106.

53. Bergson, *Time and Free Will*, pp. 112–114.

54. In the lecture course "Bungaku no Gairon," Kuki discussed poetry's relationship with quantitative and qualitative time. On the quantitative side Kuki singled out the measurability of Japan's poetic rhythm—twelve syllables divided in the 5/7 or 7/5 pattern. According to Kuki, poetic rhythm was related to human breathing: a poetic verse comes into being on condition that it can be sung in a breath. The French alexandrine line is also made of twelve sounds (hexameter); the Italian hendecasyllable is made of eleven sounds; the English iambic pentameter is made of ten sounds; the German tetrameter and pentameter iamb are made of eight or ten sounds. But the temporality of poetry is not quantitative; it is qualitative. Kuki argued that the temporality of poetry is duration *(durée)* and that the rhythmic patterns actually underscore the tensions of duration characterizing the flow of poetry. The accent in Italian poetry, for example, always falls on the tenth sound (qualitative time) independently of whether the verse is a hendecasyllable (eleven sounds), a dactyl (twelve sounds), or a trochee (ten sounds)—the so-called quantitative time. The accent endows quantitative time with quality. The same result is brought about by the length of the vowels, whether short or long, as we can see in Greek and Latin poetry. Modern poetry has replaced the length of the vowels with the accent. The more attention to sound a poem discloses, the more the poem is caught in its qualitative time of duration. See *KSZ* 11, pp. 148–154.

55. For a discussion of Kuki's philosophy and everydayness see Harry Harootunian, *Overcome by Modernity: History, Culture, and Community in Interwar Japan* (Princeton: Princeton University Press, 2000), pp. 221–250.

56. *KSZ* 1, p. 185, n. 90.

57. *KSZ* 1, p. 248. English translation by Light, *Shūzō Kuki and Jean-Paul Sartre*, p. 82. I have modified the translation slightly.

58. Robert McAlmon and Kay Boyle, *Being Geniuses Together: 1920–1930* (London: Hogarth Press, 1984), pp. 303–304.

59. *KSZ* 1, pp. 117–120. "A Seafood Restaurant." [Man] Oh, the sea, the sea/Born in an island country in the Far East/I pine for the blue sea,/The shore scattered with seashells,/White sand bathing in the morning sun,/The smell of seaweed, the sound of waves,/I wonder, you who grew up in Paris,/Do you understand my feelings?/Tonight let us go to Prunier/On Victor Hugo Avenue.//Pillars designed with the pattern of scallops,/Lamps shaped as sea crabs,/Watery foam on the walls,/Fish on the counters,/The ceiling a light turquoise,/The rug the crimson color of seaweed,/A faint floating light,/A scent more fleeting than a dream,/Like breathing at the bottom of the sea/My favorite seafood restaurant.//[Woman] What was your favorite dish?/Salmon roe sandwich,/Sea urchin in its shell/Sprinkled with lemon juice,/The chowder bouillabaisse/A specialty from Marseilles,/Lobsters the thermidor style/Not the American style,/I too like/The steamed flatfish Paris style.//For a dress I will choose clothes of black silk./Don't you like the way my figure looms over the silver wall,/One snowy white rose on my breast,/Pearls for

necklace,/A platinum watch on my wrist,/A white diamond ring,/A hat the green color of laver/I will pull down over my eyes coquettishly?/Let me please make my lipstick heavy./Do you still insist I am princess of the sea?

See also *KSZ* 1, p. 185, n. 92:

Maruseru to	Won't I find consolation
Aniesu to kuu	In the seafood
Puriunie no	Of Prunier,
Sakana ryōri ni mo	Where I eat
Nagusamanu ka na	With Marcel and Agnès?

60. *KSZ* 1, p. 175, n. 16:

Mata no yo no	Who is that talking
Kinu no iro nado	Of colors of garments and suchlike
Makuai no	Again tonight
Opera no rō ni	During the intermission
Kikaseshi wa dare	In the Opéra lobby?

KSZ 1, p. 186, n. 99:

Butōkai	This evening I will go
Waga shi no hiraku	Neither to the dance party
Opera e mo	Nor to the Opéra
Koyoi wa ikazu	My teacher is opening—
Heya ni fumikaku	I will write a letter in my room.

61. *KSZ* 1, p. 183, n. 79:

Sugishi toshi	The flowers I saw
Komo no umibe ni	On the shore of Lake Como
Mishi hana no	Last year
Parī ni mo saki	Bloom in Paris as well—
Haru no hi to naru	A spring day has come!

62. *KSZ* 1, p. 185, n. 94:

Makishimu no	The endless
Sakaba no odori	Dance at the barroom
Hatenu ma ni	Of Maxim—
Shiroki te o tori	I take the white hand
Yo no machi ni izu	And emerge on the streets at night.

63. *KSZ* 1, pp. 148-150. "Monte Carlo." Oh, how I want to gamble!/Hurry to the casino./Oh, I want to see a dance!/Peep in the barroom.//Yearning after what/Did I come to the southern lands?/Wishing for what/Did I come to Monte Carlo?//Let's get intoxicated by the blue expanse of water/In the shadow of the yucca tree!/Let's catch some shrimps,/Smelling the fragrance of seaweed!//Oh, how starved I am for an amorous glance!/Enter a teahouse./Oh, how I pine for skin!/Go to a brothel.

64. See William Wiser, *The Crazy Years: Paris in the Twenties* (New

York: Athenaeum, 1983), pp. 20-21. Kuki alludes to the "Sphinx" in the following poem in which he questions his own identity (*KSZ* 1, pp. 139-140). "Self-Questioning." Somehow I wonder/What on earth are you?/Long ears and a tail you have,/Aren't you of the same species as a horse?/And yet you look like a deer.//In the African desert/Lives an odd monster./Its body no different from that of a beast,/Its head just like a human face,/They call it a sphinx.//In the countryside of America/There is an odd bird,/Face blue like a gourd in the morning,/Becoming ruddy in evening,/They call it a turkey.// Somehow I wonder/What on earth are you?/By rolling yourself backward/ Try to unriddle the puzzle/Tangled inside your navel!

65. This word appears in several poems that Kuki did not publish, such as the following from his "Practice Project of Short Poems" (Tanka Shūsaku) (*KSZ, Bekkan,* p. 109):

Ame fureba	Women of pleasure at the street corners
Kasa sasu yowa no	Chatting casually
Yukizuri ni	With passersby,
Koto ihikakuru	Their umbrellas unfolded in the dead of the night
Tsuji no asobi onna	When it rains.

66. *KSZ* 1, p. 175, n. 8:

Tomoshibi no	The smiling profile
Moto ni Ivonnu ga	Of Yvonne
Emu yokogao wa	Under the light
Doga no e yori ya	Seems to come out more starkly
Idete kiniken	Than from a painting by Degas!

67. *KSZ* 1, p. 175, n. 15:

Yamite yaya	Having fallen ill
Hō no hosoriken	Her cheeks will be slightly thinner—
Donīzu ga	When Denise
Emeba koyoi wa	Smiles, how charming
Namamekashikere	This evening will be!

68. *KSZ* 1, p. 177, n. 30:

Koyoi shi mo	Saying,
Roshia no kouta	Let's sing the little Russian song
Shiyo mōshite	This evening,
Rina ga nuretaru	If only Rina would live
Me ni zo ikimashi	In the damp pupils of my eyes!

69. *KSZ* 1, p. 178, n. 35:

Torikago ni	A goldfish
Kingyo no oyogi	Swims in the birdcage;
Minazoko ni	A canary chirps

Kanaria no naku	Underwater—
Mariannu ka na	It must be Marianne!

70. *KSZ* 1, p. 178, n. 39:

Ruīzu ga	Louise
Ware o mukaete	Welcomes me
Yorokobase	And makes me happy—
Nihon no nui no	She leaves wearing
Kinu tsukete izu	A garment of Japanese embroidery.

71. *KSZ* 1, p. 178, n. 40:

Pansechiu to	How hard to forget even
Anrietto ga	Henriette's
Namamekite	Charming
Iitsuru kuse mo	Habit of speaking
Wasuregatakari	When she says, "Penses-tu?"

72. *KSZ* 1, p. 183, n. 72:

Janīnu ga	Faintly a light rain
Mune naru bara no	Falls dampening
Kurenai o	The crimson
Kosame honoka ni	Of the rose
Nurashitsutsu furu	On Jeannine's chest.

73. *KSZ* 1, p. 185, n. 87:

Furusato no	My heart smells
"Iki" ni niru ka o	A fragrance similar to
Haru no yo no	The "stylishness" of my homeland
Rune ga sugata ni	In the figure of Renée
Kagu kokoro ka na	On a spring night.

74. *KSZ* 1, p. 189, n. 119:

Ivetto ga	Feigning not to know
Mi no uebanashi	I listen
Ōuso to	To Yvette
Shiredo soshiranu	Boasting about herself
Kao o shite kiku	Though I know it's a big lie.

75. *KSZ* 1, pp. 160–163. "The Russian Song." [Man] You say, why is your face so sad?/Suzanne, you/Ask repeatedly, worried silly./Since that Saturday evening!/Since that Saturday evening/When we heard the Russian song together!/Somehow I grew sad in my heart/In a way I cannot say.// [Woman] That must be why!/That much I noticed—/Your pupils charmed/By the woman who sang the free and easy little song/With an amorous, coquettish voice:/You stared at her steadily./Her blonde hair,/The looks of a temptress, the shape of her mouth,/Bulging breast, twisted gait,/Her thin

legs./I know, men are all alike,/Fickle, whimsical!/You must be dying for a Slavic girl,/Before even realizing it, you have grown tired/Of a Parisian woman like myself/With a smooth brown cut./Since that evening, since that evening/You changed completely./Despite the hot hot kiss/I gave your mouth/You wouldn't return a single lukewarm kiss.//[Man] Suzanne,/You shouldn't say such silly things!/That was not the love and the song of a young girl,/It was a sailor's song of a man fifty years old./The dark moan, the dreadful suffocation,/The pitiful lamentation, the sharp anguish/Of the Volga flowing, never coming to an end,/From eternity to eternity,/Through nights of dark in the Russian wilderness,/My heart from its very bottom/Resonated with the same vibration/Of the baritone who sang that song./Since that evening, turning its back to love/My heart has been sad.

76. *KSZ* 1, p. 181, n. 62.

77. *KSZ* 1, p. 194, n. 160:

Nanitonaku	Drawn somehow
Hi ni akugaruru	By the lights
Yoiyoi wa	Every evening
Gion no machi ni	I scoop up delicious *sake*
Umasake o kumu	In the streets of Gion.

78. *KSZ* 1, p. 194, n. 157:

Yukurinaku	By chance
Saigyōan no	I passed the corner
Kado suginu	Of Saigyō's hermitage—
Kyō ni sumu mi ni	For me living in Kyoto
Sachi nashi to sezu	This is not without blessings.

79. *KSZ* 1, p. 194, n. 158:

Kamogawa no	Cold is the water sound
Mizuoto samushi	Of the Kamo River—
Kyōdan ni	Standing in the classroom,
Tachi utsusomi wa	This present body
Horobi yuku nari	Goes extinct.

80. *KSZ* 1, p. 194, n. 159:

Oshiego no	A pupil of mine
Torawarete naki	Has been taken away and was not home—
Uchi toeba	When I visited him,
Hiei no yama wa	Clear was the winter sky
Fuyuzora ni sumu	Of Mt. Hiei where he lived.

81. *KSZ* 1, p. 194, n. 162:

Tatakai ni	Rousing
Hito shinuran to	A stern heart that says,
Ogosoka no	"People will die

Kokoro okoshite   In battle,"
Mizukara o semu   I blame myself.

82. For a comparison of Bergson and Heidegger's philosophies of time see Kuki's essay "Jikan no Mondai: Berukuson to Haideggā" (The problem of time: Bergson and Heidegger), which Kuki published in May 1929 in the journal *Tetsugaku Zasshi*. See *KSZ* 3, pp. 295–337.

83. Kuki Shūzō, "Bungaku no Keijijōgaku," in *KSZ* 4, pp. 31–40. A complete translation of this essay is included in this book.

84. Here I am using Heideggerian language to explain Bergson's temporality.

85. Gilles Deleuze, *Bergsonism*, trans. Hugh Tomlinson and Barbara Habberiam (New York: Zone Books, 1988), p. 59.

86. Henri Bergson, *Creative Evolution*, trans. Arthur Mitchell (Mineola: Dover, 1998), p. 4.

87. Kuki, "Bungaku no Keijijōgaku," in *KSZ* 4, pp. 40–45.

88. "The primary phenomenon of primordial and authentic temporality is the future." See Martin Heidegger, *Being and Time: A Translation of Sein und Zeit*, trans. Joan Stambaugh (Albany: State University of New York Press, 1996), p. 303.

89. Kuki, "Bungaku no Keijijōgaku," in *KSZ* 4, p. 34.

90. Kuki discusses these issues in the section "Time and Literature" of *Bungaku no Gairon*, in *KSZ* 11, pp. 137–161.

91. Kuki, "Bungaku no Keijijōgaku," in *KSZ* 4, p. 33.

92. *Analects* 9:16; English translation by Arthur Waley, ed., *The Analects of Confucius* (New York: Vintage, 1938), p. 142.

93. Kuki, *Bungaku no Gairon*, in *KSZ* 11, pp. 136–137.

94. Martin Heidegger, *The Concept of Time*, trans. William McNeill (Oxford: Blackwell, 1992), p. 20E.

95. *KSZ* 1, pp. 128–129.

96. Kuki, "Bungaku no Keijijōgaku," in *KSZ* 4, pp. 45–52. Kuki noticed a similarity between the arts and religion since both were concerned with the notion of "eternity." The difference was that while religion dealt with the potentiality of the infinite *(sempiternitas)* and, therefore, its temporal nature was a metaphysical present *(keijijōgaku genzai)*, art was centered on the notion of the present power of eternity *(aeternitas)* and, therefore, its temporal structure was phenomenological *(genshōgakuteki genzai)*.

97. Kuki, *Bungaku no Gairon*, in *KSZ* 11, pp. 139–140.

98. Light, *Shūzō Kuki and Jean-Paul Sartre*, p. 50.

99. For Bashō's original text see Kon Eizō, ed., *Bashō Kushū*, SNKS 51 (Tokyo: Shinchōsha, 1982), p. 226, n. 635.

100. Light, *Shūzō Kuki and Jean-Paul Sartre*, p. 59. With regard to Japanese painting (Nihonga), Kuki says that the flux of Tao is captured in Japanese art

by the *line* that is dynamic. He argues: "It can hold the future within the present; it can hold one space within another; it can move." Black and white—the privileged colors in Japanese art—indicate a taste for simplicity and fluidity "arising from nostalgia for the infinite and from the effort to efface differences in space." The four characteristics of Japanese painting—the absence of exact perspective, the free composition not bound by realism, the importance of the line, and the preference for ink painting—are all "expressions of a pantheist idealism." They "all are methods for gaining liberation from space." Ibid., pp. 54–55.

101. Kanno Akimasa, ed., *Kuki Shūzō Zuihitsu Shū* (Tokyo: Iwanami Shoten, 1991), pp. 147–148. See the translation of this essay in this book.

102. Kuki defines painting, sculpture, and architecture as "spatial arts" while considering literature and music "temporal arts," arts that bring about qualitative time, fluid and continuous time, which is different from the quantitative time of the clock. For Kuki the difference and, at the same time, similarity between literature and music is that in poetry, rhythm brings together the disjunctive 5/7 pattern, while in music, melody brings together the disjunctive notes. Mutual permeation is achieved in poetry by rhyme, which allows sounds to come together. Unlike music that lasts only the space of a performance (*tansōsei* or one-layeredness), poetry has a multilayered temporality (*jūsōsei*), thanks to its ability to bring together different temporalities such as the time of the speaker, the times of what was spoken about, as well as the fiction of making things past present. A *haiku* does not last for only the six seconds it takes to read it. It also brings with itself the continuity of ideal time, the reverberation of past time. As we know from *Bungaku no Gairon*, Kuki was indebted to Max Dessoir (1867–1947) for the distinction he made between temporal arts, spatial arts, and spatio-temporal arts. In the temporal arts Kuki includes literature and music. He argues for the difference between these two arts by concentrating on the fact that the temporality of music corresponds to the time of the actual execution. But the temporality of literature is not limited to, for example, the few seconds that it takes to read a *haiku*. The poetic composition possesses an internal richness of time that overlaps with the actual time it takes to read the poem. For Kuki, literature's peculiar relationship with time is similar to the relationship that painting has with space. He classifies painting as a spatio-temporal art, or an art of movement, together with dance and drama. Unlike sculpture and architecture, which are spatial arts occupying a well-defined space, painting contains within itself a larger space than the one that the painting itself actually occupies. In the same course on literature, Kuki also mentioned Karl Jaspers's (1883–1969) definition of music, architecture, and sculpture in terms of their relationship with a "real present" *(wirkliche Gegenwart)*. Painting and literature, by contrast, are seen as "visions of a present unreality" *(Visionen eines gegenwärtig Unwirklichen)*. Painting and literature are "illusions of representation" *(Illusionen der Vorstellung)* brought about by color in painting and

language in literature. Kuki defined the temporality of literature according to the unreal representation *(unwirkliche Vorstellung)* produced by language. See Kuki Shūzō, *Bungaku no Gairon,* in *KSZ* 11, pp. 143–148.

103. See Henri Bergson, *The Two Sources of Morality and Religion,* trans. R. Ashley Audra and Cloudesley Brereton (Notre Dame: University of Notre Dame Press, 1977).

104. A photographic reproduction of the inscription appears in Iwaki Ken'ichi, ed., *Nishida Tetsugaku Senshū,* vol. 6 (Tokyo: Tōeisha, 1998), p. 400.

Free Verse

The original text appears in *KSZ* 1, pp. 114–171.

1. [Text: *Kaze. Puratanu no nure o fuku/aki no kaze yo,/omae no yō ni jiyū ni/fukasete kure.//Minikui mono mo/kasarazu ni,/hazubeki koto mo/ kakusazu ni,//sono mama,/arinomama,/hito o osorezu,/yo o ojizu,//mune no zange o/katarasete kure./Kokoro no nageki o/utawasete kure.//Puratanu no nure o fuku/aki no kaze yo,/omae no yō ni jiyū ni/fukasete kure.*]

2. [Text: *Omoide. Hito no yo no/michi wa ogurashi./Tasogare no/ kokage wa sabishi.//Wasureezu,/kano kaori./Maboroshi ni miyu,/kano sugata.//Omoide ni/kokoro kizutsuki,/akugare ni/inochi nayamu.//Hito no yo no/michi wa ogurashi.//Yūsareba/utsusomi sabishi.*] We hear in this poem the echo of Henri Bergson's words: "Sensations and tastes seem to me to be objects as soon as I isolate and name them, and in the human soul there are only processes.... We are now standing before our own shadow: we believe that we have analyzed our feeling, while we have really replaced it by a juxtaposition of lifeless states which can be translated into words, and each of which constitutes the common element, the impersonal residue of the impressions felt in a given case by the whole society." See Bergson, *Time and Free Will,* p. 133. Bergson is the author of *Essai sur les Données Immédiates de la Conscience* (1889), *Matière et Mémoire* (1896), *Le Rire* (1900), *Introduction à la Metaphysique* (1903), *L'Évolution Créatrice* (1907), *Les Deux Sources de la Morale et de la Religion* (1932). He was awarded the Nobel Prize for literature in 1928.

3. Prunier, one of the best seafood restaurants in Paris, is located at 16 Victor Hugo Avenue in the capital's 16th Arrondissement (Trocadéro, Bois de Boulogne). The restaurant was founded in 1925. The famous Art Déco mosaics glitter and the white marble counters overflow with the impeccably fresh shellfish displayed like precious jewels.

4. [Text: *Sakana Ryōriya. Aa, umi, umi/tōi higashi no shimaguni ni umareta boku wa/aoi umi ga koishii,/kaigara no ochite iru hamabe,/asahi o abita shiroi suna,/mo no nioi, nami no oto,/Pari sodachi no omae ni wa/boku no kimochi ga wakaru kashira./Kon'ya wa Vikutoru Yūgōgai no/Puryunie e ikō.//Hashira no moyō wa hotategai,/dentō no katachi wa umigani,/kabe ni*

wa mizuawa,/nageshi ni wa sakana,/tenjō wa usui mizuiro,/shikimono wa kurenai mo no iro,/honoka ni tadayou hikari,/yume yori awai kaori,/umi no soko de iki suru yō na/ano boku no suki na sakana ryōriya.//Osuki na oryōri wa nan deshitaro,/sake no ko no sandowicchi,/remon no mi o kakeru/kara no mama no uni,/Marusēyu meibutsu no/yoseni no buiyabēsu,/ebi wa Amerikafū de naku/terumidōru no hō deshō,/watashi mo suki na no wa/ Parifū ni mushita karei.//Kimono wa kuroji no kinu ni shimasu wa,/gin no kabe kara sugata ga ukidete ii deshō,/mune ni masshiro na bara no hana o hitotsu,/kubikazari wa shinjū,/ude ni wa hakkin no tokei,/yubiwa wa shiroi daiya,/bōshi wa aosa no yō na midoriiro no o/mabuka ni, iki ni kaburu wa./ Kuchibeni o koku sasashite chōdai,/otohime da nante mata ossharu no?]

5. *Contes d'Hoffmann* (Tales of Hoffmann) is the only grand opera of Jacques Offenbach (1819–1880), French musician and composer. The opera was inspired by the work of Ernst Theodor Amadeus Hoffmann (1776–1822), a German composer, music critic, and illustrator who wrote tales of the supernatural collected as *Die Serapionsbrüder* (1819–1921) *and Die Lebensansichten des Katers Murr* (1820–1822). *Tales of Hoffmann,* completed by Ernest Guiraud, was not produced until after Offenbach's death.

6. Publis Vergilius Maro (70–19 B.C.), the greatest of Roman poets, enjoyed the patronage of Maecenas and Augustus. Works include *Eclogae* or *Bucolica,* a set of ten poems (42–37 B.C.); *Georgica,* four books on rural topics (36–29); and the great epic of the founding of Rome, *Aeneis* or *Aeneid* (30–19).

7. Saint Augustine of Hippo (354–430), early Christian church father and philosopher. Works include *De Vera Religione* (ca. 390), *De Doctrina Christiana* (397–428), *De Trinitate* (400–416), *Confessiones* (ca. 400), and *De Civitate Dei* (413–426).

8. Baruch Spinoza (1632–1677), Dutch philosopher of Portuguese-Jewish parentage. Among his works are *Tractatus Theologico-Politicus* (1670), *Ethica Ordine Geometrico Demonstrata* (1677), and *Tractatus Politicus* (unfinished, 1677). In his *Ethics* Spinoza distinguishes between a *natura naturans* (anything that is in itself, all the attributes expressing the infinite substance, that is, God) and a *natura naturata* (anything that follows from the necessity of the nature of God, anything that is in God). Such a necessity is absolute freedom since it acts *causa sui* and is unconditioned. To know for Spinoza is to free oneself from the mistakes of the imagination and those of the passions in order to catch the existence of things from the point of view of eternity *(sub specie aeternitatis).* Intuitive knowledge corresponds to the coincidence of our mind with the idea of our mind in God. In this coincidence the mind finds its eternity. By ascending to God we reach our true freedom since we come to understand the wholeness of our being. The love of self becomes intellectual love for God. And God, by loving himself, loves all humanity. See Baruch Spinoza, *Ethics,* trans. G.H.R.Parkinson (Oxford: Oxford University Press, 2000).

9. [Text: *Monban no Musuko. Antoanetto ga karima shite/sunderu ie*

*no monban no/hitori musuko no Furansoa,/kotoshi jūyon no bishōnen,/
chūgakkō no kyūchū no/yūtōsei de gohōbi o/itsumo morau to, shōjiki na/
oyaji ga sakujitsu hidarite ni/hageta kiseru o mochinagara,/hokuhokugao de
ittakke.//Kyō nichiyō no yūgata ni,/Antoanetto no te o totte/odorigaeri no
jidōsha no/tobira o akete oritatsu to,/genkanmae no isu ni kake,/bōshi o
kabutta Furansoa,/kotoshi jūyon no Furansoa,/ore no ofuru no erikazari/
mune ni musunde, ratengo no/kobunten o motte ita.//Oo, Furansoa,
Furansoa,/kotoshi jūyon no bishōnen,/yūbe wa nan no kimagure ka,/ano
'Hofuman no Monogatari' no/'Utsukushii yo no koi no yo' to,/utatte nagasu
funauta o/omae wa shikiri ni hamonika de/tonari no heya de fuiteta na./Iki
na tsutome o oretachi ni/shiro to wa dare ga oshieta ka.//Kotoshi jūyon no
Furansoa,/ sono utsukushii Ratengo o/o-manabi, o-manabi, o-manabi yo,/
toshi hete itsuka Virujiru ni/manako o nurasu hi mo arō,/Oogyusutan no
Zangeroku/yonde wa inoru hi mo arō,/mata Supinoza no eigō no/sugata no
moto ni utsushiyo no/urei o warau hi mo arō.//Oo, Furansoa, Furansoa,/
kotoshi jūyon no bishōnen,/o-manabi, o-manabi, Ratengo no/meishi,
daimeishi, keiyōshi,/dōshi no henka o o-manabi yo,/Antoanetto no tomoda-
chi no/odori no sukina ojisan mo/chūgakkō no sensei to/onnaji koto o iu
nado to/fushigigatte wa ikenai yo.]*

10. This is probably a reference to the art historian Kojima Kikuo (1887–
1950), a close friend of Kuki, who studied in Europe from 1921 to 1926 and
was appointed professor of art history at the University of Tokyo in 1937.

11. Jean Désiré Gustave Courbet (1819–1877), leader of the new realist
school, was constantly at odds with the academic establishment.

12. Édouard Manet (1832–1883) followed a mixture of realism and im-
pressionistic technique. His depictions of nudes and casual city life often scan-
dalized Paris. He encouraged Monet and other impressionists and was an
important forerunner of impressionism.

13. Claude Monet (1840–1926) developed the technique of rendering light
and color as actually perceived, perfecting a style known as impressionism.

14. Amano Teiyū (1884–1980) was a professor of philosophy at the Uni-
versity of Kyoto. In *Dōri no Kankaku* (The sense of rationality; 1937) he cri-
tiqued totalitarianism, privileging instead the self-genesis of action and the
freedom of the will that is born out of a sense of rationality. After World War
II Amano became minister of education and made efforts to revive the study
of ethics in Japan. He translated Kant's *Critique of Pure Reason (Junsui Risei
Hihan)* into Japanese.

15. In the *Critique of Practical Reason* Kant introduces the notion of moral
law that works as an imperative, the producer of an order in a categorical way.
It orders an action as if this action were objectively necessary. This is the law of
duty that determines the will. To act according to reason is the fundamental
moral rule. Kant argues that one's way of acting must be universal. People
must behave according to laws that they would like to become natural laws.

Others must be treated as an end, not as a means. We should not reduce people to instruments for our own ends. See Immanuel Kant, *Critique of Practical Reason*, trans. Mary Gregor (Cambridge: Cambridge University Press, 1997).

16. Modeled after a Greek temple, La Madeleine was begun in 1764 but was not consecrated as a church until 1845. A columnade of Corinthian columns encircles the building and supports a sculptured frieze. The inside, crowned by three ceiling domes, is lavishly decorated with fine sculptures, rose marble, and gilt.

17. René Descartes (1596–1650) established in *Discours de la Méthode* (1637) the ideal of mathematical certitude in all scientific and philosophical thought. He also laid the foundation of analytic geometry. Among his works are *Meditationes de Prima Philosophia* (1641), *Principia Philosophiae* (1644), *Les Passions de L'Âme* (1649), and *Opuscula Posthuma, Physica et Mathematica* (1701).

18. Blaise Pascal (1623–1662) originated with Fermat the mathematical theory of probability. Works include *Lettres Écrites par Louis de Montalte á un Provinciale de ses Amis,* popularly known as *Provinciales* (1656–1657), and *Pensées,* published (1670) from manuscript notes left by him.

19. "Nel mezzo del cammin di nostra vita/mi ritrovai per una selva oscura/che la diritta via era smarrita./Ah, quanto a dir qual era è cosa dura/ esta selva selvaggia e aspra e forte/che nel pensier rinova la paura!/Tant'è amara che poco è piú morte;/ma per trattar del ben ch'io vi trovai/dirò dell'altre cose ch'i' v'ho scorte." See Dante Alighieri, *La Divina Commedia: Inferno,* ed. Natalino Sapegno (Florence: La Nuova Italia Editrice, 1955), pp. 4–5.

20. [Text: *Aki no Ichinichi. Shanzerizē no namiki/kiiro ni somatte chiriyuku maronie no ha,/kesa kimi ga boku no yado e kita no wa jūji goro,/ hanashi o shita, tabako o sutta,/hirumeshi o kutta, sanpo o shita,/kafé de ikonda, kaiga tenrankai o mita,/ima wa mō yūgure/kimi mo boku mo aikawarazu no kawarimono,/gakusei no jidai, yoku ichiya o katariakashite/ kimi wa yokuasa kaette itta./Toki o chōetsu shi, toki o hitei suru sube,/yōi no yō de, yōi de nai sube,/kimi wa sono meijin da, sono tensai da,/ryūgaku kigen ga kirete mo kaeranai gurai wa betsu ni fushigi ja nai./Da ga kimi wa mō fune o kimeta ka,/kichō suru to mata kōgi o shinakucha naranai na,/bungei fukkōki no geijutsu ga daimoku nara/jōron gurai de ichigakunen wa tatsu no darō,/Girisha no chōkokushi nara/kigenzen goseiki no nakaba atari made susumu ka,/Furansu gendai no kaiga ni tsuite nara/Kūrubē, Manē, Monē,/ konna iriguchi de tomaru no darō,/sakki mo tenrankai de kimi no hihyō o kiite iru to/gobun no ichi mo minai uchi ni/heisa no fue ga natte oidasareta ja nai ka.//Aa, kirei da, furigaette mitamae,/murasaki iro no sora ni sabita ochitsuita iro no gaisenmon,/itsu mite mo ii na,/sō ieba A wa imagoro nani o shite iru darō,/Nihon e kaette kara mō ichinen tatta/natsuyasumi go no shingakki,/ Kanto no rinrigaku no kōgi de mo shite iru ka,/are hodo no dōtokuteki jinkaku wa metta ni nai na,/donna ni tsukareta ban de mo 'nanji no gimu o*

nase' to itte/nemui me o kosurinagara yokujitsu no kōgi no shirabe o suru hito da,/kategorisheru inperachibu ga are made ni ikita chikara ni natte iru seikaku o/kimi wa hoka ni mita koto ga aru ka,/mō jūnenmae ni natte shimatta,/kōtō gakkō ya daigaku no koro,/sannin de yoku Yodobashi no suidō no tsutsumi o sanpo shitakke na,/rengesō no saku haru no hi, susuki no nabiku aki no kure,/kaerimichi no Shinjukudōri,/yūkaku no mae o aruite kuru sannin,/sannin to mo onna no koto nado o wadai ni noseta koto wa/ tada no ichido mo nakatta,/boku wa ano koro ga koishii,/mada mada kibō ni michite ita,/jinsei wa utsukushikatta.//Itsu no ma ni ka Konkorudo no hiroba e kita na./Oberisuku ga itsu mo tatte iru no wa naze ka?/Furansujin wa konna ni tou./Utsukushii madoren o misetsukerarete iru kara da,/Furansujin wa konna ni kotaeru./Share o itte fuzakeru hansui no kokumin da,/da ga De-karuto o umi, Pasukaru o unda,/hoshi o umu konton wa saiwai naru ka na./ Aa, Sēnu no hō o mitamae,/sunda sora ni kakatte iru ano mikazuki,/puratanu no kodachi no ue ni matataite iru ano utsukushii hoshi,/konton yori idete konton ni hairu inochi,/eien no naka ni matataku mijikai jinsei,/kimi mo boku mo mō han o sugiyō to shite iru,/Nel mezzo del cammin di nostra vita.../boku wa yappari sabishii yo,/yami o tadoru mono no kodoku, miezaru kage o ou mono no hiai,/keijijōgaku no nai tetsugaku wa sabishii,/ ningen no sonzai ya shi o mondai to suru keijijōgaku ga hoshii./Kyō wa ii aki no ichinichi datta,/dokka e yūmeshi de mo kuwō ka.]

21. The yin principle is related to the moon, the night, the negative, and the feminine; the yang principle is related to the sun, the day, the positive, and the masculine.

22. [Text: *Fugōryō. Kage ni wa kage no sachi ga aru,/hi ga ataranai dake ja nai./Kōri wa kōri no aji ga aru,/yuzamashi nado no rui ja nai./Shiraga o nuitatte/kurokami wa haenu./Kangan datte/nyokan ni narenu./Seigō fugō wa kyoku to kyoku/izure otoranu kōtei da./Mujun genri wa o-ki no doku/chinba de katate de mekkachi da./In ni homare are./Yō ni homare are./Zen yo/ka ni nioe./Aku yo/hana sake.*] The title of this poem comes from Immanuel Kant's *Versuch, den Begriff der negativen Grössen in die Weltweisheit* (Experiment, the concept of the negative dimension in the sphere of the world; 1763).

23. Euclid (fl. ca. 300 B.C.), Greek geometer, founded a school in Alexandria during the reign of Ptolemy I Soter. His main work, *Stoicheia* (Elements) remained the chief source of geometrical reasoning and methods until the nineteenth century. He also wrote *Data, On Divisions, Optics, Phenomena,* and more.

24. [Text: *Gūzensei. Heikō chokusen no kōri,/nozomidōri/shōmei ga dekita?/Iya, kihon yōkyū o tekkai shita?/Mondai no chūshin to natte iru no wa,/nichokkaku ni hitoshii?/Nani, hyakuhachijūdo ni tarinai?/Arekisandoria de mitsuketa furuhon/nisennen mae no kikagaku genron,/mushi ga kutte iyō to kutte imai to/Yūkuriddo wa erai hito,/uchū no sugata o sen to ten to ni tsukurikae/omae to ore, ore to omae/meguriai no himitsu,/koi no hanritsu./*

Kore wa jinsei no kika,/nantoka toite wa kuremai ka./Kō naru inga no chokusen o miyo/otsu naru inga no chokusen o miyo/futatsu no heikōsen wa majiwaranu ga kotowari,/fushigi ja nai ka heikōsen no majiwari,/kore ga gūzensei,/konton ga haranda kinsei,/inga non nami no yosuru ga mama/futari ga hirotta shinjūdama.]

25. [Text: *Benshōronteki Hōhō. Tamashii yo/jigoku, gokuraku/taiihō yue beso o kaku./Niramiai wa ame no kumo,/tsuifuku-kyoku mo/umarenu zo yo.//Akebono no no ni sumu/kumanbachi to himeyuri,/tsurunde mitsu o tsukuri,/dare ga toku tokoro zo/kami to majo,/chigitte ningen o umu.//Inochi no ritsu wa kore/sei, han, gō,/rogosu no kakuchō/utau wa hōshi,/yoki ka na sanbyōshi/warutsu o odore.*] This poem echoes Bergson's words: "Hence a thesis and an antithesis which would be vain for us to try logically to reconcile, for the simple reason that never, with concepts or points of view, will you make a thing." See Bergson, *The Creative Mind*, pp. 207–217.

26. Here Kuki refers to Bergson's notion of "quantitative time," that is, a time made into space, the time of the watch, inauthentic time.

27. "Moshi moshi, kame yo, kamesan yo" is the beginning of the song *Usagi to Kame* (Rabbit and tortoise; 1901) by Ishihara Wasaburō. The original text and music appear in Horiuchi Keizō and Inoue Takeshi, eds., *Nihon Shōka Shū* (Tokyo: Iwanami Shoten, 1958), p. 106.

28. "Verse" in Japanese is *ku;* "nine" is *kū.*

29. By "pure heterogeneity" *(junsui ishitsu)* Kuki refers to "qualitative time." To live in "qualitative time" means to live in a world free of regrets for the past since one realizes that life actually incorporates all possibilities. This thought derives from Bergson's idea that life is in continuous flux—what Bergson called *"durée"* (continuity; Jpn. *jizoku*).

30. It means "to count."

31. This refers to the regrets that a person has once he starts thinking, "Oh, if only I had done this, or if only I had done that." Such a regret is an indication that the person is still imprisoned in quantitative time.

32. The meteor, the flash of lightning, the melody, and the color are examples of pure duration, change, heterogeneity.

33. [Text: *Junsui Jizoku. Kūkan ni kesō shite/jikan nante kechi na shiseiji,/umu no ga somosomo no machigai,/kaikon to yara roku de nashi no bakemono/yo na yo na omae o nayamasu mono no sei da./Moshi moshi kame yo kamesan yo/usagi ni makeru kaji yarō./Mizu ni tadayou miyakodori/ahiru ni oikosaremai zo./O-toshi wa sanjū ikutsu desu/aikawarazu misoji hitomoji no kenkyū ka/go, shichi, go, shichi, shichi no goku da to ka?/Jūshichi, jūyon no niku ga seikaku ja to?/Jūni, jūni, nana no sanku ga genkei da?/Ku no kiriyō ga warui kara uta no tsukurinaoshi ka ne/'ku' to 'kū' o hakichigaeru na./Ku wa sūji de wa dete konai./Somosomo dōshitsu wa dakyō no moto,/junsui ishitsu no fushi o mamore./Kako no sōki mo/toki ni yorikeri,/kabidarake no kanōsei ni yubi o oru wa/haisha no narai./Kokoro ni sakebe/*

ryūsei/denkō/senritsu/shikisai.] The title of this poem is the translation of Bergson's *"durée pure."*

34. [Text: *Jinsei no Odori. Unmei yo/watakushi wa omae to odoru no da./ Hisshiri to daita mama./Yosome ni wa mittomonaitte?/Sonna koto wa dō de mo ii./Unmei yo/unmei yo/omae to odoru no da./Watakushi wa ureshii,/ watakushi wa sabishii./Oo, utsukushii ongaku./Hoshi no yozora no/sora no ochi kara hibiite kuru/tenkyū no senritsu da.*]

35. When the Chinese characters indicating "horse" *(ba)* and "deer" *(ka)* are read together, in Japanese they mean "foolish" *(baka)*.

36. [Text: *Jimon. Ittai omae no shōtai wa/nani ga nandaka wakaranai./ Mimi wa nagai,/shippo mo aru,/uma no tagui ja nai ka,/shika no yō de mo aru na.//Afurika no sabaku ni wa/kimyō na obake ga sunde iru./Karada wa kemono ni kotonarazu,/kubi wa sanagara ningenzura,/sufinkusu to iu yatsu ja.//Amerika no inaka ni wa/henchikirin na tori ga iru./Asa no aida wa aobyōtan,/yū to nareba akaragao,/shichimenchō to ka iu mono ja.//Ittai omae no shōtai wa/nani ga nandaka wakaranai./Dengurigaeshi de mo utte,/heso no naka de motsureteru/nazo o hodoite misete kure.*]

37. [Text: *Tango. Tomoshibi yo/tamashii wa kagayaki o motomezu,/ mabayuki hikari o keshite/yami to nare.//Parī no sora no tsuki yo/mado yori hisoka ni hairite/shizuka ni aoku/rokoko no hiroma o terase.//Kiiro no bara yo/hito wa sugishi koi o yumemimu,/fukeyuku aki no yo o/iyatakaku ibure.// Shiraga no gakushi yo/minami no kuni no kano furuki/vioron o torite/'Hiai no Tango' o hike.//Aruzenchin no onna yo/ito to tomo ni furuete/shikyō no kanashimi o/ennaru aruto ni utae.//Hyōhaku no tōhō no hito yo/uree o tsu-masaki ni komete/toshima no onnayakusha to/mugon no mama ni odore.*]

38. In the revised version published in the journal *Myōjō* (Morning star) in October 1926, Kuki clarified that this was "a yellow Positivist" *(kiiro no jis-shōronsha)*. The same thing applies to the "Metaphysician," while "the Kritic Philosopher" is "white."

39. This is a reference to Wolfgang Amadeus Mozart's (1756–1791) opera *Die Zauberflöte* (The magic flute; 1791). The birdcatcher is Papageno who runs to the rescue of Pamina, the queen's daughter, with the aid of his magic silver bells and the help of Prince Tamino, whose flute has magic properties.

40. [Text: *Kiiroi Kao.* **Ōshūjin:** *Zuibun kiiroi o-kao desu na./Minami no kuni no Supein ya/Itariakuni no jūmin wa/tsuyoi hizashi ni tamarikane/chairo no kao o shite imasu ga/kiiroi koto wa gozaimasenu./Kō mōshite wa shitsurei desu ga/Shinajin to Nihonjin to wa/mansei no ōdanbyō to yara ni kakatte…/ to, kō watakushidomo Ōshūjin wa/jitsu no tokoro kangaete iru no desu.//* **Jisshōronsha:** *Sore wa sukoshiku hidoi yō desu./Hifu no shikiso no ari basho to/ōdanbyō no kiiro to wa/zonsuru sō ga chigaimasu./Wareware no senzo wa/dōmo kabocha to mikan to o/kuisugita ka to omowaremasu./Kōga ya Kōkai no mizu o mo/nomisugita ka mo shiren desu.//* **Keijijōgakusha:** *Jinshū no betsu wa sententeki desu./Wareware wa zensei de itazura o shimashita,/*

*kamisama ga hidoku okotta,/suru to onidomo ga yatte kite/nigeru wareware
o funzukamae/atama kara obutsu o hirikaketa desu./Wareware no kiiroi kao
wa/seigi no kami no zankoku na noroi o/eien ni kinen suru no desu.//Hihyō
Tetsugakusha: Mateki no naka no torisashi no/ronpō o mane suru wake de wa
nai ga/kiiroi tori mo aru yō ni/kiiroi ningen mo aru no desu./Seisei wa shichi-
mendō na betsu mondai,/jijitsu wa jijitsu to shite ataerarete iru./Yō suru ni
kiiro jinshū to iu gainen no/datō no han'i o kakuritsu shite/kachi no ue kara
mite ikeba yoi./Sate, dōshitara kiiroi kao ga shiroku naru ka?/Kōshite mondai
o junri kara/jissen no ryōiki ni utsushimashō.*]

41. Saint-Germain-des-Prés started to develop in the sixth century near
the abbey that Childebert build up, counseled by Bishop Germain, in order to
shelter treasures of the surrendered Vandals, such as Saint Vincent's tunic.
This church and monastery became rapidly the richest one in France, and after
the death of Bishop Germain its name was changed into Saint-Germain-des-
Prés. The suburb continued to develop and became, in the seventeenth cen-
tury, a center of literature and theater life. The area continued to blossom in-
tellectually and artistically, especially in the nineteenth century when painters
such as Delacroix, Ingres, and Manet and writers such as Balzac and George
Sand settled there. In the twentieth century Saint-Germain-des-Prés, with its
numerous cafés that have created their own circles and even their own litera-
ture, has continued to be synonymous with literary and artistic life.

42. Literally "the inhabitants of the capital" *(miyakobito).*

43. Henry IV (1553–1610), king of France and Navarre, to whom a leg-
end attributes the saying "Paris is well worth a Mass," thus indicating that his
conversion to Catholicism would only have been a piece of policy devoid of all
contrition. Henry is well remembered among the Bourbon kings because of his
numerous amorous affairs, for it was generally known that he fathered a num-
ber of bastards.

44. [Text: *Serenādo. Gakushi yo/sono serenādo o/mō ichido/hiite kure.//
Kyonen no natsu,/San Jeruman no utena,/miyakobito no moyōshi no/hare
no en.//Shizuka ni nagaruru Sēnugawa,/sora ni niou yūgetsu,/oka no kanata
yume yori mo awai/tomoshibi no katamari no Parī.//Anri yonsei no tei no
rankan,/tagai ni totta te to te,/seien na Eriannu wa/rirairo no kinu o kite ita.//
Ano toki, ano toki/onaji senritsu o kiita./Ima wa fuyu no yo,/hitorikiri no
watakushi.//Gakushi yo/sono serenādo o/mō ichido/hiite kure.*]

45. [Text: *Monte Karuro. Bakuchi ga shitakeri ya/kajino e isoge./Odori
ga mitakeri ya/sakaba o nozoke.//Ore wa nani o shitōte/nangoku e kita?/Ore
wa nani o negōte/Monte Karuro e kita?//Yukka no hakage de/aounabara ni
yowō./Mo no ka o nioide/ebi de mo torō.//Irome ni ueteri ya/o-chaya e
haire./Hada ga koishikeri ya/jorōya e maire.*]

46. [Text: *Ginnan no Ha. Ginnan no ha yo/hitotsu ga futatsu ni natta no
ka./Ichō no ha yo/futatsu ga hitotsu ni natta no ka./Fushigi na katachi,/iyō
na sugata,/katsute, sai yutaka na shijin ni/koi no kokoro o/sasayaita de wa*

*nai ka./Katsute, sugureta tetsujin ni/uchū no himitsu o/katatta de wa nai
ka./Sore da noni dōshite/nanji wa ima/bunretsu ni nayamu tamashii ni/sono
itamashii sugata o/mazamaza to/utsushite miseru no da./Miyo/miginaru
nomi, hidarinaru bachi,/haiiro no nōmiso, kurenai no chishio,/sono washi-
gatai mujun,/sono taezaru tōsō,/kakushite horobita tamashii no ikutsu o/
shitte inai to demo omou no ka./Ginnan no ha yo/nanji wa futatsu ni sakete
iru./Ichō no ha yo/nanji wa futatsu ni warete iru.*]

47. Literally *Perilla frutuscens crispa*, a kind of beefsteak plant *(nigakusa)*.

48. [Text: *Kodoku. Kodoku!/Amari ni mo tōtoki hibiki,/nanjira wa sono
shirabe o/kikishi koto naki ka.//Goishi yo/nanjira wa mina manmaru nari./
Seimei wa gara ni nashi,/nanisurezo bangō o mochiizaru ka.//Ichi, ni, san,
yon/so o kaigō to nazuke yo./Kachi, kachi, kachi, kachi/so o danshō to yobe.//
Nanjira wa keijijōteki no/kodoku o shirazaru ka./Kano itsukushiki jitsuzai
no sugata o/mishi koto naki ka.//Makoto no kodoku wa/tsukanoma mo
kobochiezu,/makoto no kodoku wa/ai mo yūjō mo kore ni furezu.//Uchi yori
waku/fudan no sekiryō,/nigakusa no hakanasa,/mitsu no amasa,//nanjira/
katsute ajiwaishi koto naki ka./Goishi yo/manmaru no katachi o nageke.*]

49. "Do not give dogs what is sacred; do not throw your pearls to pigs. If
you do, they may trample them under their feet, and then turn and tear you
to pieces." See the Sermon on the Mount, Matthew 7:6.

50. *Akoya no kai* is the *Pinctada martensii*.

51. [Text: *Buta (Buta no mae ni jisō no shinju o nageatauru nakare) Akoya
no kai no tamamono no/shinju o buta ni yattakke./Buta wa shinju o
marunomi shi,/kyū, kyū, kyū to hanasaki de/kogoto o itte nukarumi o/acchi
kocchi to kobashiri shi,/hiriri to tareta fun no naka/goran, shinju mo
kegareiro./Akoya no kai no tamamono no/shinju o buta ni yattakke.*]

52. In 1918 Kuki married Nakahashi Nuiko, the widow of his brother
Ichizō who had died the previous year. They were divorced in 1931.

53. [Text: *Kyaku. Nihon no koto o/katatte kure/kogoe ni katatte kure//
ano nakaniwa no mokuren wa/tsubomi o ikutsu/tsukete ita//mokkoku no
aoi edaburi wa/gonen mukashi ni/kawaranu ka//ki no ji o iwau/oyaji no
kami wa/yuki no yō ni nattarō na//Nuiko wa asayū/yosome ni mo/sabishii
kao o shite iru ka//Nihon no koto o/katatte kure/kogoe ni katatte kure.*]

54. Sometimes compared to a giant wedding cake, this extravagant build-
ing was designed by Charles Garnier for Napoléon III in 1862. The Prussian
War and the 1871 uprising delayed the opening of the building till 1875.

55. [Text: *Sanpo. Honobono to koki murasaki ni/rira no hana niou haru
no hi/uchihisasu Parī no machi o/sozoro ni mo hitori waga yuku//Madorēn
mitera no hashira/nibiiro o shitagaikoshi mi wa/hana o uru shōjo o miredo/
dare ga tame ni hana o motomemu//nuka tarete miyako no ōji/tobotobo to
Opera e kureba/uchidoyomi yosete wa kaesu/hito no nami ikaga subeki zo/
/izukata e ware wa ikamu ka/maronie no midori ni moete/yuruyaka ni mizu
no nagaruru/Sēnugawa sashite ya ikamu//wabibito wa nani o motomemu/*

akashia no wakaba no kaoru/Burōnyu no mori ni kakurete/kagiroeru haru o nagekamu.]

56. [Text: *Roshia no Uta. Dōshite sonna sabishii kao o shiterutte?/ Shuzannu, omae wa/baka ni ki ni shite ikudo mo kiku ne./Ano doyōbi no ban kara da yo,/Roshia no uta o issho ni kiita/ano doyōbi no ban kara da yo,/ore wa nandaka iu ni iwarenu/sabishii kokoro ni natte shimatta.//Sō deshō,/sono kurai ni wa kizuiteru wa./Ano adappoi iki na nodo de/jaraketa kouta o utatta onna o/anata no hitomi wa torokekitte/jitto mitsumetemashita mono./Ano burondo no kami/otokotarashi no metsuki, kuchitsuki,/fukureta o-chichi, yojireta koshitsuki,/hosokkoketa ashi./Shitteru wa, otoko wa minna sō yo,/ uwaki, utsurigi,/Surabu no onna koishiindeshō,/buriyun no kami o kirina-deta/Parīonna no atashi ni wa/itsu no ma ni ka akitandeshō./Ano ban kara, ano ban kara/anata wa maru de kawatte shimatta./Atsui atsui seppun o/ anata no kuchi ni shitatte mo/uranamanurui seppun kiri/kaeshicha kurenai mono.//Shuzannu,/baka o itcha ikenai,/musumekko no iro ya uta ja nai,/ano gojūotoko no funauta da./Roshia no arano no yami no yo o/eien kara eien ni/ nagarete tsukinai ano Voruga no/kurai umeki, sugoi musebi,/itamashii nageki, ōkii modae,/sore o utatta ano bariton ni/ore no kokoro ga donzoko kara/onaji hibiki de tomonari shita./Ano ban kara da, koi ni mo somuite/ore no kokoro wa sabishiinda.*]

57. A hill in the Ueno area of Tokyo.

58. The steep *butte* (hill) of Montmartre has been associated with artists for two hundred years. Théodore Géricault and Camille Corot came here at the start of the nineteenth century, and in the twentieth century Maurice Utrillo immortalized the streets in his works. The name of the area is ascribed to martyrs tortured and killed in the area around A.D. 250—hence *mons martyrium.* The cemetery of Montmartre, dating from 1795, lies west of Montmartre and north of the boulevard de Clichy. This has been the resting place for many luminaries of the creative arts since the beginning of the nineteenth century. Besides Heinrich Heine, the composers Hector Berlioz and Jacques Offenbach (who wrote the famous cancan tune), the poet Alfred de Vigny, and the painter Edgar Degas are buried here.

59. [Text: *Haine no Haka. Aki no hiyori no/Haine no haka./ Tsutsumashiyaka na sekichū,/kanso na ukibori,/jojō shijin o katadoru/yonsuji no ito no tategoto,/esupuri no hito o arawasu/tsubasa hirogeta chō no sugata,/ kanashimi no hito o shinobaseru/utsumuita kyōzō.//Okutsuki o kazaru/ kurenai aoi,/shiroi bara,/kuroi daria,/kiiroi kiku./Sekichū no rakugaki o miyo,/kazu kagirinai sanbi no ku,/junreisha no kokumei,/sankeijin no shomei./ Watakushi wa damatte kubi o tareta.//Katsute seinen no jidai/watakushi mo sono sanbisha de atta./Aki no sabishii hana no yō na/shi o yonde/kokoro yuku bakari/yo o nakiakashita koto mo atta./Mukaigaoka no shibafu ni/hitori-mi o yokotaete/Ueno no kane o kikinagara/sono shi o yaku shita koto mo atta.// Sono nochi toshi hete/Rain no kishi ni hodochikai/minami Doitsu ni sunda*

koro,/kyōyō aru utsukushii fujin ga/tsuki no yo no barukon de/sono shi o gin-shō shita toki,/kanshōteki na shijin da to/arifureta riyū de/naze ni watakushi wa sugenaku/kenashisatta no ka.//Kokyō o ushinatte/sasurai no sei o okutta shijin,/ikoku ni hitori/hichō o utatta shijin,/ima no watakushi wa sono shijin ni dōjō suru./Seinen no jidai ni sukanakatta/odoke to fūshi no hanmen,/ima wa sore mo wakaru dake ni watakushi mo toshi o totta./Asu wa shoten e itte/ Haine no shishū o motomeyō.//Yūhi ga katamuita/horohoro to ko no ha ga ochite kita./Sachi usui Doitsujin,/Monmarutoru no kaede no moto ni/nemutte iru Doitsujin,/Parī no yo no hoshi ga/mamonaku akashi o tsukeru de arō./ Chekkusurovakia no gakusei ga/kono bozen de jisatsu o shita no wa/chōdo kyonen no imagoro de attarō.] Heinrich Heine (1797–1856), German poet and critic, resided in Paris from 1831. His work was notable for sardonic wit and arrogant radicalism. He composed the volumes of verse *Gedichte* (1821), *Buch der Lieder* (1827), *Neue Gedichte* (1844), and *Romanzero* (1851). These works contain some of the best-loved German lyrics, many of them set to music by Schumann, Schubert, and others. His prose works include *Reisebilder* (1826–1831), *Französische Zustände* (1832), *Geschichte der neueren schönen Literatur in Deutschland* (1833), *Der Salon* (1834–1840), *Lutezia* (1854), and *Vermischte Schriften* (1854). Verse satires include *Deutschland: Ein Wintermärchen* (1844) and *Atta Troll: Ein Sommernachtstraum* (1847).

60. *"Hana"* specifically refers to cherry blossoms, the mark of spring.

61. [Text: *Waga Kokoro. Haru kureba hana wa nioedo,/samidori ni ko no ha mo yuredo,/waga kokoro mono o nagekai/waga omoi hakanakarikeri.// Shōjoshi to tomo ni odoredo,/kuchibiru no kurenaki o suedo,/waga kokoro mono o nagekai/waga omoi hakanakarikeri.//Hashikeyashi tamashii hitotsu/ waga mono to shiritsutsu yobedo,/waga kokoro mono o nagekai/waga omoi hakanakarikeri.//Utsuriyuku yo ni sumu kagiri,/utsushimi no iki suru kagiri,/ waga kokoro mono o nagekai/waga omoi hakanakaruramu.]*

62. [Text: *Hedo. Ore wa tokidoki hedo o haku./Shozai no isu ni koshi kakete/hitori shigoto o shite iru to/futto hakike ga yatte kuru//muga muchū de tachiagari/mado kara ōrai e kubi o dashi/gerori, gerori/kurushimagire ni haku hedo wa//chōsen azami, matsubaudo,/mahimahitsuburi, akagaeru,/ kani no harawata, kurage no ko,/usagi no kintama, hato no kimo.// Kuidōraku no tenbatsu da na,/shōka furyō no shōko da na,/gerori, gerori/ sake no nioi mo suru zoino.//Haori hakama wa chikazuku na,/kesa to koromo wa tōku ore,/gakuseibō wa yoritsuku na,/onna, kodomo wa nigete yuke.//Ore wa tokidoki hedo o haku./Mōchōen ja arumai na,/ninshin no hazu mo arumai na,/komatta kitsune ni tsukareta wai.]*

Short Poems

The original text appears in *KSZ* 1, pp. 174–195.

1. Edgar Degas (1834–1917) was associated with impressionism. His

best-known works include *La Repasseuse, Bouderie, Sur la plage, La Classe de Danse, Miss Lola au cirque Fernando, Mlle. Fiocre dans le ballet de "La Source,"* and *Le Viol.*

2. Located between the western edges of Paris and the Seine, the park Bois de Boulogne offers a vast belt of greenery for strolling, riding, and boating. In the mid-nineteenth century, Napoléon III had the Bois designed and landscaped by Baron Haussmann along the lines of Hyde Park in London.

3. Alphonse Daudet (1840–1897) is the author of such plays as *Le Frère aîné* (1867), *L'Arlésienne* (1872), and *L'Obstacle* (1891). He wrote novels and story collections including *Le Petit Chose* (1868), *Lettres de mon moulin* (1869), *Les Aventures prodigieuses de Tartarin de Tarascon* (1872), *Le Nabab* (1877), *Tartarin sur les Alpes* (1885), and *L'Immortel* (1888).

4. The Latin Quarter is the ancient area of Paris lying between the Seine and Luxembourg Gardens. Since the Middle Ages this riverside quarter has been dominated by the Sorbonne; it acquired its name from the early Latin-speaking students.

5. Literally "Do you think?"

6. Paris's best-known and most popular thoroughfare was a desolate marshland until about 1667, when the master landscape-garden designer André Le Nôtre created a tree-lined avenue that he named the Champs-Elysées. It has been the "triumphal way" ever since the homecoming of Napoléon's body from St. Helena in 1840.

7. Mephistopheles is one of the seven chiefs of medieval demonology. He is best known to modern readers as the cold, scoffing, relentless fiend of Goethe's *Faust.*

8. Although in Paris this church is known as La Madeleine, its full name is the church of Saint Mary Magdalene, or Sainte-Marie Madeleine.

9. Claude Debussy (1862–1918), French composer, greatly influenced the symbolist poets and impressionist painters. His major works include *Deux arabesque* (piano, 1888), *Suite bergamasque* (piano pieces, 1890–1905), *Prélude à l'après-midi d'un faune* (symphonic poem, 1894), *Nocturnes* (1899), *Pelléas et Melisande* (opera, 1902), *La Mer* (tone poem, 1905), *Douze Préludes* (piano, 1910–1913 and 1915), *Jeux* (ballet, 1913), songs, and chamber music.

10. This green haven dates back to 1778, when the Duc de Chartres commissioned the painter-writer and amateur landscape designer Louis Carmontelle to create a magnificent garden. The result was an exotic landscape full of architectural follies in the English and German style. In 1852 the park was acquired by the state and made into a chic public park. A few of the original features still remain. Among them is the *naumachia* basin—an ornamental version of a Roman pool used for simulating naval battles.

11. Kuki provides this *furigana* reading for the phrase "Thé dansant" (tea dance), which actually appears in the original text.

12. Jules Claretie (1840–1913), French writer, was director of the Comédie-Française from 1885. Among his novels were *Une Drôlosse* (1862), *Amours d'un interne* (1881), and *Le Prince Zilah* (1884). Among his plays are *Les Mirabeau* (1879) and *Monsieur le Ministre* (1883).

13. This is a reference to *"wasurenagusa" (Myosotis scorpioides)*.

14. This is the name of a brand of cigarettes that was popular in Europe in the 1920s.

15. Charles-Pierre Baudelaire (1821–1867) is regarded as the earliest and finest poet of modernism in French, harbinger of later symbolists. Among his works are the novel *La Fanfarlo* (1847), essays in *Les Paradis Artificiels* (1860), *Curiosités esthétiques* (1868), and the volume of verse *Les Fleurs du Mal* (1857; expanded 1861; definitive edition 1868), which led to his prosecution for obscenity and blasphemy.

16. *"Yayoi"* indicates the third lunar month and the spring season.

17. In 1756 Madame de Pompadour and Louis XV opened a porcelain factory near Versailles at Sèvres to supply the royal residences with tableware and objects of art. Thus began the production of exquisite dinner services, statuettes, Etruscan-style vases, romantic cameos, and porcelain paintings depicting grand châteaux or mythological scenes.

18. A reference to Kant's *Kritik der reinen Vernunft* (Critique of pure reason; 1781).

19. The Sorbonne, seat of the University of Paris until 1969, was established in 1253 by Robert de Sorbon, confessor to Louis IX, for sixteen poor scholars to study theology. From these modest origins the college became France's center of scholastic theology. The college's opposition to liberal eighteenth-century philosophical ideas led to its suppression during the revolution. It was reestablished by Napoléon in 1806, and the seventeenth-century buildings were replaced. In 1969, the Sorbonne split into thirteen separate universities, but the building still holds some lectures.

20. Honoré Daumier (1808–1879), French caricaturist. He was on the staff of *La Caricature* (1832) when one of his caricatures of Louis-Philippe caused his arrest and a six-month prison term. Later he joined the staff of *Charivari* where he caricatured bourgeois society. He completed some 4,000 lithographs and 4,000 illustrations. He is also known as a serious painter in the impressionist manner (from 1848) and a skilled sculptor.

21. A reference to Charles Baudelaire's *Les Fleurs du Mal* (1857; expanded 1861) and Immanuel Kant's *Critik der praktischen Vernunft* (1781; rev. 1787).

22. Friedrich Nietzsche (1844–1900), German philosopher and poet, wrote *Also sprach Zarathustra* between 1883 and 1885.

23. The Sacré-Coeur basilica, dedicated to the Sacred Heart of Christ, was built as a result of a private religious vow made at the outbreak of the Franco-Prussian War. Two businessmen, Alexandre Legentil and Rohault de Fleury,

promised to finance the basilica should France be spared from assault. Despite the war and the Siege of Paris, invasion was averted and work began in 1875 to Paul Abadie's designs. The result has never been considered particularly graceful, but the basilica is vast and impressive and is one of France's most important Roman Catholic buildings.

24. Iwashita Sōichi's sister, with whom Kuki had been romantically involved, eventually became a nun.

25. Saigyō (1118–1190), Japanese Buddhist priest-poet, is considered one of the greatest masters of the poetic form called *waka*.

26. Kuki plays on the double meaning of the word *"sumu,"* which means "to live" and "to be clear." The poet implies that his pupil has become a monk at the Enryakuji temple on Mt. Hiei, the center of Tendai Buddhism.

27. The pleasure quarters of the ancient capital Kyoto are located in Gion.

28. Naruse Mukyoku (1884–1958) was a scholar of German literature. Like Kuki he was a professor at the University of Kyoto.

Rhyming Poems

Kuki appended these poems to "Nihonshi no Ōin" (Rhymes in Japanese poetry), an essay originally written in 1931 and amply revised before being included in *Bungeiron* (Essays on the literary arts; 1941). My translation of Kuki's poems follows the revised version of 1941. See *KSZ* 4 (Tokyo: Iwanami Shoten, 1981), pp. 454–513. Kuki composed these poems to disprove the widely held prejudice that Japanese poetry cannot rhyme. The poems are true tours-de-force whose essential value is formalistic, a feature that the English translation can hardly maintain. After a lengthy discussion of different types of rhyme in world poetry, and after providing a variety of examples of rhyming poems from ancient and modern Japanese poetry, Kuki ends his essay with an explanation of the formal characteristics of the poetic experiments translated here. He indicates that "Thoughts Originating from Herbs" is the combination of four *sedōka* (head-repeated poems). Among the dialogical poetic genre known as *sedōka* Kuki includes narrative poems from the *Kojiki* made of four verses with a pattern of 12/7/12/7 syllables, the first verse rhyming with the third and the second verse rhyming with the fourth.

"To Ms. D" and "A Solitary Life" are examples of *chōka* (long poems usually followed by one or more envoys) with flat rhymes *(rima piana)*. The same rhyme is used in the three verses of the envoys.

"Onogoro and Intercourse" and "Konohana no Sakuyabime" are examples of *imayō* (present-day song), popular songs that were widespread in the middle of the Heian period, usually sung by female entertainers. They are both alternate rhymes *(ABAB)*.

"Poetry," "Journey," "One Night," "Squirrel," and "Bookbinder" are examples of the Italian sonnet *(sonetto)*, a fourteen-line poem composed of eight- and six-line stanzas. Stanza 1 is known as the octave; stanza 2 is called the sestet.

"Bat" and "The Sleepy Inland Sea" are examples of short couplets: two rhymed lines.

Among the quatrains, "Heart" is an example of a refrain in *rima piana*.

"Meeting Bridge," "Monte Carlo," "The Carnival of Nice," and "A Wish" are regular alternate rhymes *(ABAB)*; "Wind," "Farewell to Paris," "Grieving Mr. Iwashita Sōichi," and "Credo Quia Absurdum" are irregular alternate rhymes.

"A Stroll" and "Renunciation" are examples of regular envelope rhymes; "Cointreau" and "Luxor" are irregular envelope rhymes *(ABBA)*.

"Fontainebleau" and "The Geometry of Gray" are a combination of quatrains and couplets. In the latter poem Kuki uses a character rhyme *(manmaru* and *daen*, both words meaning "round").

"Arabesque," "Tango," and "Mediterranean Sunset" are examples of tercets *(terzina)*, three lines of any length and any meter, with any rhyme pattern.

"Repentance" and "Evening in the Alps" are examples of cinquains, five-line stanzas; "Dialectic" is a sestet; "The Ruins of Karnak" is a ten-line stanza.

"Flower Picking," "Three Comma-Shaped Figures in a Circle," and "Contingency" do not follow any specific meter. They are in *rima piana*. "The Negative Dimension" and "Destiny" do not follow any specific meter or any fixed rhyme.

  1. [Text: *Kisō Hasshi. 1—Rengesō, tanpopo, sumire/tsuminishi wagimo/mizu hisa ni furu hatsushigure/itamu muragimo//Atemonaku samayou akino/obana ho ni saku/sabishisa ni tsuchikau ai no/keijijōgaku// 2—Shida, shinobu, zenmai, warabi/oeru tsuyujimo/banshū no ureba aosabi/omoiganashi mo//Nani iro ni inochi karakusa/suriteba yokemu/ nubatama no kuroki maganusa/oru mo ningen.*]

  2. [Text: *Madomoaseru D ni. Kasumi tatsu Burōnyu no mori/wakakusa no komichi no hotori/haru no hi no amaki yume umu/sumirebana omoide ni tsumu/shizuyaka ni hohoemu hitomi/kimi koso wa waga yo no nozomi/ aimiru ni ajiwaitsukizu/wakarete wa ieji kono kizu/hito shirezu iku shizuku otsu/namida mote soto hana hitotsu/kawatoji no furuki shishū ni/irete saru tōki sototsukuni/murasaki no nioi usenamu/shika wa are mune ni ikuramu/ yashioji no umi no ochikata/kimi ga misugata.// Henka: Burōnyu no mori ni saku hana/wakaruru hi tsumite kimigana/mune ni yobu kana.*]

  3. In 1940 Kuki transferred from the Kusakawa district in Kyoto, where he had lived for many years near the Nanzenji, to the Yamashina area outside the city. In Yamashina Kuki spent the last two years of his life.

  4. The Engi era corresponds to the years 901–923, during the reign of Emperor Daigo (r. 897–930). According to a legend, Semimaru was the fourth son of Emperor Daigo. On the life of the blind musician and poet Semimaru

see Susan Matisoff, *The Legend of Semimaru, Blind Musician of Japan* (New York: Columbia University Press, 1978).

5. Mt. Otowa is located east of the Higashiyama district in Kyoto. In the past it marked the boundary between the capital and Ōmi province.

6. [Text: *Dokkyo. Yamashina wa kyō no hingashi/kakuresumu sato ni arurashi/inishie no Engi no miyoyu/Semimaru no na nomi ni kikoyu/biwa-goto no ito no yonnomiya/ito yoshi to tsukurishi kariya/manakai no mine wa Otowayama/asayū ni utsuru sono sama/kiri tateba sumie ni kawari/kumo yukeba masshiroki tobari/harube wa na no hana saku/manjushage aki hamo akaku/natsu ni wa kaoru kisokei/fuyu no hi ni mawaru hidokei/hitori i ni na-zumu utsusomi/hito sawa no densha o utomi/machi towade sugishi ikuhi yo/utsuyufu no komoru onogayo/wabinureba fumi o himotoku/muragashi no oku//Henka: Uchihisasu miyako no higashi/Yamashina no sato no mura-gashi/konure makanashi.*]

7. [Text: *Onogoro to Maguhai. Izanagi Izanami futahashira/kamiunabara o kakinaseri/shitataru shio ni namigashira/okite Onokorojima nareri//Mizu no mihashira meguru toki/aite wa kawasu ana ni yashi/kuraki kumido ni mohimo toki/maguhai suru ni maga wa nashi.*] This poem refers to the creation of the land by the deities Izanagi and Izanami. The myth appears in the third chapter of the *Kojiki* (Records of ancient matters; 712): "At this time the heavenly deities, all with one command, said to the two deities Izanagi no Mikoto and Izanami no Mikoto: 'Complete and solidify this drifting land!' Giving them the Heavenly Jeweled Spear, they entrusted the mission to them. Thereupon, the two deities stood on the Heavenly Floating Bridge and, lowering the jeweled spear, stirred with it. They stirred the brine with a churning-churning sound; and when they lifted up [the spear] again, the brine dripping down from the tip of the spear piled up and became an island. This was the island Onogoro." English translation by Donald L. Philippi, *Kojiki* (Tokyo: University of Tokyo Press, 1968), p. 49.

8. The name Konohana no Sakuyabime is written with characters meaning "princess flowery tree."

9. [Text: *Konohana no Sakuyabime. Kasasa no misaki no nagisabe ni/tamatama aishi otome ari/makeru magatama ruri ni beni/unane wa yuki to miru bakari//Na mo uruwashi no azusayumi/haru wa konohana sakuyabime/utsuroiyasuki ka ni nazumi/hitoyo musubishi kari no ime.*] In the myths of the *Kokjiki*, Konohana no Sakuyabime appears as the daughter of Ōyamatsumi no Kami, the consort of Ninigi no Mikoto, and the mother of Honosuseri no Mikoto, Honoakari no Mikoto, and Hikohohodemi no Mikoto. "Thereupon Amatsuhiko no Ninigi no Mikoto met a lovely maiden at the Cape of Kasasa. He asked: 'Whose daughter [are you]?' She replied: '[I am] the daughter of Ōyamatsumi no Kami, and my name is Kamuatatsuhime. [I am] also called Konohana no Sakuyabime.'" See Philippi, *Kojiki*, pp. 144–147.

10. "The blind turtle sticking its head in the hole of a floating log" is a

Buddhist metaphor for something that is impossible. [Text: *Shi. Uragirishi kotoba wa mugoku/shi wa kanashi jōka no matsuro/itsushika to tsumetaki mukuro/tonauru wa nani no daimoku//Moji ikutsu tobiishi o oku/Kara no moji, hibiki wa utsuro/Yamatomoji, iro wa usuguro/ichi, ni, san, shi, go, roku//Wakuraba ni koko o yogirite/nagai suru tamashii magite/ikifuke to yobinamu wa dare//Umareshi hi inochi o tatsu/shinishi ku wa odoru koto mare/mekuragame, ukiki o matsu.*]

11. [Text: *Tabi. Fuyu no hi no usuki ni hitori/aozora o shitaite haruka/ nanro o tadorite ikuka/tamachihau Kannu no hotori//Nagisabe ni mure tatsu chidori/nami koete tobu kage kasuka/tabi to wa nani o nageku ka/ kanran no kokage no yadori//Yūsareba sōbi wa akaku/mimoza kiiro ni honobono to saku/shizukesa wa hana no tsuku iki//Furusato no sanizurau imo/yume ni mite mi ni sozoro ni mo/sora o yuku kumo zo koishiki.*]

12. [Text: *Aru yo. Sakazuki ni tsuida sake/aoi tabako no kemuri/kabe ni akari ga utsuri/heya ni tada hitori dake//Tsubaki no hana no nasake/tokei no hari no miburi/tsui ni musubanu nemuri/madobe ni shiramu yoake// Asazora ni izaru kumo/itaru tokoro furusato/watashi mo mata mayowō// Doko kara kita kono kumo/damatte iru omae to/futari de sake o nomō.*]

13. [Text: *Risu. Aoba no mori o atemonaku hitori yuku/pyonpyon to odotte deta karen na risu/watashi o miru ya ina ya megurasu kibisu/kashiwa no ki ni kakenobotte shita o muku//Haru wa ano sakurasō ga omae o suku/ natsu no yo wa kozue de hoshi to kawasu kisu/aki wa kinoko no chippoke na marui isu/fuyu wa shippo ni chirachira to yuki ga tsuku//Odokesuki no risu yo, risu yo tada odore/mushin ni hanete ki kara ki e kakenobore/omae wa itsumo tada nikoniko to warau//Shikashi watashi wa kureyuku aoba no mori/ atama o tarete urei no michi o tadori/ningen no nayami to kanashimi o omou.*]

14. Molière (1622–1673), French actor and playwright, is the author of *Le Misanthrope* (1666), *Tartuffe* (1667), *L'Avare* (1668), *Le Bourgeois Gentil-homme* (1670), and *Le Malade Imaginaire* (1673).

15. Jean de La Fontaine (1621–1695), French poet, is the author of *Fables* (1668–1694), some 240 poems based on traditional fables.

16. Auguste Comte (1798–1857), French philosopher and founder of positivism, is the author of *Système de Politique Positive* (1851–1854).

17. Maximilien-Paul-Émile Littré (1801–1881), French lexicographer and philosopher, is the author of *Dictionnaire de la Langue Française* (1863–1873).

18. [Text: *Seihonya. "Pēji o shirabeta ka, hyōshi o umaku hare/nori no kawaki ga warui na, kyō wa donten"/kozō o furimuku oyaji no kita hanten/ Darutoa-gai, seihonya no shūjin wa kare//Segawa no kinji ga bonyari uku tasogare/dekiagatta no wa Moriēru, Rafonten/Konto no seiji taikei, Ritore no jiten/shūjitsu hataraite soto e deru no mo mare//Hyakkaten e kayotteru jūkyū no musume/"otōsan" to yobu to shigoto no te o yasume/nikkori warainagara shokutaku ni suwaru//Kisaku na okami o nakushita no wa kono natsu/eikyū ni kaeru hazu no nai mono o matsu/Parī no yoru, Sakure Kōru no kane ga naru.*]

19. [Text: *Kōmori. Ware wa kōmori/furusumori//Haru no tasogare/yo ni kogare//Idete tobedomo/tobu midomo//Tsubasa ga usuku/shikuhakku//Kao wa hairo/me wa oboro//Na no hana sakari/usuakari//Chōchō ga tobu/yume o yobu//Oeba maboroshi/nagareboshi//Nageku mo oroka/nan to shiyo ka.*]

20. [Text: *Nemuru Seto Naikai. Umibe no yado/yoru no mado//Sora ni wa kin no hoshi/mizu ni wa rin no mushi//Nemuru Seto Naikai/mimamoru tōdai//Patto akaku/satto kuraku//Haru no yoi/nan no omoi//Tamashii no kataware/muragimono akugare//Tōi shima/yume miru ima//Yawarakai sazanami/migiwa no sen o kizami//Oto mo naku/nagareboshi ga ko o kaku.*] "Seto Naikai" (Sea within channels) indicates the long expanse of water between Honshū and the islands of Shikoku and Kyūshū.

21. [Text: *Kokoro. Haru kureba utsusomi no yado/hana hiraki wakaba kaoredo/muragimono kokoro uruhoi/nibiiro no ame no monomoi//Fue no ne ni tachite odoru mo/fumukara ni kiyuru ayagumo/muragimono kokoro uruhoi/nibiiro no ame no monomoi//Hashikeyashi tamashii hitotsu/te ni dakedo tokienu himitsu/muragimono kokoro uruhoi/nibiiro no ame no monomoi//Chie no mi no ajiwai o shiri/ikizuku ni shiroku tatsu kiri/muragimono kokoro uruhoi/nibiiro no ame no monomoi.*]

22. [Text: *Yukiaibashi. Wakuraba no/yukiai no hashi/sakariba no/gaitō akashi//Itsu nariki/yoi no kawabata/sozoroariki/mikakeshi sugata//Omoide ni/kokoro itamedo/akugare ni/inochi nayamedo//Gūzen no/kanadeshi jazu/yukijimono/yukite kaerazu.*]

23. [Text: *Monte Karuro. Monte Karuro e/monbi ni ojare/sui na minatoe/suiro o kiyare//Kajino wa kochira/saikoro korori/kafe wa achira/saifu ga karari//Umi wa aoao/ushio wa makkuro/tō no tsurizao/toranse maguro//Koko wa irozato/ageya mo gozare/koyoi dake na to/ajimite tamore.*]

24. [Text: *Nīsu no Shanikusai. Kyō wa kekkō na karunavaru/taiso na taiko no bakabayashi/tsukehige tsukete karaibaru/yakko mo yan ga te chidoriashi//Minamikunibare no yoi hiyori/tsuji no hiroba de sore odore/wakai shū, kodomo, otoshiyori/morote o utte ondo tore//Tatta, tararara, tattatta/tsuji no hiroba de sore odore/tatta, tararara, tattatta/morote o utte ondo tore//Yuki ka arare ka kami no kona/yukiau hito ni patto kake/hanagassen ja min goto na/mimoza mo yuri mo bara mo kake//Hana yori hade na haregi kite/odoru onago wa choito dare/bureikō ja to kaishaku shite/kisu no hitotsu o kurete yare//Tatta, tararara, tattatta/odoru onago wa choito dare/tatta, tararara, tattatta/kisu no hitotsu o kurete yare.*]

25. [Text: *Negai. Zae takaki takumi are/tama no ono ute ritsu/sumiishi ni sachi wa mare/araragi no naru hi itsu//Utagami no manago dare/aozora e fume yo in/tsuchikure no hitotsu ware/niji no iro yume ni mimu.*]

26. [Text: *Kaze. Suzukake no ure/takaku mau aki no kaze/watashi ni mo mawasete kure/jiyū o ibuku kaze//Minikui katachi o mo/tsukurowazu/magatta wadachi o mo/kakusazu//Tamatama/onore ni ubenawazu/arinomama/hito ni habakarazu//Niku no zange o/sotchoku ni katarō/rei no sange*

o/tanteki ni utaō//Suzukake no ure/takaku mau aki no kaze/watashi ni mo mawasete kure/jiyū o ibuku kaze.]

27. [Text: *Parī no Wakare. Sasurai no mi ni yadokashita Parī yo/hatsuaki no machi ni ko no ha no ochiru kure/tsuki ga maroraka ni sunde akarui yo/ satte yuku watashi o wasurezu ni kure//Shanzerizē no maronie/Burōnyu no mori no akasha/Sēnu no kawazoi no ie/Nōtorudamu no Seibo Maria//Monsō no en ni asobu hato/Ryukusanbūru no niwa ni odoru suzume/Monmarutoru no sakaba no kiiroi mado/nanyara no tsuji no hanauri no musume// Sorubonnu no sabita tobira/kyōju no yaseta omokage/Madorēnu no utsuku-shii hashira/odoriko no yasashii nasake//Sasurai no mi ni yadokashita Parī yo/ kaette yuku watashi wa nani o iō/Parī yo, Parī yo/watashi wa damatte sarō.*]

28. [Text: *Aa Iwashita Sōichi Kun. Shizuka ni yukeri/Kamiyama fuku-seibyō inchō/rei wa ten ni kaeri/tsuchi ni mitsuru aichō//Tsumetaki te no nenzu/ikinaki mune no jūjika/me wa tojite akazu/koe wa kiku ni yoshinaki ka//Namiyorishi raisha/shimeyaka ni mamoru tsuya/misa no motarasu isha/ nageki o kesu ni tarazu ya//Yo mo sugara nakeri/mada wakaki kangofuchō/ susono ni fuyu no hideri/kesa kanashi Fujisanchō.*] Iwashita Sōichi was Kuki's best friend at the Daiichi Kōtōgakkō and at Tokyo University. Iwashita became a Catholic priest and wrote *Shinkō no Isan* (Legacy of faith) and *Chūsei Tetsugaku Shisōshi Kenkyū* (Study of the intellectual history of medi-eval philosophy). Iwashita became the director of a hospital for lepers at the foot of Mt. Fuji. Under the influence of Iwashita, Kuki entertained the thought of joining the Trappist monastery in Hokkaidō. During his studies at the Uni-versity of Tokyo, Kuki was baptized in the church of St. Francis Xavier in Kanda. See Kuki's essay "Remembering Mr. Iwashita Sōichi" in this book.

29. *Epoche* means "withholding of assent and dissent," that is, suspense of judgment. According to Edmund Husserl, the phenomenologist must per-form an *epoche*—that is, suspend judgment—with regard to the existence of objects of consciousness. In analyzing, for example, the essence of perceived objects, we must not assume that such objects as trees and tables exist and causally engage with our sense organs but must focus exclusively on the essen-tial structure of perceptual consciousness. We must suspend, or "bracket," the "natural attitude" to the world.

30. Hanayagi and Fujima are two schools of classical Japanese dance. The Hanayagi school was founded by Hanayagi Jusuke (1821–1903); the Fujima school was founded by Fujima Kanbē (d. 1769).

31. The Heideggerian term *"Entwurf."*

32. The Heideggerian term *"Geworfenheit."*

33. [Text: *Credo Quia Absurdum. Harawata yo/itaki o kakotsu ka/ kudachi yuku nagayo/sanrime no ichirizuka//Kaikiteki jikan/yukite wa mo-doru yū to mu/saketaru shukan/sake no kaori o homu//Tawareo no epoke/ wabibito no sekai—nai—sonzai/ukina tatsu (iroke)/kakkoteki manzai// Shikari,nagahonryō/kakuritsuron o fue de fuke/Hanayagi Fujima no gen-*

shiryō/sorobandama de pinto yuke//Hideri wa hideri/ame wa ame/kitsune no yomeiri/sobae no mezame//Aware ekusutashisu/tenkyū no tōkī/tetsugaku uete shisu/hitō no tōki//Mogura tsubasa o ete/tasogare no sora ni tobu/bara toge o soroete/ningen no chi ni kobu//Mujun no oborozukiyo/goshiki no hikari/shinkō usuki ko yo/kami wa zennō nari//Nan no ōnō zo/kike, kyōfu no chie/hanritsu no hozo/"hairi no yue ni shinzu" to ie.] "I believe because it is absurd." This is an inexact quotation from Tertullian's *De carne Christi*, a diatribe against the gnostic Marcion, who had sought to remove the apparent contradiction in believing that God became man. Tertullian responded, angrily, that the very impossibility of the incarnation was the mark of divine agency. The saying is often used, unsympathetically, to express the idea that religious belief is irrational.

34. [Text: *Sanpo. Honobono to murasaki usuku/rira no hana niou haru no hi/otomego no kinu wa momo to hi/uchihisasu Parī waga yuku//Madorēnu hokora no hashira/nibiiro o shitaikitsuru mi/kamigaki no kado ni tatazumi/te ni osedo omoki tobira//Tamaboko no miyako no ōji/Etoaru e ashi o hakobeba/jodōsha ni umoruru hiroba/sanshikibata nani no gyōji//Izukata zo kokoro no arika/inishie no chie no ka hanatsu/furubumi no tana no namitatsu/masokagami Mishieru tōri ka//Wabibito wa nani o negawamu/shizukeki Burōnyu no mori/wakakusa o fumitsutsu hitori/kagiroi no haru o nagekamu.*]

35. [Text: *Akirame. Haiiro ga katta tamashii/jinsei no nakaba o tadori/oboeta akirame to satori/yonareta to de mo iurashii//Ikutabi ka tsumazuki mo shita/sono tsudo yoromeite taore/hitai ni kizutsuita onore/unmei to ka no kao mo mita//Geta no ne wa utsuro na oto/kotokoto to soranari shiteru/kuchi ni wa hagekoketa kiseru/hakidasu yatsu wa hitorigoto.*]

36. [Text: *Koantorō. Parī no yo no machi/fukeyuku shurō/kobin no koantorō/hakanai haru no sachi//Nibiiro no nikkei no kawa/chōzume ni chōji no heta/hana saku rira no eda/mizu nemuru Sēnu no kawa//Arazumogana no hashiradokei/bōn, bōn, gozen niji/kanjō no yume, kannō no niji/odoru shinzō, togaru shinkei.*]

37. Tutankhamen is believed to have ruled Egypt from 1334 to 1325 B.C. He was probably the twelfth ruler of Egypt's Eighteenth Dynasty.

38. [Text: *Rukusōru. Rakuda inanaku Afurika/Rukusōru no haru sangatsu/konjiki no yume o isago ni ugatsu/Tsūtankamon no arika//Hanazono no yū o yuku/sora ni matataku hoshi/Niru no mizu ni kage o otoshi/neppū kasuka ni ikizuku//Heriotorōpu nioi/būgenverea kaori/utsubokazura muragari/hitori tatsu ejiputoaoi//Tokage wa tasogare o nuu/ware wa utsukushiki mono o koi/Kureopatora no na ni yoi/kurenaki hanabira o suu.*]

39. [Text: *Fontenburō. Fontenburō no mori/Furansoa issei no miyai/haru o utsusu ike ni ukabu shiratori/amoru no asobu sakai//Hitotsu no tamashii ga ureinagara/maronie no kibamu aki no kure/higo ni esa o yari ni kitara/kogoe de tsugete kure//Gogatsu no hana ni umoreta rokoko no tei no ato/mikaerinagara watashi ga tachitatta to.*]

40. [Text: *Haiiro no Kika. Yume o tsutsumu manmaru/mawari mawarite ikuhi/kidō wa daen/shōten ni moeru hi//Samete wa sankakkei/kakudo no umu rikutsu/zuhyō wa kukei/hoshi no na ikutsu//Marui shikaku/= hanritsu/ tamashii no jikaku?/∞ tairitsu//Haiiro no kika/jinsei o toku ki ka.*]

41. The Greek version of Egyptian Asar (variant: Ausar), Osiris was the god of the dead and the god of the resurrection into eternal life. Osiris was the first child of Nut and Geb, thus the brother of Set, Nephthys, and Isis, who was also his wife. By Isis he fathered Horus, and according to some stories Nephthys assumed the form of Isis, seduced him thus, and from their union was born Anubis.

42. An early deity—probably the best-known Egyptian deity represented only as an animal and never as a human with an animal's head. Apis was most closely linked with Ptah, and his cult center was Memphis. Primarily a deity of fertility, he was represented as a bull crowned with the solar disk and uraeus-serpent. A sacred Apis bull was kept in Memphis, and there is a great mass burial of Apis bulls, the Serapeum (named for his composite relative Serapis), located there.

43. [Text: *Arabesuku. Oshirisu, Apisu, ushi no kami/wani no ha, ja no me, shishi no kami/rinne tensei to wa no nami//Tendō yōgi, kika genri/seitai kaibō, chi wa rinri/miira wa kuchizu kinenri//Tsūtankamon, kinjitō/papirusu emaki, shishinzō/meiki chinpō mujinzō//Kuroro no katsugi, hohokamuri/jirin no kazari, horegusuri/Kureopatora wa iro o uri//Jitsugetsu, seishin, natsume-yashi/Kōkai, sabaku, Niru no ashi/mukashi mo ima mo kawarinashi.*]

44. [Text: *Tango. Tamashii wa hae o negawazu/kie yo akashi no tomoru kazukazu/hoshigarisuru wa matama nasu yami//Pari no tsuki en ni aeka/ rokoko no yo masame ni miru ka/ukiizuru uzu no bi no kami//Haru nare ya kaguwashi no yoi/isaribi no wananaku wa koi/muragimono nayameru katami//Yotsu no o no vioron no nushi/hikiizuru tango no fushi/hoo ni tsutau namida no amami//Utagoe wa yoki jukōon/furusato o omou Minyon/haro-baro ni yume miru minami//Rira no hana niou otome to/mihitotsu ni odoru tabibito/nagaremizu inochi no kiwami.*]

45. [Text: *Chichūkai no rakujitsu. Gin'iro no kanran no hayashi kara/ niyoyaka ni nankoku no kaze ga fuku/ryūzetsuran no mukō wa unabara// Apenin no sanmyaku mo kage usuku/bonyari kiri no naka ni toketa mama/ yūhi ga Chichūkai e ochite yuku//Omoiokosu no wa Bōshū no hama/barairo ni wananaku kishibe no nami/kanata ni wa murasaki no Fuji no yama// Utsukushii mono ni majitta nigami/inochi ni kuikomu urēi no kizashi/ watashi o osōta kasuka na nayami//Are wa mada shōnen no hi no watashi/ yatto koi nado o shirisometa koro/itsu no mani ka nijūnen no mukashi//Ima chōdo ano shunkan no kokoro/sokkuri mō ano mama no kimochi da/chigau to ieba tada toki to tokoro//Watashi wa yappari moto no watashi da.*]

46. [Text. *Kui. Ivu—Akai akai iro/sasoi no wana no ringo/nande nande shiro/waruzare no hebi no ingo/kaeranu kami no kago. Perusefone—Amai*

amai aji/ure ni ureta zakuro/ubenai ga towa no haji/magamagashii utsuro/ hi no me minu shiko no muro. Izanami no Mikoto—Tada hitokuchi tada hitokuchi/ozomashii yomotsuhegui/ima wa ima wa mō guchi/sakidatanu kui/toga yue no kotodo no mukui.]

47. Jungfrau is a great snowy mountain, a center for tourism in the Bernese Alps. Its spectacular North Face towers nearly 10,000 feet from the valley below. At 11,412 feet (3,478 meters) this is the highest point in Europe that is reachable by railway, from which Jungfrau's summit is a short, icy climb up the northeast ridge.

48. [Text: *Arupusu no yū. Okiki, okiki, suzu no ne/rinrin, kororin, rin/ ushi asobu one/kororin, rin/kororin, rin//Are, asoko ni yagi/kuroi iwa no hotori/makka na hana wa shakunagi/otome ga hitori/hizamazuite otsuge no inori//Tatte iru no wa bokudō/yūzora o/miterun darō/junboku na kao/ sanrei no isao//Itsunomani hi ga ochita/yuki no hada o goran/barairo ni natte kita/Yungufurau no sōran/Arupusu no yōran//Sumitōtta aozora/anna ni kage o yadoshi/mizuumi no naka ni hora/ikutsu ka mabataku hoshi/oo, utsukushii maboroshi//Okiki, okiki, suzu no ne/rinrin, kororin, rin,/ushi asobu one/kororin, rin/kororin, rin.*]

49. [Text: *Benshōhō. Jigoku, gokuraku/taiihō yue beso o kaku/tabi wa michizure/niramiai wa ame no kumo/tsuifuku-kyoku mo/toki hazure// Kumanbachi to himeyuri/tsurunde mitsu o tsukuri/hatsunatsu no no o megumu/zenshin to majo/aiyō shite ichinyo/hito no ko o umu//Inochi no kakuchō/sei, han, gō/izaiza onto tore/meshii no hōshi/yoki ka na sanbyōshi/ warutsu o odore.*]

50. The god protector of Thebes.

51. Literally "the *ba*-bird." The *ba*, often represented as a bird or a human-headed bird, symbolized the vital principles of human beings. The word *"ba"* is usually translated as "soul," but this translation is not entirely correct. An exact translation cannot be given, but the word may be related to another word *"ba"* that means "power" or "force."

52. [Text: *Karunakku no haikyo. Yozora harewatarite koyoi tsuki maroshi/atemonaki sasurai no tabibito hitori/yukiyukedo hateshinaku sa- baku wa hiroshi/oto ni kiku Amon ga shinden no hotori/sayū ni tsuranaru yōtōshishin zō/kuroki kage kazu ikutsu utateki isō/Eru no kawakami Ejiputo no Karunakku/kike, are wa nandori, kusushiki fushizuke/bai no tori, bai no tori, hō, hō to naku/tamashiidori to nari tobimajiwau sayofuke//Hōkei no daimon, ensui no hashira/ sobiyuru oberisuku, umoruru ishizue/kobotarete hizumeru gyūshin no kashira/kono kōhai, kono sangeki, nan no yue/katsute yūkyū no inochi o yume mishi ka/aware, ima nakigara no nemureru wa chika/mokumoku to shite kabe o kazaru ukibori/inishie no Ramusesu no hae o katare/shōkeimonji no shishi, dachō, wani, kotori/koe o soroete utae Tēbe no homare//Ureitsutsu samayoeru onore mo katsute/kokoro ni tokoshie no shinden o tatenu/sono hi mishi yume ima kotogotoku satte/mabayuki*

maboroshi mo mata subete kienu/wazuka ni nokoru wa nani zo, horobi no ato/isago no naka ni umoruru shishimura no yado/aogi miyo Afurika no yozora o takaku/tsuki wa sumu, shirogane no iro ao o obu/kike yo, tamashii no koe, bai no tori naku/ayashiku nakite shisha no nikutai o yobu.] The Karnak Temple complex in Luxor, Egypt, includes many singular temples dedicated to Amun, his wife (Mut), and their son (Khonsu), the moon deity. Since the Arab conquest, it became known as "al-Karnak" (the fort).

53. [Text: *Hanatsumi. Arupusu no yama/yuki no yama/yūbae no yama/ hana no yama/tsumu wa enji no eboshisō/mihanadairo no minezuhō/ yaeshakunagi no yashihozaki/unran kazura komurasaki/usuyukigusa wa rikyūjiro/takane nadeshiko shinkuiro/ichiyōchidori, iwagikyō/ruri to nando no shōrindō/mine no kiiroi kinpōge/mahora no maroi iwarenge/kai no kasayuri, kirimagire/mushitori kurau tsubosumire/hi ni moete saku yamagiran/ ukon ni hikaru yama botan/Arupusu no yama/yuki no yama/yūbae no yama/ hana no yama.*]

54. [Text: *Mitsudomoe. Yoriatsumaidokoro maku/kuchinawa no sama o kaku/mondokoro mitsudomoe/isonokami furinishi e/mitsu ni shite itsu/itsu ni shite mittsu/chihayaburu kami no gofu/mi ni tsukeshi mononofu/takanaru wa tomo no oto/toberu ya no sakasagoto/ou ni maboroshi/kou ni harukeshi/ mitasarenu kokoro ari/towa ni toku ito no mari/uchinaru katachi o omoe/ awareshiki wa mittsudomoe/hitahita to namida waku/nagaruru ni uzumaki o maku.*]

55. [Text: *Unmei. Unmei yo/kōshite uta o utai/watashi wa omae to odoru/shikkari to omae no nikutai/dakishimete watashi wa odoru/yosome ni wa migurushiitte?/nan to miyō ga katte/unmei yo/unmei yo/omae to odoru/ utainagara omae to odoru/watashi wa ureshii/watashi wa kanashii/kono kimochi/kore ga watashi no inochi/are utsukushii ongaku/senritsu ga maru o kaku/hoshi no yozora no/ano sufaira no/sō de aru chōwa/daiya no hanawa/ unmei yo/watashi wa omae to odoru/omae to odoru.*]

The Genealogy of Feelings

Kuki included this essay, "Jōcho no Keizu: Uta o Tebiki to Shite" (1938), in his *Bungeiron* (Essays on the literary arts; 1941). See *KSZ* 4, pp. 170–222.

1. For the original text of the poems quoted here see Ōta Mizuho et al., eds., *Shin Man'yōshū*, vol. 2 (Tokyo: Kaizōsha, 1938).

2. "Joy is a delightful excitation of the soul, wherein consists the enjoyment it has of the good which the impressions of the brain represent to it as its own....Sadness is an unpleasant languor, wherein consists the distress which the soul receives from the evil or defect which the impressions of the brain represent to it as belonging to it." See René Descartes, *The Passions of the Soul*, trans. Stephen Voss (Indianapolis: Hackett, 1989), pp. 69–70. The

original text appears in Descartes (1596–1650), *Les Passions de L' Âme* (1649) (Paris: J.Vrin, 1955), pp. 131–132.

3. "*Joy* is man's passage from a less to a greater perfection. *Sorrow* is man's passage from a greater to a less perfection. I say passage, for joy is not perfection itself. If a man were born with the perfection to which he passes, he would possess it without the emotion of joy—a truth which will appear the more clearly from the emotion of sorrow, which is the opposite to joy. For that sorrow consists in the passage to a less perfection, but not in the less perfection itself, no one can deny, since in so far as a man shares any perfection he cannot be sad. Nor can we say that sorrow consists in the privation of a greater perfection, for privation is nothing. But the emotion of sorrow is a reality, and it therefore must be the reality of the passage to a lesser perfection, or the reality by which man's power of acting is diminished or limited." See Baruch Spinoza (1623–1677), *Ethics* (*Ethica Ordine Geometrico Demonstrata* or *Ethics Demonstrated According to a Geometric Order;* 1677), trans. James Gutmann (New York: Hafner, 1949), p. 175.

4. Ezureshi Rochō (b. 1907), a native of Tochigi prefecture, is the author of the poetry collection *Sawarabi* (Early bracken; 1933).

5. Katagiri Ryō, a native of Nagano prefecture, was a farmer who became a student of the folklorist and poet Orikuchi Shinobu (1887–1953).

6. Kawabata Chie (1887–1933), a native of Kobe, is the author of the poetry collection *Shiroi Ōgi* (White fan; 1932). Her collected works, *Kawabata Chie Zen Kashū*, were published in 1934 by Ritsumeikan University Press.

7. Kawada Jun (1882–1966), a native of Tokyo, is the author of numerous poetic collections, including *Gigeiten* (The arts' heaven; 1918), *Washi* (Eagle; 1940), and *Tōki* (Return to Kantō; 1952). A scholar of ancient poetry, Kawada published a series of essays on the poetry of Minamoto no Sanetomo, Saigyō, Fujiwara Teika, and the poets of the *Shinkokinshū*.

8. Okuyama Shūho, a native of Kagoshima, participated in movements of colonial literature, especially in Manchuria.

9. Kawanaka Yūkō, a native of Fukui prefecture, was a student of Orikuchi Shinobu.

10. Kuki refers to the last Korean king, Sunjong (r. 1907–1910) of the Yi dynasty, whose death in April 1926 inspired an outpouring of grief among the Korean people during a period of Japanese colonial rule.

11. Kuki refers to *La Psychologie des Sentiments* (The psychology of feelings; 1896) by Théodule-Armand Ribot (1839–1916), who is considered the father of French scientific psychology. Among Ribot's major works are *Logique des Sentiments* (The logic of feelings; 1905) and *Essai sur les Passions* (Essay on the passions; 1907). See T.Ribot, *La Psychologie des Sentiments* (Paris: Félix Alcan, 1911), p. 45.

12. Kabuki Fumi, a native of Sakai, was a schoolteacher.

13. Ōe Takeo, a native of Sapporo, was a poet.

14. Kanbara Katsushige (1892–1966), a native of Chiba prefecture, is the author of poetry collections such as *Tanagumo* (A rack of clouds; 1928) and *Gyokushō* (The jewel camphor tree; 1951).

15. Ōno Tamotsu (b. 1898), a native of Chiba prefecture, was a professor at Waseda Middle School.

16. Ōmura Gorō (1895–1968), a native of Ikeda in Osaka prefecture, is the author of the poetry collection *Hanayabu* (A bush of flowers; 1941).

17. Kawai Takako (b. 1898), a native of Gifu prefecture, was a student of the poet and literary scholar Sasaki Nobutsuna (1872–1963).

18. Nakamura Kenkichi (1889–1934), a poet from Funo village in Hiroshima prefecture, is the author of such famous poetry collections as *Rinsenshū* (Collection of the forest's spring; 1916), *Shigarami* (A weir; 1924), and *Keiraishū* (Collection of light thunders; 1931).

19. Kuki refers to Georges Dumas's *La Tristesse et la Joie* (Sorrow and joy; 1900). Kuki's library also includes the two volumes of Dumas's *Traité de Psychologie* (Treatise on psychology; 1923–1924) and *Le Sourire: Psychologie et Physiologie* (Smiling: Psychology and physiology; 1906). For a list of Kuki's books see *Kuki Shūzō Bunko Mokuroku* (Kobe: Kōnan Daigaku Tetsugaku Kenkyūshitsu, 1976).

20. Katō Sugie, a native of Mie prefecture, was an elementary-school teacher.

21. Kawasaki Togai (1884–1934), a native of Wata village in Nagano prefecture, wrote the poetry collection *Yamamori* (Mountain ranger; 1927).

22. Katō Tōri (1882–1944), a native of Matsushima village in Aomori prefecture, is the author of the poetry collection *Katō Tōri Shū* (Collection of Katō Tōri; 1919).

23. Kaitatsu Yoshifumi (b. 1871), a native of Shizuoka prefecture, was a poet and writer of children's stories.

24. Kaneko Kun'en (1876–1951), a native of Tokyo, is the author of the poetry collections *Sameta Uta* (Disillusioned poems; 1910), *Kusa no Ue* (On the grass; 1914), and *Shizumareru Ki* (The still tree; 1919).

25. This is a reference to the myth of the Sun-Goddess Amaterasu who shut herself in a cave as a result of a conflict with her brother Susanowo. In an attempt to bring Amaterasu out of the cave in order to restore the sun in the sky, the deity Ame-no-Tajikarawo "took her hand and pulled her out," thus causing joy and relief among all deities. See Philippi, *Kojiki*, pp. 81–86.

26. Kawatani Tose was a native of the southern Kawachi district of Osaka prefecture.

27. Kanasawa Chōzaburō, a native of Aomori prefecture, was a railway worker.

28. Kuki uses the Chinese translation of the Sanskrit word *"vedanā,"* which corresponds to the modern expression *"kankaku"* (sense, sensation). In Buddhist philosophy *ju* (sensation, perception) is one of the five aggregates

(skandha) forming the human personality together with form *(shiki, rūpa)*, conception *(sō, samjnā)*, volition *(gyō, samskāra)*, and consciousness *(shiki, vijñāna)*.

29. *Yuishikiron* is the translation by Hsüang-tsang (ca. 596–664) of Dharmapāla's *Vijnapti-matrata-siddhi*. See the French translation by L.de la Vallée Poussin, *La Siddhi de Hiuen-tsang* (Paris, 1928).

30. Kaneda Chizu (1902–1934), a native of Nagano prefecture, is the author of the posthumous *Kaneda Chizu Kashū* (Collected poems of Kaneda Chizu).

31. Karakita Rison, a native of Nagano prefecture, was a student of the poet Wakayama Bokusui (1885–1928).

32. Katō Michiko, a native of Aichi prefecture, was an elementary-school teacher.

33. Katsuta Motobumi, a native of Sapporo, was a businessman.

34. Kamiyoshi Taeko was a native of Tokyo.

35. Ōta Fujiko, a native of Nagano prefecture, was a student of the poet Ōta Mizuho (1876–1955).

36. Kawaguchi Rei was a native of Shiga prefecture.

37. "Since love is pleasure with the accompaniment of the idea of an external cause, and hatred is pain, also with the accompaniment of the idea of an external cause, this pleasure and this pain will be species of love and hatred. But since love and hatred are related to external objects, we shall refer to these emotions by other names. We shall call pleasure, accompanied by the idea of an internal cause, 'glory,' and the pain that is the contrary of this we shall call 'shame.' It must be understood here that the pleasure or pain arises from the fact that a man believes himself to be praised or blamed; otherwise I shall call pleasure, accompanied by the idea of an internal cause, 'self-contentment,' and the pain that is the contrary of this I shall call 'repentance.' Further, since it can come about that the pleasure with which someone imagines himself to affect others is only imaginary, and each person endeavors to imagine everything that, he imagines, affects him with pleasure, it can easily happen that a person who glorifies himself is proud and imagines that he is pleasing to everyone, when in fact he is annoying to everyone." See Spinoza, *Ethics,* trans. Parkinson, pp. 187–188.

38. Kaneto Sōshi (b. 1908), a native of Ibaraki prefecture, was a schoolteacher.

39. Kanazawa Hisako, a native of Nagano prefecture, was a student of the poet Imai Kuniko (1890–1948).

40. Kawashima Sonoko (b. 1893) was born in Lyon, France, and lived in Tokyo. She was a student of Ōta Mizuho.

41. Kashiwahara Toshirō was a native of Kumamoto prefecture.

42. Ebihara Hamatoshi, a native of Ibaraki prefecture, was a dentist.

43. Ōi Hideko, a native of Hyōgo prefecture, was a student of Kaneko Kun'en.

44. Ōtsuji Mieko was a native of Kyoto.

45. Ōhashi Matsuhei (1893–1952), a native of Oita prefecture, worked as an editor of the *Shin Man'yōshū* (New collections of ten thousand leaves), from which Kuki takes all his examples. Among his poetic collections are *Tanboku* (Pale India ink; 1951) and *Yūgiri* (An evening mist; 1957).

46. Kōmura Kasumi was a native of Tokyo.

47. Ōkuma Chōjirō (1901–1933), a native of Hachiōji in Tokyo prefecture, is the author of *Ōkuma Chōjirō Zenkashū* (Collected poems of Ōkuma Chōjirō; 1933).

48. Katō Toshiko (b. 1907) was a native of Tokyo.

49. Ōtsuka Gorō (b. 1897), a native of Nagano city, was a middle-school teacher.

50. Kawasaki Ishimatsu (b. 1899), a native of Hokkaidō, worked in the steel industry.

51. Kaneya Shōji, a native of Fukushima prefecture, was a high-school teacher.

52. Ōkoshi Kōchō, a native of Ibaraki prefecture, was an elementary-school teacher.

53. Ōtsuka Takeshi was a native of Saitama prefecture.

54. Kakegai Yoshio (b. 1905), a native of Tokyo, was a student of the poets Yosano Tekkan (1873–1935) and Yosano Akiko (1878–1942).

55. Ōtsuka Torao (1902–1937), a native of Saga prefecture, was a journalist.

56. Ōkubo Hitō (1894–1925), a native of Nagasaki prefecture, was a student of the poet Saitō Mokichi (1882–1953).

57. Kawakami Ichirō, a native of Okayama prefecture, was a student of Orikuchi Shinobu.

58. Ōmura Tsuruko (1906–1934) was a native of Kyoto prefecture.

59. Ōmori Hiromu, a native of Hyōgo prefecture, was an elementary-school teacher.

60. Ōnishi Hajime (1864–1900), a native of Fukuoka, is the author of several philosophical works including *Ryōshin Kigen Ron* (Treatise on the origin of conscience; 1904). His essay "Waka ni Shūkyō Nashi" (There is no religion in *waka*; 1887) is translated in Marra, *Modern Japanese Aesthetics*, pp. 83–92.

61. Kamiya Masae (b. 1907), a native of Tokyo, was a student of the poet Hosoi Gyotai (1889–1962).

62. Kawashima Fumiko was a native of Matsumoto city.

63. Ōkawa Sumie, a native of Mito city, was a student of the literary scholar Takasaki Masahide (1901–1982).

64. Katayama Hiroko (b. 1878), a native of Tokyo, is the author of the poetry collection *Hisui* (Kingfisher; 1916).

65. Kawai Ichiro (b. 1901), a native of Aichi prefecture, was a rice dealer.

66. Kaneko Fukyū (1892–1970), a native of Sado Island, is the author of

the poetry collections *Nami no Ue* (On the waves; 1916), *Dokkyo* (Solitary life; 1937), and *Ariso Nami* (Waves on a reefy coast; 1967).

67. Ōsawa Isamu was a native of Gunma prefecture.

68. Ōtsuka Etsuyo was a native of Yokohama.

69. Kawabata Yasuto, a native of Nagasaki prefecture, was a school-teacher.

70. Kawabata Shunpo (b. 1904), a native of Chiba prefecture, was an elementary-school teacher.

71. Ōta Toshiko was a native of Nagano prefecture.

72. Ochiai Naobumi (1861–1903), a leading Japanese literary scholar from present-day Miyagi prefecture, was an advocate of the reform of *tanka* poetry. His literary works, *Ochiai Naobumi Bunshū*, were collected in 1927 by the poet Yosano Tekkan (1873–1935).

73. Kamizawa Hiroshi was a native of Tokyo.

74. Kōsaka Nobukatsu, a native of Miyagi prefecture, was an elementary-school teacher.

75. Okumura Okuemon was a native of Shiga prefecture.

76. Okuda Kazuo (b. 1912), a native of Hokkaidō, was a carpenter.

77. Ōno Toraji (1908–1931), a native of Saitama prefecture, is the author of the posthumous *Ōno Toraji Kashū* (Collected poems of Ōno Toraji; 1931).

78. Okimoto Shigetora, a native of Kōchi prefecture on the island of Shikoku, was an elementary-school teacher.

79. Ōta Seikyū (b. 1909), a native of Nagano prefecture, is a famous scholar of Chinese literature and the author of poetry collections such as *Kokuho no Naka ni* (In the fortunes of a state; 1950), *Ajia no Kao* (The face of Asia; 1960), and *Sakugen* (Going upstream; 1973).

80. Ōhashi Moyo (b. 1893) was a native of Ibaraki prefecture.

81. Kaneko Shinsaburō, a native of Gunma prefecture, was a school-teacher.

82. Ōta Mizuho (1876–1955), a native of Nagano prefecture, is the author of ten volumes of collected works including the poetry collection *Unchō* (Birds on the clouds; 1922) and the theoretical work on poetry *Tanka Ritsugen* (Proposal on *tanka;* 1921).

83. Emura Jōken, a native of Kyoto, was a middle-school teacher and a student of the poet Ōta Mizuho.

84. Kawabe Morihei (b. 1913), a native of Gunma prefecture, was a postal worker and a student of the poet Tsuchiya Bunmei (b. 1890).

85. Kawaguchi Kozue (b. 1900), a native of Aichi prefecture, was a hair-dresser.

86. Ebato Hakuka (b. 1887), a native of Chiba prefecture, was an elementary-school teacher and a student of the poet Wakayama Bokusui (1885–1928).

87. Kawachi Eisō (b. 1913), a native of Hokkaidō, was a student of the poet Hashimoto Tokuju (b. 1894).

88. Kanaoka Masao (b. 1891), a native of Chiba prefecture, was a farmer.

89. Kanazawa Tanetomi (1889–1961), a native of Ikeda city in Osaka prefecture, is the author of the poetry collections *Mitsurin* (Jungle; 1930) and *Kokūhen* (Many empty spaces; 1957).

90. Kagami Masako (b. 1894), a native of Osaka, was a high-school teacher.

91. Kawazu Teruko, a native of Ōtsu, was a student of the poet and literary scholar Oyama Tokujirō (1889–1963).

92. Ōshita Mitsuo (b. 1909), a native of Aichi prefecture, was a schoolteacher.

93. Ōya Ichizō (1908–1928) was a native of Niigata city.

94. Katagishi Yoshikumi, a native of Toyama prefecture, was a farmer.

95. Ōkuro Tomiji, a native of Akita prefecture, worked as an agricultural expert.

96. Katō Meiji (1911–1970), a native of Nagano prefecture, wrote mainly children's stories such as *Tsuru no Koe* (The voice of cranes; 1960).

97. Ebisawa Kinzō, a native of Yokohama, sold stationery. "Hungry ghost ships" *(segakibune)* refers to ships that were used to offer prayers for the souls of people who had died by drowning.

98. Kawamura Senshū, a native of Kyoto, worked for his native city.

99. Okunuki Nobumitsu (b. 1902), a native of Fukushima prefecture, worked for an insurance company. He is the author of the poetry collection *Asagiri* (Morning fog).

100. Ōishi Issaku, a native of Yamanashi prefecture, was a schoolteacher.

101. Katō Tōryō, a native of Kanagawa prefecture, was a student of the poets Shimaki Akahiko (1876–1926) and Saitō Mokichi.

102. Ōno Kazuo, a native of Yokohama, worked in the dyeing industry. He was a student of the poet Uematsu Hisaki (1890–1964).

103. Kanamori Hiroshi, a native of Kumamoto prefecture, was a schoolteacher.

104. Katō Isami (b. 1902), a native of Miyagi prefecture, was a student of the poets Kumagai Takeo (1883–1936) and Hashimoto Tokuju.

105. Ōtsuka Taiji, a native of Tokushima prefecture, was a businessman and a student of the poet Matsumura Eiichi (1889–1981).

106. Kamata Keishi (1893–1980), a native of Chiba prefecture, managed the Yakumo Shorin and Hakugyoku Shobō publishing houses.

107. Ebara Seichō, a native of Yamaguchi prefecture, was a landowner.

108. Okuda Tomio, a native of Nagano prefecture, worked at the Mitsukoshi department store.

109. For the original text see *Gūzensei no Mondai* in *KSZ* 2, pp. 214–217. For a French translation see Kuki Shūzō, *Le Problème de la Contingence*, trans. Omodaka Hisayuki (Tokyo: University of Tokyo Press, 1966), pp. 160–163.

110. For the original text see *Ningen to Jitsuzon* in *KSZ* 3, pp. 142–176.

111. Ōki Yūji (1895–1963), a native of Gunma prefecture, wrote a series of children's stories such as *Tsukiyo no Basha* (The carriage of a moonlight night; 1950) and *Hoshi no Kodomo* (Children of the stars; 1950).

112. Ōya Jūei, a native of Kawasaki city, was a maker and seller of wooden sandals *(geta)*.

113. Kagoshima Juzō (1898–1982), a native of Fukuoka, is the author of poetry collections such as *Chōseki* (Ebb and flow; 1941) and *Gyorin* (Fish scales; 1952).

114. Kamada Kichisaburō, a native of Miyagi prefecture, was a school-teacher.

115. Kanbayashi Fumiko (b. 1883) was a native of Uji city.

116. Kageyama Masaharu, a native of Aichi prefecture, was a journalist. During his two and a half year imprisonment, he wrote the poetry collection *Higanshū* (Collection of merciful prayers; 1936). The poet refers to his mother's outstanding ethical standards, which provide her with a knowledge far greater than that acquired from books.

117. Kuki refers to Kant's *Kritik der praktischen Vernunft* (1788): "Two things fill the mind with ever new and increasing admiration and reverence, the more often and more steadily one reflects on them: the starry heavens above me and the moral law within me." See Kant, *Critique of Practical Reason,* trans. Gregor p. 133.

118. Kawai Chioko was a native of Tokyo.

119. Kawazoe Yukiko (1897–1931), a native of Kōchi prefecture, was a student of Ōta Mizuho. Her poetry collection *Sugi no Shizuku* (Drops from a cryptomeria; 1932) was published posthumously.

120. Kuki Shūzō, *Ningen to Jitsuzon* (Tokyo: Iwanami Shoten, 1939).

121. Kuki Shūzō, *Bungeiron* (Tokyo: Iwanami Shoten, 1941).

122. *Man'yōshū* 4:741. *Odorokite* (to be surprised) literally means "to wake up." In the eighth century the word *"yume"* (dream) was actually pronounced *"ime."* Ōtomo no Yakamochi (d. 785), son of Tabito, is considered to be the last compiler of the *Man'yōshū.* He is one of the Thirty-Six Poetic Geniuses *(sanjūrokkasen).*

123. *Man'yōshū* 3:340. Ōtomo no Tabito (665–731), son of Yasumaro, made Dazaifu in Kyushu a literary center.

124. *Man'yōshū* 4:518. Ishikawa no Iratsume was intimate with Prince Ōtsu, the third son of Emperor Tenmu (r. 673–686).

125. *Man'yōshū* 10:1951.

126. *Man'yōshū* 3:373. Yamabe no Akahito (fl. 724–737) is counted among Japan's Thirty-Six Poetic Geniuses.

127. *Man'yōshū* 2:218. Kakinomoto no Hitomaro (d. 708–715?) worked at the court for three sovereigns: Tenmu (r. 673–686), Jitō (r. 690–697), and Monmu (r. 697–707). He is considered one of the Thirty-Six Poetic Geniuses.

128. *Man'yōshū* 8:1658. This poem was sent by Empress Kōmyō, daughter of Fujiwara no Fubito, to her husband Emperor Shōmu (r. 724-749).

129. *Man'yōshū* 17:4016. Takechi no Kurohito was a courtier during the reigns of Jitō (690-697) and Monmu (697-707).

130. *Man'yōshū* 5:796. Yamanoue no Okura (660-733), allegedly of Korean descent, was a learned scholar who spent two years doing research in China.

131. *Man'yōshū* 10:1990.

The Metaphysics of Literature

This essay, "Bungaku no Keijijōgaku," was originally part of a course, "Bungaku no Gairon" (Outline of literature), which Kuki delivered at Kyoto Imperial University in 1940. Kuki included this essay in his last book, *Bungeiron*, which was published posthumously in 1941. See *KSZ* 4, pp. 7-59.

1. Hōnen (1133-1212) was the founder of the Pure Land (Jōdo) sect of Buddhism.

2. Kaibara Ekiken (1630-1714) was one of the major Neo-Confucian scholars of the Edo period.

3. Nishikawa Joken (1648-1724) was an astronomer and geographer of the Edo period.

4. Satō Nobuhiro (1769-1850) was an economist of the late Edo period.

5. A reference to Henri-Louis Bergson's (1859-1941) *Durée et Simultaneité* (Duration and simultaneity; 1922). See Bergson, *Duration and Simultaneity*.

6. A reference to Martin Heidegger's (1889-1976) *Sein und Zeit* (Being and time; 1927). See Heidegger, *Being and Time*.

7. Tamenaga Shunsui (1790-1843) is the author of popular fiction known as "books on human feelings" *(ninjōbon)*.

8. Kiyomoto Enju Daiyū (1777-1825) is considered the founder of the art of Kiyomoto songs.

9. Unkei's (d. 1223) statue of the priest Muchaku (1212) is kept in the Kōfukuji of Nara.

10. Sesshū Tōyō (1420-1506) is considered the greatest priest-painter of the late Muromachi period.

11. Matsuo Bashō (1644-1694) is the most renowned Japanese poet of *haikai*.

12. Chikamatsu Monzaemon (1653-1724) is Japan's most renowned dramatist of the Edo period.

13. Ryūtatsu (d. 1611), a monk of the Nichiren sect at the Kenponji temple in Sakai, created ditties that were popular at the beginning of the Edo period.

14. The original text says, "Verweile doch, du bist so schön!" This is a quotation from *Faust* by Johann Wolfgang von Goethe (1749-1832).

15. The English physicist and mathematician Isaac Newton (1642–1727) taught at Cambridge University (1669–1701) and was president of the Royal Society (1703–1727). According to Voltaire, Newton conceived the idea of universal gravitation after seeing an apple fall in his garden.

16. "Two things fill the mind with ever new and increasing admiration and reverence, the more often and more steadily one reflects on them: the starry heavens above me and the moral law within me." See Kant, *Critique of Practical Reason*, trans. Gregor, p. 133.

17. Augustine (354–430) is the well-known early Christian church father and philosopher.

18. Théodore Géricault (1791–1824) inaugurated the romantic movement in French art.

19. Auguste Rodin (1840–1917) is the well-known French sculptor.

20. This verse comes from the poem "Chikumagawa Ryojō no Uta" (Consolation of the weary heart of the traveler to the Chikuma River) by the novelist Shimazaki Tōson (1872–1943).

21. This is the opening verse of the poem "Oefu" from Shimazaki Tōson's poetic collection *Wakanashū* (Anthology of young herbs; 1897).

22. This is a quotation from Charles Baudelaire's "Le Goût du Néant" from his *Les Fleurs du Mal*. See Francis Scarfe, ed., *The Complete Verse: Baudelaire*, vol. 1 (London: Anvil Press Poetry, 1986), p. 160.

23. *Man'yōshū* 2:137. See Kojima Noriyuki, Kinoshita Masatoshi, and Satake Akihiro, eds., *Man'yōshū*, 1, NKBZ 2 (Tokyo: Shōgakukan, 1971), p. 137, in which the fourth verse reads *"chirimagai ni."* The meaning is the same.

24. The English translation is by Edwin A. Cranston, *A Waka Anthology, 1: The Gem-Glistening Cup* (Stanford: Stanford University Press, 1993), p. 207.

25. *Kokinshū* 9:410 by Ariwara no Narihira (825–880). See Okumura Tsuneya, ed., *Kokin Wakashū*, SNKS 19 (Tokyo: Shinchōsha, 1978), p. 157.

26. A *haiku* by the mid-Edo poet Yosa Buson (1716–1783). See Iida Ryūta et al., eds., *Nihon Meiku Shūsei* (Tokyo: Gakutōsha, 1991), pp. 242–243.

27. The English translation is by Makoto Ueda, *The Path of Flowering Thorn: The Life and Poetry of Yosa Buson* (Stanford: Stanford University Press, 1998), p. 159.

28. A *haiku* by Buson. See Iida, *Nihon Meiku Shūsei*, p. 221.

29. English translation by Ueda, *The Path of Flowering Thorn*, p. 180.

30. A *haiku* by Buson. See Iida, *Nihon Meiku Shūsei*, p. 234.

31. A *haiku* by Buson. See Iida, *Nihon Meiku Shūsei*, p. 221.

32. A reference to the Italian *verso sdrúcciolo*.

33. A reference to the Italian *verso tronco*.

34. *Man'yōshū* 6:971. See Kojima et al., *Man'yōshū*, 2, p. 157.

35. For an English translation of the entire poem see Cranston, *Waka Anthology*, p. 327.

36. A famous dancer from Kyoto, Shizuka was the lover of the legendary

Minamoto no Yoshitsune (1159–1189). During the battles between Yoshitsune and his brother, the shogun Yoritomo (1147–1199), Shizuka was captured at Mt. Yoshino and forced to leave Yoshitsune. She was sent to Kamakura, Yoritomo's capital, where she danced her love for Yoshitsune in front of the shogun and his wife Masako. This episode is portrayed in several *nō* pieces, such as *Yoshino Shizuka, Futari Shizuka, and Funa Benkei.*

37. This quotation comes from the poem *Fan Chao* (Reflection) by the Chinese poet Tu Fu (712–770). See Takagi Masakazu, ed., *Tōshisen,* 3, *Chūgoku Kotensen* 27 (Tokyo: Asahi Shinbunsha, 1978), p. 235.

38. A *haiku* by Bashō in which the first line reads *"nagaki hi mo"* (even in long days). See Kon Eizō, ed., *Bashō Kushū, SNKS* 51 (Tokyo: Shinchōsha, 1982), n. 295, p. 107.

39. The English translation is by Makoto Ueda, *Bashō and His Interpreters: Selected Hokku with Commentary* (Stanford: Stanford University Press, 1992), p. 155.

40. *Man'yōshū* 4:653, in which the third verse reads *"tamasaka ni"* (fortuitously). The poem is by Ōtomo Surugamaro. See Kojima, *Man'yōshū,* 1, p. 354.

41. The English translation is by Ian Hideo Levy, *Man'yōshū: A Translation of Japan's Premier Anthology of Classical Poetry,* vol. 1 (Princeton: Princeton University Press, 1981), p. 300.

42. *Kokinshū* 9:419 by Ki no Aritsune. See Okumura, *Kokin Wakashū,* p. 162.

43. *Man'yōshū* 3:378 by Yamabe no Akahito. See Kojima, *Man'yōshū,* 1, pp. 245–246.

44. English translation by Levy, *Man'yōshū,* p. 198.

45. *Man'yōshū* 1:37. See Kojima, *Man'yōshū,* 1, p. 84.

46. English translation by Levy, *Man'yōshū,* p. 57.

47. A *haiku* by Bashō. See Kon, *Bashō Kushū,* 635, p. 226.

48. Natsume Sōseki (1867–1916) is considered the major Japanese novelist of the Meiji period. He wrote *Kokoro* (Heart) in 1914.

49. The English translation is by Edwin McClellan, *Kokoro: A Novel and Selected Essays* (Lanham, Md.: Madison Books, 1992), p. 1.

50. Nagai Kafū (1879–1959) wrote this work in 1937. Kafū wrote stories of Tokyo life including *Sumidagawa* (1909), *Ude Kurabe* (1917), *Ajisai* (1931), and *Tsuyu no Atosaki* (1931).

51. The English translation is by Edward Seidensticker, *A Strange Tale from East of the River and Other Stories* (Tokyo: Tuttle, 1972), p. 106.

52. The *Taketori Monogatari,* written during the early Heian period, is celebrated by the author of *The Tale of Genji* as "the ancestor of all tales."

53. Adapted from Helen Craig McCullough, trans., *Classical Japanese Prose: An Anthology* (Stanford: Stanford University Press, 1990), pp. 28–29. For the original text see Noguchi Motohiro, ed., *Taketori Monogatari, SNKS* 26 (Tokyo: Shinchōsha, 1979), p. 9.

54. *Genji Monogatari* is the work of Murasaki Shikibu (978?–1014?), who wrote the best-known story of the Heian period around the year 1000.

55. The English translation is by Royall Tyler, *The Tale of Genji* (New York: Viking, 2001), p. 3.

56. English translation by McCullough, *Classical Japanese Prose*, p. 29, with a slight variation.

57. English translation by Tyler, *Tale of Genji*, p. 3.

58. The Hikone Screen is a six-panel *byōbu* created between 1624 and 1644. One screen is painted with scenes from the pleasure district in the foreground and landscape in the background.

59. Kuki refers to the clay over wood and metal tableaux such as the one on the death of Shaka on the north side of the pagoda and the tableaux of the Yuima-Monju debate on the east side. These works are dated A.D. 711.

60. The Phoenix Hall (Hōōdō) is a representation of Amida's Western Paradise inside the Byōdōin, a temple situated on the banks of the Uji River southeast of Kyoto.

61. "Going up a mountain track, I fell to thinking. Approach everything rationally, and you become harsh. Pole along in the stream of emotions, and you will be swept away by the current. Give free rein to your desires, and you become uncomfortably confined. It is not a very agreeable place to live, this world of ours. When the unpleasantness increases, you want to draw yourself up to some place where life is easier. It is just at this point when you first realize that life will be no more agreeable no matter what heights you may attain, that a poem may be given birth, or a picture created. The creation of this world is the work of neither god nor devil, but of the ordinary people around us; those who live opposite, and those next door, drifting here and there about their daily business. You may think this world created by ordinary people a horrible place in which to live, but where else is there? Even if there is somewhere else to go, it can only be a 'non-human' realm, and who knows but that such a world may not be even more hateful than this?" English translation by Alan Turney, *The Three-Cornered World* (Tokyo: Tuttle, 1968), p. 12. Natsume Sōseki wrote *Kusamakura* in 1906.

62. *Man'yōshū* 11:2373. See Kojima, *Man'yōshū*, 3, p. 177.

63. English translation by Cranston, *Waka Anthology*, pp. 250–251.

64. A *haiku* by Bashō singing the day before the Tanabata festival on the seventh day of the Seventh Month. See Kon, *Bashō Kushū*, 539, p. 195.

65. *Man'yōshū* 3:318 by Yamabe no Akahito. See Kojima, *Man'yōshū*, 1, p. 226.

66. English translation by Levy, *Man'yōshū*, p. 178.

67. A *haiku* by Buson. See Iida, *Nihon Meiku Shūsei*, pp. 213–214.

68. English translation by Ueda, *Path of Flowering Thorn*, p. 128.

69. Andō Hiroshige (1797–1858) is considered the most famous print-maker of the Tokugawa period.

70. Marcel Proust's (1871–1922) *A la Recherche du Temps Perdu* was published between 1913 and 1927.

71. The English translation is by Frederick A. Blossom, *The Past Recaptured* (New York: Albert & Charles Boni, 1932), pp. 400–401.

72. Hayashi Fumiko's (1903–1951) extensive work includes the titles *Hōrōki* (Wandering; 1928–1930), *Bangiku* (Evening chrysanthemum; 1948–1949), and *Ukigumo* (Floating clouds; 1949–1950). Kuki describes a meeting with Hayashi Fumiko in the short essay "A Record of Short Songs," which is translated in this book.

73. Tanizaki Jun'ichirō (1886–1965) is the author of *Chijin no Ai* (A fool's love; 1924), *Tade Kuu Mushi* (Some prefer nettles; 1928), *Sasame Yuki* (The Makioka sisters; 1943–1948), and *Kagi* (The key; 1956). He wrote *Ashikari* in 1932. For an English translation of this story see Tanizaki Junichirō, *The Reed Cutter and Captain Shigemoto's Mother: Two Novellas*, trans. Anthony H. Chambers (New York: Knopf, 1994), pp. 1–53.

74. A son of Emperor Takakura, Go-Toba (1180–1239) reigned from 1183 until 1198. He was exiled to Oki Island during the Jōkyū disturbance of 1221. His villa was located south of the Minase River in Settsu province, today's Osaka prefecture.

75. Murasaki Shikibu (978?–1014?), the famous author of *Genji Monogatari*, lived during the mid-Heian period.

76. Ōda Noburaga (1534–1582) ended the Ashikaga shogunate and began to unify Japan after conquering central Japan in 1582.

77. A reference to the vendetta of the forty-seven loyal retainers immortalized in Takeda Izumo's (1691–1756) *Kanadehon Chūshingura* (The treasury of loyal retainers; 1748).

78. Sugawara no Michizane (845–903) was a poet and politician of the early Heian period. His collections of Chinese composition include *Kanke Bunsō* (Sugawara poems; ca. 900) and *Kanke Kōshū* (A later Sugawara collection; 902).

79. Kagawa Kageki (1768–1843), *waka* poet and critic, is the author of the poetry collection *Keien Isshi* (A shoot from the Judas-tree garden; pub. 1830).

80. Enomoto Kikaku (1661–1707), a renowned *haikai* poet, edited the collection *Kareobana* (Withered pampas plumes) to honor Matsuo Bashō in the year of his death (1694).

81. Tu Fu (712–770), one of the greatest poets of China, adopted an itinerant mode of life after failing to pass the imperial examination.

82. The Chinese poet Po Chü-i (772–846), known in Japan as Hakurakuten, became the favorite poet of Heian times.

83. Ōe no Masahira (952–1012), a scholar of Chinese studies, served under Emperor Ichijō (r. 986–1011).

84. Ōe no Masafusa (1041–1111), *waka* and *kanshi* poet, compiled the *Wakan Rōei Gōchū* (Ōe's notes on the *Wakan Rōeishū*) and *Gōki* (Ōe's own record).

85. Saigyō (1118–1190) is the author of the poetry collection *Sankashū* (The mountain hut).

86. The writer Tokuda Shūsei (1871–1943) is considered one of the "four pillars" of Japanese naturalism.

87. Chikamatsu Monzaemon (1653–1725), the most renowned writer of *jōruri* of the Edo period, wrote *Sonezaki Shinjū* in 1703. The play was first performed on 20 June 1703, less than a month after the events described took place (22 May 1703). For an English translation see Donald Keene, trans., *Major Plays of Chikamatsu* (New York: Columbia University Press, 1961), pp. 39–56.

88. Soga no Yagorō (1877–1948) is the founder of the genre of Japanese comedy together with his brother Jūrō.

89. Okamoto Kidō (1872–1938), playwright and novelist, wrote the play *Shuzenji Monogatari* in 1911.

90. The novelist Kurata Hyakuzō (1891–1943) wrote the play *Shukke to Sono Deshi* in 1916.

91. The renowned eighteenth-century literary scholar Motoori Norinaga (1730–1801) developed this argument in his treatise on poetry, *Isonokami no Sasamegoto* (Personal views on poetry; 1763). The original text of Kuki's quotation appears in Hino Tatsuo, ed., *Motoori Norinaga Shū*, SNKS 60 (Tokyo: Shinchōsha, 1983), p. 305.

92. The English translation is by Sanford Goldstein and Seishi Shinoda; see Ishikawa Takuboku, *Romaji Diary and Sad Toys* (Tokyo: Tuttle, 1985), p. 45. The quotation comes from "Poems to Eat," an article serialized in the Tokyo *Mainichi* newspaper from 30 November to 7 December 1909.

93. *Man'yōshū* 1:29; English translation by Levy, *Man'yōshū*, pp. 53–54. The original text appears in Kojima, *Man'yōshū*, 1, pp. 80–81.

94. *Man'yōshū* 2:219 by Kakinomoto no Hitomaro. See Kojima, *Man'yōshū*, 1, p. 179. The original text has *"mishiku wa"* in the fourth line.

95. English translation by Levy, *Man'yōshū*, p. 141.

96. *Man'yōshū* 7:1092 by Kakinomoto no Hitomaro. See Kojima, *Man'yōshū*, 2, p. 209.

97. *Man'yōshū* 3:316 by Ōtomo Tabito. See Kojima, *Man'yōshū*, 1, p. 225.

98. English translation by Levy, *Man'yōshū*, p. 177.

99. *Man'yōshū* 8:1471 by Yamabe no Akahito. See Kojima, *Man'yōshū*, 2, p. 315.

100. *Man'yōshū* 3:337 by Yamanoue Okura. See Kojima, *Man'yōshū*, 1, p. 234. In the original the fourth line is *"sore sono haha mo."*

101. English translation by Levy, *Man'yōshū*, p. 186.

102. *Man'yōshū* 3:328 by Ono no Oyu. See Kojima, *Man'yōshū*, 1, p. 231.

103. English translation by Levy, *Man'yōshū*, p. 183.

104. *Man'yōshū* 3:266 by Kakinomoto no Hitomaro. See Kojima, *Man'yōshū*, 1, p. 210. In the original the fourth line is *"kokoro mo shinoni."*

105. English translation by Levy, *Man'yōshū*, p. 162.

106. *Man'yōshū* 2:211 by Kakinomoto no Hitomaro. See Kojima, *Man'yō-shū*, 1, p. 175.

107. English translation by Levy, *Man'yōshū*, p. 137.

108. *Man'yōshū* 6:924 by Yamabe no Akahito. See Kojima, *Man'yōshū*, 2, pp. 136-137.

109. English translation by Cranston, *Waka Anthology*, p. 310.

110. A *haiku* by Bashō. See Kon, *Bashō Kushū*, 270, p. 99.

111. English translation by Ueda, *Bashō and His Interpreters*, p. 140.

112. A *haiku* by Bashō. See Kon, *Bashō Kushū*, 294, p. 107.

113. English translation by Ueda, *Bashō and His Interpreters*, p. 154.

114. A *haiku* by Bashō. See Kon, *Bashō Kushū*, 523, p. 189.

115. English translation by Ueda, *Bashō and His Interpreters*, p. 251.

116. A *haiku* by Buson. See Shimizu Takayuki, ed., *Yosa Buson Shū*, SNKS 32 (Tokyo: Shinchōsha, 1979), p. 133.

117. This poem is by Emperor Wen of the Wei dynasty (r. 220-226).

118. Miyoshi Tatsuji (1900-1964) is the author of many poetry collections, including *Sokuryōsen* (A surveying ship; 1930) and *Rakuda no Kobu ni Matagatte* (Sitting on a camel's hump; 1952). See *Miyoshi Tatsuji zenshū* 1 (Tokyo: Chikuma Shobō, 1964), pp. 334-335.

119. Hagiwara Sakutarō (1886-1942) is the author of the poetry collections *Tsuki ni Hoeru* (Howling to the moon; 1917), *Aoneko* (Blue cat; 1923), and *Hyōtō* (Iceberg; 1934). See *Hagiwara Sakutarō Zenshū* 1 (Tokyo: Chikuma Shobō, 1975), p. 37.

120. *Man'yōshū* 3:3253-3254 by Kakinomoto no Hitomaro. See Kojima, et al., *Man'yōshū*, 3, pp. 390-391, in which *"wa ga"* and *"ware wa"* are *"a ga"* and *"are wa."*

121. The English translation is from Nippon Gakujutsu Shinkōkai, ed., *The Man'yōshū: One Thousand Poems, Selected and Translated from the Japanese* (Tokyo: Iwanami Shoten, 1940), p. 59. For a discussion of this poem and its translation see Roy Andrew Miller, "The 'Spirit' of the Japanese Language," *Journal of Japanese Studies* 3(2) (Summer 1977): 270 ff.

122. Kawabata Yasunari (1899-1972), winner of the 1968 Nobel Prize for literature, wrote *Yukiguni* in 1947. For an English translation of the novel see Kawabata Yasunari, *Snow Country: A Novel*, trans. Edward G. Seidensticker (Tokyo: Tuttle, 1957).

123. *Man'yōshū* 5:892 by Yamanoue no Okura. See Kojima, *Man'yōshū*, 2, pp. 95-97. [Text: *(Mon)—Kaze majiri ame furu yo no/ame majiri yuki furu yo wa/sube mo naku samuku shi areba/katashio o toritsuzushiroi/ kasuyuzake uchisusuroite/shiwabukai hana bishibishi ni/shika to aranu hige kakinadete/are o okite hito wa araji to/hokoroedo samuku shi areba/ asabusuma hikikagafuri/nunokataginu ari no kotogoto/kisoedomo samuki yo sura o/ware yori mo mazushiki hito no/chichi haha wa uekoyuramu/me*

kodomo wa koite nakuramu/kono toki wa ika ni shitsutsu ka/na ga yo wa wataru// (Kotae)—Ame tsuchi wa hiroshi to iedo/a ga tame wa saku ya narinuru/hi tsuki wa akashi to iedo/a ga tame wa teri ya tamawanu/hito mina ka a nomi ya shikaru/wakuraba ni hito to wa aru o/hitonami ni are mo nareru o/wata mo naki nunokataginu no/miru no goto wawakesagareru/ kakafu nomi kata ni uchikake/fuseiho no mageiho no uchi ni/hitatsuchi ni wara tokishikite/chichi haha wa makura no kata ni/me kodomo wa ato no kata ni/kakumiite ureisamayoi/kamado ni wa hoke fukitatezu/koshiki ni wa kumo no su kakite/ihi kashiku koto mo wasurete/nuedori no nodoyoioru ni/ itonokite mijikaki mono o/hashi kiru to ieru ga gotoku/shimoto toru sa-toosa ga koe wa/neyado made kitachiyobahinu/kaku bakari sube naki mono ka/yo no naka no michi.]

124. English translation by Cranston, *Waka Anthology*, pp. 361–363.

125. "At this time there were seven maidens playing on the plain of Takasa-jino. Isukeyorihime was among them. Ōkume no Mikoto, seeing Isukeyori-hime, said to the emperor in a song: 'Seven maidens/walking along/the plain Takasajino/in Yamato—/which of them will you wed?' At the time Isukeyori-hime was standing out in front of those maidens. Then the emperor, looking upon the maidens, knew in his heart that it was Isukeyorihime standing out in front, and replied in a song: 'The eldest maiden/standing slightly out in front,/ her will I wed.' Then, when Ōkume no Mikoto announced the emperor's will to Isukeyorihime, she saw the tattooing around the eyes of Ōkume no Mikoto; thinking it strange, she sang: '*Ame tsutsu/chidori mashi toto*—/why the tat-tooed eyes?' Then Ōkume no Mikoto sang in reply: 'The better to meet/ maidens face to face/are my tattooed eyes.' Then the maiden promised to serve the emperor." See Philippi, *Kojiki*, pp. 180–181.

126. See Nishimiya Kazutami, ed., *Kojiki, SNKS* 27 (Tokyo: Shinchōsha, 1979), p. 121.

127. English translation by Cranston, *Waka Anthology*, p. 17.

My Family Name

The original text, "Jibun no Myōji," appeared in the March 1938 issue of *Bungei Shunjū*. It was included in *Ori ni Furete, KSZ* 5, pp. 58–71.

1. *Kuki* (九鬼) literally means "nine devils."

2. The English translation is by Richard Wilhelm and Cary F. Baynes, *The I Ching or Book of Changes* (Princeton: Princeton University Press, 1977), p. 294.

3. Chang Heng-ch'ü (also known as Chang Tsai; 1020–1077) was a Neo-Confucian who drew his inspiration from the *Book of Changes*.

4. Wang Ch'ung (27–100?), a thoroughly independent thinker, has often been classified as a member of the Miscellaneous school.

5. The English translation is by Wing-Tsit Chan, *A Source Book in Chinese Philosophy* (Princeton: Princeton University Press, 1963), p. 300.

6. Monk Takuan (1573–1645) belonged to the Rinzai school of Zen Buddhism. He became the first abbot of Daitokuji.

7. Hiraga Gennai (1728–1779) wrote *Nenashigusa* (Rootless grass) in 1763. In the same year he wrote his masterpiece, *Fūryū Shidōken Den* (The dashing life of Shidōken).

8. Fuse Shōō wrote fifteen volumes of moral tales, *Shōō Dōwa*, in 1814.

9. A field located at the foot of Mt. Adatara in Fukushima prefecture. Legends indicate that the field was a meeting place for devils.

10. Raimundus Lullus (ca. 1230–1315) became famous through his teaching, which was referred to by his followers as the "Great Art" or *"Ars magna."* As with God and his qualities in theology, or the soul and its characteristics in psychology, Lullus had arrived at the conclusion that, in each scientific field, there are a few fundamental terms and principles which can be accepted without further explanation or additional inquiry.

11. Jakob Böhme (1575–1624), German mystic whose philosophy was mainly concerned with the problem of evil.

12. Aleksei Nikolaevich Kuropatkin (1848–1925) became Russia's minister of the army.

13. General Kuroki Tamemoto was commander of the First Division of the Japanese army in Manchuria during the Russo-Japanese War.

14. Miki Kiyoshi (1897–1945), Japanese philosopher, developed a synthesis of Marxism and liberal democracy.

15. Heinrich Rickert (1863–1936) was a Neo-Kantian philosopher from whom Kuki received private instruction on Kant's *Critique of Pure Reason*.

16. The English translation is by Cranston, *Waka Anthology*, p. 310; *Man'yōshū* 2:925.

17. *Man'yōshū* 10:1863.

18. Jpn. *ugui (Tribolodon hakonensis)*.

19. Kojima Kikuo (1887–1950), art historian and critic, introduced Western art on the pages of the journal *Shirakaba* (White birch).

20. Mt. Akagi, one of the Jomo Three Mountains, is located in the eastern part of Gunma prefecture.

21. Jpn. *iwana (Salvelinus pluvius)*.

22. *Honji suijaku* indicates the religious practice of presenting local deities *(kami)* as manifestations of original buddhas.

23. 1688–1703.

24. Sakanoue no Tamuramaro (785–811), famous general of the early Heian period.

25. A collection of stories *(setsuwa)* edited in 1254 by Tachibana Narisue.

26. Toba, located at the northeastern end of the Shima-hanto peninsula in Mie, flourished as the castle town of the Kuki family who ruled this region

from the seventeenth century. It was also a landing spot for visitors on the sea route to Ise-jingū shrine.

27. The bean-scattering ceremony *(setsubun)* marks the division between winter and spring. The term originally referred to the eve of the first day of any of the twenty-four divisions of the lunar year known as Setsu. Later it came to be applied more specifically to the last day of the Setsu called Daikan (great cold), which corresponded to the eve of Risshun (the first day of spring), the new year's day of the ancient lunar calendar and the traditional beginning of spring. A ritual observed during *setsubun* is the expulsion of bad luck and evil demons by tossing beans (mostly soybeans) into the air while saying *"fuku wa uchi, oni wa soto"* (fortune in, demons out).

Negishi

This essay appears in Kuki's *Mihappyō Zuihitsu* (Unpublished essays). See *KSZ* 5 (Tokyo: Iwanami Shoten, 1981), pp. 224–232. Negishi is the name of an area in the Taito district of Tokyo.

1. Okakura Tenshin (1862–1913), who worked together with Ernest F. Fenollosa for the reappreciation of Japanese art, was director of the Tokyo School of Fine Arts from 1889 to 1898. He is the author of *The Ideals of the East* (1903), *The Awakening of Japan* (1904), and *The Book of Tea* (1906).

2. A reference to the Kantō earthquake of 1923.

3. In 1889, when the Tokyo School of Fine Arts opened, Hashimoto Gahō (1835–1908) was given the position of chief professor of painting. Later, in 1898, when Okakura resigned as director of the school to found the Japan Fine Arts Academy, Gahō followed him there to become the principal instructor in the new institution.

4. Kawabata Gyokushō (1842–1913) was a renowned painter in the Japanese style (Nihonga).

5. Renba, a Chinese general of the Warring States period, developed such an intimate relationship with Lady Rinshōjo that they wanted to be together in life and in death.

6. The word "day" is in *katakana* in the original Japanese. The text says *"haetori dē,"* in which *"dē"* is a borrowed word from English.

7. It would be impossible to translate this sentence without losing the sense of the joke. The speaker plays with the English word "day" and the Japanese colloquial expression *"dai."* This word is used in Japanese at the end of informal interrogative sentences, as in *"Nan dai?"* (What's that?), *"Nani o itte yagaru'n dai?"* (What on earth are you saying?). The expression *"dai"* undergoes a phonetic transformation into *"dee"* in an even more informal context: *"Nan dē? Nani o itte yagaru'n dē?"* Here lies the joke. The speaker emphasizes the similarity of *"dē"* with the English word "day" (a word that

was becoming increasingly popular in Japan), thus introducing a further vowel alteration by changing *"dē"* into *"dei."* Professor Omodaka is actually making fun of Japanese custom of importing foreign terms, such as "day," by using an almost homophonic word in Japanese.

Remembering Mr. Okakura Kakuzō

This essay appears in Kuki's *Mihappyō Zuihitsu, KSZ* 5, pp. 233–239. From internal evidence it appears to have been written in 1937.

1. Saitō Makoto (1858–1936) became a politician after serving as an admiral in the navy. For eight years from 1906 he served as minister of the navy. He was appointed governor-general of Korea in 1919 and became the thirtieth Japanese prime minister in 1932 after the coup d'état. He was assassinated in the 26 February incident of the following year.

2. Rokumeikan was a dance hall in Tokyo and the symbol of Westernization in Japan.

3. Yokoyama Taikan (1868–1958), Shimomura Kanzan (1873–1930), and Hishida Shunsō (1874–1911) became the leaders of the Nihonga movement in the late Meiji and Taishō periods. They forged a lasting friendship during their student days at the Tokyo School of Fine Arts. All three taught at their alma mater, resigned when Okakura left, and helped him form the Japan Fine Arts Academy.

4. Okakura Yoshisaburō (1868–1936) is the author of *Kokugo Tōya to Rajio* (Linguistic education and radio).

5. Present-day University of Tokyo.

6. Hamao Arata (1849–1925), the founder of Tōkyō Bijutsu Daigaku (Tokyo University of Fine Arts), became president of the University of Tokyo and minister of education.

Remembering Mr. Iwashita Sōichi

This original text, "Iwashita Sōichi Kun no Omoide," appeared in the April 1941 issue of *Katorikku Kenkyū* as an obituary of Iwashita Sōichi. It was included in *Ori ni Furete, KSZ* 5, pp. 142–150.

1. Raphael von Koeber (1848–1923) taught philosophy and aesthetics at the University of Tokyo from 1893 to 1914.

2. Kuno Fischer (1824–1907) was professor of philosophy and German literature at the University of Heidelberg.

3. *Études d'Histoire de la Philosophie* by the French philosopher Émile Boutroux (1845–1921).

4. The Neo-Scholastic revival in Belgium has been chiefly fostered by two

great centers of learning: the College of the Jesuits of Louvain and the Institut Supérieur de Philosophie. The peculiar character that distinguishes the Institute of Louvain from earlier centers of Thomism is chiefly due to the initiative of its first president, Desiré Mercier (b. 1851). Under the direction of Mgr. Mercier, a course of philosophy has been published to which Mercier himself has contributed the volumes *Logic, Criteriology, General Metaphysics,* and *Psychology.*

5. Maurice de Wulf (b. 1867) is the author of *History of Medieval Philosophy* (1900) and *Introduction à la Philosophie neo-scolastique* (1904).

6. As vicar of St. Mary's Oxford, John Henry Newman (1801–1890) exerted a profound spiritual influence on the Church of England. Joining the Catholic Church in 1845 he became the first rector of the Catholic University in Dublin and was made cardinal by Pope Leo XIII in 1879.

7. Edited by Paul Hinneberg, the book contains articles by Wilhelm Dilthey, Theodor Lipps, Wilhelm Münch, Hermann Ebbinghaus, Rudolph Euchen, and others.

8. Theresa of Lisieux (1873–1897), French Carmelite nun, is a saint of the Roman Catholic Church. Her original name was Thérèse Martin, and her religious name was Theresa of the Child Jesus; she is known as the Little Flower of Jesus. The youngest of five daughters of a watchmaker, she became, as proclaimed by Pope Pius XI, "the greatest saint of modern times." At the age of fifteen she was permitted to follow two of her sisters into the Carmelite convent at Lisieux. There she spent the remaining nine years of her life and died of tuberculosis.

9. This is the first of James Cardinal Gibbons's (1834–1921) apologetic books, later followed by *Our Christian Heritage* and *The Ambassador of Christ.*

10. François-Alfred-Désiré Ligneul was a prolific writer on church-related matters, especially between 1896 and 1902.

11. Sylvain Lévi (1863–1935)—a French orientalist who wrote on Eastern religion, literature, and history and is particularly noted for his dictionary of Buddhism.

12. Maurice Blondel (1861–1949), dialectical philosopher, formulated a "philosophy of action" that integrated classical Neoplatonic thought with modern pragmatism in the context of a Christian philosophy of religion.

13. Iwamoto Tei (1869–1941) was a philosopher.

14. Amano Teiyū, translator of Kant in Japanese, became Japan's minister of education.

15. Iwanami Shigeo (1881–1946) was the founder of the Iwanami Press.

A Recollection of Henri Bergson

The original essay, "Kaisō no Anri Berukuson," appeared in the March 1941 issue of *Risō.* It was included in *Ori ni Furete, KSZ* 5, pp. 135–141.

1. Ishii Kikujirō (1866–1945) was a career diplomat. Beginning in 1890, he was an attaché at the Japanese legation in Paris, a consul in Korea, the secretary in the Beijing legation during the Boxer Uprising of 1900, the director of the Foreign Ministry's Commerce Bureau, minister of foreign affairs, special ambassador to the United States, ambassador to the United States, ambassador to France, and president of the Council and Assembly of the League of Nations.

2. A reference to Bergson's notion of *"élan vital."*

3. Ernest F. Fenollosa (1853–1908), Salem-born Harvard graduate, became professor of philosophy at Tokyo University (1882–1885), curator of the Imperial Museum of Japan, and curator of oriental art at the Museum of Fine Arts in Boston.

4. Herbert Spencer (1820–1903), an English philosopher, advocated extreme individualism and applied the doctrine of evolution to sociology.

5. A reference to *Essai sur les Données Immédiates de la Conscience* (Essay on the immediate data of consciousness; 1889).

6. Theresa of Ávila (1515–1582), Spanish Carmelite nun, doctor of the church, one of the principal saints of the Roman Catholic Church, one of the greatest mystics, and a leading figure in the Counter-Reformation.

7. Octave-Auguste-Louis Hamelin (1856–1907), professor of philosophy, was one of the best representatives of realism in France.

8. Jacques Chevalier (1882–1962) wrote a book on his teacher, Henri Bergson. Chevalier was France's education minister from 14 December 1940 to 25 February 1941.

9. Emile Antoine Bourdelle (1861–1929), French expressionist painter and sculptor.

10. A reference to Frédéric Lefevre.

11. For an English translation of this piece see Light, *Shūzō Kuki and Jean-Paul Sartre,* pp. 71–74.

12. Pierre Laval (1883–1945) was premier of France from 1931 to 1932 and from 1935 to 1936. He was executed by the French authorities for collaboration in October 1945.

13. William James (1842–1910), American psychologist and philosopher, is considered one of the founders of pragmatism.

14. Alfred North Whitehead (1861–1947), English mathematician and philosopher, was professor of philosophy at Harvard University from 1924 to 1936.

15. Charles Péguy (1873–1914), French writer, socialist, and vigorous defender of Dreyfus, founded the journal *Cahiers de la Quinzaine.* He was killed at the battle of the Marne.

16. Rabindranath Tagore (1861–1941), Indian Bengali poet, was awarded the Nobel Prize for literature in 1913.

Tokyo and Kyoto

The original text, "Tōkyō to Kyōto," probably written in 1937, appears in *Mihappyō Zuihitsu, KSZ* 5, pp. 190–194.

Contingency and Destiny

The essay "Gūzen to Unmei" was originally a thirty-minute lecture that Kuki delivered on the radio on 23 January 1937. It was included in *Ori ni Furete, KSZ* 5, pp. 25–35.

1. Makkhali Gosāla was a contemporary of the Buddha whose systematization of the universe was akin to the tradition of the Jaina. His followers were known as Ajivakas, which probably refers to their practice of extreme austerities, love of solitude, and disdain for any kind of comfort.

2. Wang Ch'ung (27–100?) is often classified as a member of the Miscellaneous school.

3. Saigō Takamori (1828–1877) led the imperial loyalist troops in the overthrow of the Tokugawa shogunate and restoration (Meiji Restoration) of the emperor in 1868.

4. For the complete story, titled "On Redemption," see Friedrich Nietzsche, *Thus Spoke Zarathustra: A Book for None and All*, trans. Walter Kaufmann (New York: Penguin, 1966), pp. 137–142.

5. Yamaga Sokō (1622–1685) was a military strategist and a philosopher. He developed a Neo-Confucian code of honor for the samurai class expounded in *Yamaga Gorui* (1665).

Contingency and Surprise

The essay "Gūzen to Odoroki" was originally a thirty-minute lecture that Kuki delivered on the radio on 5 March 1939. It was included in *Ori ni Furete, KSZ* 5, pp. 125–134.

1. Heracleitus (ca. 540–480 B.C.) took fire to be the principal element of cosmology. He was later interpreted by Plato to have claimed that all things are in constant flux.

2. Epicurus (341–270 B.C.), Greek philosopher, adopted the atomistic doctrine of Democritus.

3. Gottfried Wilhelm Leibniz (1646–1716), German philosopher and mathematician, developed a rationalistic system of metaphysics based on his theory of monads.

4. Sextus Tarquinius (d. 496 B.C.?) raped Lucretia, the wife of Tarquinius Collatinus, and was driven from Rome with his father Tarquinius Superbus (534–510 B.C.), who was the seventh and last king of Rome.

5. Friedrich Wilhelm Joseph von Schelling (1775–1854), German philosopher, was a leading figure of German idealism.

6. Pūrana Kāśyapa, Maskarī-Gośāliputra, Sañjaya, Vairātīputra, Ajita Keśakambala, Kakuda Kātyāyana, and Nirgrantha Jñatiputra were all contemporaries of the Buddha.

7. Skt. *hetu-pratyaya;* Jpn. *innen.*

8. For an explanation of this metaphor see "Rhyming Poems," note 10.

9. Although Kuki uses the spelling "Onokoroshima" in order to maintain the sound *"koro"* found in *"korokoro"* (churning sound), scholars have adopted the spelling "Onogoroshima." See Nishimiya Kazutami, ed., *Kojiki,* *SNKS* 27 (Tokyo: Shinchōsha, 1979), p. 28. See also Philippi, *Kojiki,* p. 49.

A Joke Born from Contingency

The original essay, "Gūzen no Unda Dajare," appears in *Mihappyō Zuihitsu,* *KSZ* 5, pp. 209–210.

1. A reference to the philosopher Watsuji Tetsurō (1889–1960).
2. Area of Kyoto.
3. *Oncorhynchus masou ishikawae.*
4. *Astrocongere myriaster.*
5. A scholar of French philosophy and translator of René Descartes.

Sound and Smell

The original essay, "Oto to Nioi: Gūzensei no Oto to Kanōsei no Nioi," appears in *Mihappyō Zuihistu, KSZ* 5, pp. 167–168.

1. The word "thrill" appears as such in the original text. In the Japanese syllabary it would sound *"suriru."*

A Record of Short Songs

The original essay, "Kouta no Rekōdo," appears in *Mihappyō Zuihitsu, KSZ* 5, pp. 169–170.

1. Hayashi Fumiko (1904–1951), a Japanese novelist, is the author of realistic novels of women's lives in Japan.

2. This is the last verse of Charles Baudelaire's *Le Gout du Néant* (Longing for nothingness): "O avalanche, will you take me with you when you fall?" The English translation is by Francis Scarfe, *The Complete Verse: Baudelaire,* vol. 1 (London: Anvil Press Poetry, 1986), p. 160.

My Thoughts on Loanwords

The original essay, "Gairaigo Shokan," appeared in the newspaper *Tōkyō Asahi Shinbun* on 3 May and 6 May 1936. It was included in *Ori ni Furete, KSZ* 5, pp. 91–99.

    1. For an explanation of this joke see "Negishi," note 7.

    2. Kuki's expression mixes the feminine language of the geisha with a couple of English words: "*ōpun de doraibu oshashitara dō dosu?*"

    3. German word for "beggar."

    4. German word for "hut."

    5. Originally a loanword from the Portuguese "*gibão*," "*juban*" became so assimilated into the Japanese language that it came to be written with Chinese characters (襦袢).

    6. "*Ābento*" comes from the German "*Abend*" (evening).

    7. "*Sorudo*" stands for the French word "*solde*" (bargain sale).

    8. From the German "*spurlos verloren.*"

Tradition and Progressivism

The original essay, "Dentō to Shinshu," probably written in May or June 1936, appears in *Mihappyō Zuihitsu, KSZ* 5, pp. 207–208.

Bibliography

NKBZ   *Nihon Koten Bungaku Zenshū*
SNKS   *Shin Nihon Koten Shūsei*

Alighieri, Dante. *La Divina Commedia: Inferno.* Edited by Natalino Sapegno. Florence: La Nuova Italia Editrice, 1955.

Amano, Teiyū, ed. *Kuki Shūzō Bunko Mokuroku.* Kobe: Kōnan Daigaku Tetsugaku Kenkyūshitsu, 1976.

Arisaka, Yoko. "Beyond 'East and West': Nishida's Universalism and Post-colonial Critique." In Fred Dallymayr, ed. *Border Crossings: Towards a Comparative Political Theory.* Lexington, Mass.: Lexington, 1999.

Aristotle. *The Poetics.* Translated by W. Hamilton Fyfe and W. Rhys Roberts. Cambridge, Mass.: Harvard University Press, 1927.

Bergson, Henri. *Creative Evolution.* Translated by Arthur Mitchell. Mineola, N.Y.: Dover, 1998. First published in 1911.

———. *The Creative Mind: An Introduction to Metaphysic.* New York: Philosophical Library, 1946.

———. *Duration and Simultaneity: Bergson and the Einsteinian Universe.* Translated by Mark Lewis and Robin Durie. Manchester: Clinamen, 1999.

———. *Essai sur les Données Immédiates de la Conscience.* Paris: Presses Universitaires de France, 1946. First published in 1889.

———. *Time and Free Will: An Essay on the Immediate Data of Consciousness.* Translated by F.L.Pogson. London: Allen & Unwin, 1971. First published in 1910.

———. *The Two Sources of Morality and Religion.* Translated by R.Ashley Audra and Cloudesley Brereton. Notre Dame: University of Notre Dame Press, 1977.

Botz-Bornstein, Thorsten. "Contingency and the 'Time of the Dream': Kuki

Shūzō and French Prewar Philosophy." *Philosophy East and West* 50(4) (October 2000): 481–506.

Bourdieu, Pierre. *The Political Ontology of Martin Heidegger.* Cambridge: Polity Press, 1991.

Chan, Wing-Tsit, ed. *A Source Book in Chinese Philosophy.* Princeton: Princeton University Press, 1963.

Cranston, Edwin A. *A Waka Anthology, 1: The Gem-Glistening Cup.* Stanford: Stanford University Press, 1993.

Daitō, Shun'ichi. *Kuki Shūzō to Nihon Bunkaron.* Tokyo: Azusa Shuppansha, 1996.

Deleuze, Gilles. *Bergsonism.* Translated by Hugh Tomlinson and Barbara Habberiam. New York: Zone Books, 1988. First published in 1966.

Descartes, René. *Les Passions de L'Âme.* Paris: J.Vrin, 1955.

———. *The Passions of the Soul.* Translated by Stephen Voss. Indianapolis: Hackett, 1989.

Dilworth, David A., Valdo H. Viglielmo, and Augustin Jacinto Zavala, eds. "Kuki Shūzō." In David A. Dilworth, Valdo H. Viglielmo, and Augustin Jacinto Zavala, eds., *Sourcebook for Modern Japanese Philosophy.* Westport: Greenwood Press, 1998.

Ferry, Luc, and Alain Renaut. *Heidegger and Modernity.* Chicago: University of Chicago Press, 1990.

Fujinaka, Masayoshi. "Kuki Tetsugaku ni Okeru Keijijōgakuteki Jitsuzon no Mondai." *Shisō* 2 (1980): 69–86.

Hagiwara, Sakutarō. *Hagiwara Sakutarō Zenshū.* 15 vols. Tokyo: Chikuma Shobō, 1975–1978.

Harootunian, Harry. *Overcome by Modernity: History, Culture, and Community in Interwar Japan.* Princeton: Princeton University Press, 2000.

Heidegger, Martin. *Being and Time: A Translation of Sein und Zeit.* Translated by Joan Stambaugh. Albany: State University of New York Press, 1996. First published in 1927.

———. *The Concept of Time.* Translated by William McNeill. Oxford: Blackwell, 1992.

———. "A Dialogue on Language Between a Japanese and an Inquirer." In Martin Heidegger, *On the Way to Language,* trans. Peter D. Hertz. San Francisco: Harper & Row, 1971.

———. *Introduction to Metaphysics.* Translated by Gregory Fried and Richard Polt. New Haven: Yale University Press, 2000.

Heisig, James W. *Philosophers of Nothingness: An Essay on the Kyoto School.* Honolulu: University of Hawai'i Press, 2001.

Heisig, James W., and John C. Maraldo, eds. *Rude Awakenings: Zen, the Kyoto School, and the Question of Nationalism.* Honolulu: University of Hawai'i Press, 1994.

Hino, Tatsuo, ed. *Motoori Norinaga Shū. SNKS* 60. Tokyo: Shinchōsha, 1983.

Horiuchi, Keizō, and Inoue Takeshi, eds. *Nihon Shōka Shū.* Tokyo: Iwanami Shoten, 1958.

Iida, Ryūta, et al., eds. *Nihon Meiku Shūsei.* Tokyo: Gakutōsha, 1991.

Ishikawa, Takuboku. *Romaji Diary and Sad Toys.* Translated by Sanford Goldstein and Seishi Shinoda. Tokyo: Tuttle, 1985.

Ishimatsu, Keizō. "Haideruberuku no Kuki Shūzō." In *Kuki Shūzō Zenshū Geppō,* 1. Vol. 2. Tokyo: Iwanami Shoten, 1981.

Isoya, Takashi. "Gengo to Shite no Kuki Shūzō, Jō: Yōroppa Gengo Shisō no Juyō to Chōkoku." *Shisō* 2 (1980): 106–140.

———. "Gengo to Shite no Kuki Shūzō, Ge: Sonzairon kara Kigoron e no Kakyō." *Shisō* 3 (1980): 104–134.

———. "Kuki Shūzō ni Okeru Chisei no Shukusai." *Shisō* 11 (1978): 1–26.

Iwaki, Ken'ichi, ed. *Nishida Tetsugaku Senshū,* vol. 6. Tokyo: Tōeisha, 1998.

Kanno, Akimasa, ed. *Kuki Shūzō Zuihitsu Shū.* Tokyo: Iwanami Shoten, 1991.

Kant, Immanuel. *Critique of Practical Reason.* Translated by Mary Gregor. Cambridge: Cambridge University Press, 1997.

———. *Critique of Pure Reason.* Translated by J.M.D. Meiklejohn. New York: Prometheus Books, 1990.

———. *Essai pour Introduire en Philosophie le Concept de Grandeur Négative.* Translated by Roger Kempf. Paris: J.Vrin, 1949.

Karatani, Kōjin. "One Spirit, Two Nineteenth Centuries." Translated by Alan Wolfe. In Masao Miyoshi and H.D. Harootunian, eds., *Postmodernism and Japan.* Durham: Duke University Press, 1989.

Kasulis, Thomas P. "The Kyoto School and the West: Review and Evaluation." *Eastern Buddhist* 15(2) (Autumn 1982): 125–144.

Kawabata, Yasunari. *Snow Country: A Novel.* Translated by Edward G. Seidensticker. Tokyo: Tuttle, 1957.

Keene, Donald, trans. *Major Plays of Chikamatsu.* New York: Columbia University Press, 1961.

Kim, Hakkhyon. "Iki, Iki, Mott: Nihon no 'Iki' to Chōsen no 'Mott.'" *Bungaku* 54(5) (1986): 63–77.

Kojima, Noriyuki, Kinoshita Masatoshi, and Satake Akihiro, eds. *Man'yōshū,* 1. *NKBZ* 2. Tokyo: Shōgakukan, 1971.

———, eds. *Man'yōshū,* 2. *NKBZ* 3. Tokyo: Shōgakukan, 1972.

———, eds. *Man'yōshū,* 3. *NKBZ* 4. Tokyo: Shōgakukan, 1973.

Kon, Eizō, ed. *Bashō Kushū. SNKS* 51. Tokyo: Shinchōsha, 1982.

Kuki, Shūzō. *Bungeiron.* Tokyo: Iwanami Shoten, 1941.

———. "A Consideration of *Fūryū.*" Translated by Michael Bourdaghs. Unpublished manuscript.

———. *"Iki" no Kōzō.* Tokyo: Iwanami Shoten, 1979.

————. *Kuki Shuzō Zenshū*. Edited by Amano Teiyū, Omodaka Hisayuki, and Satō Akio. 12 vols. Tokyo: Iwanami Shoten, 1981.

————. *La Struttura dell'Iki*. Translated by Giovanna Baccini. Milan: Adelphi, 1992.

————. *Le Problème de la Contingence*. Translated by Omodaka Hisayuki. Tokyo: Tokyo University Press, 1966.

————. *Ningen to Jitsuzon*. Tokyo: Iwanami Shoten, 1939.

————. *Reflections on Japanese Taste: The Structure of Iki*. Translated by John Clark. Sydney: Power Publications, 1997.

Lacoue-Labarthe, Philippe. *Heidegger, Art, and Politics: The Fiction of the Political*. Oxford: Blackwell, 1990.

Levy, Ian Hideo. *Man'yōshū: A Translation of Japan's Premier Anthology of Classical Poetry*. vol. 1. Princeton: Princeton University Press, 1981.

Light, Stephen. *Shūzō Kuki and Jean-Paul Sartre: Influence and Counter-Influence in the Early History of Existential Phenomenology*. Carbondale: Southern Illinois University Press, 1987.

Lippit, Seiji M. *Topographies of Japanese Modernism*. New York: Columbia University Press, 2002.

McAlmon, Robert, and Kay Boyle. *Being Geniuses Together: 1920-1930*. London: Hogarth Press, 1984.

McCullough, Helen Craig, trans. *Classical Japanese Prose: An Anthology*. Stanford: Stanford University Press, 1990.

————. *Kokin Wakashū: The First Imperial Anthology of Japanese Poetry*. Stanford: Stanford University Press, 1985.

Marra, Michael F., ed. and trans. *A History of Modern Japanese Aesthetics*. Honolulu: University of Hawai'i Press, 2001.

————, ed. *Japanese Hermeneutics: Current Debates on Aesthetics and Interpretation*. Honolulu: University of Hawai'i Press, 2002.

————. *Modern Japanese Aesthetics: A Reader*. Honolulu: University of Hawai'i Press, 1999.

Matisoff, Susan. *The Legend of Semimaru, Blind Musician of Japan*. New York: Columbia University Press, 1978.

Mikkelsen, J. Mark. "Reading Kuki Shūzō's *The Structure of Iki* in the Shadow of *Le Affaire Heidegger*." In Hiroshi Nara, trans. and ed., *The Structure of Detachment: The Aesthetic Vision of Kuki Shūzō*. Honolulu: University of Hawai'i Press, 2004.

Miller, Roy Andrew. "The 'Spirit' of the Japanese Language." *Journal of Japanese Studies* 3(2) (Summer 1977): 251-298.

Miyoshi, Tatsuji. *Miyoshi Tatsuji Zenshū*. 12 vols. Tokyo: Chikuma Shobō, 1964-1966.

Nagai, Kafū. *A Strange Tale from East of the River and Other Stories*. Translated by Edward Seidensticker. Tokyo: Tuttle, 1972.

Nakano, Hajimu. "Kuki Shūzō and the Structure of Iki." In J. Thomas

Rimer, ed., *Culture and Identity: Japanese Intellectuals During the Interwar Years*. Princeton: Princeton University Press, 1990.

Nara, Hiroshi, trans. and ed. *The Structure of Detachment: The Aesthetic Vision of Kuki Shūzō*. Honolulu: University of Hawai'i Press, 2004.

Natsume, Sōseki. *Kokoro: A Novel and Selected Essays*. Translated by Edwin McClellan. Lanham, Md.: Madison Books, 1992.

―――. *The Three-Cornered World*. Translated by Alan Turney. Tokyo: Tuttle, 1968.

Nietzsche, Friedrich. *Thus Spoke Zarathustra: A Book for None and All*. Translated by Walter Kaufmann. New York: Penguin, 1966.

Nippon Gakujutsu Shinkōkai, ed. *The Man'yōshū: One Thousand Poems, Selected and Translated from the Japanese*. Tokyo: Iwanami Shoten, 1940.

Nishimiya, Kazutami, ed. *Kojiki*. SNKS 27. Tokyo: Shinchōsha, 1979.

Noguchi, Motohiro, ed. *Taketori Monogatari*. SNKS 26. Tokyo: Shinchōsha, 1979.

Ōhashi, Ryōsuke. "The Hermeneutic Approach to Japanese Modernity: 'Art-Way,' 'Iki,' and 'Cut-Continuance.'" In Michael F. Marra, ed., *Japanese Hermeneutics: Current Debates on Aesthetics and Interpretation*. Honolulu: University of Hawai'i Press, 2000.

Okumura, Tsuneya, ed. *Kokin Wakashū*. SNKS 19. Tokyo: Shinchōsha, 1978.

Omodaka, Hisayuki. "Kuki Sensei o Shinonde." *Shisō* 2 (1980): 65–68.

Ōno, Keiichirō. "Kuki Shūzō ni Okeru Shi to Tetsugaku: Shisō no Keisei o Megutte." *Shisō* 2 (1980): 87–105.

Ōta, Mizuho et al., eds. *Shin Man'yōshū*. Vol. 2. Tokyo: Kaizōsha, 1938.

Parkes, Graham. Review of *Authenticating Culture in Imperial Japan: Kuki Shūzō and the Rise of National Aesthetics* by Leslie Pincus. *Chanoyu Quarterly* 86 (1997): 63–69.

―――. "The Putative Philosophy of the Kyoto School and the Political Correctness of the Modern Academy." *Philosophy East and West* 47(3) (July 1997): 305–336.

Philippi, Donald L., trans. *Kojiki*. Tokyo: University of Tokyo Press, 1968.

Pincus, Leslie. *Authenticating Culture in Imperial Japan: Kuki Shūzō and the Rise of National Aesthetics*. Berkeley: University of California Press, 1996.

Proust, Marcel. *The Past Recaptured*. Translated by Frederick A. Blossom. New York: Albert & Charles Boni, 1932.

Ribot, Théodule-Armand. *La Psychologie des Sentiments*. Paris: Félix Alcan, 1911.

Sakabe, Megumi. *Fuzai no Uta: Kuki Shūzō no Sekai*. Tokyo: TBS Buritanika, 1990.

Scarfe, Francis, ed. *The Complete Verse: Baudelaire*. Vol. 1. London: Anvil Press Poetry, 1986.

Shimizu, Takayuki, ed. *Yosa Buson Shū. SNKS* 32. Tokyo: Shinchōsha, 1979.

Shimomise, Eiichi. "Kuki Tetsugaku to Gūzensei no Mondai." *Shisō* 3 (1980): 76-103.

Spinoza, Baruch. *Ethics.* Translated by G.H.R. Parkinson. Oxford: Oxford University Press, 2000.

———. *Ethics.* Translated by James Gutmann. New York: Hafner, 1949.

Takagi, Masakazu, ed. *Tōshisen,* 3. *Chūgoku Kotensen* 27. Tokyo: Asahi Shinbunsha, 1978.

Tanaka, Kyūbun. "Kobayashi, Kuki, Miki ni Okeru 'Sōzōryoku' Ron no Shosō: Nihon ni Okeru 1930 Nendai no Shisōteki Kadai." *Rinrigaku Kiyō* 2 (1985): 114-133.

———. *Kuki Shūzō: Gūzen to Shizen.* Tokyo: Perikansha, 1992.

———. "Kuki Shūzō and the Phenomenology of *Iki.*" In Michael F. Marra, ed., *A History of Modern Japanese Aesthetics.* Honolulu: University of Hawai'i Press, 2001.

Tanizaki, Junichirō. *The Reed Cutter and Captain Shigemoto's Mother: Two Novellas.* Translated by Anthony H. Chambers. New York: Knopf, 1994.

Tezuka, Tomio. "An Hour with Heidegger." In Reinhard May, *Heidegger's Hidden Sources: East Asian Influences on His Work,* trans. Graham Parkes. London: Routledge, 1996.

Tyler, Royall, trans. *The Tale of Genji.* New York: Viking, 2001.

Ueda, Makoto. *Bashō and His Interpreters: Selected Hokku with Commentary.* Stanford: Stanford University Press, 1992.

———. *The Path of Flowering Thorn: The Life and Poetry of Yosa Buson.* Stanford: Stanford University Press, 1998.

Viswanathan, Meera. "An Investigation into Essence: Kuki Shūzō's 'Iki' no Kōzō." *Transactions of the Society of Japan* 4 (1989): 1-23.

Waley, Arthur, ed. *The Analects of Confucius.* New York: Vintage, 1938.

Watson, Burton, trans. *The Complete Works of Chuang Tzu.* New York: Columbia University Press, 1968.

Wilhelm, Richard, and Cary F. Baynes. *The I Ching or Book of Changes.* Princeton: Princeton University Press, 1977.

Wiser, William. *The Crazy Years: Paris in the Twenties.* New York: Athenaeum, 1983.

Yamamoto, Yuji. "An Aesthetics of Everyday Life: Modernism and a Japanese Popular Aesthetic Ideal, *'Iki'.*" M.A. thesis, University of Chicago, 1999.

Yasuda, Takeshi, and Tada Michitarō. "*'Iki' no Kōzō*" o Yomu. Tokyo: Asahi Shinbunsha, 1979.

Index

Amano, Teiyū, 50, 244, 271–272, 289n. 14, 304n. 14, 343n. 14
Aristotle, 202, 257
Augustine, 30, 32–33, 36, 37, 48, 178, 242

Baudelaire, Charles-Pierre, 85, 93, 180, 314n. 15
Becker, Oskar, 9
Bergson, Henri, 3, 9, 18, 22, 30, 31, 35, 40, 41, 240, 242, 248–252, 255, 302n. 2, 307nn. 25, 26; pure duration, 23–26, 174, 307n. 29
Blondel Maurice, 244, 343n. 12
Böhme, Jakob, 219
Borel, Émile, 10
Boutroux, Émile, 10, 242
Bréhier, Émile, 9
Bungaku no Gairon (Outline of literature), 12, 19, 22, 32–36, 295n. 54, 301n. 102
Bungaku no Keijijōgaku (The metaphysics of literature), 5, 30–33; 292n. 16; temporality of art, 175–178; temporality of drama, 199–202; temporality of literature, 178–192; temporality of novels, 195–199; temporality of poetry, 202–209; theories of time, 192–195
Bungeiron (Essays on the literary arts), 12, 169, 315, 332

Chevalier, Jacques, 250, 251, 344n. 8
Chikamatsu, Monzaemon, 21, 200, 337n. 87
Choses Japonaises (Things Japanese), 28
Claretie, Jules, 81, 314n. 12
contingency, 10–18; and surprise, 264–270; three modalities, 257–263
Courbet, Jean Desiré Gustave, 49, 304n. 11

Daudet, Alphonse, 71, 313n. 3
Daumier, Honoré, 92, 314n. 20
Debussy, Claude, 79, 313n. 9
Degas, Edgar, 67, 312n. 1
Dentō to Shinshu (Tradition and progressivism), 1, 284–285
Der Begriff der Zeit (The concept of time), 35–36
Descartes, René, 50, 126, 164, 305n. 17, 324n. 2
Dessoir, Max, 301n. 102
Dumas, Georges, 130, 326n. 19

Epicurus, 267, 345n. 2

Fenollosa, Ernest F., 248, 344n. 3
Fischer, Kuno, 242, 342n. 2
Fujita, Tsuguji, 28

Géricault, Théodore, 37, 178, 311n. 58
Glockner, Hermann, 14–15

Goethe, Johann Wolfgang von, 22, 41, 176, 255, 332n. 14
Gūzensei no Mondai (The problem of contingency), 10, 164

Hagiwara, Sakutarō, 207
Hahen (Fragments), 4, 24, 51-54, 291n. 15
Hamao, Harata, 240, 342n. 6
Hamelin, Octave-Auguste-Louis, 250, 344n. 7
Hashimoto, Gahō, 232, 236, 341n. 3
Hayashi, Fumiko, 197, 275-276, 336n. 72
Heidegger, Martin, 2, 8, 9, 14, 18, 30, 32, 35-36, 37, 174, 255-256; Marxist interpretations, 3
Heine, Heinrich, 63-64, 311n. 58, 312n. 59
Heracleitus, 267, 345n. 1
Hiraga, Gennai, 218, 227, 340n. 7
Hishida, Shunsō, 237, 342n. 3
Hōnen, 174, 332n. 1
Hoshizaki, Hatsu, 6
Husserl, Edmund, 9, 30, 33-34, 217, 320n. 29

Iki no Kōzō (The Structure of Iki), 1, 6-7, 244, 284-285
Ishii, Kikujirō, 248, 250, 344n. 1
Ishikawa, Takuboku, 203
Iwamoto, Tei, 244
Iwanami, Shigeo, 245, 343n. 15
Iwashita, Sōichi, 110, 241-247, 315n. 24, 320n. 28

James, William, 252, 344n. 13
Jaspers, Karl, 301n. 102
Jōcho no Keizu: Uta o Tebiki to Shite (The genealogy of feelings: A guide to poetry), 5; objective feelings, 135-145; subjective feelings, 125-135; tension and relaxation, 157-163

Kaibara, Ekiken, 174, 332n. 2
Kant, Immanuel, 19-21, 91, 93, 166, 177, 306n. 22, 314n. 18, 331n. 117

Karatani, Kōjin, 2, 3
Kawabata, Chie, 126, 132, 133, 136, 144, 145, 161, 162, 325n. 6
Kawabata, Gyokushō, 232, 341n. 4
Kawabata, Yasunari, 209-210
Kiyomoto, Enju Daiyū, 175, 332n. 8
Koeber, Raphael von, 241, 242, 243, 255, 342n. 1
Kojima, Kikuo, 49, 223, 304n. 10, 340n. 19
Kuki, Ryūichi, 6, 14, 60, 68, 228, 235, 238, 239, 243, 278
Kuki, Shūzō: and Bergson, 248-252; and contingency, 10-18; critique of, 3; and Marxism, 1, 284-285; and nothingness, 18-23; and Okakura Kakuzō, 228-240; and poetry, 4, 36, 39-40; quality and quantity, 23-30; and rhymes, 12-13, 292n. 19; studies in Europe, 9; temporality, 30-40
Kurata, Hyakuzō, 201
Kyō no Fuyu (Winter in Kyoto), 30, 97-98
Kyoto school, 2

Leibniz, Gottfried Wilhelm, 267, 345n. 3
Lemestre, Marthe, 29
Lullus, Raimundus, 219, 340n. 10

Makkhali, Gosāla, 257, 345n. 1
Manet, Édouard, 49, 304n. 12
Matsuo, Bashō, 39-40, 175, 184, 205
McAlmon, Robert, 28-29
Mercier, Desiré, 242, 343n. 4
Miki, Kiyoshi, 221
Miyoshi, Tatsuji, 206
Monet, Claude, 49, 304n. 13
Motoori, Norinaga, 203

Nagai, Kafū, 186
Nakahashi, Nuiko, 61, 71, 290n. 3, 310n. 52
Naruse, Mukyoku, 99, 275, 315n. 28
Natsume, Sōseki, 186, 191, 196
Newman, John Henry, 242, 343n. 6
Newton, Isaac, 176, 333n. 15
Nietzsche, Friedrich, 38, 262-263

Nihon Ideorogīron (Essay on Japanese ideology), 2
Nihonshi no Ōin (Rhyme in Japanese poetry), 5, 12, 100–121, 315
Ningen to Jitsuzon (Man and existence), 164, 167
Nishida, Kitarō, 2, 18, 41, 245, 271, 287n. 5
Nishikawa, Joken, 174, 332n. 3
Nishitani, Keiji, 287n. 5

Ochiai, Tarō, 272, 346n. 5
Okakura, Kakuzō (Tenshin), 6, 229, 231–233, 234, 235–240, 341n. 1
Okakura, Kazuo, 232, 236
Okakura, Yoshisaburō, 237, 342n. 4
Okamoto, Kidō, 201, 337n. 89
Omodaka, Hisataka, 234, 278
Ōnishi, Hajime, 141, 328n. 60
Ōta, Mizuho, 150, 329n. 82
Oto to Nioi (Sound and smell), 40, 273–274

Parī no Mado (Windows of Paris), 4, 60–65
Parī no Negoto (Sleep talking in Paris), 4, 15, 54–60, 291n. 15
Parī Shinkei (Paris mindscapes), 4, 45–51, 66–79, 291n. 15
Parī Shōkyoku (Sonnets from Paris), 18, 79–97, 291n. 15
Pascal, Blaise, 50, 305n. 18
Péguy, Charles, 252, 344n. 15
Pincus, Leslie, 2–3
Plato, 141
Proust, Marcel, 192

Ribot, Théodule-Armand, 127–128, 325n.11
Rickert, Heinrich, 7, 9, 14, 221, 291n. 11

Rodin, Auguste, 37, 178
Ryūtatsu, 175, 332n. 13

sabi, 168
Saigyō, 97, 197, 254, 315n. 25
Sakabe, Megumi, 8
Sartre, Jean-Paul, 9, 18
Satō, Nobuhiro, 174, 332n. 4
Schelling, Friedrich Wilhelm Joseph von, 267–268, 346n. 5
Semimaru, 101, 316n. 4
Shimazaki Tōson, 333nn. 20, 21
Shimomura, Kanzan, 237, 342n. 3
Shin Man'yōshū (New ten thousand leaves), 125–126, 328n. 45
Soga no Yagorō, 201, 337n. 88
Spencer, Herbert, 249, 344n. 4
Spinoza, Baruch, 48, 126, 135, 164, 222, 303n. 8, 325n. 3, 327n. 37

Tagore, Rabindranath, 252, 344n. 16
Takuan Zenshi, 218, 340n. 6
Tamenaga, Shunsui, 175, 332n. 7
Tanabe, Hajime, 2, 287n. 5
Tanaka, Hidenaka, 243
Tanaka, Kyūbun, 6
Tanizaki, Jun'ichirō, 197, 336n. 73
Tokuda, Shūsei, 198
Tōkyō to Kyōto (Tokyo and Kyoto), 3, 253–256
Tosaka, Jun, 2

Valéry, Paul, 12, 13, 271

Wang, Ch'ung, 257, 269, 345n. 2
Watsuji, Tetsurō, 271, 288n. 5
Whitehead, Alfred North, 252, 344n. 14
Wulf, Maurice de, 242, 343n. 5

Yamaga, Sokō, 263, 345n. 5
Yokoyama, Taikan, 237, 342n. 3
Yosa, Buson, 181, 191, 206, 333n. 26

About the Editor

MICHAEL F. MARRA is professor of Japanese literature at the University of California, Los Angeles. He has served on the faculties of the Osaka University of Foreign Studies, the University of Tokyo, the University of Southern California, and the University of Kyoto. Among his numerous publications are *The Aesthetics of Discontent: Politics and Reclusion in Medieval Japanese Literature* (1991), which was named a finalist for the 1991 Hiromi Arisawa Memorial Award; *Representations of Power: The Literary Politics of Medieval Japan* (1993); *Modern Japanese Aesthetics: A Reader* (1999), a companion volume to *A History of Modern Japanese Aesthetics* (2001); and *Japanese Hermeneutics: Current Debates on Aesthetics and Interpretation* (2002).

Production Notes for Marra/*KUKI SHŪZŌ*
Cover design by Santos Barbasa Jr.
Text design and composition by inari in Sabon.
Printing and binding by The Maple-Vail Book Manufacturing Group.
Printed on 60 lb. Sebago Eggshell, 420 ppi